THE RISE AND FALL OF MORRIS ERNST, FREE SPEECH RENEGADE

THE RISE AND FALL OF MORRIS ERNST, FREE SPEECH RENEGADE

· Samantha Barbas ·

The University of Chicago Press
Chicago and London

The University of Chicago Press, Chicago 60637
The University of Chicago Press, Ltd., London

Published 2021
Printed in the United States of America

30 29 28 27 26 25 24 23 22 21   1 2 3 4 5

ISBN-13: 978-0-226-65804-9 (cloth)
ISBN-13: 978-0-226-65818-6 (e-book)
DOI: https://doi.org/10.7208/chicago/9780226658186.001.0001

Library of Congress Cataloging-in-Publication Data

Names: Barbas, Samantha, author.
Title: The rise and fall of Morris Ernst, free speech renegade / Samantha Barbas.
Description: Chicago : University of Chicago Press, 2021. | Includes bibliographical references and index.
Identifiers: LCCN 2021001494 | ISBN 9780226658049 (cloth) | ISBN 9780226658186 (e-book)
Subjects: LCSH: Ernst, Morris L. (Morris Leopold), 1888–1976. | Civil rights—United States—Biography. | Lawyers—United States—Biography.
Classification: LCC KF373.E7 B37 2021 | DDC 340.092 [B]—dc23
LC record available at https://lccn.loc.gov/2021001494

CONTENTS

Introduction · 1

1 Early Years · 7
2 Williams · 18
3 New York · 26
4 Greenbaum, Wolff, and Ernst · 38
5 Adventures · 50
6 Free Speech Lawyer · 67
7 To the Pure · 84
8 The Sex Side of Life · 99
9 Sex Wins in America · 116
10 Troubled Times · 127
11 Freedom for the Thought That We Hate · 141
12 *Ulysses* · 152
13 The Importance of Being Ernst · 176
14 Defending the New Deal · 190
15 The Champion of Freedom · 208
16 The National Lawyers Guild · 219
17 Ernst vs. Hague · 232
18 Controversy in the ACLU · 250
19 The Turning Tide · 270
20 Ernst at His Worst · 292
21 Desperate Moves · 314
22 Utopia 1976 · 341

Acknowledgments · 355
Notes · 357
Index · 411

INTRODUCTION

A small, dark-haired man with wire-rimmed glasses, bow tie, and tweed jacket stood, dragged on his cigarette, and held up a dog-eared book with a blue cover. Using the word *fuck*, he said, was a sign of integrity.

The book was James Joyce's *Ulysses*, the revolutionary, stream-of-consciousness novel that had been banned under the notorious Comstock laws for more than a decade. The scene was a New York City courtroom in the fall of 1933, and the man was Morris Ernst, a civil liberties lawyer who adored controversy.

Ernst sought to prove to the judge, John Woolsey, that *Ulysses* was not obscene—that it would not corrupt even those members of society "whose minds are open to such immoral influences."[1] The word *fuck*, Ernst argued, was "cleaner and less revolting" than paraphrases of it. It had "more integrity than a euphemism used every day in every modern novel to describe precisely the same event." That is, it meant same thing as "they slept together."

Replied Woolsey, "But, Counselor, that isn't even usually the truth!"[2]

Nevertheless, Woolsey ruled in favor of *Ulysses*, and the decision was upheld on appeal. Legalized, *Ulysses* went on to sell thousands of copies. This was a historic triumph for the nation's literary culture, and it also made Ernst rich. He had made a shrewd deal with the publisher: if he won the case, he would receive royalties on every copy sold.[3]

Morris Ernst was one of the best-known liberal lawyers in the country. An eminent attorney in private practice, an early leader of the American Civil Liberties Union (ACLU) and its general counsel for more than twenty-five years, Ernst was renowned for his work in free speech, especially the fight against literary and artistic censorship. With his trademark bravado, Ernst came to the defense of sex education manuals, nudist treatises, burlesque shows, and risqué films and novels. In the decades before World War II, no one did more than Ernst to extend legal protections to literature, art, theater, and movies.[4]

Battling censorship was only one of Ernst's free speech causes. Believing that democracy, freedom, and human enlightenment depended on "the free play of ideas in the marketplace of thought," Ernst worked tirelessly to expand that "marketplace" on a variety of fronts. Ernst authored scores of books, columns, and articles in which he publicized and popularized his civil libertarian views. In 1939 Ernst won a major Supreme Court ruling, *Hague v. Committee for Industrial Organization*, which established streets and parks as "public forums," constitutionally protected venues for public discussion. Convinced that social progress came from the clash of opinions, even hateful ones, Ernst advocated the ACLU's viewpoint-neutral stance on free speech and defended the rights of Nazis he abhorred.

The 1930s and '40s saw a sea change in civil liberties and free speech rights. The public and the courts moved toward greater tolerance of unpopular views and advocacy of free expression. After decades of suppression, "speech started to win," observed First Amendment scholar Harry Kalven Jr.[5] One of America's preeminent defenders of the rights to speak and to "see, read and hear," as Kalven put it, Ernst was a pivotal figure in this development. There was no one in the country, opined one commentator, who had not benefited from Ernst's court victories.

* * *

Ernst was a diminutive, compact, energetic man, described by friends as a "human dynamo," and he thrived on causes and "crusades," as he called them. In the 1930s and '40s, he was one of the nation's most prominent liberals, at the forefront of countless organizations and initiatives. For a while Ernst served as a legal advisor to the NAACP and helped pioneer the legal strategies of the nascent civil rights movement. Organized labor was another of Ernst's "causes." Ernst helped his best friend, syndicated columnist Heywood Broun, form the American Newspaper Guild, and in a landmark Supreme Court case, successfully defended newspaper workers' right to organize. In 1936 Ernst formed the National Lawyers Guild to unite attorneys working for progressive social goals. As counsel for Margaret Sanger's birth control movement, Ernst litigated cases that legalized the dissemination of contraceptives and information about contraception.

Ernst defended the underdog but at the same time had no qualms about representing the wealthy and powerful. Ernst's law firm of Greenbaum, Wolff, and Ernst, which he cofounded in 1915, took civil liberties cases pro bono, along with paid cases in banking, media, and publishing law. His law practice was lucrative, and Ernst enjoyed fine homes, fashionable suits, visits to swanky nightclubs, and soirees with his celebrity friends, including Franklin and Eleanor Roosevelt, novelist Edna Ferber, Heywood Broun, Fiorello La Guardia, and J. Edgar Hoover. According to one magazine account:

> To call him a lawyer is to designate only a small part of the role he plays. He is a literary man. . . . writes serious books. . . . He is counsel for *The New Yorker*, the American Newspaper Guild, and the ACLU. His most intimate friends include many newspaper liberals and radicals, and he is a member of the crowd of "highbrows" known as the Algonquin Club. . . . In Washington he has entrée into offices of dozens of leading public officials.[6]

Sincere ideological commitments propelled this "human dynamo" forward, as did profound insecurities. A Jew of relatively humble background who had attended night law school and started his career as a shirt-factory manager and a furniture salesman, Ernst saw himself as a perpetual outsider and craved public acceptance and recognition. Ernst was a shameless self-promoter, vain and obsessed with his image. Quipped *Scribner's Magazine* in 1938, "a perfect example of Morris Ernst bearing the torch of public service is one that lands him in the headlines of every newspaper in town."[7]

* * *

In the 1940s Ernst became consumed by a new cause: fighting Communism. Ernst was convinced that Communists were infiltrating liberal groups he was involved with, including the ACLU and the National Lawyers Guild, tarnishing their images, disrupting their work, and subverting them to antidemocratic purposes. Ernst became obsessed with "purging" his organizations of Communist influence and was one of the most vigilant anti-Communists on the Left.

In one of his most disgraceful episodes, Ernst became a promoter and defender of the FBI. Duped by J. Edgar Hoover and the FBI's skillful public relations machine, Ernst came to believe that Hoover was the nation's most valiant fighter against the Communist menace and had been unfairly maligned by liberals who questioned the FBI's civil liberties record. Ernst served as an informal public relations agent for the FBI, quashing criticism, writing laudatory articles, and going so far as to alert Hoover when the ACLU was planning to criticize the FBI. Though Ernst did not "name names," he damaged the cause of civil liberties. As journalist Harrison Salisbury put it, Ernst's endorsement functioned as a kind of left-wing "Good Housekeeping Seal of Approval," deflecting potential liberal criticism of the FBI.[8]

When Ernst died in 1976 at the age of eighty-seven, he was lauded as one of the most influential civil libertarians of the century. The following year, the press revealed Hoover and Ernst's correspondence, obtained by the ACLU through a Freedom of Information Act request, and Ernst was damned in the press as an FBI "spy" within the ACLU.[9] Before long, he fell out of the spotlight, with mentions of his life and work confined largely to academic discussions of free expression and censorship history. The life of this complex man, a key figure in the ACLU who transformed free speech and was at the center of some of the twentieth century's most significant civil liberties causes, has yet to be examined in depth. It deserves to be.

* * *

A biography of Ernst is long overdue. Ernst was eager for one to be written but skeptical that it could be done. "It's sheer madness," he advised a potential biographer. "Everyone has given up. It's madness for anyone to try . . . the only thing anybody could do is to tell the story in terms of a diluted person who runs from one thing to another and has no main streams."[10]

Ernst was right: writing his life has been no easy feat. He left behind a massive collection of personal papers—590 boxes of archival material, as well twenty-one published books and hundreds of other writings on topics ranging from the Supreme Court to obscenity to extrasensory perception. (Ernst calculated that he wrote more than a million words per year.) Ernst's correspondence is scattered throughout the collections of prominent organizations and individuals of his time, including in the voluminous files of the ACLU. Even with his huge achievements, Ernst had a penchant for exaggeration, which also posed challenges for a biography. Especially in his old age, Ernst circulated fibs about himself, embellishing his accomplishments and experiences, a habit that no doubt reflected his insecurities and craving for recognition. As such, Ernst's claims had to be approached with caution and required particular efforts to verify and corroborate. Perhaps the most egregious of Ernst's assertions—now circulated on the internet as fact—was that Ernst was a founder of the ACLU. Ernst was not, in fact, an ACLU founder and did not become seriously involved with the organization until half a decade into its career.

Morris Ernst was a quirky, lovable man with many virtues and no shortage of flaws. He was generous and patient but at the same time vindictive and thin-skinned. He was brilliant, but his thinking could be sloppy and contradictory. Ernst was warm and generous, with many true friends, yet he could betray his colleagues without the slightest pang of conscience. He was shrewd and strategic but at the same time whimsical and impulsive, often plunging ahead without plan or direction.

One of Ernst's most remarkable qualities was his unflagging hopefulness—his "glandular optimism," he called it. One colleague, Harriet Pilpel, recalled that if Ernst saw a law that was unjust, he refused to accept it. According to Pilpel, "He believed in change and he set about changing things."[11] Ernst refused to be limited by what was; he never stopped thinking about what could be. Morris Ernst dreamed of a better world, set out to make it, and in many ways succeeded.

1
EARLY YEARS

> More than once, after a radio or television appearance, or after the publication of newspaper or magazine stories connecting my name with some case or cause, I have received abusive letters. Many of these letters have contained the same, usually poorly scrawled injunction: "You dirty kike, go back where you came from."
>
> When such letters have a return address, I answer them. I have a standard form of reply: Do you mean Alabama?[1]

A lifelong, liberal, city-proud New Yorker, Morris Ernst spent the first year after his birth on August 23, 1888, in Uniontown, Alabama, which sits one hundred miles west of Montgomery, in the fertile part of the state known as the Canebrake. In the 1880s, as the cotton economy flourished, the town of two thousand people was a thriving trading center with fine hotels, well-stocked general stores, and elegant homes.

Though there were few Jews in the South, German Jews owned many of Uniontown's leading establishments, and their impact on the region was profound.[2] They prospered as artisans, financiers, and merchants, and their wealth and enterprise supported growing communities. There was relatively little anti-Semitism in the South at the time; southerners who hoped to imitate northern industrial and commercial accomplishments often welcomed Jews into their villages and towns.[3] It was not uncommon for German Jews to make their first money in the South and then move to New York, where they amassed even greater fortunes. Mayer Lehman, founder of the banking house Lehman Brothers, started out as a cotton dealer in Montgomery in the 1850s. The banker Joseph Seligman and his brothers ran general stores serving towns and plantations in the Alabama countryside.[4]

The Jews of Uniontown owned banks and dry goods stores, built elaborate homes, and joined lodges and civic groups. Family names in the town rolls included Proskauer, Adler, Marx, Wolf, Maier, Hertz, Loewi, Goldsmith, and Markstein. In the 1880s there were seventy-six Jews in Uniontown, enough to form a temple and a social club.[5] They learned English, adopted American lifestyles, and stood among the town's leading citizens. This was the path that Morris Ernst's father, Carl Ernst, had followed.

* * *

In 1869, seventeen-year-old Carl Ernst arrived in Uniontown with nothing more than a mattress, a spoon, and the clothes on his back. Born in Pilsen, Bohemia (then part of Austria-Hungary, now the Czech Republic), Carl came to America fleeing poverty, anti-Semitism, and compulsory service in the Austro-Hungarian military. Carl hailed from a German-speaking Jewish family and followed an older brother, Moritz Leopold ("M.L."), who had put down roots in Uniontown a few years earlier.[6]

Carl was strong, hardworking, and tremendously driven. For six years he labored as a "pack peddler," selling soap, spices, linens, and household trinkets to rural families from an enormous knapsack he hauled on his back. Peddling was a common, even ubiquitous start for Jewish immigrants at the time.[7] The work was grueling. Carl braved storms, heat waves, rabid dogs, and threats of attack and theft. His clothes and shoes were tattered, and hunger was never a stranger.

Yet in time Carl learned English and saved enough to start his own business. With his brother M.L. and another German Jew, Simon Mayer, he founded a general store: Ernst Brothers & Mayer, on Uniontown's main street.[8] Soon it was the town's leading general store, selling an array of dry goods from clothes to perfume to coffins.[9] Carl and M.L. started a small bank on Main Street and also began dabbling in real estate. By the time Carl naturalized in 1882, he and M.L. owned fifteen city lots and Carl had a sizable nest egg.[10]

Carl went north each spring to buy goods for his store. He bought shirts from Henry Bernheim, a high-status German Jew from Alsace-Lorraine who owned the shirt company Bernheim, Dreyfus, and Herman. Carl, who was eager to climb the social ladder, saw much in Bernheim as a partner. Bernheim, too, had started out as a peddler, after immigrating in 1850 at the age of twenty-five.[11]

Bernheim had five daughters and three sons. He saved up to send two of his children to college, including Sarah, his youngest daughter, who graduated from Hunter College—the only public college for women at the time—in 1884 at the age of eighteen.[12] Its graduates typically became teachers.[13] Bernheim was eager to marry off his daughters, and by the time Carl met Bernheim in 1884, all of them had wed except Sarah. The spark between eighteen-year-old Sarah and thirty-two-year-old Carl was immediate, and they were married in a year.[14]

Their first child, Magdalen, was born in June 1886. Morris Leopold, named after Carl's brother, came two years later, on August 23, 1888. The local newspaper, the *Canebrake Herald*, reported that "a son makes Mr. Carl Ernst smile sweeter than ever."[15] An attractive boy with vivid brown eyes and dark curls, Morris was mischievous and full of energy. He and his cousin Montrose, M.L.'s younger son, who lived next door, delighted in playing practical jokes, such as emptying all the sugar bowls. Morris spoke early and asked lots of questions. He was inquisitive, talkative, and extremely bright.

* * *

The years in Uniontown were flush times for the Ernsts. Carl's businesses flourished, and Sarah was happy, at least for a while. Sarah's sister Rachel had married Simon Mayer, Carl's business partner, and they lived in nearby Demopolis. When Mayer died in 1888, Rachel moved to New York, and Sarah grew restless.[16] In October 1889, the Ernsts also moved to New York, where Carl and M.L. set up a land-speculation office on Liberty Street, buying tracts that later became choice locations in the city.[17] In February 1894 Carl and Sarah had a third child, George Goodman.

The family's trajectory continued upward. Their first home in

New York was, like many immigrant homes, on the Lower East Side but they soon moved to Harlem, amid a large population of middle-class German Jews, including Carl and Sarah's siblings.[18] Both the Ernsts and the Bernheims were highly successful, and the extended clans, which included several of Carl's brothers who immigrated after him, boasted lawyers, bankers, and doctors.

The Ernsts lived well. Two live-in Irish maids and a cook served the family. Heavy dinners were laid out formally each night, with fine plates and linens.[19] Tailors came over weekly to fit Sarah for dresses. The family took long summer vacations to seaside and mountain resorts, often with a gaggle of relatives.[20] But clothes and possessions were not important to the Ernsts nor considered proper subjects of discussion. The family members considered themselves people of culture and ideas, and young Morris imbibed these nonmaterialistic values.

Morris's childhood was sheltered, confined largely to his family and their tight-knit German Jewish enclave.[21] Even though Carl was considered Austrian, the Ernsts identified with the Bernheims' upper-middle-class community, whose members prized education and the arts, philanthropy, upward mobility, and cultural assimilation. At its glittering center were the Strausses, Loebs, Lehmans, Lewisohns, and Schiffs, princely families behind major mining, commercial, and banking fortunes. Later dubbed "Our Crowd," they were among the most prominent and prestigious Jews in the nation.[22]

Morris was thus shielded from the brunt of anti-Semitism, which was on the rise, as large numbers of poor Eastern European Jews began arriving on the nation's shores. Hotels, social accommodations, and educational institutions adopted exclusionary policies, announcing "Hebrews Need Not Apply."[23] Even established Jews turned against the newcomers, who seemingly threatened to cast all Jews in a negative light. In an interview much later in his life, Morris recalled that "we looked down on the Poles."[24]

Well-off and assimilated, the Ernsts avoided much of the animus suffered by their less privileged coreligionists. At the same time, within the status-conscious German Jewish enclave, the family experienced discrimination. Carl's Austro-Hungarian origins put them lower in the "pecking order" (in Morris's words) than German Jews and even further below wealthy, acculturated English Jews.[25] From a young age, Morris was conscious of being an outsider—not only a Jew in a largely Protestant nation but socially beneath his more well-heeled Jewish peers.

Like many upwardly mobile Jews, Carl and Sarah were mostly religiously nonobservant. The family went to temple only on holy days, mainly to see and be seen. The Ernsts, like others in their community, were members of Temple Israel, a liberal Reform congregation on Fifth Avenue and 125th Street. The temple was led by Maurice Harris, a young, dynamic rabbi from England who tried to Americanize Judaism by abolishing traditional rituals and introducing English-language prayers into services.[26] Among the temple's trustees were Cyrus Sulzberger, merchant, philanthropist, and father of future *New York Times* publisher Arthur Sulzberger, and prominent judge Samuel Greenbaum, father of Morris's future law partners, Eddie and Laurie.[27]

For a few years Morris attended Sunday school, where he won an award for his Hebrew studies. The prize was a green-covered book titled the *Battles of the War of the Confederacy*, which had the unexpected effect of turning him off religion. This odd gift contributed to his growing conviction that religion was irrational. Though he remained proud of his Jewish heritage, Morris never set foot in a temple again.

* * *

Carl and Sarah left their distinct imprints on Morris. Carl was a dedicated and hardworking father but formal and emotionally distant. Haunted by memories of his peddling days and determined to provide his children every opportunity and comfort, he worked constantly, as many as eighty hours a week. Morris learned from Carl the value of diligence and effort, but affection was scarce. Morris "had no real communication system" with his father, he recalled.[28] By contrast, he adored the bright, creative, and free-thinking Sarah. His mother was intense, serious, and sophisticated-looking, if not beautiful, with sharp, aquiline features accentuated by large, round, gold-rimmed spectacles.

Thanks to Carl's good fortunes, Sarah devoted herself to her passion in life, the pursuit of knowledge and culture. She raced through dozens of novels weekly and ran up large bills at secondhand bookstores. Each night she read aloud to the children—fairy tales and Greek myths when they were young, then such classics as *Ivanhoe*, *Vanity Fair*, and *Leatherstocking Tales*.[29] Carl sat in on the recitations; they were as much an education for him as they were for the children.

Well-read, educated, and engaged with public affairs, Sarah was a woman ahead of her time. Her social views were liberal, and she was regarded as a "modern thinker." "Intellectually and culturally adventurous" is how the Bernheims described her. Sarah took the children to concerts, operas, museums, and plays, and she subjected them to music and dancing lessons. Each summer she dispatched Morris to camps, which were seen as extremely progressive. Camp Marienfeld in Keene, New Hampshire, combined a left-wing curriculum with outdoor recreation. The students lived in tents, heard lectures on the evils of materialism, and slept in the nude.[30]

Sarah was forward-looking in her views on sex, too, which influenced Morris greatly. When he was in his early teens, Sarah bought him a sex education text, "a suppressed and very modern book in regard to matters sexual." [31] It referred to syphilis, which "scared the daylights" out of him. It was his mother's sophisticated attitudes, he speculated, that led him to crusade against censorship laws.[32]

Sarah taught Morris the importance of generosity, charity, and "doing good." "Be good sweet child and let [others] be clever," she would say in lectures on "the golden rule" and "patterns for decent living." Sarah volunteered extensively, impressing on the children the importance of kindness toward the less fortunate. She also taught religious tolerance by example. Sarah's best friend was a bright woman named Nellie Sweeney, a fellow Hunter College graduate and unmarried teacher who was a devout Irish Catholic. Sarah and Nellie's friendship, Morris felt, led to the "evaporation of differences between Jews and Catholics" in his mind.[33]

Sarah never pressured Morris to succeed but gently encouraged him to use his potential. She taught him to set an alarm every day and to wake before it went off. When Morris was fourteen, even though he was afraid, Sarah sent him to Princeton, New Jersey, to attend Woodrow Wilson's inauguration as president of the university there. She put train fare in one hand and a cold sandwich in the other. His mother's confidence meant the world to him.[34] He wrote half a century later, "I shall die in debt to my mother."[35] Though they would not bear fruit immediately, Sarah planted in her son the seeds of courage, fortitude, and self-reliance. "Most fears," she told him, were "completely invalid."[36]

* * *

In 1900, while she was doing charity work in the slums, Morris's beloved mother Sarah came down with tuberculosis.[37] It was for all intents and purposes a death sentence. Marked by a hacking cough, bloody sputum, and a general wasting away of the patient, the dreadful and incurable disease was one of the most feared illnesses in the world. High altitudes, sun, and dry air were thought to encourage remission, and well-off patients were shipped to mountain sanitaria in desperate and usually futile pursuit of relief.

For the next eight years, Sarah battled fiercely for her life. Carl sent her to expensive resorts in the Catskills, the Adirondacks, and the Rockies. She returned to New York between treatments. George and Magdalen went with her, while Morris stayed behind.[38]

While Sarah was away, Morris lived with Rachel Mayer, Sarah's older sister. A generous, sentimental woman who never remarried after Simon Mayer's death, "Aunt Ray" resided with the Bernheims and her sons Leo and Arthur in the Bernheims' enormous home in West Central Harlem. Rachel never remarried, she said, because she wanted to express her love for Simon through her devotion to his sons. Rachel ran the house for the Bernheims in exchange for room and board.[39]

Art and Leo Mayer became Morris's main companions in his teenage years. The Mayer brothers were bright and ambitious, and each would go on to have distinguished careers—Leo as a surgeon and Art as a film executive and critic.[40] Art, who was two years older than Morris, was Morris's buddy, and Leo, four years older, became his role model and mentor. The bond between Morris and the Mayers was fierce. Rachel called Morris her "near-son."[41] Art Mayer recalled, "Next to Leo and myself my mother loved [Morris] more than anyone else in the world."[42]

Meanwhile, Morris longed for Sarah. Heartfelt letters shuttled between them daily. In her precise hand, she penned maternal cautions:

> I want to caution you in this hot weather about your clothes. Moths are very active in the heat and you'd not want anything to destroy the few good things you have. Let me know how you fare in your examinations and whether they seem difficult. Good bye for today. Lovingly, Mama. PS. Have you bought socks? Did you wear that lovely hat to go out driving with Judge Greenbaum and his wife?[43]

It was "a love affair at a distance," Morris recalled. It was in those years that he "started to learn . . . the difference between alone and lonely."[44]

* * *

Though he was later renowned for his exuberance and confidence, this man who would call himself a "glandular optimist" was a brooding and confused adolescent. Until his late teens, Morris was timid, awkward, and aloof from his peers. Even the love of Sarah, Rachel, and the Mayer brothers could not conquer his deep insecurity, borne of his mother's absence and anxieties around abandonment, the family's lesser status within the elite German Jewish community, and no doubt some measure of internalized anti-Semitism. This insecurity would drive much of his life's efforts—his frenetic, compulsive activity, his relentless search for the spotlight, and his quest to attract the attention and praise of others by being smart, charming, and provocative.

His teenage depression and lack of confidence were so profound as to raise concerns. In 1904, when Morris was sixteen, the head of

Camp Marienfeld wrote a worried letter to Sarah. "Morris has been a good camper—unselfish, generous, and willing to do even more than his own share," he observed. "He is too prone, however, to see the dark side of things . . . the boy [has a] tendency towards pessimism. I think this became more marked after the disappointment about the examinations."[45] Morris was an unfocused student and struggled with exams. He later described his teenage self as "afraid of being hurt," "afraid of defeat, afraid of rejection, afraid to try anything."[46]

He fretted about his looks. Although he was in fact strikingly handsome, with olive skin and thick, wavy black hair, he was embarrassed by his pointed, crooked nose and was convinced he was ugly.[47] Fully grown, he was only five foot six and weighed 135 pounds.[48] Morris was never athletic, though as an avid hiker and tennis player he was always fit. One of his earliest heroes was Teddy Roosevelt, president when Morris was in high school. One summer on vacation in the Catskills (in 1901, when he was thirteen) Morris was playing tennis, and word came to the court that President McKinley had been shot and that Roosevelt would succeed him. Throwing his racket in the air, he yelled, "Hurrah for Teddy!" Morris, who considered himself a "physical coward" and blanched at the sight of blood, admired Roosevelt for his energy, ruggedness, and brazenness.[49]

"There were . . . boys who . . . were sophisticated who made me feel quite meager, inadequate, and frightened," he recalled. "I was usually desolate for a friend. . . . I was frightened and lonely for sure."[50]

* * *

In his early years of schooling, Morris attended Public School 89 at 135th Street and Lenox Avenue. After Carl's fortunes picked up, when Morris was thirteen, Morris started at Horace Mann School, a prestigious private school in Morningside Heights in the shadow of Columbia University. Horace Mann had been founded in 1887 as a working laboratory, a coeducational experimental school run by the Teachers College of Columbia to test progressive educational theories under the observation of Teachers College students.[51] It became one of New York's finest high schools, with a selective admissions policy to keep its "social tone" above that of the public schools of the city.[52]

Morris graduated from Horace Mann High School in 1905. The school's curriculum was modern and forward-looking, so progressive that the boys were taught sewing and the girls tended the campus garden.[53] Horace Mann launched many who would become prominent in New York liberal intellectual and legal circles, including ACLU lawyers Dorothy Kenyon (class of 1904) and Osmond Fraenkel (class of 1905), as well as the celebrated newspaper columnist Heywood Broun, who was a year behind Morris. Broun, who was over six feet tall and weighed more than two hundred pounds, was the center on the football team. Although Morris and Broun became friends later in life, they were not close at Horace Mann. Morris knew Broun from a distance and looked up to him.

Horace Mann left little impression on Morris. Even though the school's teachers were considered the "pick of the city," he found them smarmy and dull.[54] His English teacher Helen Bartlett Baker, who happened to be Broun's aunt, was his most influential instructor. Baker, in the words of one Broun biographer, "had the gift for shaming an unprepared student while making him feel that her interest never flagged."[55]

Morris had unreasonably high aspirations for himself. Inspired by Art and Leo Mayer, who went to Harvard, fifteen-year-old Morris took the university's entrance exams for English, Latin, German, History, and French. The dean of Harvard sent him a letter informing him that "you have failed to pass a single examination."[56] The failure was so comically spectacular that Morris kept the letter under the glass on his office desk his entire career.[57]

Morris had never heard of Williams College, a small liberal arts college in Western Massachusetts at the foot of the Berkshire Mountains, until Helen Baker, who believed in the virtues of liberal arts colleges, pushed for her students to attend Williams.[58] Morris became intrigued at the prospect of going to a small college where he might make friends instead of a large school where he would fade into the crowd.[59] When the family was on vacation in nearby Great

FIGURE 1. Morris Ernst and his sister, Magdalen, on a family trip to Pilsen, Bohemia, circa 1891. Courtesy of Stephanie Begen.

Barrington, Massachusetts, in the summer of 1904, Morris went up to Williamstown for an interview. Sarah had dressed him in an unusual hat, "with the front of it furled high up," and it made him especially self-conscious.[60] Nonetheless, he was accepted, and the following August he made his way to the Berkshires. It was there that this painfully insecure boy began to find his voice and himself.

2
WILLIAMS

It was an unlikely place for Morris Ernst's transformation. Founded in 1841, Williams College had graduated governors, senators, and presidents, including James Garfield, class of 1856. Williams drew much of its student body from the *Social Register*, the same source that fed Princeton, Harvard, Yale, and other Ivy League schools. The college was remarkably homogeneous even by standards of the day—Anglo-Saxon, Protestant, and elite. "Williams was a wealthy man's college, an Ivy League college [attracting] wealthy boys" who attended "Groton, Exeter and other swank schools," Ernst recalled. "They knew each other . . . their relatives had gone to Williams."[1]

Set on 450 acres in the small town of Williamstown, Massachusetts, 150 miles west of Boston, the picturesque campus was known for its classical architecture, rolling hills, brilliant fall colors, and white winters. The campus atmosphere was of a conservative, country club type, with heavy emphasis on athletics and socializing. Students were expected to present themselves formally at all times, and there were strict dress codes. Freshmen were not allowed to smoke on the street, to go outside without coats or hats, or to wear corduroy, the privilege being reserved for upperclassmen.[2] Social leaders looked down on bookworms and "greasy grinds" who became too interested in their coursework.[3]

Ernst was one of three Jews in his class. Williams was an unusual choice for Jews, not so much because of formal discrimination but because the school was mostly unknown outside elite social circles.[4] Most Jewish students at Williams came from well-off German Jewish families that could afford an expensive private education.[5] Several of this cohort would become quite successful, including Herbert

Lehman (class of 1899), future governor of New York, and Raoul Fleischmann (class of 1906), who founded Fleischmann's Yeast and provided financial backing for the *New Yorker*. Though anti-Semitism existed in the backdrop of campus life, overt hostility was rare; Jews were not yet enough of a presence on campus to be seen as a threat.[6]

One can imagine the awe and trepidation Ernst felt when he arrived in Williamstown in the summer of 1905, just days after his seventeenth birthday. The pristine, white-columned buildings and halls with names of great founders and forebears like Chapin and Sawyer and Hopkins highlighted the privilege that came with a Williams education and also how out of place he was. Clumsily, he tried to fit in. Thinking it would make him look "collegiate," he wore his required freshman hat, a black hat with a green button, cocked oddly to one side.[7] He was jealous of popular students who went to Albany for a night at the theater and drank at bars in nearby North Adams. Nothing terrified him more than trying to fit in with the "sophisticated boys."[8]

* * *

Fraternities were the heart of social life at Williams.[9] Most students belonged to fraternities. For outsiders like Ernst, frats were generally off-limits because almost all chose members in the first semester and therefore depended on family connections.

Only one fraternity didn't elect in the first semester—Alpha Zeta Alpha, a small local fraternity.[10] AZA had been founded by a group of prominent alumni, concerned with the exclusiveness of the fraternity system, who sought a new organization where academics rather than financial status would be the chief criterion for membership.[11] AZA elected Morris in January of his freshman year.[12] It was the only Williams fraternity that accepted Jews; Herbert Lehman had been an early AZA member.[13] That's how Ernst got to know Lehman.

AZA was the "home of rather serious and not too well-dressed youngsters," as Ernst put it.[14] Most of its seventy-five members were at the bottom of the class in terms of family income and had to work their way through college doing jobs like waiting tables.[15] When it came to scholarship, however, the AZA boys were usually at the top of their class.[16] AZA turned out more "honor men" than any other fraternity at the college. If a member's grades started to slip, there was a collective effort to shore him up.[17]

During his junior year Ernst moved into the fraternity house. The brothers gave one another nicknames, and Ernst's was "Dutch," a variant of *Deutsch*, the German word for "German," because of his Germanic background.[18] For the first time, in this group of outsiders, Ernst felt that he belonged. AZA was, Ernst recalled, one of the most "extraordinary experiences" of his life.[19]

* * *

Classes were less stimulating. His whole life, Ernst maintained that his college education was woefully inadequate.[20] The Williams curriculum was lax, consisting mostly of electives.[21] But much of the boredom was Ernst's fault.[22] Ernst was a middling student and earned near-failing grades in chemistry and math in his freshman year.[23] His grades did improve over time. At graduation the dean called him to his office to congratulate him. "You've improved two percent every six months while you have been here—all eight terms," he told him. "But oh my God, how low you started!"[24]

Only two subjects interested him-history and English. Ernst majored in English and minored in history. Lewis Perry, his English professor, taught one of Ernst's favorite classes: English Drama from 1642 to 1902.[25] Ernst studied American history with Professor T. C. Smith, known for his two-volume biography of President James Garfield. He wrote his thesis with Smith, an essay on "The Failure to Recharter the Bank in 1811."

Edward "Ted" Morgan Lewis, assistant professor of public speaking, was one of the most popular professors on campus. During his freshman year, Ernst took Lewis's class Argumentation and Debating, a notoriously easy "gut" course consisting mostly of memorizing and reciting.[26] The uninspiring class notwithstanding, Lewis became Ernst's first real role model and "idol"—in his eyes "more or less a hero."[27]

* * *

Lewis's story was a rags-to-riches tale. Born in 1872 in Wales, Lewis as a child had moved with his family to impoverished rural New York. Lewis delivered groceries while studying by lamplight using borrowed textbooks. After high school, he saved enough to attend Williams. Lewis made a stunning impression on his classmates as a campus leader and star pitcher and captain of the baseball team.[28]

When it came time to fund his graduate studies, Lewis turned to baseball. While working on his master's degree in ministry at Williams, Lewis achieved fame as a pitcher for two National League baseball teams, the Boston Beaneaters and the Boston Americans. In an era when baseball was notorious for fighting and rowdyism, Lewis was unusual—a college man and a religious one who refused to pitch on Sundays and was nicknamed "Parson Lewis." At the age of twenty-nine, Lewis retired from baseball, returning to Williams, where he taught and was nicknamed the "Pitching Professor."[29]

Ernst revered this tall, eloquent, noble-looking man. Lewis sensed Ernst's admiration—and also his loneliness. Lewis invited Ernst to have dinner with his family in his home, a common practice on the small campus where students had close relationships with faculty. Ernst latched onto Lewis, went to his house in the evening, and helped him wash dishes while they discussed the issues of the day.

It was not only Lewis's attention to Ernst that made a difference. Lewis also revolutionized Ernst's views on government.[30] In 1905, when Ernst started at Williams, the Progressive movement had captured the imagination of idealistic, reform-minded Americans. "A burst of energy that fired in many directions across America" between 1900 and 1920, Progressivism was a response to social problems created by massive socioeconomic changes of the previous generation—the transformation of the United States from a largely agrarian society into an urban, mechanized, industrial one, with devastating and inhumane consequences.[31]

Industrial laborers, including child workers, toiled long hours in unsafe factories. Poor immigrants lived in dirty tenements while industrial barons enjoyed gilded lifestyles. Workers were trapped in a cycle of low wages, frequent accidents, periodic unemployment, and early death. Rural areas were beset by poverty and ignorance.

Consumers were sickened by tainted foods. Municipal governments were wracked by inefficiency and graft. Under the boss and the political machine, corruption, waste, and mismanagement flourished. Bitter conflict between labor and capital resulted in violent strikes.

Buoyed by seemingly unbounded faith in the possibility of reform through regulation, Progressives sought to use government to ameliorate these ills. Their indignation fueled by muckraking exposés such as Upton Sinclair's *The Jungle* (1906) and Lincoln Steffens's *The Shame of the Cities* (1904), reformers joined together in hundreds of diverse groups, social clubs, and charitable organizations to reshape the social order. Led by social workers, ministers, and intellectuals, Progressives sought legislation to break up monopolies and big banking interests, eliminate poverty, increase standards of living, and make relationships between business, labor, and consumers fairer. They worked to open settlement houses for the poor and build parks, playgrounds, and better schools. They called for minimum wage laws, accident insurance, women's suffrage, and child labor laws. Although many of the measures they called for were redistributive, Progressives accepted industrial capitalism and sought primarily to control and ameliorate it. One of the themes of the Progressive movement was the pernicious influence of "private power" that subverted the public interest. Progressives envisioned a harmoniously functioning society in which the power of "special interests" such as big business would cede to the "general interest" or common good. Offering a new vision of shared social responsibility, they challenged entrenched Gilded Age values of individualism, laissez-faire, and property rights.[32]

Presiding over his tiny kitchen table, Lewis spoke animatedly about David Lloyd George, the Welsh radical and future British prime minister whose New Liberal Party established the foundations of the modern English welfare state. Denouncing the existence of hideous poverty alongside incalculable wealth, Lloyd George described taking care of the aged, ill, and disabled as fundamental responsibilities of government. Lewis told Ernst about social insurance, workmen's compensation, old age pensions, and minimum wage, programs that had been implemented in Europe and that were being advocated by American reformers but had yet to be widely adopted in the United States. Lewis introduced Ernst to ideas that were "shocking, new, [and] delightful," in Ernst's words.[33] Lewis taught Ernst that government was more than a "device to get roads built, maintain them, . . . and furnish the army and navy"[34]—that it should have "a relation to people's lives."[35]

Through Lewis, Ernst found his voice. Lewis urged Ernst to go out for the debate team, and Ernst found he was a natural. By the end of the year he was one the finest debaters on campus. Morris was elected captain of the freshman debate team and also made varsity debate, competing against nearby colleges such as Amherst, Brown, Dartmouth, and Wesleyan.[36]

Debate became the entrée into a whirlwind of activity. Ernst discovered he had an ability to speak eloquently, think quickly, and persuade others. Fueled by this new awareness of his talents, he joined dozens of campus groups, often taking on leadership roles. Extracurricular activities became an appealing way for Ernst to find companionship, pursue intellectual interests, and win recognition from his peers. It was in this period that Ernst developed a lifelong trait that he called "exhibitionism"—showing off, making a scene, seizing the spotlight. The attention of his peers was a powerful antidote to his insecurity, and Ernst came to crave it.

Ernst never became one of the "sophisticated boys," but he found a niche in the school's civic-minded and intellectual crowds. In his sophomore year he was elected vice president of two literary societies and an officer of the German Society, devoted to German language study.[37] After an arduous competition, Ernst was chosen for the editorial board of the school newspaper, the *Record*. In this coveted position, he handled alumni news and for a while served as editor in chief.[38]

Ernst's newfound confidence invigorated his social life. Weekends found him playing tennis, hiking in the Berkshires, and going to vaudeville shows.[39] Ernst also began taking trips with his cousin Art Mayer. These long-distance journeys were both symbolic of and a catalyst for his budding independence. After his freshman year he and Mayer took an extended summer jaunt in Europe. They got free passage to Liverpool by signing on as "cattle stiffs," joining a "tough crowd of men" who made their living taking care of livestock on steamships.[40] The boys hiked through France and Switzerland with knapsacks. Ernst fondly recalled "lush honey and butter and rolls, and sunsets on glaciers, and simple people."[41] Black-and-white Kodak snapshots depicted two tanned, fit, shirtless young men climbing hills, wading through streams, enjoying their freedom and having the time of their lives.

Ernst and his cousin had brief flings with women; it was Ernst's first romantic encounter. In Milan, Ernst met an attractive woman from Philadelphia, and Mayer also met a "girl he liked." The two young men came back to the United States with the two young women on a Dutch steamship—they paid their way this time—and after parting ways on arrival, Ernst, bolder than ever, began his sophomore year.[42]

* * *

During Morris's junior year, two tragedies befell the Ernst family. In the Panic of 1907, the first worldwide financial crisis of the twentieth century in which the New York Stock Exchange fell by 50 percent, Carl lost nearly all his wealth, which he never recovered.[43] Meanwhile, Sarah was in a sanitarium in Colorado Springs, fighting for her life. On February 15, 1908, at the age of forty-one, she succumbed to tuberculosis.[44] Ernst found out about her death while on campus. For the first time in his life, "he bawled in front of utter strangers."[45]

Despite this spontaneous expression of grief, Ernst was developing a capacity to compartmentalize distressing emotions, a skill that would serve him well over the years. The death of his beloved mother did not slow him, and he continued his frenzied campus participation. With his debate partner Eddie Greenbaum, a friend from Horace Mann School, Ernst led the debate team to victories against Wesleyan, Amherst, Dartmouth, and Brown. He continued to edit the *Record* and also edited the 1909 *Class Book*, or yearbook.[46] Perhaps his greatest achievement, at least in his mind, was his election that spring to Gargoyle, an elite senior honor society. Only a handful of students were chosen each year—those who "had fostered the

FIGURE 2. Alpha Zeta Alpha fraternity, Williams College, circa 1907, with Morris Ernst in back row, third from left. Courtesy of Harry Ransom Center, University of Texas at Austin.

Williams spirit and done most to better the college."[47] He had been gunning for membership. The society had a pin with a Gargoyle on it, and when he got it, he threw out all his bow ties—Ernst had a fashion of wearing bow ties—because he couldn't wear the pin with the ties on.[48]

In June 1909 Morris graduated from Williams College with a BA in English. He won second place in a class vote for the "most energetic" student, after his friend George Van De Carr.[49] His *Class Book* entry predicted his future trajectory: "Ernst has specialized in debating and literary work and his progressiveness and energy around college have given him a reputation as one of the most energetic and most likely to succeed."[50] The awkward freshman with the downward gaze and off-kilter hat had become one of the most respected young men on campus.

3

NEW YORK

And yet, Morris Ernst's distinguished college career didn't get him very far. An English degree, even from an elite school like Williams, didn't open doors for a young Jewish man of Ernst's position. Morris's father Carl couldn't support his son, and full-time graduate school was out of the question. Unlike many of his Williams classmates, Ernst lacked the social and family connections to land a good job in business. The only thing the family had was shirts.

On his mother's side, the Bernheim family was well situated in the Jewish-dominated garment industry. Ernst's Uncle Eli, Sarah's younger brother, ran a shirt factory. Eli came up with the idea of setting up Morris in his own shirt company. Eli introduced him to two shirt makers and loaned him money to set up a factory. In 1909 the Usona ("United States of North America") shirt company was born.[1] Thus it was that the future high-profile lawyer and civil liberties champion had an inauspicious start to his career—first managing a shirt factory and later selling cheap dining room sets in a Brooklyn furniture store.

* * *

We know little about the time Ernst spent in the shirt business, other than that the garments he made were hideous—the "ugliest . . . in the world," in Ernst's own recollection.[2] Headquartered in a loft in the industrial district in Brooklyn near the polluted Gowanus Canal, the Usona company employed sixty-five male and female workers, including three below the age of sixteen.[3] Ernst's social consciousness had not developed to the point where those working conditions upset him.

A man named Sigmund Reiss, who had been a contractor for a shirt manufacturer, ran the all the machines, and Salvyn Levy did most of the selling. Ernst managed the employees and kept the books, having learned from the bookkeeper at his Uncle Eli's shirt company.[4] Ernst also dabbled in sales, which he hated. "I learned about gussets and a little bit about the disgraceful treatment accorded salesman," he remembered.[5] Ernst lived with his father and his brother George, then in high school, in an apartment on West Ninetieth Street and spent long hours commuting. The job was boring but lucrative. In what was becoming his trademark flamboyant style, Ernst sent his entire first paycheck to Williams College. He wrote directly to college president Harry Garfield, telling him he'd landed on his feet and wanted to give back.[6]

Now earning a living, Morris began thinking about marriage. He started dating Susan Leerburger, a nineteen-year-old Barnard College student from a Jewish immigrant family from Munich that had become wealthy in the furniture business. A vivacious, upbeat woman, Susan acted in plays, drew illustrations for the Barnard yearbook, and painted sets for the theater.[7] Susan was to become Ernst's first wife, and also his ticket out of the garment industry. Susan's sister Berenice was married to Charlie Baumann, who ran several furniture stores.[8] Baumann offered Ernst a lucrative position as a manager at his store in Brooklyn. In the spring of 1910 he sold out his interest in Usona to his cousin Leo Mayer and went to work for Baumann.

* * *

It was the biggest furniture chain in New York. Founded by Charlie's father Ludwig, Baumann's was famous for pioneering furniture sales on the installment plan.[9] "Ours is surely a STORE FOR ALL OF THE PEOPLE, a store where Dependable Furniture, Carpets, Draperies, and House Furnishings are sold on easy terms," read advertisements. "Liberal credit is extended to those who want it . . . the merchandise we always have in stock meets the requirements of all grades of people."[10]

Morris kept the books, pursued delinquent accounts and repossessions, and gave financial advice to Baumann. It was a position of significant responsibility for a young man, and it made Ernst feel important. Despite his distaste for sales, Ernst also worked the selling floor and did well. Each day he met dozens of working-class newlyweds trying to furnish a home on a meager paycheck. He learned how to size up his clients, how to find out the husband's income without offending him. Knowing that most young couples wanted more than they could afford, he tried to keep the sale down so the account would be quickly paid off.[11] The job also required Ernst to become a "marriage counselor" of sorts. Many couples would call up the store after a fight, asking to return the furniture. Ernst would bring them in to settle the spat.[12] In mediating disputes over furniture, he discovered he had a talent for helping people solve problems through discussion and negotiation.[13]

Ernst earned even more at Baumann's than he had at Usona but worked very long hours. The store had evening and weekend hours, and many a Saturday found him on the selling floor late into the evening, cajoling the indecisive or consoling the brokenhearted. Furniture was no more intellectually stimulating than shirts, and he found himself withering for lack of mental challenge. He recalled, "It was 1910, and I was twenty-two years old. I was not happy about my job, which included not only bookkeeping but also selling ugly furniture to newlyweds at a dollar down and a dollar a week."[14] Life had him "boxed," he wrote.[15] How he would get out was unclear.

* * *

The answer eventually came at a skating rink. Morris often went to the Saint Nicholas Ice Rink on West Sixty-Sixth Street to skate, think, and relax. One evening a friend from Horace Mann School sailed past him on the ice. Herbert Carlebach hailed from a prestigious family. Carlebach told Ernst he was working at his father's bank by day and studying law in the evening.

That ten-minute conversation was the inspiration he needed. In his senior year of college Ernst had dabbled with the idea of studying law part-time but abandoned the idea to focus on the shirt factory. The tedium of his first months in business, along with the conversation with Carlebach, invited him to reconsider that plan. "If Herb, a social butterfly, could find the time and energy to study law, why couldn't I?" Ernst wondered.[16] The deadline for enrolling in the city's largest evening law school was close at hand, and he went down to register the following day. In 1910 Morris began night law school at New York Law School.

* * *

The school was by no means prestigious. Most of the city's elite lawyers graduated from Ivy League schools such as Yale and Columbia. The school was nonetheless a pillar of the local legal community, producing lawyers who assumed key positions in the city's bar.

New York Law School was relatively new, having originated in 1891 out of a dispute at Columbia Law School over an attempt to introduce the case method of study, which had been recently pioneered at Harvard Law School and would become the dominant teaching method at American law schools. Under the case method, students read judicial opinions as a means of understanding the law. Theodore Dwight, dean and founder of Columbia Law School, opposed the case method, believing that students learned better from secondary sources, such as treatises written by legal scholars, which tended to present law not as a series of rulings but rather a "system of principles."[17] As a result of the disagreement, Dwight and other faculty left Columbia to found their own law school in lower Manhattan.[18] At New York Law School, students pursued a standard lineup of law school courses taught from textbooks and treatises such as Blackstone's *Commentaries* and *Greenleaf on Evidence*.[19] By 1904, New York Law School was the largest law school in the country. That year its founders created one of the nation's first evening divisions, with a two-year program leading to the LLB degree. In 1908 it acquired its own building at 174 Fulton Street in the financial district.[20]

The part-time, evening law school model, intended to accommodate working students, was growing and controversial.[21] The years between 1890 and 1910 witnessed a surge in part-time and evening law programs. Night law schools were criticized for their poor instruction and lax standards. Part-time law schools also attracted a disproportionate number of immigrants and second-generation immigrants, which frightened elite members of the bar. In the early twentieth century, the number of lawyers of foreign birth or foreign parentage was expanding exponentially, outpacing the rate of growth of the profession.[22] A special committee was appointed in Pennsylvania to recommend changes to bar admissions requirements that would maintain the "honor and dignity" of the bar. To identify the problem, names were read from a *New York Times* list of graduates from New York Law School. By the reader's estimate, the majority of men were "by their disposition, their character and their training naturally disposed to move along the line of a commercial or industrial life"—they were Jewish.[23]

Defenders of night law schools lauded their students' "pluck, energy, . . . and enthusiasm."[24] What night students lacked in background they made up with ambition and effort. The "devoted, studious, earnest graduate of the evening law schools, who oftentimes snatches his education, literally and not figuratively, from the jaws of want, outshines daily in the courtroom and in the office, on the bench, and at the bar, the socially prominent, pampered, often bored to death graduate of the leading day law schools," observed one law professor.[25] The "boys who went to night school were a totally different group from those who could afford day school," Ernst recalled. "Night school boys really meant it. One way or another they were taking some kind of beating to go to law school five nights a week after a full day spent working. There were no playboys . . . there was practically no such thing as attendance at night law school because 'my father wants me to be a lawyer.'"[26]

Morris himself "took a beating." It was a tiring and lonely time, and a stark contrast with his years at Williams. Each evening Ernst would come in from Brooklyn and have a hurried dinner at Whyte's Restaurant near the law school. He would attend classes for a few hours and return home by ten thirty or eleven. After a few hours of sleep he would get up, get dressed, and go back to the furniture store. He spent almost three hours a day on trains—the subway was forty-five minutes each way between his home, work, and school. His only study time was in transit. Ernst would tear out pages from his textbooks and read them standing up in the crowded train. On these rides he also read the *New York Post*, edited by Oswald Garrison Villard, the noted progressive and cofounder of the NAACP, who used the editorial page to argue for such causes as anti-imperialism, pacifism, and racial equality. The *Post*, Ernst recalled, was an extremely important influence on him, "more important than any single book." Ernst worked hard to memorize his law lessons, only to be too exhausted to recite them in class.[27] The grueling routine lasted two years.

* * *

In June 1912, Ernst received his LLB degree. Two months later, he married Susan Leerburger in a quiet ceremony at the Hotel Savoy.[28] After a three-week honeymoon in the Adirondacks, they returned to an apartment at 749 West End Avenue on the Upper West Side.

Morris wrote almost nothing about his marriage to Susan, and he kept almost no records of those years. Their marriage apparently was not unhappy, though Morris, busy pursuing his career, was by his own admission an inattentive husband. His marriage to Susan was not "spontaneous or thrilling," he would recall, but "tame and matter of fact."[29]

Susan was like Sarah Ernst in many ways, intelligent and arty and bookish. Also like Sarah, Susan was not healthy. Around 1914, Susan was hospitalized for a week, possibly in connection with a miscarriage. On June 12, 1917, Susan and Morris had a daughter, Constance, who became known as Connie. Three years later, Susan died at the age of thirty.[30]

When Morris Ernst graduated from law school, these challenges and tragedies were still in the future. Ernst faced the more immediate issue of passing the bar. He studied while working full time at Baumann's and, predictably, failed. There were two parts to the exam, one on procedure and the other on substantive law. Ernst flunked the substantive section but got high marks in procedure, even though he had no experience practicing law.[31] He passed the entire exam on the second try.

Morris needed a statement of character from another lawyer as a condition for being admitted to the bar. In desperation he went to his father, who told him to contact Joseph Proskauer, a successful New York attorney (and future state supreme court judge) who had lived in Alabama in his youth and knew Carl. Morris went to Proskauer timidly. Because Proskauer didn't know Morris, he gave him a two-page letter that sang the praises of Carl. Even with this dubious affidavit, Morris was admitted to the bar on April 14, 1913.

Ernst knew that the chances of actually practicing law were slim. There was no possibility of being hired by a law firm that was not Jewish, and there were few Jewish firms.[32] Most Jewish lawyers had to set up their own practices, which he was in no position to do. Morris knew no lawyers except two elder cousins and members of the firm that represented Baumann's. When he told them his interest in practicing law, they pooh-poohed it. He had only "the most tenuous dream of ever practicing at the bar."[33]

* * *

The year Ernst graduated marked the high point of the Progressive movement. "Never before," observes historian Arthur Link, "had the people of the United States engaged in so many diverse [endeavors] for the improvement of their political system, economy, and communities."[34] In 1912, Theodore Roosevelt ran for the presidency under the banner of the Progressive Party, on a platform including restrictions on campaign finance contributions, the establishment of social insurance, minimum wage, the eight-hour workday, and women's suffrage. Throughout the country, reformers fought for greater government intervention in economic and social life, for legislation that would protect the common good, redress inequality, reform politics, and regulate special interests. Progressives combined tremendous social idealism with faith in democracy, in the rationality of human beings, and in statistics, efficiency, and organization. They maintained that the people and their elected leaders, working through the democratic process and using the latest methods of social science research, could eliminate the most acute suffering and make life more just, tolerable, and decent for all.

New York was the heart of the movement. Facing an influx of immigrants, grinding poverty, industrial abuses, and problems of housing, crime, disease, and policing, New York was a breeding ground of social problems and vigorous efforts to end those problems. New Yorkers created an array of nonprofit organizations to tackle such issues as child labor, failing schools, political corruption, and unsafe working conditions. Lawyers, social workers, clergy, journalists, and academics were at the forefront of these efforts. They researched causes, gathered and analyzed data, created journals, lobbied for legislation, brought court cases, and founded institutions to manage and fund reform projects. There was a distinct reform community in the city; many activists belonged to several different groups with interlocking, overlapping boards of directors. Collectively, in the words of historian Mike Wallace, New York's progressives "created one of the . . . most advanced social policy complexes" in the nation.[35]

Guided by Ted Lewis's liberal vision, Ernst immersed himself in reform activity not long after his return to New York. He joined several organizations, including the City Club, a prestigious civic group that became one of his most fortuitous associations.

* * *

Founded in 1892 by lawyer Edmond Kelley as a "social club with a civic purpose," the City Club was an important force in New York reform circles. Originally concerned with "good government" and opposition to the machine politics of Tammany Hall, the group broadened its focus to work on a variety of causes, including tenement reform, workers' compensation, factory condition improvements, and child labor reform.[36] The club was a magnet for the city's well-heeled, civic-minded citizens. By 1912 more than 1,200 men were affiliated with the group, including business executives, publishers, and clergymen. The City Club had its own building at 55 West Forty-Fourth Street, a clubhouse with a wood-paneled reading room, dining room, and library, fashioned in the elegant style to which its members were accustomed.[37] Through the City Club Ernst met many men who would play important roles in his career, including Robert Moses, book publisher G. P. Putnam, and editor Walter Lippmann of the new progressive journal the *New Republic*.

Ernst faithfully attended weekly meetings and joined the Committee on Legislation, one of the most important committees, tasked with reviewing bills introduced in the state legislature, as many as five hundred a year. The City Club was a "good teacher," he often remarked.[38] The experience, he said, was like going to graduate school in public policy.

Not long after joining the City Club, the aspiring young reformer turned his attention to one of the city's most pressing crises.

In the winter of 1913 frozen bodies lined the streets. Breadlines mounted, and homeless people slept in doorways and churches. The cause of the crisis was a severe recession, the second worst economic panic in the nation's history. Levels of unemployment were brutally high. By December 1913 the number of jobless people in the city had reached 325,000.[39] Shocked to see deprivation on such a massive scale, Ernst went to the library and began researching the topic of unemployment.[40]

Before 1900 it had been widely assumed that unemployment was an issue beyond the control of the state, a problem that could be corrected only by market forces. By the second decade of the twentieth century, Progressives had begun to argue that the government had both the power and the duty to reduce unemployment and ameliorate its effects.[41] Ernst found out that England had created government-run employment exchanges and that a handful of public employment bureaus existed in the United States.[42] He read the works of Progressive economists and political scientists who argued that the existing system of connecting workers and jobs through newspaper ads and "help wanted" signs was wasteful and inefficient. Ernst agreed that a government-run system matching workers and jobs would distribute workers properly, centralize demand and supply, and decrease joblessness by eliminating "lost motion" in the employment of labor. Ernst went to Charles H. Strong, president of the City Club, urging him to take up the matter.

In December 1913 the Trustees of the City Club appointed twenty-five-year-old Morris Ernst chairman of a special committee charged with making an inquiry into the possibility of creating public employment exchanges in New York. Ernst asked John B. Andrews, head of the American Association of Labor Legislation, an advocacy group promoting workers' compensation and occupational safety laws, to join him in the study. The investigation resulted in a thirty-five-page report published the following year.

The labor market in New York was in a "chaotic condition," without a single public employment bureau, the report asserted.[43] For each job filled in New York, three dollars was spent in newspaper advertising alone.[44] Private employment agents, "employment sharks," were taking advantage of job seekers by charging extortionate fees and misrepresenting working conditions. The report recommended the establishment of a Bureau of Employment within the state Department of Labor that would organize employment bureaus in New York, Buffalo, Rochester, and other cities. The report included a draft of a tentative bill, drawn up by Ernst.[45]

The following February the City Club hosted a conference, the First National Conference on Unemployment, attended by trade unionists, employers, economists, and government officials.[46] Representatives from fifty-nine cities discussed the causes of unemployment, contemplated European approaches to the problem, and called for state and federal action.[47] Speaking before the group, Ernst declared that unemployment was the "most serious problem of modern industry." The conference voted unanimously to endorse the creation of state and municipal labor exchanges and urged the federal Department of Labor to establish a bureau coordinating their work. [48] Shortly after, the New York Board of Aldermen adopted an ordinance creating a public employment bureau in the city, and Governor Martin Glynn sent the state legislature a special message urging the establishment of a system of state employment bureaus. At the end of its session in March, the legislature passed a bill providing for a state employment exchange, and Glynn signed it.[49] Ernst's report had been crucial to the law's passage.[50]

* * *

In Progressive reform activity, Morris had found his métier and an outlet for his intellectual curiosity and prodigious energies. By 1915 he belonged to at least a dozen organizations, including the American Association of Labor Legislation and a settlement house on the Lower East Side on which he served on the board of directors. "Joining" was de rigueur in reform circles; it was fashionable to belong to multiple groups and to be listed as a member of a prestigious committee or board of directors. Ernst's name appeared on letterheads next to such legendary reformers as Florence Kelley, Lillian Wald, Mary Van Kleeck, Frederick Howe, and Pauline Goldmark.

Ernst's enthusiasm for his civic activities was "larger than life," friends recalled. Acquaintances described his penetrating eyes, fierce demeanor, "100-mile-an-hour mind,"[51] and "quick and almost sparrowlike" movements.[52] Full of energy and ideas, he created dozens of reform proposals, devising public and private solutions to such social ills as unemployment, crime, and poverty. He sent his plans to his acquaintances Herbert Croly and Walter Lippmann at the *New Republic*, who received his ideas cordially but never published them. Ernst's correspondence from this time reveals a bright, optimistic young man with genuine belief in the possibility of social betterment—often verging on righteousness—and in equal proportion, ambition and confidence, if not haughtiness and arrogance. We see a young man who truly believes he is somebody—if not now, then soon to be.

This somewhat conceited self-image was not completely unfounded. Ernst was in fact becoming well known in reform circles. Community groups asked him to speak as an "employment expert," and he was written up in the papers. Newspapers referred to him as a "prominent lawyer," even though he hadn't practiced law a day in his life.[53]

Morris Ernst's star was rising in the reform community, and he was making good money at the furniture store. He lived comfortably, attending the opera, running up big bills at Brentano's bookstore, and buying painting lessons for Susan.

But it wasn't enough. Ernst was bored, craving even more stimulation, more challenges, and more recognition. "Life had me in a corner," he later lamented. "Married, living up on West End Avenue in Manhattan, two hours in the subway six days a week, with Saturday at the store until midnight, was less than the kind of living I wanted."[54] The goal of making money for its own sake was to him simply "without meaning."[55]

4
GREENBAUM, WOLFF, AND ERNST

At the end of 1914 Ernst got a call from his friend Lawrence "Laurie" Greenbaum, a Williams College classmate. Did Ernst want to start a law firm with him, his brother Eddie, and another Columbia Law graduate, Herb Wolff? Ernst recognized it as the opportunity of a lifetime. "It didn't take me two minutes to make this decision," he recalled. "This was what I wanted to do."[1]

* * *

Ernst's friendship with the Greenbaum brothers dated back to his childhood. The brothers were sons of Samuel Greenbaum, a Jew from London who had been a judge on the New York Supreme Court since 1902.[2] The Greenbaums lived in a fashionable brownstone on the Upper East Side and had attended Temple Israel with the Ernsts.[3] Both brothers went to Horace Mann School with Ernst and also to Williams. Laurie had been in Ernst's class at Williams, and Eddie, who graduated the following year, had been Ernst's partner on the debate team. Morris looked up to the Greenbaums, who were wealthy and ran in "Our Crowd" circles. After Williams, both Greenbaums attended Columbia Law School.

The Greenbaum brothers were hard-driving and exceptionally smart. Laurie was blond and good-looking, with a dazzling range of interests and talents. Adept with numbers, he was a mathematical genius and also brilliant at law.[4] Laurie's temper was infamous. His secretary would resign when he flung a book at her in anger. Laurie taught Ernst "not to suppress," in Ernst's words—that "like champagne, if the cork is blown all is calm."[5]

Eddie Greenbaum, fifteen months younger, was more reserved

than his brother but also opinionated and forthright. Eddie became notorious for quitting the mock trial team at Columbia when it refused to accept his friend Herb Wolff because Wolff was Jewish. Eddie also quit law review because he thought the privileges law review members were given were unfair.[6] Dean Harlan Stone personally criticized him, saying that a judge's son should understand professional conventions better.[7] Of all the partners other than Ernst, Eddie would go on to have the most public career. He became a noted advocate of court reform and conducted celebrated service in the military, including serving as general and assistant to the secretary of war during the Second World War.[8]

The third partner, Herb Wolff, was a Dartmouth graduate who attended Columbia with the Greenbaums.[9] Wolff graduated from law school in 1913 and was admitted to the bar the same day as Ernst. Wolff hailed from an elite German Jewish background, and his parents were family friends of the Greenbaums.[10] Wolff's father had been a colleague of Felix Adler, founder of the New York Society for Ethical Culture, and for decades Herb Wolff sat on the board of the directors of the Ethical Culture School. Wolff was soft-spoken and warm, and his calmness balanced the tempers of his more volatile friends.[11]

At Columbia, the Greenbaums agreed to practice law together as soon as they could. After law school, the two brothers and Wolff all clerked for respected Jewish law firms. In 1913, Laurie Greenbaum began practicing in an office at 2 Rector Street in the financial district, a building that was home to several firms. The following year Wolff and Eddie Greenbaum were invited to join the practice.[12]

Later that year a cheap suite became available in the rear of the building. It was cheap because it was on the second floor, which was right at the level of the Sixth Avenue El, its trains clattering past outside the window. Laurie saw the opportunity to start the firm that he, Eddie, and Wolff had talked about. He rented the space and made arrangements. One of the first things they did was to reach out to Ernst. Laurie thought Ernst could bring a unique perspective because he had business experience and had never worked in a law office.[13]

Ernst knew he was taking a huge risk in joining the firm. Of the partners, he was the only one who was actually sacrificing something. The young lawyers didn't have a single prospective client in sight. He wrote to Ted Lewis, who remained an adviser and confidante: "As you know this move has been close to my heart for quite a number of years, and (although) there is some element of gamble mixed up in the step, I am making the change with the greatest confidence and hopes for the future." He hoped that legal practice would bring him closer to social reform work, telling Lewis that "it may open the door to further work along those lines which have always interested me and in which you first aroused a certain amount of interest."[14]

The partners signed no formal agreement. "Important relationships in life require neither pen and ink nor red seal," Ernst recalled. "Their terms are written in the spirit."[15] Ernst quit Baumann's in April 1915, and on May 15, Greenbaum, Wolff, and Ernst opened its doors.[16]

* * *

The office at 2 Rector Street was spare and grungy, to put it mildly. Greenbaum, Wolff, and Ernst consisted of four cubicles, a few beat-up desks, and an unfurnished entrance hall. Outside the window, within nearly touching distance, was the old, noisy, grinding elevated railroad, whose trains boomed so loudly when they passed by that it was impossible to talk.[17]

The practice had to be built up from scratch, and the firm's first year was incredibly lean. Each partner made less than $100 a month, and they could barely pay the secretary.[18] It took five years for Ernst to earn close to what he made at Baumann's. Even at that salary, Ernst felt he was overpaid. His part-time legal education had taught him little. What he lacked in substance he would make up in showmanship—his trademark "exhibitionism."[19]

Slowly, cases began to trickle in. Several were minor matters, such as leases, wills, trusts, and divorce and contract suits. Ernst's connections in the garment and furniture industries brought in clients. Sometimes cases came out of the blue. One day right after the office opened, a new client walked in unsolicited. "How did you get here?" the partners asked, astonished. He said he had been told that 2 Rector Street was a building with a lot of lawyers, and he walked upstairs and found them.[20]

Another morning, Ernst, who was a chain smoker, decided to have a cigarette as he was leaving the house. He usually didn't smoke until he got to the office, but that day's decision to have one earlier led to an extraordinary stroke of luck. Ernst ran to catch the double-decker bus as he always did and went up to the top floor to finish his cigarette. A few blocks up Fifth Avenue, a well-dressed man sat down next to him, and they chatted about their work. Before they parted ways, the man, a prominent jeweler who was organizing an association of retail jewelers, asked him if he would come to his house that evening and meet his business partners. It marked the beginning of the firm's work for the jewelry industry.[21] In 1916 Greenbaum, Wolff, and Ernst was retained as general counsel for the Retail Jewelers' Association of Greater New York. This role led, shortly after, to the firm becoming general counsel for the National Jewelers' Board of Trade, comprised of jewelry manufacturers and wholesalers.[22]

With the jewelry account, the firm hit the jackpot. The board's retainer was as valuable to the firm as if it had become counsel to a large industry.[23] Besides serving as counsel to the board, the lawyers were asked to handle the commercial work for thousands of its members, which in turn dealt with thousands of retailers. The firm's income nearly doubled. The work was far more than the firm was equipped to handle, however, and they had to hire a separate staff and take out more office space. The Jewelers' Board of Trade account lasted eight years and established the law firm within the business community.[24]

Through the jewelry account, Ernst attained his first real success as a lawyer. As counsel first for the Retail Jewelers' Association and then the Jewelers' Board of Trade, he was called to develop expertise in several legal fields including tax, contracts, and insurance. The jewelry account also brought him his first trial experience. The first case he took to court involved defending a small jeweler sued by a woman who had paid him sixteen dollars to reset a diamond. The stone had come out and was lost. The woman sought to recover on the basis of faulty workmanship. Ernst established that upon leaving the jeweler's, she had ridden in an elevated train, a mode of transportation known for bumps and jolts that could loosen a stone from its setting. He won the case.[25]

Though Ernst knew nothing about jewelry before 1916, he threw himself into the field and made it his own. Trade journals described him as "counsel to the jewelry trade of the United States."[26] He was feted by the board at a special luncheon at the Waldorf Hotel, where he was presented with a gold cigarette case and pencil. The pencil was engraved with the initials MLE, said to stand for "Marconi Lightning Ernst," after Guglielmo Marconi, the inventor of radio technology.[27]

* * *

From the start, Ernst was a highly unconventional lawyer. His approach to law was so unorthodox that it was shocking, recalled Newman Levy, a friend who joined the firm in 1920. Ernst felt himself unbound by legalities and technicalities—he had a "blithe disregard" for the rules, in Levy's words.[28]

Ernst developed an instrumental view of the law that he would hold his entire career. The purpose of law, he insisted, was to achieve desired outcomes, particularly when social reform and social justice were involved. An adherent of the nascent legal realist school of thought, Ernst believed that legal doctrines should reflect social conditions and that law must be a flexible and practical tool to deal with social problems.

Law was not a set of binding, formal precedents but an "invention" that was "constantly subject to change," Ernst believed. It was "professional sin" to "insist on established means which lead only to undesirable or obsolete ends," he argued. "Treat lightly old lady Stare Decisis because law is an ever-expanding process," he would say.[29] This stance made him an iconoclast in the profession and generated no small hostility from his colleagues. "The interesting question in a legal case was never 'what is the rule,'" he said, but "what *ought* the rule be so that a beneficial result may obtain?"[30]

* * *

Another distinctive feature of Ernst's legal practice was its media savviness, unusual in this age before the advent of modern public relations. Ernst was highly attuned to the importance of public image in advancing his career, and his self-promotion was shameless. Ernst quickly established connections with news reporters and before long began appearing in the papers. The *New York Times*, in particular, became a platform for his clients and causes; this exposure was facilitated by Ernst's childhood friend Art Sulzberger, who had married the publisher's daughter and was working at the paper.

Ernst became renowned for his zealous showmanship on behalf of his clients. For several years he represented the New York Market Growers Association, an association of farmers and gardeners who marketed produce in New York City. On behalf of association farmers, he opposed a pending ordinance that would provide space in public markets for middlemen. He argued in hearings that to license speculators to do business in public markets would increase the cost of living in the city. He was so cantankerous in making his point that he was thrown out of the hearing. "Adam and Eve had a hearing before they got thrown out of the Garden of Eden," Ernst shouted as he packed up his briefcase and a police officer escorted him out.[31]

* * *

With United States entry into World War I in 1917, Ernst registered for the draft as required by the Selective Service Act. He was never called to serve; under the act's classifications, he was "temporarily deferred" because he had a wife as a dependent.[32]

Ernst never recorded his thoughts on the war, unusual for someone who was so opinionated and voluble on so many subjects. He appears to have supported the war and contributed to the effort through public service.[33] For three months he took leave from his law practice to run, at the request of Governor Whitman, a clearinghouse that coordinated the work of the nonprofit employment agencies in the state.[34] He also worked part-time as an adviser for the

United States Shipping Board. Considered an "employment expert," Ernst was dispatched to shipbuilding works to investigate hiring practices and explore ways to reduce turnover.[35] He was a "dollar a year man," one of the executives who helped the government manage industry during the war at token pay, under the law forbidding the government from accepting the services of unpaid volunteers. Ernst was paid a grand total of two cents a week. Meanwhile, a group of reformers who would become among Ernst's closest friends were denouncing the war, raising hell, and laying the foundations of the modern civil liberties movement.

* * *

In 1914 a group of prominent progressives had joined together to protest efforts to prepare for war. Fearing that participation in war would endanger social reform work and democracy itself, the group, calling themselves the American Union Against Militarism, intended to "throw a monkey wrench into the machinery of preparedness."[36] Its distinguished members included settlement house director Lillian Wald; Jane Addams, founder of the Hull House settlement in Chicago; pacifist Unitarian minister John Haynes Holmes; and *Nation* editor Oswald Garrison Villard.

The AUAM marched in the streets, lobbied members of Congress, and staged protests. In their marches they dangled a huge effigy of a dinosaur, meant to symbolize brainless aggression leading to extinction.[37] When AUAM director Crystal Eastman became ill and had to resign, a young social worker from St. Louis named Roger Baldwin took her place. Energetic and charismatic, Baldwin doubled the membership within six months.[38] Within a year it was the largest peace group in the country, with a branch office in every large city and an active membership of 1,500.[39]

After the United States entered the war, Baldwin focused his work on war resisters. He lobbied to extend protections for conscientious objectors in legislation on conscription and formed, within the AUAM, a bureau that enlisted lawyers to help persecuted conscientious objectors. A divide arose when Wald and others were urging the Wilson administration to make a negotiated peace while Baldwin was criticizing the administration for prosecuting war resisters.[40] Baldwin's organization split from the AUAM and was renamed the National Civil Liberties Bureau.[41]

The NCLB coordinated the defense of draft resisters and served as a clearinghouse for information about conscientious objectors. A staff in New York and 120 cooperating attorneys throughout the United States furnished legal advice, paid bail, and assisted conscientious objectors to gain "recognition and fair treatment."[42] The NCLB also came to the defense of the Industrial Workers of the World (IWW), the radical anarchist union, after its offices had been raided by the government and its members imprisoned. The NCLB pledged to defend freedoms of speech, press, and assembly, liberty of conscience, and freedom from unlawful search and seizure.[43] It was the first organization in the nation's history devoted to the defense of civil liberties, and it came not a moment too soon.[44]

* * *

The war years saw unprecedented violations of the right of free speech. Never before had the government cracked down so harshly on dissent. President Wilson was determined to root out disloyalty, and Congress backed him with repressive legislation. The Espionage Act of 1917 made it a crime to obstruct recruiting efforts. The Sedition Act of 1918 outlawed any "disloyal, profane, scurrilous, or abusive language about the form of government of the United States."[45] Members of the radical labor movement, pacifists, Socialists, and other opponents of war were prosecuted under the acts. Under the mail censorship clause of the Espionage Act, the entire antiwar and Socialist press was banned.[46]

Private vigilante groups—so-called superpatriots–assisted the government in its crusade by attacking purported opponents of the war. The conflict became an excuse for conservative, native-stock citizens to work off hostilities against recent immigrants and others seen as "unpatriotic" and "foreign." Mobs tarred and feathered alleged war critics. Members of the American Protective League, a private organization sponsored by the Justice Department, rounded up suspected draft evaders in "slacker raids." Schools and universities joined the campaign to compel patriotism by firing teachers who espoused radical views.

There was little public protest against these acts and virtually no legal protection for the persecuted. Although freedom of speech was enshrined in the First Amendment to the US Constitution, courts, in reality, imposed few restrictions on government restraints on speech. The reigning doctrine used by courts to determine the validity of government prohibitions on speech was the "bad tendency" test, which allowed for the "punishment of such [speech] as may be deemed contrary to the public welfare." Bans or limitations on union meetings, labor demonstrations, and other expressions by unpopular or dissenting groups were upheld by courts as legitimate exercises of the state's police power to protect the public's "safety, health, and morals."[47] The Supreme Court had yet to address the First Amendment in any significant or sustained manner; there was almost no free speech jurisprudence to speak of, and the First Amendment did not yet apply to actions of state governments through the Fourteenth Amendment. Democratic theory seemingly legitimated the right of the majority to punish speech seen as disruptive, immoral, or antisocial. The Supreme Court's protections for liberty referred primarily to the protection of property rights, the right to participate in commercial activity without restraints by the government.[48]

The suppression of dissent represented a serious blow to progressives committed to equality and social justice. Mob violence, censorship, and the espionage laws shook their faith in the rationality of human beings, in the inevitability of social progress and their majoritarian view of democracy. Before the war, people such as Roger Baldwin and John Haynes Holmes had been "'armchair civil libertarians' at best," writes historian Donald Johnson.[49] Many liberals began to see the undemocratic dimensions of majority rule and would discover the First Amendment as "a principle for advancing human freedom."[50]

* * *

The assault on everything "un-American" continued after the war. The year 1919 was marked by exceptional turmoil. The Wilson administration had established the National War Labor Board, which mediated strikes on the basis of a labor code recognizing workers' rights to fair wages and to collective bargaining. With the expiration of the government-labor truce at the end of the war, workers struck everywhere. In 1919, hundreds of thousands walked out in the steel and coal industries. About 2,600 strikes took place nationwide, with many quashed by armed police and bayonet-wielding militias.[51]

The ascendance of the Bolshevik regime in 1917 and the formation of the American Communist Party led to the frenzied persecution of radicals, immigrants, and unionists.[52] Bombs were uncovered in the New York City Post Office in packages addressed to John Rockefeller, J. Pierpont Morgan, and cabinet members A. Mitchell Palmer and Albert Burleson, leading to mass arrests of alleged radicals by the Department of Justice. Congress was flooded with bills to outlaw revolutionists, and immigration authorities began deporting noncitizens with "radical" views.[53] Thirty-five states passed laws banning advocacy of "subversive" doctrines. "Red flag laws" criminalized the display of red or black flags, symbols of Communism and anarchism.

In 1917, Military Intelligence began investigating Baldwin and the NCLB for violations of the Espionage Act. Baldwin, who had refused to register for the draft, was arrested for violating the Selective Service Act, found guilty, and sentenced to prison. When Baldwin finished his term in 1919, he married a social worker and feminist, Madeleine Zabriskie Doty. Shortly after, Baldwin took off on a tour of the Midwest as a migrant laborer to observe working conditions firsthand. He became convinced that a national civil liberties organization could play an important role in advancing labor's struggle to assemble and protest. Baldwin returned to New York in 1920 to reorganize the NCLB as the American Civil Liberties Union.[54]

"There should be no control whatever in advance over what any person may say. . . . there should be no prosecutions for the mere expression of opinion, however radical, however violent," read the ACLU's statement of purpose. "There should be no law attempting to define what opinions may or may not be expressed—whether in times of war or peace. . . . All opinions, however radical, must be tolerated."[55]

The statement went on to denounce post office censorship, government control over the distribution of literature, and permit requirements for meetings held on public and private property. It attacked policies that refused admission to the United States to immigrants holding "objectionable political opinions" and the dismissal of public school teachers for their radical views. It protested illegal search and seizure and opposed "every attempt to discriminate between races in the application of all principles of civil liberty."[56]

Though the ACLU defended all guarantees in the Bill of Rights, its primary cause was freedom of speech. From the start, the organization adopted a policy of defending speech irrespective of content, so long as no acts of force or violence were committed. In its earliest years its emphasis was the right of labor unions to picket and protest. Baldwin believed that since radical union members were the most persecuted members of American society, the labor emphasis was a way of protecting civil liberties for all.[57] Baldwin referred to himself as "an exponent of free speech for its own sake, who believes free speech should be used in fighting the fight of the exploited classes."[58]

Baldwin put together a national committee made up of several dozen well-known figures representing a range of viewpoints on the left, including *Harpers' Weekly* editor Norman Hapgood, Harvard law professor Felix Frankfurter, radical economist Scott Nearing, militant unionist A. J. Muste, Socialist Party leader Norman Thomas, and Elizabeth Gurley Flynn of the IWW.[59] British-born Methodist minister Harry F. Ward, professor of Christian ethics at Union Theological Seminary, would serve as national chair for two decades.[60] A twenty-member executive committee made daily decisions for the group.[61]

Baldwin, his secretary Lucille Milner, and lawyer Albert DeSilver spent long hours building up a network of attorneys who would volunteer their services.[62] From the organization's headquarters on

West Thirteenth Street, they meticulously tracked civil liberties violations reported in the press and corresponded with persecuted dissidents seeking legal assistance. Although legal defense was an important part of the ACLU's work, test cases were not yet the organization's focus. Like many on the Left at the time, Baldwin was contemptuous of the legal system and distrusted the conservative bar and bench.[63]

Rather than changing the law through the courts, the ACLU focused on changing public opinion in an effort to render laws irrelevant and unenforceable. To that end, it issued pamphlets and press releases describing every episode of suppression that raised civil liberties issues. Other techniques for "dramatiz[ing] . . . civil liberties" included marching, picketing, protesting, and conducting "demonstrations in areas of conflict."[64] ACLU protests were replete with symbols from the founding era, including the Declaration of Independence and the Constitution.[65] When John Haynes Holmes and Norman Thomas were sent to test an ordinance that prohibited speakers from speaking in public without a permit, they took a stand on a street corner and Holmes read aloud the Declaration of Independence. Holmes got only to the truths that the signers felt were self-evident, including the "right of the people to alter or abolish their government," when the group was arrested. Holmes protested as he was led away, "I didn't say that . . . Thomas Jefferson said it." "Where's that guy?" the policeman demanded. "We'll get him too."[66]

Morris Ernst was not a founder of the ACLU, contrary to what he boasted later in life, although he did become involved with the organization early in its career.[67] Ernst's interest in social reform and his friendships with ACLU leaders, including the charismatic Roger Baldwin, would draw him into this compelling new movement.

5
ADVENTURES

On August 21, 1920, Morris's wife Susan gave birth to a stillborn son. She passed away from complications three days later. Their daughter Connie had just turned three.[1]

Susan's death upset Morris greatly, though he said little about it. Ernst was a warm and sympathetic man who experienced emotions deeply and did not shy from his feelings. At the same time, he maintained his keen ability to distract himself from sadness when it interfered with his overwhelming drive for success.

After Susan's death, Ernst immersed himself in his careers in law and social reform, and his lively social life, full of what he called "adventures." The early 1920s were productive years for Ernst, and it wasn't long before he fulfilled the prediction of the *Williams Alumni Review*: "no member of the class has been more active in good works, more stimulating in his attitude towards life than Dutch Ernst. He has . . . interesting friends who are doing big things in the world. We predict a large and useful future for the young man."[2]

* * *

Progressive activism continued in the early 1920s, though it had been undermined by the First World War. The conflict and its aftermath disillusioned many liberals, destroying their faith in democracy and social progress. The 1920s would not be a propitious time for social reform. With rising wages and economic prosperity, many Americans would find satisfaction in full employment and mass consumption, retreating from the Progressive vision for the nation.[3]

But the reform impulse did not die out completely; not all "tired radicals" gave up.[4] The Left persisted in the 1920s, fanning out into a variety of causes and organizations. Centrist liberals clustered in organizations such as the League of Women Voters and journals such as the *New Republic*, promoting specific reforms such as women's suffrage and workers' compensation. Radical groups, including the 10,000-member Socialist Party and the fledgling Communist Party of America, offered sweeping critiques of capitalism, imperialism, and race and gender inequality, among other ills.[5] In this time of disarray on the Left, there was a good deal of cross-fertilization; the general weakness of the Left drew moderates and radicals together in common pursuit of reform goals before sharper lines would be drawn in subsequent decades.

Ernst continued his prolific involvement in liberal reform groups. He remained a compulsive joiner, never able to turn down requests. The Progressive reform journal the *Outlook* described him in 1920 as "a young New York City lawyer . . . conspicuous . . . for his interest in public affairs."[6] At the same time, Ernst was becoming involved with more radical causes; this involvement had to do with Roger Baldwin.

* * *

Baldwin was the guiding light of the civil liberties movement and one of the most influential figures of the postwar Left. For all intents and purposes, Baldwin was the ACLU; he set its agenda, made most of its policy decisions, and ran the organization with an iron hand. Ernst and Baldwin met through Albert DeSilver, the ACLU's legal adviser and Ernst's colleague from the City Club. In the spring of 1921, Baldwin, who had a knack for recruiting talent to his organizations, began asking Ernst for legal advice for the ACLU.

Baldwin was a quirky man whose unusual, ascetic lifestyle belied his upper-class roots. Born in 1884 in the fashionable Boston suburb of Wellesley, he traced his origins to the "inescapable Mayflower," as he put it.[7] Trained in the conventions of a young man of his class, Baldwin learned to sing and play the piano, to draw and paint, and he had impeccable manners. Baldwin's family attended the Unitarian Church, with its emphasis on helping others, and his relatives had been involved in antislavery and municipal reform movements. Baldwin would take up social work with the same zeal and burning idealism of his New England forebears.[8]

Baldwin obtained a master's degree from Harvard and then went to St. Louis, where he directed a settlement house for the poor. In 1908 he heard anarchist Emma Goldman speak, and it changed his life.[9] Baldwin began reading Socialist, anarchist, and utopian literature and gravitating toward the radical labor movement.[10] By 1920 he had committed his life to working toward an ideal society, one characterized, in his words, by "a minimum of compulsion, a maximum of individual freedom and of voluntary association, and the abolition of exploitation and poverty."[11]

Wiry and athletic, with a long New England face and keen, twinkling eyes, Baldwin was, like Ernst, a "demon for work," possessed of "an energy that goes deeper than the nervous system," one journalist observed.[12] His personal habits were eclectic, to say the least. Weekends found him in his cabin on the Hackensack River, where he cooked his own meals, bird-watched, read Shakespeare's sonnets aloud, and swam in the nude.[13] Believing that money was corruption, as head of the ACLU he took a salary that covered nothing but bare living expenses. He worked in a spare room, wrote on scraps of paper to conserve, and acquired his shabby wardrobe by barter to avoid contact with money. Once, some friends trapped Baldwin in an expensive restaurant. Baldwin ordered a cup of coffee and then went out to a nearby bakery for a bag of rolls, which he brought back and ate while his companions dined. He carried around a little notebook in which he entered every expense, including "phone call 5 cents, newspaper 3 cents."[14]

A consummate organizer, Baldwin founded dozens of leftist coalitions. He was the driving force behind practically every committee in New York in the 1920s that was struggling for some measure of freedom. With his sparkling personality and sharp wit, he had a remarkable ability to charm people and draw them into his causes. He wielded his magnetism to the point of being manipulative. As ACLU member Ben Huebsch remarked, "I'm in the civil liberties union for a reason that has made some thousands of people members, because of Roger Baldwin."[15]

His genial good nature notwithstanding, Baldwin was a stern taskmaster and a shrewd, ends-oriented tactician. From the start of his ACLU leadership he acquired a reputation as a harsh employer who paid staff members meager salaries and treated them poorly. His personality was "a mixture of . . . enthusiasm and calculation, of the moral crusader and the smart operator," noted the *New Yorker*. "A high pressure salesman," he was a master of "pulling strings, seeing the right people, avoiding the wrong people, [and] taking advantage of technicalities."[16] Ernst called him "the dictator"—"without him there would not have been an ACLU."[17]

* * *

As the postwar antiradical purge continued, the ACLU remained consumed with its struggle against "the forces of reaction." "Never before were the forces of reaction so completely in control of our political and economic life," announced its 1921 annual report. "Never before were the civil rights guaranteed by constitutional provision so generally ignored and violated." The "machinery of suppression" included antilabor decisions of state and federal courts, the growing use of injunctions against labor unions, ordinances restricting speech and assembly, police raids on union meetings, and mob violence against unpopular speakers.[18] The Lusk Committee, a New York legislative committee formed to investigate "seditious activities," raided the offices of dozens of left-wing organizations and seized their records.[19] "Professional patriot" groups such as the American Defense Society, the National Security League, and the Daughters of the American Revolution, many backed by corporate funding, advocated muzzling critics of the status quo.[20] The period was one of bitter industrial conflict. Employers convinced courts that union organizing involved coercion and intimidation, and injunctions banning strikes and labor organizing were handed out routinely, like parking tickets. Conservatives extended their campaign to promote tradition and "one hundred percent Americanism" through so-called morals regulations.[21] Prohibition of alcohol was enacted in 1921, and the teaching of evolution was banned in some states.

The ACLU's work in these years included securing amnesty for federal war prisoners, attempting to repeal criminal syndicalism laws, ending the wartime censorship regime, raising bail for strike leaders, and arranging for lawyers to defend those leaders against "charges that ranged from littering to sedition and murder."[22] Committed to the nonpartisan defense of free speech regardless of viewpoint, the ACLU defended society's most reviled and persecuted groups, including militant labor unions, the Ku Klux Klan, and the Socialist and Communist Parties. When the Communists' secret convention in the Michigan woods was raided by FBI agents in 1922, the ACLU defended their right to assemble.[23] After Mayor Curley of Boston banned the Ku Klux Klan from marching in the streets, the ACLU came to its aid, even though ACLU leaders abhorred the Klan's repressive intolerance. During one period in 1923, the ACLU was simultaneously defending the right of the anti-Catholic KKK to hold meetings in Catholic-dominated Boston, the right of Catholics to teach school in Akron, Ohio, where the school board was dominated by the Klan, and the right of Communists to show movies in Providence, Rhode Island, against the combined opposition of the Klan and the Catholics.[24] As Baldwin put it, "civil liberty is indivisible and . . . unless we defend the SOB's rights we'll lose our own."[25]

The ACLU soon became as despised as those it defended. The group was vilified as subversives, Bolshevists, and "free speech fakers" who were perverting the meaning of the First Amendment by defending democracy's alleged enemies.[26] The Lusk Committee denounced it as a "supporter of subversive movements . . . detrimental to the interests of the State."[27] "The American Civil Liberties Union in almost every case is on the unpopular or disapproved side," observed Arthur Garfield Hays, a lawyer on the ACLU Executive Committee. "We are seldom called upon for assistance otherwise. . . . Our enemies have little doubt that we are financed from Moscow."[28] The ACLU was often accused of being an agent of Communism, although almost all of its leaders were hostile to the Communist Party and only one board member in the 1920s, William Z. Foster, was a party member. While most ACLU leaders believed in the possibility of working with Communists, they deplored the party's belief that non-Communist "reactionaries" were not entitled to free expression as well as their penchant for breaking up and heckling their opponents' meetings.[29] Baldwin sent the party two formal protests in 1925, but leader Earl Browder replied by telling them it was ridiculous to demand that they respect the civil rights of their opponents.[30]

For legal counsel Baldwin relied on Albert DeSilver and Walter Nelles, who had worked with the earlier National Civil Liberties Bureau, as well as Art Hays. A courageous, principled lawyer with a successful corporate practice, Hays was famously jailed in the course of a 1921 ACLU protest while attempting to get union coal miners the right to meet in Vintondale, Pennsylvania, a company town. In April 1921 Baldwin began consulting Ernst for legal advice.[31] How much Ernst actually believed in the ACLU's program at this point is unclear. But he was eager to help and willing to be persuaded by its charismatic leader.

* * *

In 1919 a young, handsome Harvard graduate named Charles Garland had made headlines when he refused a million-dollar inheritance from his father, a prominent Wall Street broker. "It is not mine," he told reporters. "I never did anything to earn it." Through his readings of Henry David Thoreau, Leo Tolstoy, and H. G. Wells, Garland had become opposed to private property. He refused to take money from "a system which starves thousands while hundreds are stuffed."[32]

Garland was one of many rich, idealistic men who sought Roger Baldwin's guidance.[33] Baldwin believed Garland's inheritance could help progressive organizations trying to change the social order, and he convinced Garland to entrust him with the administration of the fund, which would assist "pioneer" enterprises "directed to social and economic freedom."[34] Baldwin drew up a trust that would "finance all sorts of leftist and pioneering causes, nonpartisan and unconventional, to do what no established foundation would dream of touching."[35] Garland announced that he would pass his inheritance, about $900,000 of stocks housed at the First National Bank of New York, to the trustees.

The American Fund for Public Service, known as the "Garland Fund," was established as a Delaware corporation in 1922. Baldwin considered it part of his project to "unite the Left."[36] The new corporation's board of directors consisted of a "united front of anticapitalists" connected to labor, radical, and liberal movements, including DeSilver, ACLU chair Harry F. Ward, Amalgamated Clothing Workers Union president Sidney Hillman, Socialist Norman Thomas, *Nation* editor Freda Kirchwey, radical economist Scott Nearing, NAACP secretary James Weldon Johnson, and Communist leaders Benjamin Gitlow and William Z. Foster. Thomas was elected the new organization's president.[37]

The Garland Fund's stated purpose was to "promote the well-being of mankind throughout the world, and to use as means to that end research, publications, [and] the establishment and maintenance of charitable, benevolent, and public educational activities, agencies, and institutions." It would support "experimental movements in the field of education and industrial organization, particularly those in the interest of the producing classes and for the protection of minority groups."[38] The fund supported the abolition of capitalism; the board was agreed in its "opposition to economic oppression" and believed that workers could craft "a new political and economic power to replace capitalism."[39]

As he did with the ACLU, Baldwin ran the show, planning the agenda, directing meetings, and making key decisions. In the spring of 1923, Baldwin asked Ernst to become treasurer of the Garland Fund.[40] Ernst would handle all financial matters pertaining to the fund, including the making of investments and loans. Ernst was elected to the board of directors in 1925. Although sympathetic to many of the causes supported by the Garland Fund, Ernst was one of the only members of the board who was not opposed to capitalism. Given the Garland Fund's objective of subverting capitalism, observed one scholar of the fund, Ernst was the "least appropriate" board member.[41]

Over the next decade, the Garland Fund subsidized "almost a

hundred enterprises of pioneering character directly or indirectly related to building up the power of the organized working class," according to Baldwin.[42] From the beginning it was the fund's policy to appropriate or lend both its principal and its income. Garland instructed Baldwin that "the money should be distributed as fast as it can. . . . There is nothing that stands in the way of sensible expenditure of money so much as does the possession of too much money."[43] As the 1920s was not a fruitful time for the Left, the Garland Fund was called on to bail out dozens of struggling organizations. During its first year it gave $79,000 outright and about $136,000 in short-term loans to fifty-seven organizations, including the League for Industrial Democracy, the ACLU, the NAACP, the National Consumers League, the Sacco-Vanzetti defense, the United Mine Workers, and the Federated Press, a left-wing press syndicate.[44] Labor colleges, created to educate labor leaders to serve the labor movement, were the fund's major recipient.[45] The fund assisted a number of Communist-dominated enterprises such as the International Labor Defense, the League for Peace and Democracy, and the publications the *Daily Worker* and the *New Masses*.[46] Not surprisingly, the Garland Fund was tagged as a hotbed of "disreputable reds" and "one of the most subversive aggregations of socialists, communists, and other radicals in the United States."[47] Ernst signed checks approving the disbursal of tens of thousands of dollars to Communist groups, a fact that would come back to haunt him years later.

Initially, the Garland Fund's board of directors operated harmoniously. Writes one historian of the fund, "given the[ir] wide range of leftist political beliefs, the board worked with a courtesy, civility, and cooperation that was astonishing."[48] But eventually the board became fraught. The tension was not between Communists and non-Communists but between "big spenders," who wanted to get rid of the money as fast as possible, and the "tightwads," as Ernst called them, who feared that in giving charity they were weakening the organizations they served.[49]

Ernst was one of the "big spenders." The main "tightwads" were Baldwin and Nearing. Nearing was a radical economist whose work in the labor movement focused on wages, hours, production and living costs. Like Baldwin, he was ascetic; he wore flannel shirts and coarse trousers, and he lived on a New Jersey farm.[50] Nearing believed that the Garland Fund was an "immoral venture in corporate wealth" and that the recipients of what he perceived as charity were "taught to live parasitically and to return for a second and third handout."[51] Baldwin wrote that "the Garland Fund aimed to put left of center institutions on their feet. What the grants did was to make them permanent beggars."[52]

Ernst denounced this "hair-shirt school of thinking." The board was the "most inept you could have picked in America to handle a million dollars," he complained. The tightwads had an "emotional blockade against using the Garland Fund money wisely just because it was money."[53] They "dished out this fortune, plus dividends and profits . . . in dribbles—never quite enough to put a venture of novelty and unpopularity on its feet."[54] Scholars of the Garland Fund agree that it was not as effective as it could have been because of the board's inability to agree on any strategy and their emphasis on experiments over sustained support of a small number of enterprises.[55] Very few of the organizations supported by the fund ended up having long-term success.

The conflicts notwithstanding, Ernst carried out his tasks efficiently and effectively. With his financial savvy, Ernst more than doubled the fund's worth in the booming stock market of the 1920s. The press noted with delight that the fund designed to fight capitalism was making thousands on Wall Street. "It is an appalling situation," quipped newspapers. "The radicals are profiting by the very system they abhor. . . . Everything is topsy-turvy. What can a poor parlor Bolshevik do?"[56] Norman Thomas described the fund's success in making money on Wall Street as one of the greatest jokes of the season. The more profits the First National accumulated, the more the bank subsidized its overthrow.[57]

* * *

By 1920 the law firm of Greenbaum, Wolff, and Ernst had made its mark. Starting from nothing more than an empty room and a nameplate, it had become a busy, prosperous, highly regarded practice.[58]

The firm, identified as a "Jewish law firm," became a magnet of talent and hired the best Jewish law graduates in the city, many from Columbia Law School. The lawyers were excellent and hardworking, but the firm was not "stuffy," recalled Newman Levy. "We were definitely not Pillars of the Bar, we were just first-rate lawyers."[59]

A general-interest practice, the firm served a diverse range of clients. Much of its work had initially come from the German Jewish community, but as the firm's reputation expanded, so did its clientele. Greenbaum, Wolff, and Ernst represented a number of private clients in divorce, trusts, and estate matters. The firm also represented small unions, such as the Macaroni Workers' Union and the Bread Bakers' Union. Major clients included trade and employers' associations, such as the Jewelers Board of Trade and the New York Real Estate Board of Trade. Day-to-day work required the lawyers to wear many hats—to be "bankers, administrators, tax collectors, accountants, real estate dealers, fiscal experts . . . detectives, marriage counselors, doctors, and psychiatrists," as the firm's history put it.[60]

Ernst specialized in tax and insurance law, as well as labor and employment law. He became interested in employment law after representing several employers' associations in the garment and textile industries, as well as garment and textile unions, including the recently formed, militant union the Amalgamated Textile Workers of America. Through this work he got to know A. J. Muste, the prominent Dutch-born, Socialist, pacifist minister who led the ATWA. Ernst was proud of his ability to represent both sides in labor conflicts, later recalling that "there were lawyers . . . who were . . . confused as to how one day you represent a union and the next day represent an employer in another industry. I was never unable to sit down with the adversary . . . whether I represented the employers or labor groups in . . . clashes."[61]

Ernst's work with unions and employers' associations led him to become an advocate of arbitration as a means of settling labor disputes. Ernst was distressed by the bitterness between labor and employers and came to believe that dispute resolution tribunals, comprised of an equal number of representatives of the union and of the employers' association, presided over by an "impartial chairman," could create "industrial peace" by forcing both sides to air their grievances civilly and come to the bargaining table. The use of "impartial chairmen" was a relatively new method of settling labor disputes that had been pioneered in the garment industry during the previous decade.[62] Ernst helped negotiate several important arbitration agreements in the 1920s, including a historic agreement between silk ribbon manufacturers and the Amalgamated Textile Workers, one of the first of its kind in the textile industry.[63]

In a series of magazine and journal articles, his first published pieces, including an oft-cited 1921 piece in the *Columbia Law Review*, Ernst promoted arbitration as a way of improving labor's position, creating more equitable relations between labor and management, and eliminating "industrial warfare."[64] For several years, in one of his pet "causes," he urged his colleagues to support the creation of an agency that would collect and distribute the decisions of the "industrial judges," which he believed would contribute to the making of a body of "industrial law" that would create consistency and fairness in the field. Promoting the rights of labor—"industrial democracy," as it was known in the parlance of the time—would remain one of Ernst's crusades for the next thirty years.[65]

* * *

Susan Ernst's death overwhelmed Morris Ernst in many ways. For one, he was unprepared to deal with his new domestic responsibilities. Morris adored his young daughter Connie—"Con Con," he called her—but was impatient and temperamentally unsuited to being a caregiver. "Tonight Con cried after she was put in bed. I hate it. It's hell being [both] a mother [and] father," he complained to Margaret Samuels, the woman who would become his second wife, in 1922.[66]

Ernst eventually hired a nanny, and he and Connie moved into a family-owned apartment building on West Seventy-Third Street. Ernst's friend Charles Barnes roomed with them. Ernst had met "Barnesie" back in 1913, when Barnes helped him draft the state employment exchange bill for the City Club. A social worker and "impartial chairman" in silk industry arbitrations, Barnes, who was eighteen years older than Ernst and genteel and southern in his manner, became a big brother figure who taught Ernst a lot, in Ernst's words, "in terms of wisdom and graciousness."[67] For two years Morris and Barnesie shared daily life. They ate meals together, smoked on the front porch, looked after Connie, and stayed up late into the night shooting dice, drinking, and discussing their favorite topics of politics, work, and women.

That apartment became the site of intense social gatherings, fueled by spirited conversation and bootleg wine. Ernst was a generous, gregarious, welcoming host who enjoyed socializing and saw parties and "soirees" as a strategic way to expand his circle of influence. Starting in 1922, Ernst invited writers, artists, activists, lawyers, and intellectuals of all political stripes to his home, many of them famous or soon-to-be famous, beginning what would become a lifelong tradition.

Roger Baldwin was a frequent guest at Ernst's soirees. Ernst and Baldwin were close, but their relationship bristled with rivalry and tension. Both men shared intensity, ambition, and prodigious talents, and they admired what they saw of themselves in each other. At the same time, their quirks and idiosyncrasies repelled each other. Baldwin, who exercised power behind the scenes, never understood Ernst's spotlight seeking, and Ernst, who liked money and spent it freely, was disgusted by Baldwin's stinginess. Ernst bought a log cabin in Westchester County and loaned it to Baldwin one winter. When Baldwin gave it back, he also gave Ernst a check for all the flour, sugar, and salt he used, which he meticulously tracked.[68] However much Baldwin denounced the profit system, this man "who all his life kept track of every two-cent stamp bought" was in his own way an "arch-capitalist," Ernst believed.[69]

A. J. Muste was another companion. By 1922, the serious, idealistic minister and labor reformer had resigned as head of the Amalgamated Textile Workers' Union to become education director of Brookwood Labor College in Katonah, New York. In the 1920s, labor leaders believed that workers' cause could be achieved through education, and in several cities, unionists and college professors cooperated in the establishment of labor colleges.[70] Ernst was an advocate of labor education and often went to Brookwood to lecture.

Liberal academics, journalists, social workers, and activists affiliated with the City Club, the Garland Fund, and the ACLU were also in Ernst's social circle. Ernst was close to *Harpers' Weekly* editor Norman Hapgood, radical economist Stuart Chase, and Robert Morss Lovett, associate editor of the *New Republic* who was on the board of the ACLU. Another friend was slender, bespectacled McAlister Coleman, "Mac." A former reporter for the New York *Morning Sun*, Coleman ran a publicity agency for leftist organizations and was a protégé of Norman Thomas. Thomas, the Presbyterian minister who was an active ACLU Board member and the perennial Socialist candidate for the presidency in the 1920s and '30s, could also be spotted at Ernst's. A Princeton graduate with an aristocratic look—"high-domed head, thin gray hair, narrow nose, firm lips, and thoughtful blue-gray eyes"—Thomas was known for his righteous, indefatigable championing of the underdog and his booming voice that he could crescendo from a whisper to a roar within seconds.[71]

Other friends of Ernst's included German Jewish lawyers, publishers, and businessmen Ernst knew through family ties or through the well-connected Greenbaums. Ernst was close to Henry Morgenthau Jr., future secretary of the treasury under the New Deal, tobacco heir Howard Stix Cullman, and Lewis Strauss of the Kuhn, Loeb banking house, all Greenbaum connections. Ernst remained a friend of banker Herbert Lehman, who as head of the humanitarian organization the American Jewish Joint Defense Committee sent Ernst on a six-week trip to war-torn Poland in 1921 to help set up loan agencies in Jewish communities. Ernst dined often with Art Sulzberger of the *New York Times* and his wife Iphigene, and with Robert Moses, future "master planner" of New York. Ernst worked with Moses on several "good government" organizations, advocating such reforms as proportional representation, nonpartisan primaries, and the elimination of corrupt Tammany Hall.[72] Moses was a frequent dinner guest, and Ernst and Connie went to stay with Moses and his wife at their summer home on Long Island.

Sometime in this period Ernst reconnected with his childhood friend Heywood Broun, who had become a noted writer for the New York *World*. In the 1920s Broun was one of the best-known newspaper columnists in the nation. His syndicated column, "It Seems to Me," had a liberal bent; Broun was known for his championing of the underdog and his virulent opposition to censorship of all kinds.[73]

Broun was pugnacious and opinionated yet also soft and sentimental. Emotionally and physically, he was a mess, disorganized and pathetically riddled with doubts and neuroses. Broun's rumpled appearance was infamous. He wore frayed trousers, ratty sweatshirts, and unmatched shoes, sometimes lacking laces. Described by critics as a walking "unmade bed," Broun often looked as if his clothes had been thrown at him.[74] Unable to deal with his daily affairs, Broun looked to Ernst for practical and emotional guidance.

Broun was a key member of the Algonquin Round Table, the renowned literary circle that met weekly for lunch at the Algonquin Hotel. Broun brought Ernst into contact with members of the group, including H. G. Wells, Robert Benchley, Edna Ferber, Dorothy Parker, and Marc Connelly. By the end of the decade Ernst had become so ingrained with the social life of the Round Table that he was regarded as one of its peripheral members. And sweet, fat, vulnerable Broun had become Ernst's best friend.

* * *

The 1920s was the Jazz Age, with speakeasies, motorcars, radio, and short skirts. The decade roared, and Morris roared with them. Ernst indulged in theater and nightclubs several nights a week and thrived on the companionship of women. He had a healthy sexual appetite, which he satisfied often. A friend of his lent out his apartment as a "hookup pad." If he felt lonely, he would pick up a random woman at a nightclub and have a fling.[75]

Ernst was uninterested in marriage, though he thought he needed a mother for Connie. His family tried to set him up. In April 1922, Ernst's sister-in-law Alma, George's wife, asked him to meet a Wellesley classmate of hers, Margaret Samuels. Maggie was a reporter for the New Orleans *Times-Picayune* who was visiting New York on assignment.

Maggie was intense-looking, with sharp features, deep-set brown eyes, and fashionably bobbed black hair. She hailed from a well-off Jewish family from Natchez, Mississippi. As a high school student at the Stanton College for Young Ladies in Natchez, she became devoted to words and etymology.[76] Maggie had been editor of the Wellesley College newspaper and a noted poet on campus. She was bright, practical, and up-front, with a wry, intellectual sense of humor and a charming, matter-of-fact warmth. She was a perfect match for Morris, though it took him a while to see that.

On their first date, Morris and Maggie went to a nightclub on the East Side and then did some "petting" in Central Park in his Buick. They spent the following week together. Most of Maggie's suitors brought her to theaters and dance halls, but Morris took her to a meeting of the ACLU. Maggie went back to New Orleans, and they began corresponding. "How I love that Buick—that was the quickest I'd ever been kissed—and honestly the first time I ever kissed back at all," she gushed.[77]

Ernst thought Maggie was pleasant enough, but he was hardly enamored. He had no interest in marriage, he warned her, taunting her with stories about his exploits with other women. From the Greenbrier Resort, a luxury golf resort in the Appalachians that he visited annually with his cousin Jerome Hanauer, a prominent banker at Kuhn Loeb, he wrote that he "played 27 holes, had a swim and lost $25 at roulette, read. . . . slept, played bridge and danced . . . [with] an attractive divorcee."[78] Later he wrote that his friend "Charley" called him and told him that if he didn't use his hook-up pad, his "petting premises," he would have to look for a new tenant—"so for your sake I . . . sought me a fair damsel and held down the premises."[79]

In time, Ernst's brashness and egotism gave way to sincere affection. "I'm feeling that I want to tell you what, where & how I do—I've been lonely for you," he wrote in August 1922. He made clear that he thought of her only once in a while, though, "on a few scattered evenings when the invitations don't come in very fast."[80]

In an undated letter presumed to have been written in fall 1922, he expounded:

> I love to be with you, I enjoy reading your letters, I take a glorious vain joy in your poems, I'll get a thrill looking at your picture—but I don't stay awake nights, I don't miss you when I have good company or a big job. Truly Margaret—I never was different with Susan. It's not in me. Whether it's base, inferior, or ignoble—at least that's me. I'm so damn flexible, resourceful, self-sufficient and conceited that I can always get along with any old person or any old situation or state of facts. Every day. . . . I get more convinced we'd hit it off but . . . you [must] be satisfied with me as I am . . . not as you want or imagine me to be.[81]

Maggie's charm and persistence eventually won him over. By the end of the year, Morris was in love. "See how I've come around even though I was stout in my position to the contrary," he wrote circa December 1922, adding that"60 to 80 percent of my life is filled with law and so-called civics & City Club, but I truly miss you in the balance of 20 to 40%, around the house, evenings, theater, and in the dancing I do with random persons."[82] It was clear that the idea of marriage had crept into his mind when, in an undated letter, he wrote to her:

> We should learn our homey habits. I don't hang my clothes neatly on a chair, do you? I often don't brush my teeth at night, do you? . . . I like to read the headlines while eating breakfast, I never use toothpicks . . . I love heavy woolen pajamas in winter. I only wear one style of collar.
>
> You think I'm sloppy but not unkind, inattentive but not intentionally cruel, a little susceptible to women's wiles, but possess possibility of real morality. You know how self-centered I am and how much of my life is taken up with other matters and things than home, love, and sex. Truly Margaret dear, if we approach everything with humor, all big things with tolerance and all little things with indifference we can give each other all the joy there is in life.[83]

On March 1, 1923, Maggie and Morris were wed in a small ceremony at the home of Maggie's uncle and aunt in New Orleans.[84] Their son, Roger, was born on June 2, 1924, and their daughter Joan was born a year later. Brought up with the idea that "it was sissy to enjoy babies," Ernst never enjoyed his kids when they were young and admitted that he was "a trifle jealous" of them—"I didn't want to share Margaret."[85] Yet as his own parents had been, Ernst was devoted to his family.

His whirlwind professional life notwithstanding, Ernst's domestic life was traditional and stable. It was his contented home life, he believed, that enabled him to take up controversial causes.[86] His family was the base from which he launched ambitious visions.

6
FREE SPEECH LAWYER

Those who saw Morris Ernst in his thirties saw a "hearty hail-fellow of enormous nervous energy," in Roger Baldwin's words—a small, solidly built man with springlike motions, a friendly but cynical smile, and a "general air of being about to take off."[1]

Ernst had thick, wavy black hair and deep brown eyes that were constantly roving, canvassing the room, gauging the audience, sizing up the competition.[2] He wore round wire-rimmed glasses, bow ties, tweed jackets, and socks that were frequently unmatched. He chose bow ties because they were quicker to put on than ordinary ties, and the socks were unmatched because he was usually dressing in a hurry.

Ernst talked informally and confidently in a gravelly voice, made hoarse by constant cigarette smoking. He never engaged in pleasantries or chitchat but got straight to the point, starting his conversations with "What's your racket?" or "Tell me your story." Ernst "rarely cared much for the sensitivity of the ears of his listeners and did not hesitate to indulge the vice of repetition, often asking persons the same questions again and again," noted Malcolm Hoffmann, a friend later in life. "He was dearly loved by his friends but many were at a loss to understand him."[3]

His bluntness, persistence, and compulsion for activity made him attractive to some people and off-putting to others. Ernst loved bringing up controversial subjects, if only to set people off. His use of profanity was notorious. Baldwin recalled that Ernst was the only person he knew who would say "fuck" in a meeting with women present.[4] Noted Newman Levy, Ernst was "for years carrying on a one-man crusade to restore certain tabooed monosyllables to polite conversation, occasionally with embarrassing consequences."[5] Law professor Fred Rodell observed that Ernst's conversation "is full of [sex] and he does not duck the short words."[6]

Conceited and boastful—a manifestation of his festering insecurity around his relatively humble upbringing—Ernst was obsessed with reliving his accomplishments and successes. This was "sometimes annoying to people who do not know him well and who are unable to discern beneath his harmless vanities," observed Levy.[7] Ernst kept every newspaper clipping in which he was mentioned, admitting that the practice was unusual and that "no sane man" was so self-consumed.[8] "An evening with Morris Ernst," Levy quipped, "is a Morris Ernst evening."[9]

* * *

Ernst never expressed interest in freedom of speech during his early years with the ACLU. But exposure to the group drew him into the issue. In 1925, Ernst became involved in the free speech crusade, bringing his tenacity, zeal, and showman's ability to the battle. That year the firm of Greenbaum, Wolff, and Ernst represented exiled Hungarian count Michael Karolyi, who had been banned by the US State Department from making political speeches in the United States. Seeing the free speech implications of the case, not to mention numerous possibilities for self-publicity, Ernst turned it into a civil liberties cause célèbre.[10]

Karolyi was an international liberal icon. After the fall of the Hapsburg government in 1918, he had been president of the new republic, the Hungarian People's Republic. Karolyi gave up his vast land holdings and laid out a land reform program. His power lasted only a few months, until he surrendered his authority to the Communist regime of Bela Kun. The Hungarian pendulum swung far to the right after Bela Kun's short-lived tenure.[11] Karolyi opposed the fascist regime of Miklos Horthy that ruled Hungary from 1919 through World War II. Karolyi was exiled and migrated to London.

In 1924, Karolyi's wife came to New York, where she became ill with typhoid fever. The count applied to the American consul in

London for a visa to visit the United States. The visa was granted on the condition that Karolyi not engage in political activities either by talking or in writing. Secretary of State Charles Evans Hughes found legal authority for the "gag order" in an act of May 1918, continued in 1922, giving the president power to regulate the movements of "aliens" in and out of the country during wartime.[12] Karolyi agreed to the gag order because he was frantic over his wife's situation. He arrived in New York in January 1925. He was attacked by pro-Horthy groups. His friends wanted him to answer the attacks, but he was unable to respond because of the gag order. He was advised to consult Greenbaum, Wolff, and Ernst. The lawyers concluded that the attacks were in fact libelous but were unable to advise him to sue, which could be a violation of the State Department's edict.[13]

Ernst challenged the gag order.[14] He charted a small plane and flew to Washington, DC, to meet Hughes. According to Ernst, although Hughes publicly said that Karolyi had been gagged because he was allegedly a Communist, Hughes admitted in conversation that it was the result of pressure from the Horthy regime.[15]

In his typical fashion, Ernst started up the publicity machine, contacting reporters from the *New York Times* and the *World*, telling them that Hughes was suppressing the complicity of the Hungarian government in the gag. Ernst alleged that "they are placing dollars above free speech by giving into the demands of the Horthy government to silence Karolyi because it will help the foreign loan situation by giving into a debtor country."[16] Ernst exposed the gag order to the public, effectively defeating the State Department's goal of silencing Karolyi.

Ernst enlisted the help of the ACLU, which staged a massive rally at the Hotel Astor denouncing the "spectacle of our state department muzzling a foreign visitor on behalf of a foreign government."[17] Speaker after speaker, including Ernst, drew applause with attacks on the Horthy government, the State Department, and Hughes.[18] The ACLU adopted a resolution protesting the gag, and an ACLU delegation including Ernst went before Secretary of State Frank Kellogg, who had replaced Hughes, to try to have the order reversed.[19] Despite the protests, Karolyi remained gagged. Now all but forgotten, the "Karolyi affair" was described by the ACLU as one of the most "striking" civil liberties cases of the year.[20]

* * *

By that time, the ACLU was reporting victories, albeit few and far between. The ACLU's annual report from 1925 declared that "political, racial, and religious minorities" were finding it "easier to live because of less interference."[21] The Red Scare was fading, and the power of the "professional patriot" groups was on the wane. Recalled Baldwin's secretary Lucille Milner, "The reaction against repression which [we] had looked for had finally set in. There was less intolerance, less fear, and a decrease in civil liberties violations. All around there was proof of this."[22] Much of this was the result of the ACLU, which in exposing the divergence of official practices from constitutional ideals prodded the consciences of Americans.

The Scopes "monkey trial," a test case litigated by the ACLU, was a turning point in the free speech fight. A Tennessee law prohibited the teaching of evolution in public schools. Much of the educated populace mocked the old-fashioned, oppressive law. The ACLU formed a Scopes Defense Committee and financed a case, litigated by renowned trial lawyer Clarence Darrow with the assistance of Art Hays in 1925, in which John Scopes, a high school teacher from Dayton, Tennessee, agreed to be arrested for violating the act. Scopes was not the ACLU's typical client; he was not a militant radical but rather a soft-spoken, middle-class teacher. Although the defense technically lost the case, the ACLU had never before received such positive attention. It was the first time the organization defended a cause that the mainstream public supported.[23]

There were also triumphs in court. In 1926 Roger Baldwin was the defendant in one of the most important free speech cases of the decade. In Paterson, New Jersey, eight thousand silk workers went on strike. The mill owners obtained an injunction banning the strike, and the workers sought the assistance of the ACLU. Baldwin led a group carrying flags to the city hall. A union leader began to read the First Amendment, but police arrested him before he could finish. Baldwin turned himself in to authorities the next day, explaining that he had been involved in organizing the demonstration. He was convicted under a New Jersey unlawful assembly law. A state appeals court unanimously reversed the conviction as a violation of free speech.[24]

The ACLU defended Communist leader Benjamin Gitlow, convicted under a New York criminal anarchy law for distributing a manifesto calling for the establishment of Socialism through direct action. *Gitlow v. New York* went all the way up to the US Supreme Court in 1925. The Court did not reverse the conviction, displaying its traditional reluctance to defend the civil liberties of radicals and aliens, and the ACLU regarded it as a loss. But the Court made a historic announcement, taking the view that freedom of speech was among the privileges and immunities guaranteed by the Fourteenth Amendment against state abridgement. To the free speech scholar Zechariah Chafee of Harvard University, the decision seemed to be "the greatest victory for freedom of speech in my lifetime" and became a stepping-stone to later advances in civil rights.[25]

In 1926 the Supreme Court heard another ACLU case, this one involving Charlotte Anita Whitney, member of a prominent California family convicted under a California criminal syndicalism act for helping to establish the Communist Labor Party. The Supreme Court again upheld the conviction, concluding that the state had the right to punish those who abused their right to free speech "by utterances inimical to the public welfare, tending to incite to crime, disturb the public peace, or endanger the foundations of organized government and threaten its overthrow by unlawful means."[26]

Justice Louis Brandeis issued a concurring opinion that remains one the greatest defenses of free speech written by a member of the Supreme Court. After the war, Brandeis and Oliver Wendell Holmes Jr., dissenters in most free speech cases, began to articulate a civil libertarian theory of freedom of expression that validated the ideals of the ACLU. Though they did not become majority positions on the Court until the 1930s, Brandeis's and Holmes's views exerted profound influence on liberal legal thought.

In 1919, Holmes had devised the "clear and present danger" test, which repudiated the earlier "bad tendency" test. "We should be eternally vigilant against attempts to check the expression of opinions . . . unless they so imminently threaten immediate interference with the lawful and pressing purpose of the law that an immediate check is required to save the country," Holmes had written in *Abrams v. United States*, dissenting from a ruling upholding the prosecution of an anarchist under the Espionage Act. Holmes had also created one of the foundational metaphors of modern free speech jurisprudence, the "marketplace of ideas." Rather than quash expression for its purported "bad tendencies," the state should rely on the free trade in ideas to defuse noxious thoughts, Holmes argued.[27]

In *Whitney v. California*, Brandeis went beyond clear and present danger and insisted on a "time to answer" test—no danger stemming from an idea could be considered clear and present if there was opportunity for the public to discuss it. Underlying Brandeis's theory was the connection between free speech and the democratic process. Brandeis wrote that citizens have an obligation to take part in the governing process, and they cannot do so unless they can criticize government fully and without fear: "Those who won our independence believed that . . . freedom to think as you will and to speak as you think are means indispensable to the discovery and spread of political truth; that without free speech and assembly discussion would be futile; that with them, discussion affords ordinarily adequate protection against the dissemination of noxious doctrine . . . that public discussion is a political duty, and this should be a fundamental principle of the American government."[28] Brandeis's view of free speech as protecting "public discussion" in the "marketplace of ideas" became the foundation of Ernst's own free speech philosophy.

* * *

Not long after the "Karolyi affair," Baldwin asked Ernst to become the ACLU's chief counsel. With increasing success in the courts, the ACLU was beginning to pay more attention to legal cases, and Baldwin needed someone to coordinate the work. Albert DeSilver, Baldwin's legal adviser, had been tragically killed, and Art Hays was unable to devote as much time as Baldwin needed.[29] Baldwin wrote to

Ernst, "We need the kind of punch and imagination you have got."[30] Ernst declined the offer but agreed to act temporarily as general counsel. In August 1926 he joined the ACLU Executive Committee and began attending its weekly sessions, where civil liberties issues were debated vigorously. He recalled the meetings as a "joy and an education."[31]

There was much work to be done. In 1926, Baldwin announced an aggressive campaign to defend free speech in education, which he described as the new "battleground" of free expression. The American Legion, "Bible crusaders," and other fundamentalist organizations sought to control educational content as a means of promoting their conservative agenda. More legal restrictions on teaching were enacted than in any previous year.[32] Several states passed compulsory Bible-reading laws, flag salute regulations, and laws banning the teaching of evolution. Loyalty oaths required "100 percent Americanism" from teachers, and colleges ousted instructors who were deemed to hold radical views.[33]

Ernst pursued his ACLU efforts diligently and without pay. He was extremely productive, coordinating, among initiatives, a successful challenge to a South Dakota law brought by students expelled for failing to attend Bible-reading exercises, a Mississippi law forbidding the teaching of evolution, and the discharge of two teachers from a New York college for their radical views.[34]

In 1926 the New York City Board of Education banned ACLU members from speaking in school buildings on the grounds that the ACLU was "disloyal to American institutions."[35] Public school buildings were used as speaking venues in the evenings.[36] The board of education's regulations required that to obtain a permit to speak, all speakers must discuss "only subjects that will tend toward active support of American ideals." The ACLU applied for a permit to hold a meeting on the subject of "Old Fashioned Free Speech" featuring a slate of liberal speakers including Congressman Fiorello La Guardia, philosopher John Dewey, and NAACP leader James Weldon Johnson. The permit was denied.[37] With pride, the board of education recited that it maintained a blacklist of "subversive" organizations.[38] The ACLU brought proceedings, charging that the "blacklist" of speakers was an "arbitrary and un-American censorship over free speech."[39]

After the ACLU appealed to the New York Supreme Court, the New York City Board of Education granted hearings, at which Ernst represented the ACLU. During the hearings, the board demanded that the ACLU recant a pamphlet, *What Do You Mean—Free Speech?*, in which it quoted a letter by Thomas Jefferson urging the right of revolution. "But that is practically what Jefferson said," Ernst replied. "We can't stand for what Jefferson said in the public schools these days," replied the chairman of the board.[40] The permit was finally granted in 1928.[41] Even though it took over two years to get the permit, the incident was regarded as a victory for the ACLU. By keeping the case in headlines, the ACLU got greater publicity than anything its members might have said at their ill-fated meeting.[42]

* * *

Ernst was demonstrating to Baldwin the qualities that would make him valuable to the ACLU—his creativity and inventiveness, his formidable energy, and his ability to spot novel free speech issues and act on them forcefully. He demonstrated these traits in his work on "radio censorship," which gave him his first real recognition as a "free speech lawyer."

Radio was the most popular new communications medium of the decade: the 1920s saw a "radio boom."[43] In January 1922 there were 30 broadcasting stations; twelve months later there were 556 radio stations and about 1.5 million receivers in homes across the country.[44]

When radio technology had been first introduced in the early twentieth century, it was used only by amateurs and naval stations. Radio remained unregulated until 1912, when increasing numbers of users caused congestion of wavelengths. That year Congress passed the Radio Act, which designated the airwaves public property, to be allocated to individuals or corporations through a licensing regime run by the US secretary of commerce. Difficulties inherent in the legislation did not surface until the rapid growth of commercial broadcasting after World War I. The US secretary of commerce, Herbert Hoover, received repeated complaints about poor reception and interference in broadcasts by other stations. By 1925, there were no more available frequencies for broadcasting, and it was agreed that there could be no more channels than the 89 that existed.[45]

Congress made several attempts to pass new radio legislation. Republican Representative Wallace White of Maine introduced bills that would allow the regulation of radio to continue to be conducted by the Department of Commerce. White's bill, which passed the House in March 1926, augmented the secretary of commerce's power by empowering him to grant or deny licenses according to "the public interest, convenience, or necessity." In the Senate, Clarence Dill of Washington proposed an independent radio commission that would be a permanent body charged with full responsibility for radio, including issuing licenses.[46] In the extensive debate over radio legislation, there had been talk about ownership, business interests, and wavelength, but in the reams of testimony, no one had brought up the free speech implications of licensing—except Morris Ernst.

"For the first time in history, the problem of free speech becomes an administrative problem, for the government controls the licensing of stations and the distributing of wave lengths," Ernst asserted in hearings before the Senate Committee on Interstate Commerce in which he represented the ACLU. "In the first place censorship is exercised by the mere selection of concerns permitted to go on the air." He continued, "The Greeks' suppression of Socrates did not prevent his pupil Plato from carrying on his gospel . . . if anti-Fascist Italians in America want to start a newspaper . . . no governmental consent is necessary. . . . But with the radio we are facing a new problem. Who shall distribute the right to get on the air? What shall be the medium of such distribution?"[47]

Ernst foresaw the importance of radio as an influence on public thought. Radio was "rapidly replacing the press, pulpit and platform in the matter of molding public opinion and prejudice," and because of that, "the principle of free speech and free press should be made to apply to broadcasting," he asserted.[48] While newspapers enjoyed protections against "prior restraints"—government suppression of speech before publication—no such safeguards existed for radio.[49]

Ernst conceded the need for regulation of radio, given the limited amount of spectrum and the inevitability of government choice among applicants. Without some selective process, he wrote, "the airwaves would be like Forty Second Street at rush hour."[50] But he worried that the proposed bills would give regulators unchecked powers to limit the speech of unpopular speakers. Regulators' decisions were to be made without public input, and they did not have to report their reasoning to the public. Broadcasters denied a license had no recourse or appeal. "Radio is a public utility . . . and everything concerning its operation and its cost should be open to the public," Ernst argued. "Granted that some censorship of the air is at this time an engineering necessity, those who believe in the right of free speech must see to it that this censorship is controlled so far as possible by the listening millions of the country. To vest unchecked control in the Secretary of Commerce and a super-political Committee of Five would . . . be a partial deeding away of our aerial voices and consequently our very thoughts."[51]

At the congressional hearings on the Dill bill, covered widely in the press, Ernst offered amendments that would allow appeals to the radio commission by parties refused licenses, public input into licensing decisions, public hearings in connection with issuing and revoking licenses, and regulations that would make all records pertaining to radio available to the public.[52] Ultimately none of his measures were introduced or adopted. Congress finally passed the Radio Act of 1927, which contained elements of both the Dill and the White bills. The two key provisions in the law were the creation of a new government commission, the Federal Radio Commission (renamed the Federal Communications Commission in 1934), and the commission's mandate to regulate radio in the "public interest, convenience, and necessity." The FRC was free to control radio to serve whatever interests it deemed were within the scope of "public interest, convenience and necessity."[53] The FRC could take into consideration programming when renewing licenses, and its ability to revoke a broadcaster's license enabled it to control content. One result of the 1927 Radio Act, still debated today, was the fact that broadcasters were accorded fewer First Amendment rights than newspapers.

Through his work on "radio censorship," Ernst developed his views on free speech. Like most of the ACLU leaders, Ernst took a near-libertarian position. When it came to political speech, he advocated broad protections for speech until an overt criminal act was committed. This was even more protective than "clear and present danger." As Baldwin put it, "the place to draw the line is between words and deeds."[54]

To Ernst, freedom of speech not only protected the ability of unpopular speakers to express their ideas but also the public's opportunity to hear them. The First Amendment safeguarded the public's right to receive information—"the right to hear, the right to see, and the right to read," as he put it. This dimension of free expression was overlooked by ACLU leaders, with their traditional focus on the rights of speakers. Throughout his entire career, Ernst would espouse this view, arguing that it was only through access to the broadest range of information, including dissenting and minority views, that the public could engage in "democratic discussion" of public affairs. Freedom of speech, he wrote, was as much in the words of the speaker as it was "in the ear of the listener."[55]

* * *

The radio episode put Ernst on the national stage as a "champion of American liberties." Before long he was working the lecture circuit, employing a skill he had excelled at since college. "The era of radio," he told crowds in his gravelly voice, "is introducing the worst infringements on the sacred rights of free speech ever recorded in the pages of history."[56] He championed freedom of opinion, "freedom for the thought that we hate," arguing that "the best test of 'Americanism' in relation to free speech is not to defend those with whom we agree but . . . those with whom you disagree. Give your opponent his chance and defend him in his right to speech."[57]

With his new prominence, Ernst invited attack by the "professional patriots." For his work on the American Fund for Public Service (the Garland Fund) and the ACLU, he was identified with the "communist [and] socialist movements" and described as a "core member" of the nation's "subversive" groups.[58] Though he invited the stamp of radicalism with his activities, Ernst reacted vehemently to these accusations.

The superpatriotic Daughters of the American Revolution put out a "blacklist" of "subversives." In 1928 Ernst appeared on this list along with more than two hundred prominent figures on the left, including Jane Addams, Clarence Darrow, and Felix Frankfurter. Those who had been listed sponsored a spoof "Blacklist party." Ernst was on the planning committee, called "Daughters and Sons of the Blacklist." The invitations read, "We notice that your name appears on the roll of honor drawn up by the DAR. . . . It includes United States senators, communists, ministers, Socialists, Republicans, editors, lawyers, and housewives. . . . Some call this honor roll a blacklist." The gathering was meant "to poke fun good-naturedly at all those individuals and organizations which are so fearful of the future of these United States that they prepare black or other colored lists and use other radical methods to destroy the rights of old fashioned conservative Americans guaranteed under the free speech clauses of the federal and state constitutions."[59]

More than a thousand people wrote in for tickets. Heywood Broun was outraged that he was left off the list and wrote in jest that he was planning to bring a libel suit against the DAR for criminal omission. Broun's "case" was tried during the evening with blacklisted Clarence Darrow and Art Hays acting as counsel and Groucho Marx as a character witness.[60]

Ernst, extremely thin-skinned, threatened to sue a newspaper for libel, and he was *not* joking. The New York *World* in its description of the blacklist had described Ernst as a "socialist." He wrote to the editors, "I wish you would make it clear that I am not a socialist. I am rather of the opinion that to call a man a member of a party to which he does not belong is libel per se."[61] His commitment to free speech notwithstanding, Ernst had no problem quashing speech that criticized *him*.

* * *

By this time, Greenbaum, Wolff, and Ernst had become the preeminent law firm for the Left. The firm's tremendous commercial success allowed it to represent liberal causes at reduced rate or pro bono. As Ernst put it, "The law game as I play it is a Robin Hood venture. By that I mean that I try, on the average, to get enough fees from those who can afford it in order to permit me the luxury of taking on . . . innumerable chores in behalf of people who cannot afford to pay."[62] The firm became, in its own right, one of the major civil liberties law firms of the time and would remain so for the next forty years. The lawyers represented leftist interests such as the Garland Fund and such Garland Fund recipients as *Labor Age* magazine, the Vanguard Press, and the *New Masses*, the Communist Party's literary magazine. The firm also defended the ACLU. When the *Chicago Tribune* printed a series of articles reporting a speech made by a member of the Military Intelligence Association accusing the ACLU of being influenced by Russia—that its finances came from "Moscow and were paid through a New York lawyer"—the ACLU threatened to sue for libel, and the *Tribune* carried a retraction.[63] Some of Ernst's conservative business clients complained about this activity, but it was never enough to repel them; Ernst was just that good. When a banker client threatened that he would "quit Ernst" if he didn't give up his "radical friends," Ernst asked him, "Are you going to quit me?" The client said no, and that was the end of the matter.[64]

Greenbaum, Wolff, and Ernst was also gaining a reputation as a literary law firm. The firm became counsel for several major magazines, including the progressive reform journal the *Survey*, as well as the *New Yorker* and the *Nation*, which shared many board members with the ACLU. Ernst's friendship with Heywood Broun brought artists, writers, and playwrights to the firm as clients, including songwriter Morrie Ryskind and famed satirist Dorothy Parker. Broun himself became a client. The firm represented Broun when he broke with the New York *World* in 1928 over his columns on Sacco and Vanzetti, Italian immigrant anarchists sentenced to death for allegedly murdering a guard and paymaster during a payroll heist near Boston in 1920. Many Americans found the trial to be a miscarriage of justice; evidence against the men was flimsy, and it was believed that they had been persecuted for their radical beliefs. Head of a committee to free the convicted men, Broun wrote a controversial indictment of the Massachusetts justice system. Although the *World* was regarded as a liberal paper, publisher Ralph Pulitzer withheld two of Broun's columns. Broun criticized Pulitzer in an article in the *Nation* and was fired.[65]

Newman Levy, who had a thriving side career as a writer, brought the celebrated novelist Edna Ferber into the firm as a client. Ferber had just won the 1924 Pulitzer Prize for her novel *So Big*. Three years older than Ernst, Ferber grew up in a middle-class Jewish immigrant family in the Midwest. Small and dark-eyed, with a low voice and gracious manner, she was witty, loving, straightforward, and generous. At the peak of her career in the 1930s she was among the best-read novelists in the nation, and many critics regarded her as the greatest woman writer of her time.[66]

Ferber's 1926 novel *Show Boat* chronicled the lives of three generations of performers on the Cotton Blossom, a floating theater that traveled between small towns on the banks of the Mississippi. Soon after its publication, Hollywood studios starting bidding for rights. Later that year Ferber sold the film to Universal Studios. She signed the contract in October 1926 and hired Ernst to handle her dealings with the studios.[67]

Show Boat embroiled Ferber in a raft of legal trouble.[68] Shortly after the book was published, Tom Taggart, a retired Democratic political leader in Indiana, brought suit against Ferber and her publisher Doubleday Doran, claiming that they had violated a New York law that prohibited the use of names and identities for commercial purposes. Ferber had written about a character named Tom Taggart, who in the book was described as a gambling house owner. Doubleday agreed to remove the name from its pages.[69]

Shortly after, a similar suit was brought by a fifty-six-year-old man from Kentucky who sued Ferber for $25,000 for using the name "Little Wayne Damron" in *Show Boat*. Ferber, describing the opening of the Black Diamond Saloon, had written that the place was owned by "Big Wayne and Little Wayne Damron." The plaintiff, Wayne Damron, alleged that he was a strict teetotaler and had nothing to do with a saloon.[70] He sued under the New York law. A number of precedents at the time could have supported the claim, and Ernst and Levy worked hard to refute it, arguing in court that awarding damages to Damron would result in the "throttling of literary expression." It resulted in an important decision stating that the single use of a name in a literary work is not prohibited under New York law.[71]

"Ferber," as her friends called her, became one of Ernst's dearest friends. For the next four decades these two independent, sparkling minds would intrigue, amuse, and comfort each other. Ernst recalled, "[Ferber] . . . sees and hears all kinds of life more accurately and acutely than anyone else I know; she can brew a dish of conversation in her home with a flavor not found anywhere else I've ever been, and she has been sufficient in herself to be alone." "I can be comfortable with Edna because she knows how wrong I can be, she is aware of my weaknesses, yet she never tries to reform or change me," he wrote.[72]

Ferber described "Morrie" as a "gay, brilliant, wise, and warmhearted friend, enjoying life with the gusto of an undergraduate, . . . the most informal, lighthearted, least pompous, and the purest human being I have ever known." "I never have signed so much as a restaurant check without first consulting him—which is tough on Morris Ernst but extremely beneficial to me," she wrote. Ferber believed that "Morris Ernst is a book, not a chapter."[73]

* * *

By the age of forty, Ernst had attained prominence, influence, and considerable wealth. The family resided in an elegantly furnished, century-old brownstone at 46 West Eleventh Street in Greenwich Village that was the site of Ernst's lavish soirees. His diverse crowd included Socialists, anarchists, publishers, conservative lawyers, business executives, members of the ACLU, writers from the Algonquin set, and "newspaper boys like Broun, Socialists such as

Thomas, . . . and sweet anarchists like Carlos Tresca," Ernst boasted. He attempted to create in his living room a "marketplace of ideas," believing that debate was "the precursor necessary to thoughtful conclusions."[74]

Perhaps the ultimate symbol of Ernst's worldly success was the purchase of his majestic estate on Nantucket Island. Thanks to the generosity of the Greenbaum partners, he spent a lavish three months each year there, from June to September, carrying on his law work primarily through telephone calls or brief visits to the city. "Nearly all the business friends I know have the theory that they will retire somewhere around the age of 50," Ernst explained. "I observed that most of them either went broke after they got their income, or else died of sheer boredom not long after they retired. I decided to gamble the other way. . . . I work nine months of the year and 'retire' the other three."[75]

Ernst's "love affair" with Nantucket started when he and Maggie went up one gloomy April weekend in 1926. Staying at the White Elephant Hotel near Nantucket Harbor, Ernst looked across the harbor and saw a few houses on the other side. He found out that the area was called Monomoy. Ernst thought it would be a good place to have a house, but everyone thought it was crazy because it was infested by mosquitoes and it "took the northeast storms on the nose." In 1928 Ernst bought the largest vacant waterfront tract in Monomoy Heights and got the mosquito commissioner to drain the swamp.[76]

Construction of Ernst's home began the following year. The expansive structure was modeled on the White Elephant Hotel and designed by its architect, Edward Ludwig. Like the wood-shingled hotel, the house had two stories in the middle with one-story wings on each end. One wing was for the household staff, and the children's suites were on the other. Ernst built a pier into Nantucket Harbor for easy access. Investing in the house was a decision he wouldn't regret because "every dollar I put into that house would have been lost in the stock market" crash of 1929, he believed.[77] He eventually bought up much of the land on the island and in time became one of three major landowners in Monomoy Heights.[78]

On Nantucket, Ernst discovered two passions: carpentry and

sailing.[79] Though he had no prior experience with woodworking, he made himself a shop and turned out beautiful, ornate furniture.[80] Carpentry "compensates for the daily verbal existence of a law office," he wrote. "In New York I work with my tongue. On Nantucket I work with my hands."[81] Ernst also took up sailing. He bought a sixteen-foot "catboat" and taught himself how to sail by textbook. Sailing became his "approach to mysticism and religion."[82] "My mistress may be the law, but my truly married wife is a . . . catboat," he quipped.[83] Each summer the family sailed all over the Northeast, going as far north as the Maine coast, a part of the world he loved. Margaret, a true southern lady, wore a dress on the boat.[84]

The Ernsts' Nantucket home, with a beautiful garden, planted pines, and homemade tables and chairs, was relaxing but regimented. A dictionary and an atlas sat on the breakfast table. The children had to make something in the workshop ("You have to earn your rights," Ernst said). Even houseguests were given projects. Edna Ferber, who went there each summer, had to mow the lawn.[85] Ernst saw in Nantucket the virtues of small-town life, where an individual could interact intimately with others and participate in the community.[86] In reality, Nantucket was not so democratic; anti-Semitism was pervasive on the elite island. Morris was barred from the Nantucket Yacht Club. He never talked about it. Quietly, he started a short-lived rival organization called the Nantucket Boat Club.[87]

During summers Ernst ran around in a T-shirt and Bermuda shorts, barefoot, enjoying the feeling of sand and mud oozing up between his toes. One of his favorite activities was "rantumscooting." The term was used by islanders to describe a type of aimless driving over the rutted roads on the wild grasslands. Ernst regarded this activity as a metaphor for his unusual, unexpected life: "Many people never learn how to do it. . . . You just keep going, never knowing which turn you will take," he wrote. "You trust all paths on the moors and drive on without a single objective. Thus do you see sights and colors and animals unknown to those who clutch a map in one hand in order to get to a certain definite spot on the shore." And yet, he noted, "You are none the less sure that you can always get home."[88]

7

TO THE PURE

In the 1920s the United States was wracked by a culture war. Forces of modernism and cosmopolitanism battled against traditionalism and fundamentalism. The First World War had created restlessness, disillusionment, and questioning of established morals. Immigration, alcohol, race, religion, gender, politics, and "Americanism" became battlefields where traditionalists fought "moderns" for what seemed to be the very soul of the nation.

The new and seemingly pervasive obsession with sex sparked major controversies. Old codes of sexual ethics were being replaced by more liberal views. Starting in the early 1900s, feminists had sought to eliminate the Victorian notion that women must be chaste and guardians of public morals. As women gained social, political, and economic independence during and after the war, including the right to vote, they pursued and achieved greater sexual freedom. The popularization of Freudianism in the 1920s led to new norms of sexual openness. There was a "revolution in manners and morals" in which the country was freed from its Victorian past. This "revolution," observed historian Frederick Lewis Allen, "was one with which Nikolai Lenin had nothing whatever to do."[1]

Traditionalists reacted to these changes by seeking to ban contraception, dancing, short skirts, jazz, and "obscene" literature. Laws suppressing purportedly obscene material—the "Comstock laws"—had been on the books since the nineteenth century, but they were never enforced more vigorously than in the years after the First World War. During the early 1920s, officials seized and confiscated thousands of books. Classics by François Rabelais and Giovanni Boccaccio, as well as modern works by James Joyce, Theodore Dreiser, and

D. H. Lawrence, were "banned" or "censored"—more accurately, prosecuted for obscenity—on the grounds of their alleged potential to corrupt youth.[2] The front pages of newspapers reported bookstore raids—police burst into bookshops, seized the literary contraband, and hauled sellers to the police station. The punishment for publishing, selling, or mailing an obscene book was a fine or jail time.

The ACLU had never addressed literary censorship to that point. Even though obscenity law criminalized words and ideas, founder Roger Baldwin did not see it as implicating free expression. In his view, literature, theater, and other kinds of "nonpolitical" expression were beyond the realm of constitutional protection. A proper New Englander, Baldwin was prudish and believed that erotic matters should not be discussed in public.[3]

With his innovative views on free speech and his modern attitudes toward sex, Ernst was the first ACLU leader to suggest that literary censorship implicated freedom of speech. It became Ernst's signature cause and his most enduring contribution.

* * *

Anthony Comstock, the notorious progenitor of American obscenity law, was a crude, deeply religious man. Born in 1844, Comstock began his career as a "smut-seeker" and vice hunter when he came to New York after the Civil War. Taking a position at a dry goods house, he became appalled by his coworkers' consumption of pornography. Comstock, who had dedicated himself to a life of struggle against sins of the flesh, believed that pornography was a tool of the devil that lured young men into indulgence and crime.[4]

Comstock lobbied for the passage of a federal antiobscenity law, and the Comstock Act was passed in March 1873. The law made it a crime to send an "obscene, lewd, or lascivious" book, "pamphlet, picture, paper, print, or other publication of an indecent character" through the mail, including "any article or thing designed or intended for the prevention of conception or procuring of abortion." Under the law, the US Post Office Department also had authority to deem an obscene publication nonmailable. Comstock was appointed a special agent of the post office to assist with the law's administration. Several states passed criminal obscenity statutes, so-called little Comstock laws. Section 1141 of the New York Penal Code criminalized material that was "obscene, lewd, lascivious, filthy, indecent, or disgusting."

Comstock's other famous creation was the New York Society for the Suppression of Vice (NYSSV), a private organization formed to assist the enforcement of the state's obscenity law. In 1873, the New York legislature empowered the NYSSV to make arrests for violations of the obscenity statute, making it the only private organization in the world with the power to enforce state censorship. The organization was supported by private funding, backed by men of wealth including J. P. Morgan, copper magnate William E. Dodge, and soap dynasty founder Samuel Colgate.[5]

For forty years Comstock waged a fierce war against sexual expression. Blustering and humorless, with broad shoulders, a potbelly, and muttonchop whiskers, Comstock raided shops selling allegedly pornographic material, seizing books, magazines, and pictures. Comstock also went after abortionists, sellers of contraceptives, and advocates of "free love" and feminism. Comstock almost never prosecuted literature, in part because erotic literature was rarely published in the United States at that time. Modernism and realism did not become trends in literature until the late nineteenth century.[6]

The vice society's attack on "obscene" literature began in the World War I era.[7] New, upstart publishers such as Alfred Knopf and Mitchell Kennerley began publishing works dealing frankly with such topics as adultery and prostitution. The surge of modern literature coincided with Comstock's death in 1915. A thirty-nine-year-old lawyer named John Sumner took the reins of the NYSSV. A New England blueblood whose ancestors came over on the *Mayflower*, Sumner, a former stockbroker and lawyer in private practice, was a teetotaler, an Episcopalian, and the married father of a young daughter.[8] Observed the *New York Times*, "if you could take the liberty of clapping upon his head a flat-brimmed, steeple-crowned high hat, putting around his neck a stiff upstanding white collar and a black string tie, and on his lean body a tight-buttoned Prince Albert, you would have a living replica of Mr. Bluenose, the man whom the caricaturists had introduced to us as the embodiment of 'Puritanism.'"[9]

Sumner considered himself a "literary man" and made the prosecution of literature his signature effort. Starting in 1915, he went after respected literary works issued by legitimate publishing houses.[10] One of Sumner's first efforts was to raid the fledgling publishing house of Alfred Knopf, which resulted in the suppression of a novel. Shortly after, he commenced actions that led to the suppression of Theodore Dreiser's *The Genius*, which Sumner deemed obscene because the main character had adulterous relationships. Sumner had become such a threat that some publishers voluntarily withdrew books to avoid prosecution.[11]

Between 1919 and 1922 Sumner escalated his raids, seeking bigger and more famous targets, including parts of James Joyce's *Ulysses* that had been published in the literary magazine the *Little Review*. Authors joined together in protest, issuing manifestos against literary suppression and the NYSSV. Newspapers and magazines teemed with editorials and letters denouncing prudery and "Comstockism."

Literary censorship became a symbol and battleground of the culture war. Often likened to Prohibition, it was denounced by liberals as "paternalism gone mad." Opined one newspaper in 1922, "America today is suffering from the prohibitive complex. It is a great era for the gentleman with the sour face whose blood is so cool that he needs wristlets in August. The [censors] have stopped the circulation of books, of plays, of works of art . . . they wish to stop the use of short skirts, silk stockings, bobbed hair, tobacco, and other things which help to make life worthwhile." This "interference with the liberty of the individual is going too far."[12] The public had grown decidedly discontent with "this system of morals pampering."[13]

* * *

Because the New York Society for the Suppression of Vice policed America's literary capital of New York, it influenced the reading fare of the entire country. New York's censorship regime, however, was just one component of a broad nationwide system of control over literature. Every state had criminal obscenity laws similar to New

York's. The federal government regulated the mailing of obscenity through the Comstock law. The Tariff Act permitted the US Customs Department to refuse admission of obscene books and to seize and destroy them. During the 1920s the Customs Department banned hundreds of works from entry into the country. There was no coordination between the branches—a book that was condemned under New York's criminal law might pass through Customs, and a work banned by Customs could be approved by the Post Office Department.

The law was rigged in favor of the censors. It was nearly impossible to challenge an obscenity conviction in court. Courts accorded broad interpretation to the statutory terms *obscene*, *lewd*, and *lascivious*. The prevailing definition of *obscenity* came from the 1868 English decision in *Regina v. Hicklin*, adopted by American courts in *United States v. Bennett* (1879). Under the "*Hicklin* test," whether material was obscene depended on its potential effect on children. Something was obscene if it had a "tendency . . . to deprave or corrupt those whose minds are open to such immoral influences and into whose hands a publication of this sort may fall."[14] The government did not have to prove actual harm. The court simply had to believe that the material had a "tendency" to corrupt youth. Adult reactions to a book, the work's literary merit, and the actual readership of the book were irrelevant. Works were judged on the criterion of whether they were safe for children. Books could be condemned on the basis of isolated passages, taken out of context. Under this rule, it was often pointed out, the Bible and Shakespeare could be obscene. Courts rejected the opinions of experts and literary critics as irrelevant in determining whether a work was fit for public consumption. Whether material was offensive and would corrupt minors was said to be a question of fact that was the province of the jury. Under existing law, there was no free speech issue. The state had the same right to safeguard its youth from dirty books as it did to protect them from unsafe foods and toxic waste.

Ernst might not have gotten involved in the censorship issue had it not been for the firm's involvement in a customs case. In the summer of 1927, the Customs Office seized three hundred copies of a purportedly obscene novel by an unknown author named John Herrmann. The firm represented Herrmann. The unexceptional seizure of this unexceptional book launched an extraordinary phase of Ernst's career.

* * *

In 1926 Robert McAlmon's Contact Editions of Paris, a noted publisher of avant-garde works, issued Herrmann's first novel, *What Happens*. A thinly veiled account of Herrmann's own experiences, *What Happens* described wild behavior among high school and university students in Michigan.[15] Herrmann used the story to comment on what he saw as the hypocrisies of conventional middle-class morality.[16] The book was widely reviewed; critics agreed that it was not well written but was exceedingly candid. H. L. Mencken called it "crudely done" but "plainly sincere."[17]

In July 1927, Contact Editions sent three hundred copies of *What Happens* to Herrmann on a French steamship. The books were seized by the Customs Bureau in New York on the charge of violating Section 305 of the 1922 Tariff Act, the prohibition on importing obscene books. When Hermann heard about the seizure, he was distraught. The penalty for violating the Tariff Act, the destruction of the books, threatened his nascent literary career. A friend of Herrmann's contacted Eddie Greenbaum. Herrmann was penniless and hoped that the firm would take the case pro bono, which it did.[18] *United States v. Three Packages of Bound, Obscene Books* was assigned to twenty-four-year-old John Wildberg, who had just joined the firm.

Wildberg sent a letter to the collector of Customs protesting the seizure. He made arrangements to appeal the decision to the director of Customs in the Treasury Department, per established procedure. The brief relied on standard arguments in literary obscenity cases at the time: that the book was not obscene because it presented a pitiable figure and condemned rather than glorified vice; that it was no more explicit than other popular novels and plays; and that the reviews of respected literary critics made clear that the book was not lewd.[19]

The government identified sixty-two passages as having the "tendency . . . to deprave and corrupt." Among passages deemed obscene included those with scenes involving sex and drinking, as well as words such as "masturbation" and "whore."[20] The firm appealed the decision to federal court. This was unusual; most importers who lost their cases before the Treasury Department assumed, correctly, that further appeals would be futile. Under existing law, Customs Bureau decisions could be overturned only if they were wholly unjustified—"arbitrary and capricious."[21]

United States v. Three Packages of Bound, Obscene Books case came up before a stern and sober judge named John Knox. Ernst argued the case. It was his first obscenity case, and it was eye-opening. The prosecutor, hoping to secure as unenlightened a jury as possible, eliminated prospective jurors who read such "sophisticated" literary magazines as Mencken's *American Mercury*.[22] After the jury was seated, the prosecutor spent most of an entire day reading several allegedly obscene passages to them and argued that *What Happens* was obscene because it conveyed "lascivious thoughts" to the young.[23]

The New York Court of Appeals had long held that expert testimony was inadmissible in obscenity cases. Morris was unfazed. Recalled Newman Levy, "Morris, with his regrettable disregard for precedent, decided to overrule the Court of Appeals."[24] Ernst lined up his big-name writer and journalist friends to testify, including Heywood Broun and H. L. Mencken.[25] Predictably, the judge prohibited the testimony. "The state of mind of the community represented by a jury is the judge of what is obscene," Knox ruled. "On that point there is no necessity for the calling of literary experts."[26]

Hermann was Ernst's only witness. Ernst put the author on the stand to testify that the book presented the truth in a frank literary style and that Herrmann had no wish to "cater to debasing thoughts." While Herrmann was testifying, Knox looked up from his copy of the book and remarked, "In these days of musical comedies and modern novels I hesitate to define 'obscene,' but as far as I've read, it certainly seems this book falls within the meaning of the word." [27] At the end of Herrmann's testimony, Ernst took a volume of Shakespeare from his briefcase, hoping to read it to illustrate how the dramatist described passionate love more graphically than Herrmann did. Knox ordered him to sit down. "You are here to show that this book is obscene, not that Shakespeare is."[28]

The jury upheld the seizure. Knox congratulated the jurors, telling them he had been on the point of ordering a verdict for the government before they deliberated. All the imported copies of *What Happens* were destroyed.[29]

* * *

The defeat humiliated and outraged Ernst. He was disturbed by the judge's obvious bias and the hypocrisy of the jurors, who claimed to be appalled by the book yet read tawdry tabloids during court intermissions. Several sought Ernst out after the hearing to tell him to advise Herrmann to change the word *masturbate* to "play with oneself" or "self-abuse." He was so frustrated that he began studying obscenity law, determined to master it. He read not only case law but also histories and sociologies of obscenity. Appalled and fascinated by what he found—the free speech implications were manifest—he set out to write a book.[30]

A few weeks after the trial, Ernst contacted ACLU member Ben Huebsch, publisher of Viking Press, with a proposal for a book on the "status of the law in connection with the definition of obscenity." In January 1928 he got a contract and a $500 advance. Ernst arranged to coauthor the book with William Seagle, a Columbia Law graduate who wrote freelance on legal subjects for magazines.[31] They put the book together quickly, in about six months. Seagle did almost all the research and much of the writing.

It was an unhappy experience for both of them, and they squabbled constantly. Ernst was a sloppy and cavalier writer; he scribbled out his first impressions on yellow pads without corrections or rewriting, which he forced on Seagle. One point of contention was that Seagle feared that the book itself would be prosecuted for obscenity and wanted to tone down some of the statements. When the manuscript was submitted to Viking in June, Ernst was so disgusted with Seagle—and so convinced that the book was going to be a hit—that he bought out Seagle's rights for $2,900.[32]

More than three hundred pages long and richly detailed, *To the Pure: A Study of Obscenity and the Censor* was a landmark work, the first book-length, comprehensive analysis of obscenity law in the United States. Approaching the topic from historical, legal, and sociological angles, the book sought to make the case for the liberalization, if not the complete elimination, of obscenity law. It was heralded as the most important work on obscenity at the time and was regularly cited in other writings on the subject. Lawyers would regard it as a blueprint for structuring obscenity defenses, and its arguments established the foundation for Ernst's attacks on censorship over the next decade.

* * *

The main premise of *To the Pure* was that "obscenity" was an illusion. Society had been led to believe that "that there is such a concept as The Obscene," but obscenity was a fiction, an amorphous concept whose definitions were as fleeting as fashion, varying with official whim and public tastes. "Obscenity is . . . only a superstition of the day—the modern counterpart of ancient witchcraft."[33]

Ernst and Seagle demonstrated how obscenity law had long been used by authorities to quash ideas, sexual or otherwise, that threatened the status quo.[34] The targets of obscenity prosecutions changed over time. In England, when religious authority reigned supreme, censorship had been used to suppress criticism of the church.[35] As the power of the church waned, political censorship took the place of religious censorship, and attacks on the government were taboo. When sedition laws were struck down and criticism of the state was permitted, the object of censorship became sex. "The purpose of authority remains always the same," they wrote, "but the index of censorship changes."[36]

The status of women in a society, its material resources, its attitudes toward sex, and its religious beliefs determined what a society considered obscene. In societies with great demand for population, birth control and homosexuality were proscribed, Ernst and Seagle argued. At the same time that definitions of obscenity were determined by social factors, they could also be subjective, dependent on such factors as "what the judge had for breakfast." Books that had been banned in Boston were judicially cleared in New York. Sometimes books were condemned at trial but given a clean bill of health on appeal. Often, courts accepted high-priced limited editions but condemned the same book when it was published in a cheap mass edition.

The vagueness of the law was terrifying. Few words were as imprecise as the "six deadly adjectives" that were the basis of obscenity laws: "obscene, lewd, lascivious, filthy, indecent, and disgusting." These "fine phrases" "conceal the ugliness, bitterness, stupidity, and confusion of judges, juries, district attorneys, moralists, and vice secretaries which go to make the myth of obscenity in action," Ernst and Seagle wrote. "No two persons agree on such definitions. . . . Judges differ to such an extent that courts divide by narrow margins. . . . Juries disagree with judges." The law's vagueness induced a "chilling effect," forcing writers to censor themselves to avoid prosecution. "Authors have to adapt their ideas to an unknown measure and jails invite those who cannot guess the contemporary meaning of obscenity."[37]

Because censorship of obscenity involved the suppression of knowledge, it raised a free speech issue, they argued. Obscenity law dealt with "the spread of thought and wisdom," therefore there was "no single group of statutes which is more important."[38] The effects of censorship went beyond the suppression of literature. The censor's long arm reached into history, art, science, and education. In their drive to eradicate sex from society, censors corrupted the writing of history, quashed artistic expression, and stifled the free exchange of opinion. In restraining sex education, obscenity law kept youth ignorant of facts that could save their lives. "The spirit of this censorship has so penetrated into the very interstices of our civilization that it has affected almost every kind of human endeavor," they wrote. "These restrictive mandates have exercised a pervading influence in the subconscious recesses of individual minds and have colored the thinking of generations."[39]

To the Pure closed with the radical suggestion that with the exception of prohibitions on pornography aimed at children, obscenity law should be completely abolished. Ernst and Seagle made clear that they were not in favor of "smutty books" and that they believed some explicit material could injure both children and adults. But the law was ill suited to prevent such threats, they argued. Mechanisms outside the law, such as parents' control over children's reading and publishers' refusal to traffic in such material, could deter pornography without the law's chilling effects. Acknowledging the unlikely repeal of the Comstock laws, Ernst and Seagle concluded that the best alternative was judicial liberalization—that the courts would refuse to enforce them strictly or would use definitions of obscenity that conformed to social norms. Obscenity should be determined according to "living standards"—the real-life views and sensibilities of ordinary people—not rigid judicial formulae or the outdated prudery of vice hunters. They concluded:

> We have endeavored to weigh the advantages and disadvantages of censorship. The scales weigh heavily in favor of freedom and liberty . . . and a free market for thought.[40]

* * *

Ernst and Seagle's analysis of obscenity as an outdated fiction struck a nerve. Reviews of the book sparkled. The *Saturday Review of Literature* called it "learnedly and amusingly written . . . [a] work which everyone who has had to do with books in any way will read."[41] According to the *Bookman*, *To the Pure* was "so honest, so logically reasoned, so sensible and so enjoyable that it might appeal to the shade of Mr. Comstock himself, if he has learned anything in Heaven."[42] Wrote another reviewer, "The most unsettling document I have ever read on this theme. For it reveals that everyone is hopelessly muddled on the subject of obscenity. The fashions in taboos change even quicker than fashions in hats."[43] The book made the *Nation*'s list of distinguished publications for 1928.[44]

Despite the praise, the book was a commercial failure, selling only 2,786 copies. Ernst contributed $2,000 of his own money for publicity; Viking apologized that there was not a better return on his investment. But the book paid off handsomely for Ernst, in ways he could not have imagined. *To The Pure* defined Ernst as the leading legal expert on obscenity.[45] It brought him, in a sudden and rather remarkable fashion, into a series of historic censorship cases.

* * *

In 1927, British author Radclyffe Hall had written the novel *The Well of Loneliness* to "smash the conspiracy of silence" around the taboo subject of lesbianism. Hall was a British upper-class woman who self-identified as a lesbian, wore masculine clothes, and called herself "John."

Partially autobiographical, *The Well of Loneliness* follows the life of Stephen Gordon, an Englishwoman from an upper-class family whose "sexual inversion" is apparent from an early age. Stephen reads psychologist Richard von Kraft-Ebbing's *Psychopathia Sexualis* and discovers that she is an "invert." Stephen cautiously embraces her identity, becoming an author in London and then in Paris, where she is introduced to urban gay culture. Throughout, she struggles with the loneliness and difficulty of living a homosexual lifestyle. The novel portrays "inversion" as a natural, God-given state, and makes the plea, "Give us also the right to our existence."[46]

The Well of Loneliness was published by the British publisher Jonathan Cape in July 1928. Only months after publication, the British home secretary declared it obscene. Cape's offices were raided and the publisher was charged with violating the Obscene Publications Act of 1857. As a result of the British controversy, the American publishing house of Alfred Knopf backed out of its contract with Hall.[47]

The book was then picked up by the recently formed Covici-Friede publishing company. Pascal Covici was a forty-year-old Chicago bookseller, and Donald Friede was a wealthy twenty-seven-year-old who had served as vice president of the publishing house Boni and Liveright. Friede had recently been involved in a censorship test case in Boston in which he had sold a copy of Theodore Dreiser's *An American Tragedy* to a Boston police officer and was convicted of violating the state's obscenity law. Friede was in the midst of appealing the conviction when he and Covici opened their firm.

As soon as they acquired *The Well of Loneliness*, Covici and Friede, who had heard about *To the Pure*, got in touch with Ernst.[48] They knew that Sumner would be coming after the book. During the British controversy, Sumner had declared *The Well of Loneliness* "literary refuse."[49] Sumner believed that "inversion," a "pathological problem," was a proper matter for medical study but not for literature. Covici and Friede gave Ernst the galleys, and when he read them he was sure he could defend the book.

A fledgling firm, Covici-Friede could not afford Ernst's high fees. Ernst proposed a shrewd contingency fee deal. If they won the case, he would earn a twenty-five-cent royalty on every copy sold.[50] He was confident that he would win the suit and that the publicity would drive up sales not only of *The Well of Loneliness* but also *To the Pure*. Covici and Friede agreed, and Ernst laid out a detailed plan. He instructed them to notify Sumner immediately of their intent to publish. Ernst wanted to make sure Sumner went after the publisher, rather than a bookseller that might be intimidated into pleading guilty or would make an inadequate defense.

Covici-Friede released *The Well of Loneliness* on December 15, 1928.[51] Two days later Sumner showed up at the Covici-Friede office and purchased a copy. Covici, Friede, and Ernst waited for the summons to arrive. In anticipation of formal charges, Covici and Friede moved the book's plates to New Jersey to continue publishing.[52]

* * *

Even before Sumner bought the book, Ernst began preparing his defense. He collected affidavits from psychiatrists, literary critics, and other experts, including Edna Ferber, Theodore Dreiser, Sinclair Lewis, John Dos Passos, F. Scott Fitzgerald, H. L. Mencken, and Upton Sinclair, that he would attempt to introduce in court to make the argument that a book could not be declared obscene solely for its theme and that the subject of lesbianism was not obscene. Sending publicity releases to all of his newspaper friends, who previewed the case in their columns, Ernst effectively "tried" the case in the press even before proceedings began.

Sumner returned to the Covici-Friede office on January 11, 1929, and seized 865 copies of the book.[53] It was described as "the most sensational raid in months." Covici and Friede were arraigned in the court of Magistrate Hyman Bushel.[54] The state's brief admitted that *The Well of Loneliness* was a "well-written, carefully constructed piece of fiction" containing "no unclean words" but claimed that the theme of lesbianism was obscene.[55]

"The test of obscenity is a 'living standard' and must be judged by the "mores of the day," Ernst argued. "To suppress the *Well of Loneliness* because of its theme would involve as a corollary the condemnation of hundreds of other volumes now extant and would prevent the proper enlightenment of the public on an important social problem. To single out the *Well of Loneliness* at a time when the mores of the day not only permit but encourage the free exchange of ideas on the subject would be tantamount to arbitrary discrimination and the most vicious form of censorship." He asked, "Who is to determine that one literary subject is more dangerous than another?" And "Who can say that the unorthodox emotional complications of *The Well of Loneliness* will have more disastrous social consequences than the incest of Oedipus, the sadism of *Uncle Tom's Cabin*, the abortion of *The American Tragedy*?"[56]

The judge refused to dismiss the complaint and sent the case to the Court of Special Sessions for trial, declaring that the book presented "unnatural and depraved" relationships in a way that "extolled" them.[57] Both Ernst and the publishers, who had been sure of victory, were caught off guard.[58] "We will fight this case to the bitter end," Covici told the press. "We've only rolled up our sleeves and begun to fight."[59]

At the hearing, Ernst argued that the discussion of a "delicate social problem" could not violate the law "unless the manner in which it was treated tended to corrupt minds." The court agreed and cleared *The Well of Loneliness* of charges of obscenity.[60] The significance of the ruling went beyond *The Well of Loneliness*. In declaring that discussion of a controversial sexual issue did not in itself violate the law so long as the treatment was dignified, the decision had significant implications for the depiction of sex in literature.[61]

Ecstatic, Covici and Friede took out a full-page ad in the *New York Times Book Review*: "The Most Controversial Book of the Century [Banned] in England and vindicated by an American Court." They also rushed out a "Victory Edition." For twenty-five dollars, readers could purchase a special edition printed on handmade paper with Ernst's summary of the opinion and Hall's autograph. More than 100,000 copies of *The Well of Loneliness* were sold the following year.[62] The controversy had made it a best seller, with the sale of each copy throwing a quarter into Ernst's coffers.

8

THE SEX SIDE OF LIFE

In 1928, Mary Ware Dennett, an esteemed liberal activist, sent a letter to Ernst after reading an excerpt from *To the Pure* that had been published in *Plain Talk* magazine. She explained to him that she was the "pestered author of a suppressed booklet" that hadn't been mentioned in the list of "banned books" described in the article. Dennett went on to describe how a sex education pamphlet for children she'd written, *The Sex Side of Life*, had been banned by the Post Office Department. She tried to have the ban removed, to no avail. "The most striking feature of the whole silly story is that they have absolutely refused to say what part or parts of the pamphlet are obscene," she wrote.[1] Ernst agreed to represent Dennett pro bono in an effort to remove the ban, resulting in a landmark obscenity law ruling freeing sex education material from the Comstock laws. Ernst regarded the *Dennett* case as one of the most significant of his career, with an "enduring effect on human happiness."[2]

* * *

Mary Ware Dennett was a warm, matronly looking fifty-six-year-old with a long and distinguished career in liberal activism. For a period, she rivaled Margaret Sanger as leader of the birth control movement. Dennett had also been involved in women's suffrage and was an early member of the ACLU.[3]

In 1915, Dennett confronted a dilemma when her fourteen-year-old son began writing letters home from summer camp with questions about sex. She searched libraries for information appropriate for a teenage boy and found nothing suitable.

Sex education was an emerging field at the time. Progressives and feminists allied with the "social hygiene" movement believed that problems stemming from sex, including unwanted pregnancy and disease, could be eradicated with education. The Women's Christian Temperance Union, the Young Women's Christian Association, and state boards of health published books and pamphlets, many aimed at children, that described the physical, social, and ethical aspects of sex.[4]

Dennett found that many of the sex education manuals were false or laden with euphemisms. Some were factually accurate but characterized sex as shameful. Children were told to fear venereal disease and that they had a "duty" to suppress their passions to the "sacredness of marriage." Dennett decided to write her own pamphlet called *The Sex Side of Life*.

Dennett's treatise was blunt and scientific. It described the male and female body in detail, using scientific terminology for sexual organs and functions. Explicit medical diagrams were included, and sexual intercourse was discussed. The pamphlet discussed forbidden subjects such as masturbation and venereal disease, noting that certain kinds of diseases were beginning to be treatable. Dennett discouraged masturbation, suggesting that it should only be engaged in if the sex urge was "overwhelming," but denied that it was harmful. The primary "evil" of masturbation, she wrote, was guilty feelings about it. Dennett hoped to use the pamphlet to dispel the idea that sex was shameful and that "sex emotion . . . must be curbed as much as possible." The most controversial aspect of *The Sex Side of Life* was its description of sex as pleasurable. The "climax of sex emotion," Dennett wrote, was an "unsurpassed joy," to be "proudly and serenely experienced" under the proper circumstances: "Sex relations belong to love, and love is never a business. Love is the nicest thing in the world, but it can't be bought."[5]

Dennett's son liked the pamphlet, and his friends began borrowing it. Dennett started loaning *The Sex Side of Life* to friends with teenage children. She interested a medical journal in publishing it, and it appeared in the *Medical Review of Reviews* in 1918. When there was continued interest, Dennett reprinted the text as a pamphlet. The Young Men's Christian Association (YMCA) distributed it, and it was used in teaching at the Union Theological Seminary and in public schools. Between 1918 and 1928, more than 35,000 copies were sold to educational and social service institutions, ministers, teachers, YMCAs, doctors, and parents. Dennett included with the pamphlet endorsements from several dozen prominent figures in medicine and psychology.[6]

In 1922, after the pamphlet had been in circulation for four years, the Post Office Department declared it obscene and nonmailable under the Comstock law. Dennett asked the post office to identify the obscene passages, but there was no response. She began to fill orders for the pamphlet using sealed first-class mail, which the post office could not inspect. Dennett was outraged by the ban, and in 1925 she asked that the Post Office Department take up the matter again. She was permitted to argue her case before the department, but it concluded that there was no reason to set aside the earlier ruling.[7]

Shortly after, Dennett consulted Art Hays about securing an injunction against the post office. Hays said he had "considerable doubt, amounting almost to a feeling of certainty, that the court would not overrule the Post Office Department in this case."[8] Dennett then wrote to Ernst, whose response was different.[9] Ernst was confident that "some action might be taken as to have the Post Office Department decisions reviewed in the courts."[10]

Ernst and Dennett met in October 1928, and Dennett showed him the pamphlet. Ernst offered to take the case without fee and to test the ban, which could include an appeal to the US Supreme Court. Dennett told Ernst that it "rejoiced" her that he cared "sufficiently about the whole matter of censorship as related to obscenity to be willing to tackle the problem at the root, the Post Office power."[11] Ernst and Dennett corresponded for several months; he delayed starting proceedings because he was overwhelmed with work.

At the same time Ernst and Dennett were exchanging letters, a post office inspector attached to the Washington, DC, office, on the complaint of a member of the Daughters of the American Revolution, "rigged up a decoy to order a pamphlet." A "Mrs. Carl A. Miles" from Grottoes, Virginia, requested the pamphlet from Dennett, who sent it to a post office box. Miles was an entrapper for the Post Office Department, which initiated criminal charges for violating the Comstock law.[12]

* * *

In January 1929, Dennett was indicted in the federal district court in Brooklyn.[13] The grand jury found *The Sex Side of Life* so "obscene, lewd, and lascivious" that its contents were unfit to be mentioned in the indictment and "to be spread upon the records of this honorable court." In his motion to quash Dennett's indictment, Ernst argued that the pamphlet was a "clean, serious, scientific document of great social value, sincerely, accurately, and honestly written." He stated, "All of us are aware of how in the past, as a result of prudishness and social taboos, most derived their first knowledge of sexual fact in a surreptitious underhanded fashion from other children. We are aware, too, that the entire subject was thus tinged with a dirtiness that left a lasting impression. Today we have arrived at a healthier viewpoint." Making use of prominent experts as he always did, his motion quoted at length medical and social work authorities who attested to the importance of honest sex education material for youth.[14]

Before Judge Grover Moscowitz, Ernst denied that there was anything filthy or obscene about the pamphlet and described how the *Sex Side of Life* had been published in the respected *Medical Review of Reviews* and was praised by authorities in the field. "The pamphlet is one of sincerity and integrity. There are no dirty words in it. There is nothing in the pamphlet that will create a dirty giggle or a blush." To "throttle the distribution of intelligent information on the subject is to drive the children back into the gutter."[15]

The government's attorney, James A. Wilkinson, a portly middle-aged prosecutor, was the perfect stereotype of the "Comstocks"—ignorant, obtuse, and vindictive. "If the court pleases, my adversary stated that he did not want the youth of the country to get the information from the gutter," he told the judge. "I would hate to see the youth of our nation not only descend to the gutter but go beneath the gutter and into the sewer, where this pamphlet leads them."[16]

Moscowitz had planned to uphold the indictment, but Ernst's forceful argument led him to change his mind. He told Ernst and Wilkinson that he was uncomfortable about deciding on the motion and wanted to seek other guidance. He then took the unusual step of scheduling an "open hearing" in which he would have priests, rabbis, ministers, physicians, and educators in court to "enlighten the conscience of the court on the matter."[17]

* * *

The *Nation* likened the hearing to the "ecclesiastical trials of Giordano Bruno . . . or Galileo Galilei." Next to Judge Moscowitz on the bench that morning sat Monsignor John Belford of the Church of Nativity, Rabbi Louis D. Gross of the Union Temple, and George P. Atwater of the Grace Episcopal Church. John Sumner sat in a jury seat to their right. The spectator benches were filled to capacity.[18] The proceedings were covered widely in the papers, and Moscowitz received hundreds of letters begging him to drop the case.

Ernst had arranged for twenty witnesses of "distinction and importance" to testify, including prominent representatives from the YMCA, child welfare organizations, and religious and educational institutions. Wilkinson's long list of witnesses included judges of the children's court and a doctor of the State Hospital for the Insane. Wilkinson had called representatives of insane asylums to show the "horrors of extremity in self-abuse"—the purportedly destructive effects of excessive masturbation.[19]

At the last minute, Judge Moscowitz decided that he would not hear any of the witnesses because he wanted to send the case to a jury. Instead of calling the experts to the stand, he permitted them to submit written statements. But Moscowitz was embarrassed to send away so many people who had come for the hearing, so he had Ernst and Wilkinson present the points they had previously argued.[20]

Ernst told the judge that he had a young daughter. He was not afraid for her to have the information in the pamphlet—children were more threatened by delayed information than "precocious stimulation," he argued. "Suppose the pamphlet does fall into the hands of a child under ten years old. What injury can ensue? . . . Certainly it will serve to satisfy an intellectual curiosity and I do not see why that curiosity should not be satisfied. This pamphlet gives facts about life."[21]

With "revivalist fervor," in a "flaming harangue," in the description of the *Nation*, Wilkinson denounced the book's failure to advocate chastity and self-control.[22] Wilkinson warned that the nation would suffer because ideas like Dennett's jeopardized the health of young white men, who would purportedly be weakened by masturbation and excessive sex. He raised the specter of "race suicide"—that Anglo-Saxons would die off because of the weakening of their males, leading to a nation dominated by immigrants and the "lower races." He argued, "What will happen to America if our national standard falls so low? Where will our soldiers come from in our hour of need? . . . When the clarion call of war shall sound, God help America if we haven't the men to defend her!"[23]

* * *

The absurdity of the prosecution and the outpouring of support for Dennett spurred the ACLU to get involved in the issue. As a result of Ernst's efforts, the ACLU Board of Directors came to see freedom of sexual education as a civil liberties goal and organized a committee to raise funds for Dennett's defense along the lines of its committee in the earlier Scopes trial.[24] The Dennett case became the ACLU's entrée into anticensorship work, which would find more concrete expression in its subcommittee founded in 1930, the National Council on Freedom from Censorship.

Meanwhile, Judge Moscowitz had come under congressional investigation concerning his conduct in bankruptcy cases. He postponed the Dennett trial date three times and then finally announced that he could not judge the case.[25] Moscowitz asked Ernst to withdraw his motion to quash and to have a motion to dismiss substituted so a new judge could be appointed. Before doing this, Ernst had the judge agree that all of the letters of support he had submitted would be made part of the court record. The case was transferred to District Court Judge Marcus Campbell.

Judge Campbell rejected the motion to dismiss and sent the case to trial.[26] He refused to read any of the letters, claiming that Moscowitz did not have the right to make the stipulation that brought them into the record. Campbell reassigned the case to another judge, Warren Burrows, on the assumption that Ernst would no longer want him to preside after the unfavorable ruling.[27] The trial was scheduled for April 23, 1929.

Ernst brought in a small army of experts to testify, including college professors, social workers, and physicians.[28] His first witness was a leader of the National Council of the YMCA, Abel Gregg, who was to explain how the YMCA used and distributed the pamphlet. As Ernst's questioning began, Wilkinson objected to all the defense witnesses on the grounds that the testimony was irrelevant. "We are only concerned here as to whether the pamphlet was mailed or not. The jury are the sole and exclusive judges of obscenity." Burrows agreed and prohibited Ernst from calling any witnesses.[29]

"Here we have the YMCA, the school system, and Columbia University prescribing this pamphlet and that fact is being kept away from the jury," Ernst protested. To create a record in the likely event of appeal, he asked that Gregg be recalled to the witness stand and that the court stenographer record his rejected questions. Wilkinson said that he would have made the same objections, the judge confirmed that he would have made the same rulings, and Ernst said he would have made the same exception. This was repeated with all the witnesses.[30] Recalled Dennett, "To the people gathered in the courtroom, this ruling out of all the witnesses for the defense seemed almost incredible. They hardly believed their ears. It startled them into a new realization of how laws and court rulings can be made to thwart common sense and fair play."[31]

Ernst requested that the jury be charged that "the test [of obscenity] is not whether the material would corrupt the most corruptible or subnormal people . . . the aggregate sense of the community is the test." Burrows rejected this and used *Hicklin*—"the true test [of a work's obscenity] is whether its language has a tendency to deprave and corrupt the morals of those whose minds are open to such things and into whose hands it may fall."

The first vote was eight to four for conviction. The second round brought nine votes against Dennett. On the third she lost another vote. A court attendant entered the jury room and warned them that if they didn't reach a decision, they would be held over for a "court supper." The jurors who had held out quickly changed their minds and voted for conviction. When the jury foreman announced the guilty verdict, Ernst sprang from his seat.[32] "If the Court please, I move to set aside the verdict and request a new trial . . . on the ground that the statute is unconstitutional, that the verdict is contrary to law [and] contrary to evidence."[33]

The following week, before a packed courtroom, Ernst appealed to the judge to overturn the verdict, telling him that "this is the most important case I have ever handled in my life":

> It is the modern equivalent of the trial of Galileo in 1528 when the judges decided that humanity would be corrupted if it should be said that the earth was round. . . . In Dayton, Tennessee, you are a corrupter of morals if you try to spread the facts of anthropology. Here this precious woman is found guilty of moral corruption because she has with the highest and most humanitarian motives in the world written down and transmitted to a government spy in Grottoes, Va. an honest statement of the most fundamental facts of life.[34]

Judge Burrows refused to set aside the verdict, and Dennett was fined $300. Ernst set about planning for an appeal. "This matter of Mrs. Dennett's conviction will not be allowed to rest," Ernst told the New York *Evening Journal*. "Are the people of the largest and most progressive city of the world ready to stand with the times and face . . . facts? . . . Are they going to continue in the old ways of shunning all references to sex, hiding their heads like the ostrich, saying 'I am shocked,' when they mean in reality 'I am afraid'?"[35]

* * *

The Dennett case became a cause célèbre. With the inane verdict and massive press coverage, millions of Americans who would not have been interested in censorship were drawn into the issue. Noted the

Indianapolis Times, "This miscarriage of justice has aroused citizens in all parts of the country to the menace of an archaic and unscientific attitude towards sex education."[36] Another newspaper opined, "Mrs. Dennett's case bids fair to attract worldwide attention and to rival the 'evolution' trial in Tennessee as a reflection on the intelligence of some of our judges and juries."[37]

In the fall of 1929 Ernst appealed the case to the New York City–based Second Circuit Court of Appeals.[38] "This is a test case of vital importance," read his brief. "It transcends by far the consideration of the rights of a particular defendant, or of the value of a specific pamphlet. It concerns the entire community." It stressed, "If the publication is deemed obscene, then no honest discussion of sex will be possible in present day society."[39]

The unanimous opinion by Augustus Hand, a respected liberal jurist, fully accepted Ernst's arguments and concluded that the pamphlet was not obscene:

> The defendant's discussion of the phenomena of sex is written with sincerity of feeling and with an idealization of the marriage relation and sex emotions. . . . While it may be thought by some that portions of the tract go into unnecessary details that would better have been omitted, it may be fairly answered that the curiosity of many adolescents would not be satisfied without full explanation, and that no more than that is really given. It also may reasonably be thought that accurate information, rather than mystery and curiosity, is better in the long run and is less likely to occasion lascivious thoughts than ignorance and anxiety. Perhaps instruction other than that which the defendant suggests would be better. That is a matter as to which there is bound to be a wide difference of opinion, but, irrespective of this, we hold that an accurate exposition of the relevant facts of the sex side of life in decent language and in manifestly serious and disinterested spirit cannot ordinarily be regarded as obscene. Any incidental tendency to arouse sex impulses which such a pamphlet may perhaps have, is apart from and subordinate to its main effect. The tendency can only exist in so far as it is inherent in any sex instruction and it

> would seem to be outweighed by the elimination of ignorance, curiosity, and morbid fear. The direct aim and the net result is to promote understanding and self-control.[40]

Hand's groundbreaking opinion repudiated *Hicklin* in the context of sex education material—such works were to be considered according to their effect on normally constituted persons, not the most susceptible members of society. The fact that a work might incidentally arouse lust in some persons did not make it obscene, if its "dominant theme" was not to convey obscene material. Hand also concluded that works must be evaluated as a whole, rather than on the basis of isolated passages. It was a ruling that would have far-reaching consequences.

Assistant US Attorney Herbert Kellogg sent a transcript to the solicitor general with a recommendation that application be made to the US Supreme Court for a writ of certiorari.[41] Knowing the public opposition to the case and fearing the likely possibility of the judgment being upheld, the solicitor general refused permission.[42] On July 2, 1930, the government formally dismissed the indictment. Ernst's assistant Alexander Lindey wrote to Dennett that "this means the definite conclusion of the case, in which the government received its deserved share of ridicule."[43]

* * *

In the midst of Dennett's trial, an undercover police officer visited Margaret Sanger's birth control clinic, the Birth Control Clinical Research Bureau, on West Fifteenth Street. The officer claimed, falsely, to be a thirty-four-year-old mother seeking contraception. It resulted in a police raid and criminal prosecution in which Ernst defended the clinic. The historic case, a victory for birth control freedom, marked Ernst's first involvement with the birth control movement and the beginning of his long affiliation with Sanger.

* * *

The opening of the Birth Control Clinical Research Bureau in 1923 was a milestone in Sanger's career as a reproductive rights crusader.

Sanger had started her career in the early 1900s as a visiting nurse in the slums of New York. Sanger treated poor immigrant women who struggled with unwanted pregnancy, miscarriage, and abortion, and she became interested in family limitation. A Socialist feminist, Sanger saw birth control as part of the class struggle. Access to contraception, she believed, would be a means for working-class women to liberate themselves from economic burdens caused by unwanted pregnancy. In 1912 she began writing a column on sex education for the Socialist newspaper the New York *Call* titled "What Every Girl Should Know." Censors quashed the column as obscene.[44]

Sanger challenged the Comstock law and state laws that banned the dissemination of contraception and information about contraception. In March 1914, she published the first issue of the *Woman Rebel,* a radical feminist monthly advocating the right to practice birth control. Three issues were banned from the mail, and Sanger was indicted. Sanger jumped bail and left for England. Charges were ultimately dropped. Sanger subsequently returned to the United States, where she embarked on a nationwide tour to promote birth control and was arrested in several cities.[45] Sparked in part by outrage over Sanger's persecution, a broader social movement for birth control took off. Middle-class feminists began to adopt the right to reproductive self-determination as a demand, along with other women's rights goals such as suffrage, opportunities in the professions, and access to higher education.

Sanger opened the nation's first birth control clinic in Brooklyn in 1916. After only nine days in operation, the clinic was raided, and Sanger and her staff were arrested. Although her conviction was upheld, the appeals court exempted physicians from the law prohibiting dissemination of contraceptives if they were prescribed for medical reasons. In *People v. Sanger* (1918), the New York Court of Appeals declared that birth control information could be legally dispensed by doctors and nurses, provided it was given "to cure or prevent disease." The court explained that "disease," as defined by *Webster's* dictionary, meant "an alteration in the state of the body, or some of its organs, interrupting or disturbing the performance of vital functions, and causing or threatening pain and sickness."[46] In accordance with this broad definition, a number of birth control clinics under the supervision of licensed physicians were established.

In 1921, Sanger founded the American Birth Control League to fight opposition from the Roman Catholic Church. Sanger began to soften her radical rhetoric and emphasized contraception's societal benefits to appeal to middle- and upper-class social reformers who could support her cause financially. The birth control movement was evolving into a large-scale, professional, "respectable" campaign supported by society women and educated professionals.[47] Sanger's clinic operated freely, without police harassment, until the March 1929 raid.

* * *

The undercover policewoman, Anna McNamara, presenting herself as "Anna Tierney," told a clinic nurse that she was married to a truck driver who earned forty dollars a week and occasionally drank and that she had three children who were one, three, and five years old. Tierney told the nurse that after having three children in short succession, she worried about the health consequences of having more. The nurse asked Tierney about her menstrual cycle and told her to make an appointment for a consultation.[48]

Tierney returned to the clinic and received contraceptive advice, a tube of spermicide, and a diaphragm. She came back a week later, at which time she told the clinic's director, Dr. Hannah Stone, that she was having difficulty inserting the device. Tierney was told to return in six months. The contraceptive had been given on the basis of spacing—the doctor concluded that having a child so quickly after another would cause physical harm—but the examination revealed that she suffered from prolapse of her reproductive organs and erosion of the cervix.[49]

On the morning of April 15, 1929, eight police officers raided the clinic. Catholic officials had allegedly pressured the police to shut down the clinic after learning that parishioners were getting birth control there.[50] When the raiders entered, there were fifteen women in the waiting room and more than thirty in the basement, most with babies and showing signs of poverty. Some of the patients wept, and some jeered at the police.[51] Police interrupted the examination of patients, some in various stages of undress.[52]

Officers seized articles for evidence including books on the shelves, speculums, and "metal instruments" used for medical examination. Most egregiously, police seized 150 index cards, each containing private medical information about patients. The records were dumped into wastebaskets and carted off.[53]

Stocky Mary Sullivan, head of the Police Department Woman's Bureau, oversaw the raid. Standing at the center of the reception room, she waved her arms and shouted directions. Sanger yelled at her, "You have no right to touch those files. . . . They are private property of the doctor and if you take them you will get into trouble." Sullivan shouted back, "This is *my* party! You keep out."[54]

After the raid, one of Sanger's staff called up Robert Dickinson of the Academy of Medicine and asked him for the name of a lawyer. He recommended Morris Ernst. Sanger later recalled, "Ernst had . . . won a reputation for his espousal of liberal causes. It was most encouraging to find a lawyer who was as convinced as we that the principle of law was an important issue. Although he seemed young, the moment I talked with him I recognized here was the person for us."[55] A supporter of birth control who had long recognized the connections between contraception, the elimination of poverty, and personal freedom, Ernst eagerly signed onto the case.

* * *

At the Jefferson Market Court, the assistant district attorney charged Dr. Stone, assistant medical director Dr. Elizabeth Pissort, and three clinic nurses—Sigrid Brestwell, Antoinette Field, and Marcella Sideri—with violating Section 1142 of the penal code, which criminalized distributing any "instrument, or article, or any recipe, drug or medicine for the prevention of conception." If convicted, they would be sentenced to a year in jail. Magistrate Abraham Rosenbluth released the women on condition of $300 per person bail paid pending their hearing.[56] Ernst said that the case would be carried to the highest court if needed but was sure that it would be thrown out on the basis of *People v. Sanger*.

Physicians had never supported Sanger; they resented the business lost to her clinic and Sanger's criticism of organized medicine. Yet after the raid, the majority of doctors were outraged that police should be permitted to seize privileged medical records. The taking of the records spurred the most prominent doctors and medical organizations in the city to support the birth control movement.[57]

The revered Academy of Medicine and the New York County Medical Society issued formal protests. A special committee of the academy reported that it found "unwarranted interference with the freedom of physicians engaged in the lawful practice of medicine" and "the violation of the privileged character of all records pertaining to the relation of a physician and his patients."[58] This outrage led to an apology from Police Commissioner Grover Whalen, who admitted that the Police Department erred when it handled the case.[59] But the cards were never returned. In advance of the court's decision, Whalen removed Sullivan from the post of director of the Women's Bureau.[60]

With the academy's help, Ernst arranged to have five of the city's most prominent physicians testify in court.[61] The police conduct was so egregious, and public sympathy for Sanger so overwhelming, that the clinic was receiving large donations and funds were being volunteered for the defense.[62]

* * *

On the first day of the five women's trial, five hundred spectators fought for one of a few dozen seats in the tiny courtroom. Clubwomen, doctors, clergymen, and activists filled the space to overflow and crowded the corridors and steps outside.[63] Birth control activists recognized that the trial's outcome would be crucial to the future of the movement. As Sanger biographer Lawrence Lader points out, "a defeat at this stage could wipe out all the hard-won progress of the past twelve years."[64]

The state's attorney argued that "any meddling with the sexual relation to secure facultative sterility degrades the wife to the level of prostitute." He stated, "Marital continence . . . is the only ethical course for a man when the life of the woman whom he has promised to love and cherish, the mother of his child, is placed in jeopardy. . . . Maternity demands heroism, the daily struggle to support wife and children demands heroism. Honesty in business demands heroism. . . . What is needed is self-control, not birth control."[65]

Ernst, who was in fine form that day, asked the judge to dismiss the case. He argued that a conviction would set precedent that would make every physician defend his judgment, putting the whole profession on trial.[66] Citing statistics showing that infant mortality increased when only one year elapsed between births, Ernst claimed that the dispensation of birth control was justified because the spacing of births posed a health issue. The US government had advised against closely spaced births in its own reports, he demonstrated. He said that his case would consist only of showing that the clinic physicians were licensed and acting with good faith, per the decision in *People v. Sanger*. "If the doctor is acting in good faith with the thought that the birth control information will prevent disease, that is all we have to prove," he asserted.[67]

Anna McNamara was the state's first witness.[68] Despite initially denying that she set out to deceive the doctors, she caved to Ernst's questioning and confessed that she had set out to entrap them.[69] He asked the policewoman to discuss, in graphic terms, her experience at the clinic. McNamara blushed and confessed that the doctor had examined her vagina.[70] She "found the going a bit difficult when [Ernst asked] her questions that no lady is expected to answer outside of a physician's sanctum," newspapers reported.[71]

Five eminent physicians testified for the clinic. Each asserted that under the circumstances, contraception was justified.[72] During the testimony of Dr. Foster Kennedy the proceedings devolved into chaos. Testifying that "too frequent pregnancies imperiled the mother's constitution" and endangered the unborn, Kennedy affirmed that patients who had given birth within a year should be given contraceptive advice.[73] "It would be for the mental and nervous good of that patient not immediately to become pregnant again." Judge Rosenbluth suggested that some patients might try to deceive doctors to get such advice, asking, "But what if the patient is lying? Wouldn't it be better practice to check the official birth records to find out whether the patient is telling the truth?"

"Judge," replied Kennedy, "we doctors examine a patient before we prescribe. You can forge a birth certificate but you can't forge a womb." The spectators burst out in laughter, and the judge threatened to clear the courtroom.[74]

The next witness, Dr. Lewis Harris, the former city health commissioner, deemed the doctors' examination of McNamara "unusually thorough."

"But isn't it most important to find out whether the patient is married or not?" the judge asked.

"Do you know of any situation where a doctor sends out a detective to find out whether his patients are married?" Ernst interjected. The crowd burst out into hoots and screams.

"Unless there is absolute silence I shall clear the courtroom," the judge announced. "On second thought, I shall clear it anyway. Out you go—all of you!" Court attendants herded spectators out of the room.[75]

Judge Rosenbluth spent almost two weeks considering the evidence. On May 14, 1929, he ruled in favor of the clinic, stating that "the law is plain that if the doctor in good faith believes that the patient['s] . . . health requires prevention of conception, it is no crime to so advise and instruct therein." He explained, "Good faith, in these circumstances, [is] the belief by the physician that the prevention of conception is necessary for the patient's health and physical welfare."[76] The government, he said, had the burden of proof to demonstrate that the diagnosis was made in bad faith, and it failed to present evidence that challenged the clinic's diagnosis. Henceforth, the obligation was on the state to prove that the prescription of contraception was in no way warranted. The case stood as a powerful precedent in favor of the lawfulness of contraception and represented a major victory for the birth control movement.[77]

Rosenbluth's decision also relaxed *People v. Sanger*'s "disease" requirement to include general health, "removing all barriers to legal dissemination by physicians to unmarried women as well as to wives of contraceptive information in cases where pregnancy would endanger health," Ernst told the press.[78] After the case, the clinic was filled three weeks in advance, and over the next eight years the number of birth control clinics in the country went from fifty-five to 374. Sanger deemed the ruling "one of the finest we have ever won."[79]

9

SEX WINS IN AMERICA

> The only real obscenity I know of in life is the obscenity of being uncourageous.[1]

By 1930, Morris Ernst was the main lawyer for the book industry in censorship cases and a pioneer of literary freedom. Ernst's courtroom showmanship, his connections to the press, and his eagerness to be associated with sex and controversy had yielded major victories in censorship cases. Ernst was a shrewd enough lawyer to know that First Amendment arguments wouldn't succeed, given the law at the time—courts weren't willing to broach the possibility that sexually themed material fell within the Constitution's protections. Instead, he relied on the straightforward and commonsense argument that the *Hicklin* definition was outdated and that obscenity must be judged according to the "mores of the time," as gauged, in part, by the views of literary and other experts. With this formula, Ernst litigated a series of cases over the next five years in which he undermined many of the foundations of literary censorship.

* * *

In 1930, the publishing house of Simon and Schuster reissued Arthur Schnitzler's novel *Casanova's Homecoming*. The book told the story of an aging Casanova who attempted to seduce a young girl. *Casanova's Homecoming* had first appeared in the United States in 1923, when it was published by the respected publishing house of Thomas Seltzer. It was prosecuted by the New York Society for the Suppression of Vice, and Seltzer withdrew the book. When Simon and Schuster reissued it, the NYSSV led by John Sumner raided the publisher and seized 477 copies. The publishers got in touch with Ernst. Promising to fight the action, they issued a statement that in proceeding against the novel, an "extralegal" society had "pitted its opinion against the virtually unanimous edict" of "critics, scholars, men of letters, and civilized readers generally."[2]

Ernst was determined to get the case before Magistrate Maurice Gottlieb, known for his well-reasoned decisions. Gottlieb discouraged Ernst from bringing the case before him. Looking at his calendar, he addressed Ernst in a fatherly tone, "Counsel, this is a book case. I have not read a book, excepting law books, for ten years. You don't want me on this case." But Morris insisted that Judge Gottlieb hear the case.[3]

In court, Ernst and Newman Levy argued that the book must be considered as a whole and that it could not be obscene because it had been accepted by the community, as illustrated by its extensive reviews and sale in reputable bookstores. Mobilizing the opinions of medical and educational authorities, eminent authors, and other prominent citizens as proof of the community's acceptance of the work, they argued that "the test of obscenity is a living standard. Every publication must be judged by the mores of the day. That which society accepts is moral; that which it rejects is immoral." [4]

Gottlieb gave the book a clean bill of health. "There is nothing within its covers which tends to impair the morals of anyone reading it," he concluded. "The book is not to be judged by the standard of mid-Victorian days but . . . by the standards prevailing at the present time." He bolstered his decision with Ernst's testimonials from H. L. Mencken, Sinclair Lewis, and others. "While the opinions of these men, famed in their fields, are not considered competent evidence upon a trial . . . this court cannot brush aside the comments of leaders in the field, men having the confidence of the public they serve, and substitute a prudish opinion in place of the liberal ideas advanced by those who have judged this book by the present day standard of living, and not by what would have been the judgment in days when the mode of life was entirely different."[5]

Gottlieb later telephoned Ernst. "I do not find a letter from Heywood Broun on that Schnitzler book. . . . I would like his opinion," he said. Ernst got a signed statement from Broun. After Gottlieb dismissed the charges, Ernst asked for his exhibits back, thinking he might need them in the event of further litigation. "Counsel," replied the magistrate, "it would be most inconvenient to return those letters. You see, my son is an autograph collector."[6]

* * *

By the time of the *Casanova* case, the Comstock regime was unraveling, undone by Ernst's legal victories, the publicity surrounding his cases, and the liberalizing social climate. Ernst's hatred of John Sumner was visceral, and his splenetic attacks on "Mr. Bluenose" made exciting headlines. In 1929, Ernst drafted and endorsed a bill to be introduced in the state legislature to investigate and terminate the privileges of the vice society.[7] He also prepared a bill, introduced to the state legislature by Assemblyman Langdon Post, that would change the penal code to exempt newsdealers and booksellers from prosecution for obscenity.[8]

Sumner went on the defensive with a "Clean Books Bill" that would permit an indictment to be based only on part of a book and that would forbid expert testimony in obscenity cases. Ernst appeared in Albany as attorney for New York book dealers to oppose the bill. "To the vice hunter sitting in his little office and always looking for dirt everything comes to look dirty," he told the press. "Theirs is a polite, legalized system of blackmail and duress."[9] He created a sensation by charging that the private library of the late J. P. Morgan, one of the backers of the NYSSV, contained America's best collection of erotica. "I mean . . . merely to point out the irony of the fact that Mr. Morgan bought and the Morgan library now possesses many copies of various classics which the [NYSSV], an organization which Mr. Morgan sponsored, has at times attempted to suppress. . . . and says is not fit even for adults to possess," Ernst said.[10]

Ernst engaged Sumner in a series of high-profile public debates. In late February 1930 he debated Sumner at the League for Political Education's town hall on "censorship of books, plays, and motion pictures" in which Ernst described the history of the "struggle for the right to spread ideas" and advocated "repeal of all censorship laws." He asserted, "The Vice Society cajoles people into committing crime and I have evidence of it."[11] The debates continued. "It is no function of government to ban anything a vice hunter thinks is in bad taste," Ernst said during a May 1930 debate with Sumner at the American Booksellers Association. "No man is equipped to nurse girl a community."[12]

In addition to attacking legal restraints on literature, Ernst took on film censorship. In 1915, the US Supreme Court had declared movies, as a medium, to be unprotected by the First Amendment, meaning that they could be constitutionally subjected to bans or prior restraints, unlike newspapers. In several states, film review boards screened films before exhibition and required deletions of scenes deemed "immoral" or "objectionable." Films could not be exhibited publicly without a seal of approval from the censor board.[13]

Ernst contracted to write a "quickie" book on movie censorship with the journalist and movie critic Pare Lorentz. *Censored: The Private Life of the Movies*, which appeared in March 1930, was a flippant exposé of the work of movie censor boards. There was often little logic to the required deletions, the book pointed out, and the standards most film censor boards employed were old-fashioned and prudish. The book did not receive positive reviews, and Ernst himself was not proud of it. Ernst once described the book as a "cheap . . . blast against movie censorship." Noted the *New York Times*, "If the authors had not indulged in such extensive and indiscriminate nose thumbing and profuse invective, they could have been expected to be listened to with greater seriousness."[14] Nonetheless, with its position that free speech principles applied to "lowbrow" entertainment no less than to "serious" literary or political speech, the book was significant, presaging the law's eventual views on film by more than two decades.

* * *

While state-level censorship was waning in the late 1920s, federal customs censorship was on the rise. In an attempt to coordinate the government's censorship activities, lawyers from the Customs Bureau and the Post Office Department held a conference in 1928 at which they prepared a blacklist of more than seven hundred books they considered to be nonimportable and nonmailable.[15]

On the hearings on a new tariff bill in 1929, the House of Representatives voted to amend Section 305 of the tariff bill, the section on obscenity, to include books or other printed matter "advocating or urging treason," insurrection, or forcible resistance to any law of the United States. This amendment stemmed from the wish of Customs Bureau authorities to bring the customs law into line with the postal code, which barred such matter from the mail. The ACLU protested.[16] Senator Bronson Cutting of New Mexico took the opportunity to attack the entire practice of customs censorship as "irrational, unsound, and un-American." He offered an amendment, ultimately unsuccessful, to strike out the section entirely. Ernst offered Cutting his assistance, sending him a copy of *To the Pure*, the brief in *Dennett*, and other articles on censorship.[17]

The following year a new provision was introduced to the tariff bill that allowed the secretary of treasury to admit classics and other works of established scientific value. The Senate also adopted the Smoot Amendment to take from customs officials the authority to decide what is obscene and make federal district courts the final arbiters of obscenity. Under the new procedure, customs would seize an item and forward it to the district attorney, who would institute proceedings in the district court for the forfeiture and confiscation of the book. Customs obscenity cases would be tried in the federal courts in civil forfeiture proceedings, with full guarantee of the right of jury trial and appeal, rather than in the US Customs Court.[18] This development opened up new possibilities for legal assaults on censorship.

* * *

In May 1929 the Customs Bureau in Philadelphia seized a copy of *Married Love* by Marie Stopes. Stopes was a prolific author and advocate of birth control, dubbed the "Margaret Sanger of England." Through her clinics, lectures, and books, Stopes provided information on contraception and sexual health. Her book *Married Love*, a guide to sexual relations in married life, first published in London in

1918, was a best seller in England. By 1931 it had gone through eighteen editions and fifty reprintings.[19] *Married Love* had been banned in the United States in 1921 as obscene. Since then, copies of the English edition had been smuggled into the country from time to time and surreptitiously circulated.[20] The books had been sent from England to two social workers, who took up the matter with an attorney, thinking it would make a good test case.

Independently, Stopes, who was a friend of Mary Ware Dennett, wrote to Ernst. She told him she had been following the *Dennett* proceedings and "I feel we know each other although we have not met." She explained that she had heard that a publisher called Pioneer Press would be issuing a pirated edition of *Married Love*. She asked for his help in stopping the publication.[21]

Ernst wrote back saying that he hadn't heard of Pioneer Press but that he was interested in testing the ban on *Married Love*.[22] "In the light of the *Dennett* decision, I am convinced that *Married Love* can be legalized in the United States," he assured Stopes. He urged her to mail him a copy of the book, letting him know "amply in advance on what boat the copy is coming to the United States." He wanted to start a customs test case. Ernst would notify authorities that the book was on its way so it could be seized—"I do not want it to slip through by some chance. I think we have the censors on the run at present and if you are interested in having me take up the matter along these lines, I would like to hear from you further."[23]

Stopes sent him two copies of *Married Love*, which were duly seized by customs. One of the bases of the seizure was the book's discussion of contraception. Ernst decided not to protest the Customs Bureau decision, knowing that the law was still on the side of the censors when it came to writings about birth control. But he was not about to give up on the possibility of legalizing *Married Love*. He believed that there was a chance of winning the case if the contraceptive information was expunged. Stopes's American agent wanted to get G. P. Putnam's, which had in 1920 purchased the American rights, to publish the book. Ernst met with Putnam's and agreed to participate in a test case. Putnam's would have expurgated copies sent into the United States, and if the book were cleared by customs, or by a court on appeal, Putnam's would publish it. Stopes and Putnam's agreed to Ernst's usual contingency deal of a $1,000 retainer for each court hearing, plus $1,500 for any court victory, plus 3 percent of the royalties from the book.[24]

For his censorship cases Ernst relied on his assistant Alexander Lindey, a recent law graduate and new member of the firm. A gentle, scholarly, soft-spoken man with great artistic talent, Lindey had emigrated from Budapest at the age of fifteen and worked as fabric designer before attending New York Law School, graduating in 1925. Meticulous and a genius at organization, Lindey was "the most careful craftsman in the field," according to Ernst.[25]

Lindey and Putnam's proceeded to prepare an expurgated version that deleted all mention of birth control. They sent the book to Stopes, who would return the book by ship.[26] Lindey alerted the Collector of Customs: "We are writing to you on behalf of our client . . . we wish to advise you that a revised copy . . . left England on August 29, 1930 on the Aquitania. We are transmitting this information to you because we do not wish the book to slip through the Customs without any official scrutiny. . . . In our opinion the copy in its present form is well within the law as interpreted and crystallized in the recent decision handed down by the Circuit Court of Appeals for the Second Circuit in the case of United States vs. Mary Ware Dennett."[27]

As expected, on September 13, 1930, the Customs Bureau seized the book as obscene and forwarded it to the US Attorney's office. Lindey instructed publisher Earl Balch of Putnam's to secure expert opinion from well-known educators, psychologists, and librarians in preparation for the case.[28] A month later, District Court Judge William Kirkpatrick ruled in the Philadelphia case that *Married Love* was not obscene. But the federal district attorney did not feel bound by the decision and took action against the book in January 1931.

The case was heard by a well-known liberal judge, John Woolsey. Ernst argued before Woolsey that the book could not be held obscene on the principle of the *Dennett* case; its obvious aim was to promote "understanding and self-control." Further, he claimed that the large sales of *Married Love* in England made it a classic and immune from seizure under the Tariff Act. Ernst cited changing morality as a reason to dismiss the government's complaint. "Times have changed," Ernst argued. "In view of the pictures on the Fifth Avenue buses and in the tabloids, we can't be prudish these days. We have no objective standards for passing on what is objectionable."[29]

Arguments for the defense took fifteen minutes, and arguments for the prosecution took even less because the judge cut short the federal attorney's time. Waving the prosecuting attorney to his seat, Judge Woolsey declared that the Philadelphia decision was effective in every part of the United States and announced that he was ready with his decision. Because it did not fall under the contraceptive instruction provision of the Comstock Act, the case "falls to be dealt with entirely on the question of whether the book is obscene or immoral."[30]

"The present book may fairly be said to do for adults what Mrs. Dennett's book does for adolescents," he concluded. "*Married Love* is a considered attempt to explain to married people how their mutual sex life may be happier." More specifically:

> I do not find anything exceptionable anywhere in the book, and I cannot imagine a normal mind to which this book would seem to be obscene or immoral within the proper definition of these words or whose sex impulses would be stirred by reading it.
>
> Whether or not the book is scientific in some of its theses is unimportant. It is informative and instructive, and I think that any married folk who read it cannot fail to be benefited by its counsels of perfection and its frank discussion of the frequent difficulties which necessarily arise in the more intimate aspects of married life, for as Professor William G. Sumner used aptly to say in his lectures on the Science of Society at Yale, marriage, in its essence, is a status of antagonistic co-operation. . . .
>
> The book before me here has as its whole thesis the strengthening of the centripetal forces in marriage, and instead of being inhospitably received, it should, I think, be welcomed within our borders.[31]

Shortly after, customs seized another Stopes book. *Contraception* was a scientific treatise intended for professional use by physicians. The book was originally published in England and sold more than fifty thousand copies. In fall 1930 a graduate student in chemistry from Connecticut ordered a copy for use in his research work. The copy was seized by customs when it arrived on an English steamship. Ernst and Lindey handled the case without fee.

United States v. One Book Entitled Contraception came up before Judge Woolsey, who deemed the book not obscene. Applying the principles of the *Married Love* case, Woolsey reasoned that *Contraception* "would not stir the sex impulses of anyone with a normal mind."[32] It was the first important decision liberalizing customs law with reference to importation of contraceptive information, and it set the stage for Ernst's later victory in the *Ulysses* case.

Around this time, the ACLU began using the remaining funds from the Dennett Defense Committee for anticensorship activities.[33] Ernst had convinced the ACLU that censorship of the arts raised civil liberties issues, and the ACLU formed a subcommittee called the National Council on Freedom from Censorship (NCFC) to fight censorship in theater, radio, literature, and film, with the slogan "Censorship Covers Up But Does Not Cure." Eminent artists, journalists, critics, and playwrights, including Walter Lippmann, Eugene O'Neill, Lewis Mumford, H. L. Mencken, and Elmer Rice, were among the early NCFC members. The group's activities included working for the repeal of laws providing for advance censorship of films, conducting test cases involving "arbitrary censorship by administrative officers," defending serious books and plays banned for alleged obscenity, and distributing anticensorship "propaganda."[34]

The committee was asked about its attitude on pornography. Fearing alienating the ACLU's more conservative members, it adopted the official position that it would not introduce itself into cases involving pornography and would "adopt no hard and fast rule as to the dividing line between obscenity and pornography, but simply that the test is a subjective one and that the committee will consider each case on its merits." Ernst, who sought greater freedom, railed against this position and believed the group's attitude toward pornography was "nonsense."[35]

* * *

By 1932, Ernst had scored so many triumphs in censorship cases that he could announce confidently that the Comstock laws had been practically "nullified" by the courts. In an article in the *Nation*, he summarized his victories. As a result of the *Well of Loneliness*, *Dennett*, *Casanova's Homecoming*, *Married Love*, and *Contraception* cases, "frank sexual-education tracts may be legally sent through the mails. Homosexuality is an admitted theme. Books dealing with birth control may be imported. Contraceptives may be sent through the mails to doctors or druggists for prevention of disease as well as for prevention of birth. Classics encouraging infidelity have been approved by our high courts. Crudities of expression, scatological references, have been held to be neither lewd nor lascivious. Campaigns of the sex-hunters in the United States are virtually at an end unless the vender of the picture or the tract enters the courtroom with an air of guilt and with the taint of stealth."[36]

He took a shot at the "Puritans" on the ACLU. "A very delightful strain of puritanism accompanies practically every act of the American Civil Liberties Union," he wrote. He continued:

> It is amazing that many people who belong to an organization such as the Civil Liberties Union are afraid of the right to spread sexual ideas. They endeavor to preserve their attitude of freedom of thought by opposing the obscenity laws but are outraged by what they call "pornography." This they cannot define, but they accept its prosecution as a social need. There is plenty of hiding-space behind the weasel words of any law. The twilight zone between obscenity and pornography is beyond human vision. The creed of anarchy or the fighting gospel of communism, many liberals contend, should be allowed free dissemination. A change in government even by force holds no horrors for them. Let everyone express his ideas without any interference. The danger to the State is slight, and even if it were great, did

> not Jefferson say that a revolution every decade or so is good fertilizer for a vital commonwealth?
>
> But men and women, their sexual libidos—hush, hush, there you will find danger. The hearth, the young, are threatened. Men may not go home to their wives, and wives may be educated up to a curiosity about diverse sexual experience. Very few men in or out of the scientific professions have stood up in the community and shouted: "Where is the proof that any of this sexual material is injurious? Is it not merely a matter of taste? Can obscenity be defined, and if defined, is it not a word of subjective, changing content? . . . What about the famous First Amendment to the Constitution, called the Bill of Rights, which we have all been brought up to think guarantees complete freedom of thought?[37]

The title of the article was "Sex Wins in America."

10
TROUBLED TIMES

In October 1929 the stock market crashed, and the Roaring Twenties came to a halt. Within a year, nearly sixteen million Americans, 25 percent of labor force, were unemployed.[1] Families were evicted from their homes and farms. Homeless people roamed the nation's highways and rode the rails in search of work.[2] With capitalism in crisis, thousands of Americans joined the Socialist and Communist Parties. On the breadlines and in newspapers, the public engaged in anxious debates about the nation's future. Who would control America's power and money? Would financiers continue to exploit the public? Could the nation's resources be used in the interest of society's well-being rather than for private gain?

Morris Ernst and his law firm were not hurt by the crash. The Great Depression transformed the ACLU. The economic crisis shifted national politics to the left, generating support for the ACLU's mission.[3] The social unrest also created a host of civil liberties challenges. Like the ACLU's focus, Ernst's interests would expand to address a range of social issues made acute by the Depression, including poverty, police brutality, and racial inequality. Airing his opinions in books and articles, Ernst became a ubiquitous liberal pundit at a time when his perspectives were in increasing demand.

* * *

With economic turmoil, social unrest, and radical activity stemming from the Depression, assaults on civil liberties reached record highs. Roger Baldwin told the New York *World*, "Depression always means repression."[4] In 1930 the ACLU reported six times as many civil liberties violations as the year before.[5] Lynchings were on the rise, deportations of noncitizen radicals increased, and Communist demonstrations were routinely quashed.[6] Police used "disorderly conduct" and "disturbing the peace" statutes to break up picket lines and Communist meetings.[7] "The record for the year 1930 was one of the longest in our history," recalled Baldwin's secretary Lucille Milner.[8]

The onset of the Depression coincided with Baldwin's plans to expand the activities of the ACLU, then celebrating its tenth anniversary. In 1929 Baldwin had written a memo in which he expressed that the ACLU needed to go beyond First Amendment freedoms to protect other constitutional rights. The ACLU Executive Committee called for a greatly augmented agenda including, among causes, civil rights, support for foreign nationals facing deportation battles, and a campaign against police misconduct.[9]

The ACLU had identified police as the primary violators of civil liberties, alleging that nine-tenths of attacks on freedom of speech and assembly were made by local police, which functioned as "censors and dictators."[10] This was borne out vividly when demonstrations of the unemployed around the country led to arrests and assaults. The situation was especially dire in New York.[11] At a Communist-led unemployment demonstration in Union Square on March 6, 1930, riots erupted and police attacked tens of thousands of marchers.[12] An ACLU committee led by Art Hays and Ernst demanded from Mayor Jimmy Walker a public hearing on police brutality and the ouster of police commissioner Grover Whalen, infamous for his quip that "there is enough law at the end of a nightstick."[13] The ACLU announced plans to bring suit to force out the commissioner, but before it had time to act, Whalen resigned.[14]

Ernst was also involved in the ACLU's campaign to outlaw the use of injunctions in labor disputes. In 1930 the ACLU announced a nationwide fight for state and federal anti-injunction laws, declaring the increased use of injunctions "the most serious violation . . . of the guarantees of civil liberty during the past 10 years."[15] Ernst represented the ACLU in hearings before the Senate Committee on the Judiciary on the Shipstead bill, a proposed federal anti-injunction statute.[16] When the bill failed to pass the Senate, committee chair George Norris invited Felix Frankfurter and other legal scholars affiliated with the ACLU to draft a model anti-injunction bill. The ACLU formed the National Committee on Labor Injunctions, in which Ernst participated, and the bill became the Norris–La Guardia Act in 1932. It was the preface to a new field of labor legislation that would bloom under the Franklin D. Roosevelt administration.

Though women's issues were not yet a focus of the ACLU, Ernst expressed interest in equal rights and an enlightened attitude for a male of his time. In 1929 he spoke in Albany on behalf of the Mastick-Goodrich bill, which would permit women to serve on juries in New York. Women were prohibited from serving on juries in the majority of states. Ernst warned that the exclusion of half of the country's citizens from the court system could lead to the "nullification" of its decisions.[17] "In the final analysis law is nothing more nor less than the expression of the wishes, the customs, and the modes of the people. With the jury composed only of men the jury system must fail because it represents only half of the population," he wrote. "It is about time that we men become sufficiently inwardly secure so as to permit women to serve on juries."[18]

As a result of his experience as a lawyer in difficult divorce cases, Ernst became a crusader for the liberalization of divorce laws. He castigated the law's antiquated attitude toward divorce, as indicated by the caption of the provision of the New York State Constitution listing it with other proscribed activities such as "lotteries, pool selling, and gambling."[19] He sought to amend New York's conservative divorce law to include three years' desertion as grounds for divorce. "If the bloom is off the peach for three years it ain't worth eating," he told the press, adding that he had "no present indication that [my] wife will desert me."[20]

* * *

Racial equality was another of Ernst's "causes." Through his work for the ACLU, the NAACP, and the American Fund for Public Service, or Garland Fund, Ernst made significant contributions to civil rights. He despised it when people were being "pushed around" on the basis of their "race, creed, or color," he often said. He attributed this racial consciousness, in part, to the discrimination he experienced as a Jew, recalling how "historically I was tagged as a member of a minority group . . . this made me identify with people pushed around."[21]

Ernst shared this interest with most of the ACLU leaders. The ACLU had been one of the first predominantly white, liberal organizations to pursue racial equality. During the 1920s it investigated lynchings and campaigned for a federal antilynching law. Ernst and Hays were appointed to the National Legal Committee of the NAACP, a position Ernst held until the 1960s, and Ernst volunteered his services to the organization in several high-profile cases involving police brutality, lynchings, and exclusion from public accommodations.[22]

For decades, Ernst was a vocal crusader against the American Bar Association, which had a long-standing policy not accepting black members. After receiving a pamphlet asking him to join the association, he wrote back, "Do you take in Negro members?" The reply read, "Sorry, we did not know you were a Negro."[23] In protest, Ernst refused to join the ABA, and he railed against its discriminatory practice in the *Nation*: "Why not apologize for its enactment, expunge it from the records, and abolish a discrimination ordinarily condemned by the leaders of the bar when practiced by labor unions, as well as other groups, against colored citizens."[24]

In large part through Ernst's efforts, the Garland Fund made historic contributions to civil rights. In 1926, the fund gave substantial support to A. Philip Randolph to start the union of African American Pullman porters, the Brotherhood of Sleeping Car Porters. Randolph enlisted several white speakers, including Ernst, to speak to porters' groups in a demonstration of white support.[25] Ernst was elected an honorary member of the union and regarded his membership card as one of his prized possessions. "I still cherish my honorary membership card in the Brotherhood of Sleeping Car Porters, dated January 1, 1926," he recalled. He carried it around in his wallet, a "symbol of his belief in eradicating barriers between the races."[26]

Starting in 1929, Ernst served on the Garland Fund's Negro Work committee.[27] Ernst founded the committee with journalist Lewis Gannett and NAACP head James Weldon Johnson. In 1929, it requested that the fund approve a grant to the NAACP to subsidize a major civil rights litigation campaign.[28] It produced a memo, authored principally by Ernst, calling for a "dramatic, large-scale campaign to win equal rights for southern blacks in the public schools, in the voting booths, on the railroad, and on juries in every state where they are at present denied them, and the right to own and occupy real property."[29]

"Civil liberties in the coal baronries are flourishing compared to civil liberties among the Negroes of the South," read the memo. "We believe that the largest single contribution which this Fund could make to the release of the creative energies of the producing class in America would be to finance a large-scale, widespread, dramatic campaign to give the Southern Negro his constitutional rights, his political and civil equality, and therewith a self-consciousness and self-respect which would inevitably tend to effect a revolution in the economic life of this country. . . . For the Negro problem is not simply a question of the uplift and advancement of Negro Americans; it is for historical and economic reasons bound up with all the major problems in which this Fund is interested; the problems of labor, wages, and income, democracy, wealth and privilege, education, war and peace, and a dozen others involved in the rights and status of 12 million black Americans."[30]

Rather than fight Jim Crow laws directly, the committee believed, it would be more effective to compel railroads, schools, and other public accommodations to provide genuinely equal accommodations, as required under the principle of "separate but equal." Ernst believed that mandamus proceedings conducted simultaneously in eleven states—suits brought by taxpayers that would ask courts to issue orders forcing governments to provide equal facilities—"would force a radical change. . . . The effect would be to make the Jim Crow system impossibly expensive."[31] The Garland Fund gave the NAACP a $10,000 planning grant and pledged another $90,000 for implementation. It was the Garland Fund's most important and consequential grant. Ernst assisted in finding a lawyer to coordinate the campaign. His friend Felix Frankfurter, then teaching at Harvard, suggested Nathan Margold, one of his protégés.[32]

Margold, who developed the final plan for the NAACP, rejected the strategy suggested by the committee's memo. He argued that using mandamus actions would be like "trying to empty a swimming pool with an eyedropper," in the words of historian Richard Kluger.[33] Waging the battle through such actions, Margold believed, would not be establishing new principles, "nor bringing any sort of pressure to bear which can reasonably be expected to retain the slightest force beyond that exerted by the specific judgment or order that we might obtain."[34] Margold instead put forth a more far-reaching proposal: a direct attack on the constitutional validity of segregation when coupled immediately with discrimination. But Margold's approach was too daring for the NAACP, and its legal director rejected it. The Margold report nonetheless played an important role in expanding the horizons of the civil rights movement, setting the NAACP on the path toward civil rights test litigation that would culminate twenty years later in *Brown v. Board of Education*.[35]

* * *

The ACLU continued to generate acrimony and controversy. In particular, it continued to battle accusations that it was affiliated with the Communist Party. In 1930 the notorious red-baiting congressman Hamilton Fish III, a conservative Republican from New York, launched a committee to investigate Communist activities in the United States. The Fish Committee concluded, incorrectly, that the ACLU was a Communist organization.[36] The ACLU's purported Communist ties were further highlighted when, in Gastonia, North Carolina, in 1929, seven Communist Party organizers whom the ACLU had defended were convicted of murder after a battle between striking textile workers and local police. The defendants jumped bail, provided by the Garland Fund, and fled to Russia. The disreputable incident made clear to ACLU leaders the importance of dissociating themselves from the Communists if they wanted to earn support from the mainstream.[37] After that, the ACLU Board of Directors refused to provide bail for Communist Party members "until the Communist authorities make it clear under adequate guarantees that they will not support or tolerate bail jumping."[38] The Gastonia affair heightened Ernst's distaste for the Communists, leading him to go as far as to warn Art Sulzberger of the *New York Times* against publishing news about the Communist Party, so-called red news, fearing that any publicity would aid the party's growth.[39]

At the same time it was despised in many quarters, the ACLU was becoming more widely accepted as faith in the status quo unraveled.[40] The ACLU became an institutional outlet for the increasing number of Americans who were radicalized by the Depression.[41] By 1931, it had three thousand members, eight hundred correspondents and investigators, and five hundred cooperating attorneys.[42] The publicity it received was more favorable, as the press recognized the important function it served in a period of unrest.[43] "We were firmly established. Our influence reached far and wide. . . . We had brought the Bill of Rights to life," recalled Milner.[44] The ACLU came to be viewed by many people, in the words of historian Paul Murphy, as an "agency for human relief at a time in which such relief was a crying need."[45]

The ACLU was also reaping the rewards of a more liberal judiciary, more often finding success in the courts and going there for relief. In 1930 President Herbert Hoover appointed Charles Evans Hughes chief justice of the US Supreme Court. The Hughes court would establish itself as a "free speech Court." In 1931 the Court's landmark decision in *Near v. Minnesota* invalidated a ban on a tabloid scandal sheet as an unconstitutional prior restraint. In *Near*, the Supreme Court brought freedom of the press within the liberty safeguarded by the due process clause of the Fourteenth Amendment. *Stromberg v. California*, also decided that year, struck down a law that prohibited the display of a red flag as a Communist symbol. The majority wrote in Brandeisian terms: "The maintenance of the opportunity for free political discussion . . . is a fundamental principle of our constitutional system."[46] These decisions, considered to be a revolution in free speech, made clear that the federal government was prepared to be a national monitor over freedom of expression.

In 1929 Ernst formally took the position of ACLU cocounsel, serving alongside Art Hays. Hays and Ernst were an interesting pair, with similar backgrounds, brilliance, and energy but vastly different philosophies and temperaments. Hays, who was seven years older than Ernst, had grown up in an assimilated German Jewish family that succeeded in the clothing business.[47] Hays earned his law degree from Columbia and went on to form a large commercial litigation practice, which made him rich. Like Ernst, Hays did not regard his work for business clients as inconsistent with his commitment to liberal causes. An obituary in 1954 would describe him as "the lawyer who grew rich representing corporations and grew famous defending civil liberties without pay."[48] But Hays did not share Ernst's scattered interests or flamboyance, nor his faith in the state. Ernst believed in government as a force for social good, while Hays distrusted government. Hays, who didn't believe in banning anything, may have been the most extreme civil libertarian on the ACLU.[49]

At first Baldwin worried that divided counsels might be disorienting, but the group settled the potential confusion by turning to Ernst for censorship cases and, during the New Deal, for negotiations with Washington, where Ernst wielded influence. Hays and Ernst worked well together and had great respect for each other, their differences notwithstanding. ACLU leaders "knew which one to consult to get what we wanted . . . each had specialties in the law, and in tactics," according to Baldwin. Ernst enjoyed "pulling wires behind the scenes" and working the "inside track," using his connections to make things happen. Hays preferred the open fight, the "frontal assault on the powers that be," beating them at their own game.[50] "Hays was ever the wise counselor, Ernst the smart 'fixer.'"[51]

* * *

This man who had once labored mightily to get a single byline was now a widely read liberal pundit. In the early 1930s, one could find Morris Ernst's ideas, opinions, plans, and pronouncements in an array of print venues, thanks to his connections to the press. His column in the *Nation*, "Dissenting Opinions," served as a platform for his views on a variety of topics, including birth control, censorship, tax, Prohibition, and poverty. Ernst had another outlet in the New York *Evening Post*, where editorial writer Joseph Cookman did a column called "Ahead of the News." The column featured opinions of a famous lawyer, "Malachi Forsyte," a pseudonym for Ernst.

For a few years Ernst did a column for the William Randolph Hearst-owned paper the New York *Journal American* called "Take Your Choice," debating issues in the news. Three days a week it appeared on the editorial page. The column featured opposing opinions on such questions as "Should Hitchhiking Be Illegal?" and "Are Prison Sentences Too Long?" Ernst wrote both sides. The side he agreed with was signed with his name and the opposition one signed "Patrick Stand," a play on "stand pat." The column didn't last long. Ernst believed that Hearst stopped it because of an attack he made on him in a book he had written, but in reality, Ernst said years later, the column wasn't that exciting.[52]

In 1931 Harry Hansen of the New York *World-Telegram* was going on vacation and asked Ernst to take over his book review column for the day. Which new book would Ernst like to review? he was asked. He chose *America's Primer*—his own book, which he reviewed under his nom de plume Malachi Forsyte.[53]

* * *

America's Primer was Ernst's third book and his only solo-written book to that time. It was the first of two books in which he responded to the conditions of the Great Depression. One of his many "quickie books" written hastily to capitalize on a current issue, it was very much a product of the early Depression years, which saw a vogue for "planned economies."[54]

The Depression had raised questions not only about business leadership but also about capitalism itself.[55] Conditions in the Soviet Union, which seemed relatively stable, contrasted starkly with rampant unemployment and inequality in the United States. Stalin's first five-year plan, initiated in 1928, focused on rapid industrialization, nationalization of industry, and nationalization and collectivization of agriculture. By the mid-1930s, it was supposedly producing economic miracles.

A Russian engineer, M. Ilin, wrote *New Russia's Primer* in 1930 to instruct Soviet youth in the five-year plan. The book got onto the American market, and its English translation was selected in 1931 by the Book of the Month Club. *New Russia's Primer* became a best seller in the United States, inspiring similar books by American authors, including Ernst with his *America's Primer*.[56] Like many liberals, Ernst had come to believe that a "planned economy," working within the capitalist system, was the only way to end poverty and lift the country out of the Depression, and *America's Primer* was devoted to making that point.[57]

The United States was as "devoid of any rational plan in its business and politics as Russia was dominated by too much plan," he argued. "We are the most daring of gamblers but timorous of new ideas in government. So timorous that we reject any planning of life."[58] As reported in one newspaper, Ernst characterized the "economic pattern of the United States" as a "hodgepodge" operating under "such vicious principles that it throws 6,000,000 persons out of work on a plea of overproduction, although the average per capita income of the country is below $700 a year."[59] Quoted another, "We are the richest nation in the world . . . yet we have longer breadlines, more starving and homeless people than any other nation. Millions are out of work, Wall Street is in despair, and yet we are producing more wealth per capita at any time than was ever produced by any other country in the world."[60]

Time magazine published a scathing review of *America's Primer*—and Ernst. "*America's Primer* is a phrase book for those discontented, restless, loosely anchored, ever-thinking, rarely-doing citizens of the world who discuss what Colyumist [*sic*] Heywood Broun writes, who when abnormally excited vote for socialist Norman Thomas, both good friends of Author Ernst," said the anonymous reviewer. "To him, as to lawyer Arthur Garfield Hays, liberals, workers, writers, and bohemians look for championship and defense." The *Time* reviewer described Ernst as "swarthy, small, and solidly built. Membership in the Dr. John Roach Straton Sunday Morning Bowling and Breakfast Club"—a bowling league of New York literati Ernst attended weekly—"has not prevented a gentle paunch."[61] In his typically high-strung manner, Ernst retorted in a personal letter to the editor, "Time is usually accurate, but I can bring evidence to prove that I have no paunch." He expounded, "It might be an interesting legal case to define paunch in the courts of law. I hold a doctor's certificate indicating that my waist measure is 33, chest 38, which for a height of 5 ft. 9 and a half inches [Ernst, five foot seven, exaggerated here] does not qualify me for the Atlantic City Shape contest, but nevertheless should eliminate in the future all libelous statements about a paunch."[62]

Like all of his books, *America's Primer* never caught on. It sold only two thousand copies, and the publisher melted the plates in 1934. Ernst quipped that Liggett's Drug Store, where remaindered books were sold, was the best place to get his books: "Within two weeks after publication they are on the drug counters. I am known as Liggett's friend."[63]

Shortly after, however, he did present a "plan" of sorts, appearing in the *Nation* in January 1932 under the title "If I Were a (Constitutional) Dictator." In typical Ernstian fashion, it was a "multi-point plan," a sweeping "88-point proposal" of "national and world construction":

> If I were dictator, under the Constitution, therefore, I should proceed as follows . . .
>
> Repeal all legislation giving the state power to censor ideas by control of mails, customs, movies, and so on, or by forbidding free discussion of obscenity, sedition, birth control, et cetera. Only a constitutional dictatorship can afford to allow free trade in thought and wait to act until the commission of an overt deed. . . .
>
> Procure advice from the medical profession, and on its judgment legalize abortions within that period which the profession reports as medically safe. . . . After our economic reforms are established, our birth-rate will increase—but only of wanted offspring born into adequate economic surroundings. . . .
>
> Establish unemployment insurance and thus abolish the dole system now carried on in most cities and States through soup kitchens.

Ernst also asked "governments to conduct or indirectly subsidize music, opera, theater, movies, and other forms of entertainment as they now handle playgrounds and parks. I will also want bowling alleys and hurdy-gurdies to satisfy a personal weakness."[64]

Calling for public works, low-cost housing, public employment agencies, unemployment insurance, old-age pensions, federal aid to the unemployed and poor, and minimum wage laws, Ernst's forward-looking platform presaged the New Deal.

* * *

Ernst had first met Franklin Delano Roosevelt back in 1929 when FDR, then governor of New York, appointed Ernst to the state insurance commission. The commission was charged with regulating all insurance business in New York; Ernst was considered one of the state's outstanding insurance experts. Three years later, Roosevelt summoned Ernst to his executive mansion and appointed him to the New York State Banking Board.[65] When he accepted, Roosevelt quipped, "I have one favor to ask of you. . . . Promise me that for the first year at least you won't bring the Tom Mooney case [an ACLU cause célèbre involving a wrongfully convicted anarchist] up before the Banking Board."[66]

The Banking Board had been established in 1932 to set rules for the regulation of the state's financial institutions. It consisted of nine members, four nominated by banks and four appointed by the governor. The board had a good deal of power; it fixed the interest rates that savings banks and other institutions were permitted to pay their depositors and had the power to throw out a banker whose practices were against the public interest and the safety of depositors.[67] No new bank could be opened without the consent of two-thirds of the board. Ernst was reappointed to the board by Herbert Lehman, elected governor in 1932.[68]

During the bank crisis, the closing and reopening of the banks in early 1933, Ernst threw himself into his work for the Banking Board. He was in Albany "day and night" drafting banking legislation, he wrote to a friend.[69] Ernst also volunteered his services in Washington, DC, helping draft the Glass-Steagall Act, a major component of

Roosevelt's efforts to reform the shady banking practices that had led to the crash. "I am living in Washington and Albany most of the time," he complained to "Barnesie," his friend Charles Barnes.[70]

Through this work for the Banking Board Ernst got to know Louis Brandeis, one of his lifelong idols. May 1933 was the first time he met Brandeis, at a gathering in Washington put on by columnist Drew Pearson, one of Ernst's clients. Shortly after, Ernst went to Washington to seek the judge's advice. "Many of our small independent banks were merging or being swallowed by increasingly larger ones. Was this good or bad for the people of New York, or for the banks themselves?" Ernst asked Brandeis.[71]

Before his appointment in 1916 as the first Jewish justice on the US Supreme Court, Brandeis had been known as "the People's Lawyer" for his advocacy of progressive causes. As a lawyer in private practice in Boston, Brandeis had mediated labor disputes, advocated trade unions, and broken the industrial life insurance monopoly. Brandeis advised President Woodrow Wilson on banking policy and helped establish the Federal Trade Commission. Brandeis believed that the law should be an instrument of morality and social progress, and his signature "Brandeis brief," devoted to the exposition of social facts, brought realism into the courtroom. In addition to his civil libertarian views on free speech, another component of Brandeis's philosophy was his belief that the country's economic and social problems could be attributed to "bigness," the extreme concentration of wealth and power in large corporations, financial conglomerates, and trusts. Brandeis believed that "bigness" discouraged competition and threatened to undermine democracy by robbing citizens of their initiative to develop their capacities and participate in public life.[72]

Ernst became persuaded of the "curse of bigness" when the title and mortgage companies began to fail in New York. Before the crash, a popular investment had been the guaranteed mortgage. An apartment house would be erected at a cost of $2 million, for example, with $1.5 million borrowed on a first mortgage. The mortgage would be broken up in parts; certificates, guaranteed by mortgage companies, would be sold for $10,000 or $5,000. After the crash, the certificates were worthless, which resulted in claims against the mortgage companies. In August 1933, Insurance Department superintendent George Van Schaick appointed the firm of Greenbaum, Wolff, and Ernst counsel for seven companies with $3 billion of mortgage obligations. It was an arduous job, entailing extensive litigation and the employment of fifty additional lawyers.[73]

Governor Lehman commissioned Ernst to draft legislation to deal with the mortgage crisis. Ernst helped create the Schackno Act, which authorized the state superintendent of insurance to take over defaulting mortgage guarantee companies for reorganization and prevented minorities from blocking reorganization of certificate issues. Under the terms of the act, a majority of two-thirds of certificate holders could, with the approval of the court, do anything they wished. The Schackno Act was largely Ernst's creation and was considered a landmark in emergency legislation.[74]

"In the unraveling of this mess I came to see most clearly that by and large corruption and mismanagement were in direct relationship to size, and that investors suffered losses in proportion to the size of the companies which had seduced them to invest," Ernst wrote. "I talked it all over with the Judge [Brandeis] many times. He was right. There is an optimum point to man's capacity to manage men and dollars."[75] Already Brandeisian on free speech, Ernst was henceforth a Brandeis disciple on "bigness." He maintained a cordial relationship with the judge, visiting him once or twice a year for "chats" on economic and banking policy at Brandeis's summer home in Chatham, Massachusetts. Ernst "loved" Brandeis, he would say, and he worshipped the judge the way a small boy idolized his baseball hero. Ernst wrote, "this man and his philosophy were to influence me for the rest of my life."[76]

11

FREEDOM FOR THE THOUGHT THAT WE HATE

The winter of 1932 witnessed the depths of the Great Depression. Famine and unemployment peaked. To many observers, the social fabric had completely unraveled. The civil liberties outlook was bleak. Everywhere the rights of the unemployed were violated, and their efforts to organize were brutally halted. Archaic laws disqualifying the unemployed as paupers were used to prevent voting. The Bonus March, a protest of World War I veterans to obtain cash payment of their service certificates, was quashed by US Army troops.

The presidential campaign of 1932 was fought on the issue of the Depression. Herbert Hoover ran for reelection. The Socialists ran Norman Thomas, and the Communists nominated William Z. Foster, who received less than 1 percent of the vote. The Democrats ran Franklin Delano Roosevelt, who won by a landslide. FDR pledged to reform every aspect of the economy and offered the public a "New Deal." "The only thing we have to fear," he famously said, "is fear itself."

In his first hundred days in office, Roosevelt pushed through Congress fifteen major bills creating unprecedented reforms. With the Agricultural Adjustment Act, the Securities Act, and the National Industrial Recovery Act, among other legislation, Congress committed the country to a massive program of government-industry cooperation, pledged to save homes and farms from foreclosure, accepted responsibility for the unemployed, and established federal regulation of Wall Street.[1] When it became clear that Roosevelt supported the kind of progressive social and economic programs Morris Ernst had long advocated, Ernst threw his efforts behind Roosevelt and the New Deal.[2]

* * *

The social turmoil of the Depression created new free speech dilemmas for the ACLU. In particular, the rise of political extremists on the right posed difficult questions for many civil libertarians. With Hitler's 1933 rise to power, a host of American Nazi groups sprang up, including the Silver Shirts, the Khaki Shirts, and the German American Bund.[3] Would the ACLU defend free speech for fascists?

The organization had no official policy on this, and many members said no. They opposed censorship in general but were troubled when fascists asked for the same rights as Communists, labor activists, and other dissidents the ACLU traditionally defended. ACLU board member Margaret DeSilver, widow of ACLU cofounder Albert DeSilver, opposed allowing Nazis "the liberty to organize to destroy liberty." The Nazi regime was so brutal that it "forfeits all tolerance."[4] Roger Baldwin, Morris Ernst, and Art Hays maintained their viewpoint-neutral position, arguing that it was only through unfettered public discussion in the "marketplace of ideas" that noxious philosophies could be countered.[5]

In two controversial cases in 1933, Ernst defended freedom for "the thought that we hate."[6] One involved Robert "Fighting Bob" Shuler, a Los Angeles Methodist preacher who had gained a wide following over his radio station. A conservative who held the KKK in high regard and was opposed to "Jews, Catholics, movies, jazz, liquor, and dancing," Shuler believed he had a responsibility to expose sin and corruption in Los Angeles. Shuler had many followers and also opponents. Victims of his broadcasts tried to shut him down by getting his radio station taken off the air.[7]

The Federal Radio Commission decided to hold hearings on Shuler's application for station license renewal. The Radio Act of 1927 required that broadcasters operate in the "public interest, convenience, or necessity." The FRC had received criticism of Shuler and was thus compelled to review whether the station was serving the public interest.[8] Ultimately the FRC refused to renew Shuler's license because of his promotion of "religious strife and antagonism." The FRC's decision was upheld by the District of Columbia Circuit

Court of Appeals.[9] The US Supreme Court refused Shuler's petition for certiorari, and he enlisted Ernst and the ACLU to appeal the denial.[10] Noted newspapers, "The Rev. Robert Shuler, the ACLU, Roger Baldwin, and Morris Ernst make up a queer alliance. No one ever assailed all brands of radicalism more intemperately than Shuler. No one ever defended all brands of radicalism with more enthusiasm than the American Civil Liberties Union, Baldwin, and Ernst."[11]

Ernst saw Shuler's case as an important test of the Radio Act, which he had opposed since its inception. Ernst claimed that the Supreme Court "misapprehended the nature and importance of the question presented"—that Shuler's denial, and the Radio Act itself, violated the First Amendment. He argued that the Radio Act, which vested power to grant licenses in the FRC, gave the government "unlimited powers" of censorship. "Never before in the history of the United States has there been lodged in any tribunal a power over liberty of expression such as is claimed by the FRC," he said. The vague phrase "public interest, convenience, and necessity" could be used to enact censorship based on political views.[12]

The FRC's power functioned as a "prior restraint," he claimed; the Radio Act denied to broadcasters the right of free expression that the US Constitution accorded the press. "If Reverend Shuler said offensive things he should be punished, as provided by law, but it is against all previous rules laid down by the Supreme Court to gag a man in the future for something he said in the past." He cited Louis Brandeis's dissent in *Whitney v. California*, noting that "the benefits of free speech flow not so much to man as to mankind. It matters little socially whether or not a single citizen is robbed of his say. It matters tremendously whether or not society is deprived of the incalculable benefit of free discussion."[13] The Supreme Court refused to hear the case.

For his defense of Shuler, Ernst was attacked by members of the ACLU and Jewish organizations. "Mr. Ernst as a Jew is not justified in defending the right of a vicious anti-Semite to poison minds," asserted the editor of the *Brooklyn Jewish Examiner*.[14] Noted J. George Fredman of the Jewish War Veterans, "It hurts us, who have sacrificed so much in our struggle for equality for the Jew, to think that a prominent Jewish lawyer should interest himself in a cause contrary to ours."[15] Replied Ernst, "I am convinced that Jews and all other groups in the land can only obtain real protection by preventing pre-censorship. . . . I do not believe that the Founders of this nation ever intended that freedom of speech should be allowed generally except in cases of attacks upon Jews."[16]

Ernst's defense of the right of Nazis to hold a public rally in New York generated similar hostility. In May 1933, Nazi Deputy Rudolph Hess gave a German immigrant named Heinz Spanknoebel the authority to form an American Nazi organization, the Friends of New Germany. Between 1933 and 1935, the group recruited a membership of about five thousand and was one of the largest American Nazi organizations.[17]

The Friends of New Germany tricked their way into a position of apparent leadership of the United German Societies, an organization representing one hundred societies of German Americans in New York. Spanknoebel was scheduled to appear as one of the speakers at their annual gathering, the German Day celebration, held to mark the two hundredth anniversary of German immigration into the United States. His backers pushed through a resolution to post the swastika at the celebration. Spanknoebel and his representatives went to Mayor John O'Brien for permission to use a city armory for the celebration. The mayor denied the request, expressing fear that there would be violence at the meeting.[18]

When the Nazi leader protested, the mayor granted him a three-hour public hearing.[19] Several organizations, including veterans and Jewish groups, assembled to support the permit denial. The only defenders of the right of the United German Societies to meet, even with Nazi speakers, were Ernst and Harry Weinberger, another Jewish lawyer affiliated with the ACLU. Ernst and Weinberger contended that the protection of Jewish rights depended on the safety of the "rights of every unpopular minority, even Nazis."[20] "The Mayor's order forbidding the meeting is wrong as a matter of law," Ernst said. "I'd be glad, even though I am a Jew, to fight the Nazi case on this issue." "The best protection of the Jews is to allow these people to meet and speak freely and show themselves up publicly and thereby destroy themselves by ridicule as the Ku Klux Klan did."[21] Ernst was booed and hissed. O'Brien refused to rescind his prohibition.[22]

"Are you so muddle-headed that you can see no difference between freedom of speech and press and the advocacy of hate and actual violence and murder?" wrote one ACLU member to Ernst.[23] Another correspondent, Herman Axelrod, cautioned, "Your devotion to the principle of free speech . . . should induce you not to further its destruction by its avowed enemies. . . . By aiding the [Nazis], you aid the enemies of free speech, you frustrate the very object you set out to achieve."[24] Ernst replied to Axelrod, "I feel that the only way that the Jews and other minority groups can ever get decent protection is to stand firmly on the principle of free speech and free press for all groups. . . . My contempt for the Nazi bigotry is no less than yours, I am sure."[25] Several members resigned from the ACLU in protest.

The incident led the ACLU Board of Directors to produce a historic position statement, *Shall We Defend Free Speech for Nazis in America*? If the ACLU "condoned the denial of rights to Nazi propagandists, in what position would it be to champion the rights of others?" it asked rhetorically. "Is it not clear that free speech as a practical tactic, not only as an abstract principle, demands defense of the rights of *all* who are attacked in order to obtain the rights of *any*?"[26] It remains the ACLU's position on hate speech to this day.

* * *

By the early 1930s, Ernst had become one of the preeminent lawyers for the press. Ernst represented some of the most prominent publishers and journalists in the nation, including the *New Yorker* and the New York *Post*, reporter Dorothy Thompson, and Drew Pearson, who wrote the syndicated political column "Washington Merry-Go-Round" with Robert Allen.

Much of Ernst's work for the press involved copyright, privacy, and especially libel cases. Ernst and Lindey advised publishers on potentially libelous material in books and articles and defended libel actions when they arose. Like most of the ACLU leaders, Ernst did not see libel laws as problematic from a free speech perspective; he believed that the First Amendment did not preclude an individual's right to recover for reputational harm. Ernst helped the ACLU sue its critics for libel and at times personally threatened suit over unfavorable commentary. At the same time, Ernst began to see how stringent libel laws, like obscenity laws, could constitute a form of "censorship." In 1932 Ernst and Lindey wrote *Hold Your Tongue! Adventures in Libel and Slander*, which pointed out the absurd, antiquated nature of much of libel law and advocated greater protections in the law for statements involving public figures and "matters of public concern." *Hold Your Tongue* had a small but admiring group of users, from lawyers to journalists to teachers, and it remained in print for years.

Ernst was a shrewd libel lawyer. Like all good libel lawyers, he recognized that complainants would often back down and drop their cases when they realized that by bringing suit they would put their own lives under scrutiny. In 1934 General Douglas MacArthur filed suit against Pearson and Allen, asking $1.75 million in damages. MacArthur charged that they had ridiculed him in their column by depicting him as "dictatorial, insubordinate, disloyal, mutinous, and disrespectful of his superiors in the War Department." The columnists and Ernst were worried until a Congressman told Pearson that until recently a suite on his floor in a Washington hotel had been occupied by Isabel Rosario Cooper, a Filipina actress, whose most frequent visitor had been MacArthur. Pearson found Cooper and paid for her love letters to MacArthur. Cooper disclosed that MacArthur frequently referred to Roosevelt as "that cripple in the White House."[27] Ernst informed MacArthur's lawyer that Cooper had "discussed with me at length her relations with you and has shown me various letters, etc."[28] MacArthur dropped the suit and paid Cooper $15,000 to leave the country, the money allegedly delivered by his aide, Dwight Eisenhower.[29]

Though Ernst zealously defended his media clients, he was personally cynical about the press and called himself a "professional press critic." The domination of the press by corporate interests, he believed, led to distortion and bias in the news. "The news agencies . . . color and distort the news, failing to send over the wires matter that does not fit with the prejudices of the owner," he wrote.[30] By the 1930s, the press had in fact become a big business, as big as many other industries around the country and pervaded by the conservative biases of the business leadership class. Mergers had led to consolidation in big cities and the disappearance of many well-known newspapers. During the decade the number of one-paper towns tripled. A third of newspapers were owned by chains.[31] By 1940, fourteen publishers controlled a third of all national newspaper circulation. Ernst, with his Brandeisian philosophy, believed that when big companies dominated the channels of communication, the public was prohibited from accessing news from diverse perspectives, and the marketplace of ideas did not function. The press exercised a "private censorship" of ideas that was as dangerous as state censorship, Ernst asserted. If the "three great channels of information"—radio, movies, and the press—"are really kept open," he believed, most of the nation's problems could be solved.[32]

Ernst accused the owners of the press of manipulating the meaning of "freedom of the press" to serve their self-interest. He deplored how they "perverted" the First Amendment in an effort to use it as a shield in their quest for "economic power." Waving the banner of the Constitution, "the publishers . . . opposed the Wagner Labor Act, as well as child labor, minimum wage, and most social reform legislation," he later wrote.[33] In early 1934, he said, "I have advised the newspaper owners with whom I have sat in conference that the only way they can really protect their rights of free press is to be equally vigilant for the rights of free speech and free press for all groups. I doubt if they are willing to go that far, because in the final analysis they are really only excited about free press . . . for themselves."[34] In this distrust of the press he was allied with Heywood Broun, who remained embittered since his difficulties with the New York *World* over his reporting of the Sacco and Vanzetti case.

* * *

Ernst and Broun were the closest of friends. Broun, who was unable to keep his life together, relied on Ernst for advice and emotional support. Ernst loaned Broun money, advancing him his first income tax installment when he was unable to pay. "I held his hand in all his scrapes and escapades. I represented him as a lawyer and I befriended him as a friend. . . . He could never organize his own life," Ernst recalled.[35] They made an odd pair—Broun was a huge figure in soiled, baggy clothes, while Ernst was slender, short, and elegant in his speech and appearance.[36]

Broun had long wanted to unionize journalists. In the 1920s, with Lewis Gannett and McAllister Coleman, he had tried to organize reporters, but the effort went nowhere. By the summer of 1933, with Roosevelt in office and passage of the National Industrial Recovery Act (NIRA), Broun had come to believe that the New Deal might benefit journalists.

The National Recovery Administration (NRA), the administrative arm of the NIRA, had been created, in FDR's words, to "obtain wide re-employment, to shorten the working week, to pay a decent wage for the shorter week, and to prevent unfair competition and disastrous overproduction." Under NRA supervision, each of the nation's major industries would write for itself a code that involved setting minimum wages, maximum hours, regulating overtime, and other matters related to working conditions specific to each industry, subject to government approval. Employees were guaranteed the right to organize and bargain collectively through representatives of their own choosing by Section 7a of the NIRA. Industries would also organize authorities to regulate themselves under the code. If self-regulation failed, the president could license business enterprises. Once certified, an industry could mark its establishments with the prized symbol of the NRA's Blue Eagle.[37]

The American Newspaper Publishers Association (ANPA), the national publishers association, representing large-circulation newspapers, professed to support the NRA but argued that newspapers should not come within its jurisdiction because it would interfere with freedom of the press.[38] In 1933, ANPA submitted a daily newspaper code to the NRA in Washington, DC. At hearings on the code, ANPA urged that reporters should be classified as professionals and exempted from maximum hours. They wanted an open shop and a clause inserted in the code that guaranteed "freedom of the press," meaning that the newspaper industry would not be subject to the NRA licensing procedure. Meanwhile, as the publishers resisted regulation, living conditions of reporters were declining. As newspapers merged or folded, unemployment was rampant.[39]

One afternoon at the 21 Club while having drinks, Broun dashed off a column titled "A Union of Reporters," which was published on August 7, 1933, in the New York *World-Telegram*. Noting that the newspaper industry was "planning to cheat NRA re-employment aims" by classifying editorial staff as professionals, thus forcing them to work all hours of the day and any number of hours in the week, Broun announced that there should be a "newspaper writers' union," and that he was "going to do the best [he could] to help in getting one up."[40] Broun's column struck a nerve, and he was barraged with phone calls and letters. Reporters throughout the country began getting together to talk about how to organize editorial workers. Ernst agreed to assist Broun in forming the union, a "departure from his [Broun's] real interests of nightclubs, gambling, baseball, and theater."[41]

Broun held informal meetings in his cluttered, book-lined penthouse to discuss the formation of a society of journalists.[42] Many who came did so secretly, for fear of being fired.[43] Publishers vehemently opposed unionization, which they feared would increase salaries and cause union member journalists to express prounion views in their writings. Early debates in the meetings were over the NRA Code, how best to organize journalists, and whether a union or a professional guild was the more appropriate form of organization. The journalists did not yet see the wisdom of throwing in their lot with blue-collar newspaper workers who had unionized, and they agreed to create a professional association called the Newspaper Guild. All the journalists were united in their opposition to the publishers' version of the NRA Code.[44]

Through arrangements made by Ernst, three hundred reporters, rewriters, and copy readers came together at the City Club on September 17, 1933, to form the Newspaper Guild of New York. Ernst was elected the committee's legal adviser and represented the reporters in the NRA Code hearings, in which he argued, along with

Broun, for minimum wage and maximum hour standards.[45] At a gathering in Washington in December, the American Newspaper Guild, a national organization, was formed.

The guild grew quickly. At its first convention in June 1934, it drew 125 delegates representing more than 7,000 journalists. By 1935 it had a membership of 10,000 of the 24,000 editorial workers in the country. As membership grew, the publishers became frightened. As Ernst recalled, "the publishers made plain that they would fight the Guild and everything it stood for." They were "scared stupid . . . they would do anything but recognize a guild of their favorite and most important workers."[46]

* * *

This famous defender of radicals and unionists lived in fine, high style. Two or three nights a week he frequented café society hot spots such as the 21 Club, where he drank with Broun and James Thurber, E. B. White, and Robert Benchley of the *New Yorker*.[47] Ernst maintained not one but two country homes. In January 1934 he bought a one-hundred-year-old, sixty-nine-acre farm in East Millstone, New Jersey, about fifteen miles north of Princeton. A well-known architect was engaged to restore the old Dutch Colonial dwelling, and Ernst went there most every weekend.[48]

Despite his flamboyant and ostentatious lifestyle, which Roger Baldwin believed was an effort to mask his insecurities, Ernst thrived on routine in his personal affairs. It was a point of pride that for decades he had the same secretary, maids, and law partners.[49] His family life remained stable and contented. In 1929, Maggie Ernst had found her calling when she began working as a librarian and teacher at the City and Country School in Greenwich Village. Considered to be at the forefront of progressive education, the school promoted independent thinking and student participation in education, a novel approach to learning in that time.[50] During her eighteen years at the school, she developed a method of teaching spelling by means of word study. She also wrote several books on etymology, including *In a Word*, featuring illustrations by James Thurber, which was published to stellar reviews in 1939.[51]

The Ernst children were cared for and educated impeccably. Connie and Roger attended grammar school at the City and Country School and then went to junior high school and high school at the progressive, Quaker George School in Bucks County, Pennsylvania. In 1935 Connie started as a drama major at Bennington College in Vermont, where she gained a reputation as one of the most charming and sociable young women in her class.

When Ernst's daughter Joan was six months old, she contracted spinal meningitis and became completely deaf. Ernst crusaded to restore her hearing. When medical experts told him her case was hopeless, Morris, undaunted, consulted radio engineers. He believed they could "find some wavelength that could get into Joan's nerves, through either the bone or the ear." After years of experimentation, they developed an apparatus which permitted her to hear partially. Ernst called it "his miracle."[52]

Joan developed into an "exciting person," Ernst wrote. He recounted, "She dove off a twenty-foot springboard at the age of five and sailed a boat alone at the age of eight. She grew into a horrible chatterbox and makes our dinner meal quite unbearable by incessant gossip about Hollywood. She covers the murder stories in the news with great personal thrills."[53] Maggie and Morris refused to treat Joan as "handicapped," going as far as to refuse to learn sign language. Their philosophy was that "we let our kids get bumped by life."[54]

12
ULYSSES

In the early 1930s, James Joyce's *Ulysses* was the most notorious banned book in the United States. Using a stream-of-consciousness style to describe twenty-four hours in the life of a lower-middle-class Dubliner named Leopold Bloom, Joyce's classic, published in 1922, was brilliant, dense, convoluted, complex, and legally obscene. *Ulysses* was the "only volume of literary importance still under a ban" in the country, Ernst declared.[1] He set out to "liberate" it, and the celebrated case, resolved by the Second Circuit Court of Appeals in 1934, was not only a landmark in the law of literary censorship but also a turning point in Ernst's career.

* * *

Joyce's novel had a long history of suppression in the United States. *Ulysses* had been banned even before Joyce finished writing it. In 1918, as he was completing *Ulysses*, Joyce sent chapters to the New York–based literary magazine the *Little Review*, which published them in installments. The Post Office Department confiscated the issues and burned them.[2] Shortly after, the New York Society for the Suppression of Vice had obscenity charges brought against the *Review*'s editors for having published the chapter in which Bloom masturbates while watching a young woman on the beach.[3] John Quinn, a noted literary lawyer and patron of the arts, defended the editors in court. Despite Quinn's persuasive argument—*Ulysses* was so dense and convoluted that no one could possibly understand it, much less be debauched by it, he argued—a three-judge panel, using the *Hicklin* test, concluded that the book had the potential to corrupt youth and was therefore obscene. After the New York decision, no American publisher was willing to take a chance on *Ulysses*. The book was eventually issued in Paris in 1922, under the imprint of the avant-garde bookstore Shakespeare and Company. Joyce gave Sylvia Beach, the bookstore's proprietor, the world rights to *Ulysses*.[4]

The ban on the book notwithstanding, *Ulysses* found a wide and receptive audience in the United States. Blue paperbound copies were smuggled into the country and sold at fantastic prices, sometimes as much as fifty dollars.[5] Joyce won critical acclaim for *Ulysses*; articles and treatises were written about it, its style was widely imitated, and the book achieved masterpiece status. Observed critic Harry Hansen in 1933, a generation of Americans coming of age in the 1920s grew up "with the idea that [*Ulysses*] is a literary Bible."[6]

Because *Ulysses* could not be legally published in the United States, it could not be copyrighted.[7] Samuel Roth, an infamous publisher of pornography, seized on this opportunity and began to publish bowdlerized installments of *Ulysses* in his magazine *Two Worlds Monthly*. Joyce sued Roth over the unconsented use of his name. One hundred sixty-seven of Joyce's literary friends, including T. S. Eliot, D. H. Lawrence, and Thomas Mann, signed a petition protesting the "appropriation and mutilation" of Joyce's work. Joyce won an injunction in 1927.[8] Meanwhile, US Customs officials seized copies of the book that were imported from Paris. In 1928, the US Customs Court, in an action titled *A. Heymoolen v. United States*, affirmed the exclusion of *Ulysses* as an obscene book.[9]

Joyce, who was living in Paris, launched a search for a reputable American publisher. Aging, syphilitic, and nearly blind, he was desperate for money, and it was rumored that Roth was going to sell another pirated edition, publishing as many as twenty thousand copies.[10] A few US publishers, sensitive to the changing cultural climate around sex and the more liberal obscenity rulings in the New York courts, began to discuss the possibility of bringing out an American edition of *Ulysses*. But no one was willing to commit to it; with the legal restrictions in place, publishing *Ulysses* was a still a risky proposition.[11]

Ernst knew about the renewed interest in *Ulysses*, and in the summer of 1931 he had asked Alexander Lindey to help him find a publisher that might be willing to publish the book and cooperate in a test case to remove the ban. Ernst planned to deploy the same strategy he had used in the *Contraception* and *Married Love* cases—he would have a copy of *Ulysses* imported from France and seized by the Customs Office under the Tariff Act as an obscene book, and then he would challenge the seizure.[12]

In August, Lindey had a lengthy conversation with Sylvia Beach's sister, Holly Beach Denis, about the possibility of an American publisher obtaining the rights and participating in the "legalization of *Ulysses*."[13] Denis said that she was "tremendously interested" and that Sylvia Beach would likely cooperate if a suitable publisher could be found. Shortly after, Lindey wrote to Ernst, "I . . . feel very keenly that this would be the grandest obscenity case in the history of law and literature, and I am ready to do anything in the world to get it started. What do you suggest?"[14]

"Tell Mrs. Denis that I want to see her," Ernst replied. "I am sure I can get a good publisher."[15]

Two months later, Ernst lunched with Ben Huebsch, ACLU member and vice president of Viking Press. Viking had published Ernst's *To The Pure*, as well as Joyce's *Dubliners* and *Portrait of the Artist as a Young Man*. In a letter after the lunch, Ernst told Huebsch he was confident that because of his recent victories in obscenity cases, *Ulysses* can "now be tested (in court) with the real hope of gaining immunity for it." Ernst assured Huebsch that he had little to lose under his plan. Because customs actions proceeded against the book, rather than its publisher or mailer, no one risked fines or jail sentences. Huebsch didn't have to spend a dime on publishing *Ulysses* until the court approved it—the fight would be waged over an imported copy of the Shakespeare and Company edition. Success in the customs case didn't mean that it was completely safe to publish *Ulysses*, however, Ernst warned. The book could still be seized by the post office, and the publisher could be charged under state obscenity laws. The approval of *Ulysses* by a federal tribunal, however, made subsequent actions against the book "highly improbable," according to Ernst.[16]

As an incentive to get Viking to publish *Ulysses* and sponsor the case, Ernst offered Huebsch his usual deal. His normal fee was a retainer of $1,000. If the case were appealed to the Supreme Court, fees and costs could run as high as $8,000. Ernst proposed a contingency arrangement in which he would be paid a retainer of $500 and an additional $500 for each subsequent appeal. The maximum would be $2,000 if the case went all the way to the Supreme Court. In exchange for the reduced rate, Ernst wanted 4 percent of the book's royalties. Ernst knew he had a good chance of winning the case and that the publicity around the litigation would drive up the book's sales.[17] Huebsch agreed and approached Sylvia Beach about obtaining the American rights to *Ulysses*. When she demanded $25,000, Huebsch balked.[18] Huebsch then wrote to Bennett Cerf, the young president of Random House, who had also expressed interest in publishing *Ulysses*. Huebsch told Cerf that it was fine for him to try to acquire the rights from Beach.[19] Around the same time, Robert Kastor, a New York stockbroker who was the brother-in-law of Joyce's son, approached Cerf and asked if Random House was interested in publishing *Ulysses*.[20]

Cerf was thrilled at the possibility of issuing the first legal edition of *Ulysses*. It would bring Random House, then a fledgling company (only six years old), into major prominence in the publishing world.[21] Cerf and Ernst met in March 1932, and Ernst offered him the same contingency deal he had presented to Huebsch.[22] Meanwhile, under pressure from Joyce, Sylvia Beach agreed to give Joyce the world rights to *Ulysses*. By the end of the month, Random House had worked out a contract with Joyce in which Joyce received $1,500 and the firm obtained the US rights to the book.[23] Ernst would litigate the customs case, and if the book were cleared, Random House would publish it. Under the final agreement with Random House, Ernst would receive 5 percent of the royalties if the book were legalized and published. Cerf "had not the faintest doubt" that Ernst would win the case. Ernst, he was sure, could handle the litigation "better than anyone else in the country."[24]

* * *

Ernst set the wheels of the "grandest obscenity case" in motion in 1932 when he instructed Cerf to have a copy of *Ulysses* sent from Paris to Random House's office in New York. Cerf wrote to Joyce's secretary Paul Leon asking him "to purchase the latest edition of *Ulysses*." Knowing the courts' resistance to hearing expert testimony in obscenity cases, Ernst had come up with the idea of pasting positive reviews of *Ulysses* into the book itself, which would be introduced as evidence. Cerf advised Leon, "if there has been printed . . . any circular containing opinions of prominent men or critics on this book, paste a copy of the circular into the front of the book. It is important that this circular be actually pasted into the book, as if it is separate we may not be able to use it as evidence when the trial comes up, but if these opinions of respected people are actually pasted in the book, they become, for legal purposes, a part of the book, and can be introduced as evidence." Leon was told to notify Cerf what ship the book would be coming in on so that Cerf and Lindey could alert authorities. Cerf explained, "It is necessary that they catch this book or all our efforts in this matter will have been in vain."[25]

The main argument Ernst planned to make in court was by then a familiar one—that the question of whether a work was obscene should be determined by contemporary social standards, and it was "undisputed" that the public accepted *Ulysses*. Ernst planned to demonstrate this by showing the accolades the book had won from literary critics, professors, and other "prominent men" whose sentiments reflected public opinion. Ernst instructed Lindey to have Random House send more than five hundred letters to esteemed writers and intellectuals surveying their opinion on *Ulysses*.[26] Cerf was also told to put together a massive file containing essays, articles, and positive reviews of *Ulysses*, as well as statements from "prominent critics, librarians, authors, physicians, psychologists, welfare workers, and the like," attesting that *Ulysses* had major "literary, scientific, [and] sociological value."[27] Random House also sent a circular to one hundred colleges and universities, asking whether Joyce was used in courses.[28] Nine hundred letters were sent to librarians, querying whether *Ulysses* was on their shelves or whether they would like to have it in their collections.[29] By the end of May, Random House had received favorable responses from several important literary figures, including George Jean Nathan, Theodore Dreiser, John Dos Passos, and F. Scott Fitzgerald. Hundreds of librarians said they wanted to have copies of the book and saw *Ulysses* as having major literary importance.[30]

On April 27, 1932, Leon telegrammed Cerf that he had shipped a copy of *Ulysses* on the SS *Bremen*, scheduled to arrive in New York on May 3. Leon had pasted positive reviews into the book's cover; he also sent several articles praising *Ulysses* that he hoped Ernst could use in his "speech before either the lower or the higher court."[31] Lindey alerted the collector of customs:

> A copy of James Joyce's novel, entitled *Ulysses*, has been dispatched into this country, addressed to our client. We are informed that the volume left on the *Bremen* on April 28, and is due at the port of New York on Tuesday, May 3, 1932.
>
> We are transmitting this information to you because we do not wish the book to slip through the Customs without official scrutiny. As you may know, *Ulysses* during the last two decades has been praised by critics as probably the most important contribution to the world literature of the twentieth century. Entirely apart from its profound literary significance, we are convinced that *Ulysses* is not violative of the Tariff Act. In saying this we are not unmindful of the adverse attitude of your department with regard to the book in the past. We feel, however, that in view of such recent decisions as [the *Dennett, Married Love*, and *Contraception* cases] there is no longer any legal sanction for such attitude.[32]

A few days later the book showed up at Random House—it had passed through customs. Furious, Ernst personally marched the package over to the customs office and demanded that it be searched.[33] When the inspector opened it and found *Ulysses*, he muttered, "Oh, for God's sake, everybody brings that in. We don't pay attention to it." Ernst insisted that he seize it. On May 8, the book was officially seized by customs.[34] Lindey urged customs officials to forward the book to the Offices of the United States Attorneys for proceedings.[35] On May

24, 1932, *Ulysses* was sent to the US Attorney for the Southern District of New York for "forfeiture, confiscation, and destruction of the book in accordance with the provisions of Section 305a of the Tariff Act of 1930."[36] The battle over *Ulysses* had begun.

* * *

From the start, the US Attorney's office was ambivalent about prosecuting *Ulysses*. A few weeks after the book reached the office, Lindey called Samuel Coleman, assistant US Attorney in charge of the Civil Division. An honest and earnest young attorney, highly regarded by Ernst and Lindey, Coleman apologized to Lindey that he was taking so long to move against *Ulysses*. He was reading the book carefully to figure out whether it was obscene, he explained, but was "having a difficult time." Lindey offered to send him interpretive works, such as Paul Jordan-Smith's *A Key to the Ulysses of James Joyce* (1927). Coleman declined, saying he preferred to form his own opinion.[37] In late July, Coleman reported to Lindey, who relayed the information to Ernst, that he had finally finished *Ulysses* and that although he liked it very much and regarded it a "masterpiece," he thought it was probably obscene under federal law.[38] But Coleman did not want final responsibility for making the decision and turned the case over to his superior, US Attorney George Z. Medalie, who had prosecuted the cases against Marie Stopes's *Married Love* and *Contraception* .[39]

Like Coleman, Medalie had mixed feelings about *Ulysses*. Medalie was impressed by Joyce's writing and the critical praise for the work. At the same time, he was concerned about its many "four-letter Anglo Saxon words" and the sexual frankness of some of the unconscious streams of thought in the novel, such as the libidinous musings of the character Molly Bloom describing her thoughts as she had an affair ("I was coming for about 5 minutes with my legs round him I had to hug him after O Lord I wanted to shout all sorts of things fuck or shit or anything at all").[40] Worried about the possibility of failing to secure a conviction and embarrassing the office, especially after the losses in the Stopes cases, Medalie proceeded cautiously. Finally, after weeks of stalling, Medalie called Lindey and told him he would have to proceed with the prosecution. Medalie thought *Ulysses* might well be obscene. At the very least, the liberal prosecutor believed that the issues in the case were important enough to merit a hearing and that the time had come to at last settle the legal status of the notorious book.[41]

For the next fourteen months, while at the same time prosecuting the government's case, Medalie, Coleman, and another young prosecutor, Assistant US Attorney Nicholas Atlas, went out their way to help Ernst and Lindey secure a favorable hearing for *Ulysses*. Medalie agreed with Ernst that it would be best if a progressive, open-minded judge heard the case—in particular, Judge John Woolsey, who had presided over the Stopes cases. Ernst got Medalie to promise that he would "not start anything" in the *Ulysses* case until Woolsey got back from his vacation in October.[42] Ernst and Lindey also convinced Medalie to sign a stipulation agreeing to the facts in the case and that the case would be decided by motion.[43] Ernst and Lindey wanted to avoid a jury trial because juries usually sided with the government in obscenity cases.[44] On December 9, 1932, the US Attorney's office, declaring 260 passages obscene, officially began proceedings against *Ulysses*.

Throughout the spring and summer of 1933, Ernst, Lindey, and Coleman maneuvered to get the case before Woolsey. Every time it looked as though the case was about to be assigned to another judge, the trio arranged to stall the proceedings.[45] When it appeared that the case would go before Judge Frank J. Coleman, a "straitlaced Catholic" and "about the worst on the bench for us," in Lindey's words, Sam Coleman managed to have the hearing delayed so that it would be reassigned.[46]

In the meantime, Ernst and Lindey did something tricky. In March 1933, they arranged to have another copy of the book sent from Paris. Their plan was to get the book admitted under the classics provision of the Tariff Act, permitting the "admission of so-called classics or books of recognized and established literary or scientific merit into the United States, when imported for noncommercial purposes." "Classic" status permitted only the importation of a single copy for personal, noncommercial use. It was not a declaration that the book was not obscene—a work could be a classic and admissible under the exemption yet still obscene and excludable under the general provisions of the Tariff Act. Ernst and Lindey nonetheless believed, with good reason, that an official designation of *Ulysses* as a classic might persuade the US Attorney's office to give up the prosecution and admit the book. At the very least, a declaration that the book had "exceptional literary merit" would no doubt strengthen their case.

This copy, like the previous one, also slipped through customs.[47] Lindey personally brought the copy to the customs office and filed a formal application for the admission of *Ulysses* under the classics provision.[48] He made clear to state that in doing so he was not conceding that the book was obscene.[49] Lindey based his petition on the "undisputed reputation" of Joyce as an author of "first-rate importance," and *Ulysses*'s "worldwide acclaim"—"it has been said by some that *Ulysses* is the most important book that has ever been written. . . . In introducing the stream of consciousness method and developing it to a high degree of perfection Joyce has, in *Ulysses*, made an epochal contribution to letters. There can be no doubt that his book is a modern classic in every sense of the word." As evidence that *Ulysses* was a "modern classic," Lindey attached to the petition several book reviews, as well as the testimonials and surveys Random House had gathered.[50] On June 16, 1933, *Ulysses* was admitted to the United States as a classic, and the decision made the *New York Times*.[51]

Sam Coleman was livid. For months, he had cooperated with Ernst and Lindey, and he felt embarrassed and betrayed. Via Ernst, Coleman told Lindey he thought they had "put a fast one over."[52] Coleman feared that the clearance of the book under the classics provision had ruined the government's case. Ernst and Lindey urged Coleman to concede defeat and consent to the book's admission. But the US Attorney's office continued the prosecution, and eventually Coleman resumed his cordial mood and continued to work with Ernst and Lindey in getting the case before Woolsey. The hearing was delayed to July 25, 1933, and then again to August 8, to avoid an unfavorable judge. It was finally scheduled for late August, when Woolsey would be sitting. "Don't let it get away from Woolsey,"

Ernst reminded Jonas Shapiro, a partner at the firm who also worked on the case.[53]

On August 30, 1933, both sides presented their motions informally before Judge Woolsey. Shapiro represented Greenbaum, Wolff, and Ernst, and Coleman argued for the government. Shapiro gave Woolsey the imported copy of *Ulysses* with the pasted-in reviews, as well as the testimonials and other documents that Random House had gathered. The date for the formal argument on the motions was set for October 2, to give Woolsey time to read the book.[54] Woolsey had the entire month of September off, having earned the leave by presiding that spring over the longest criminal case in US history, a 109-day fraud trial. The *New York Times* reported that Woolsey would be spending most of his vacation at his estate in rural Petersham, Massachusetts, 75 miles east of Boston, poring over Joyce's 752-page tome.[55]

* * *

Fat, moonfaced, ruddy-cheeked, and bald, Woolsey, a fifty-six-year-old former admiralty lawyer from a prominent New York family, was one of the most eccentric judges on the federal bench. A passionate devotee of English literature, nicknamed the "literary jurist," Woolsey was said to collect first editions of Samuel Johnson and to peruse pages of Chaucer in between court reports.[56] Woolsey was an aspiring literary stylist in his own right; his judicial opinions, though often short on legal analysis, sparkled with witty turns of phrase and rhetorical flourishes ("whimsicality . . . mingled with wisdom" and "humor [mixed] with legal lore," noted the *New York Times*). Fashioning himself an English country gentleman, he sported octagonal gold-rimmed glasses, a custom-made soft collared shirt, and a loose silk cravat, which he secured with a gold ring.[57] An eccentric collector, Woolsey hoarded fine paintings, ship models, pewter mugs, and antique furniture, including tall clocks, of which there were at least ten in his New York apartment.[58] Woolsey planned to spend his break holed up in his wood-paneled study reading *Ulysses* and critical works on *Ulysses*, so-called satellite texts that would help him gain "complete understanding of the book."[59] He had no idea how difficult it would be until he started—it was, he recalled, one of the "hardest [times] of my life."[60]

While Woolsey was wrestling with *Ulysses* in Petersham, Lindey bombarded the judge with letters, memoranda, testimonials, survey results, satellite texts, and other material.[61] Lindey mailed them to the judge's New York chambers, which forwarded them to Woolsey's country estate. In September, Lindey reported to Cerf that he had sent Woolsey a twelve-page preliminary memorandum outlining the defense's position.[62] In October, three weeks before the scheduled hearing, Lindey offered the judge a formal brief with a note attached, stating that "we feel that you may wish to be apprised of the claimant's legal contentions in advance of the argument."[63]

Written mostly by Lindey with contributions from Ernst, the exhaustive, fifty-six-page brief presented arguments that were by that time familiar weapons in Ernst's anticensorship arsenal. The first was that the *Hicklin* test, although still the reigning rule, was "patently unfair, unreasonable, and unsound." The sturdy, normal adult "must serve as the criterion" in obscenity law, not the vulnerable child. "The test of obscenity is a living standard," the brief continued; *Ulysses* should be judged according to the moral sensibilities of the time, not the squeamish tastes of religious zealots or old-fashioned prudes.[64]

The public had become candid when it came to sexual matters, and Americans no longer blinked at the things that made the Victorians blush. In 1900, a woman who went to a beach in an outfit without sleeves and a long skirt would have been jailed, but women now went to the shore with their limbs and midriff exposed. The press no longer referred to rape with the euphemism "statutory offense," Ernst and Lindey wrote. Tabloids carried "stories of passion and lust, of crime and perversion, told with graphic vividness." "Sex discussion" was accepted in popular literature, and divorce and remarriage were no longer verboten. "The standards of yesterday, the abhorrence of any mention of certain biological functions, the excessive prudery, the sex taboo, are as definitely dead today as the horse-drawn carriage. . . . We have developed sturdier tastes and grown wiser in the process."[65]

Ulysses was not obscene under contemporary social standards, Ernst and Lindey argued in their brief, because "public opinion, crystallized in the statements thereto annexed, vigorously repudiates any imputation of obscenity with respect to *Ulysses*." Joyce's reputation, the praise of critics, the inclusion of the book in libraries, and its proposed publication by a reputable publishing house indicated that *Ulysses* had been widely accepted and was wholly in tune with the temper of the times. Moreover, *Ulysses* was a "modern classic," having been officially designated such by the US government. "The federal government has officially paid tribute to the greatness of *Ulysses*," and the book "cannot therefore be deemed obscene."[66]

Furthermore, *Ulysses* lacked "intrinsic and extrinsic features" that were hallmarks of obscene works. It was not published pseudonymously; the title was circumspect, and the style, complexity, and length of the book deterred the smut seeker from picking it up, let alone being corrupted by it. The language was "baffling," at times incomprehensible, and "the construction is almost unbelievably involved." Citing *Dennett*, the brief argued that the book must be judged in its entirety, not on the basis of isolated passages. "The Court has read the book and knows that such portions of it as may conceivably be challenged are a negligible fraction of the whole." It continued, "It is true that *Ulysses* employs a few Anglo-Saxon words to denote certain human organs and functions. However, this does not render it obscene. Such words recently appeared in Ernst and Seagle's *To the Pure*."[67]

Ulysses continued to torment Judge Woolsey. He spent night after night "reading and re-reading the book and became frantic trying to get the author's idea," he recalled. When Woolsey returned to New York in early October, he sheepishly reported to prosecutor Nicholas Atlas that he had only been able to get through a small portion of the book and would have to postpone the arguments.[68] The hearings were rescheduled for November 6, then delayed once again, then finally set down for the morning of Saturday, November 25, 1933, over a year and a half after the book was seized.

* * *

Rather than hold his hearings in the gloomy federal court building, Judge Woolsey held his arguments in the tiny, elegant courtroom on the sixth floor of the building of the New York City Bar Association. That morning forty to fifty spectators, including Margaret Ernst, John Sumner, Bennett Cerf, and Cerf's business partner Donald Klopfer, crowded into the cramped, exquisitely furnished space.[69] Woolsey, dressed in a rumpled robe, sat behind a finely crafted wooden bench. Ernst, Lindey, Coleman, and Atlas occupied a row of handsome colonial-era chairs at the front of the room. Laid out on the tables before them were blue-bound bootleg copies of *Ulysses*.[70] Woolsey, who had heard Ernst in court many times, greeted him warmly and told him that he should feel free to smoke his cigarettes in the courtroom.[71]

Coleman spoke to the judge first. He began by asking Woolsey not to think of him as a "puritanical censor." Coleman then claimed that the government was helpless to act against *Ulysses* because "the only way to win is to refer to the great number of four-letter words used by Joyce." Ernst turned to Coleman and asked why it was impossible to say those words in the court. "Because there is a lady in the courtroom," Coleman said—referring to Maggie. "But that's my wife; she's a former newspapergal and a present schoolteacher," Ernst laughed. "She's seen all these words on toilet walls or scribbled on sidewalks by kids who enjoy them because of their being taboo."[72]

Coleman conceded *Ulysses*'s literary importance but insisted that obscenity was so "woven into its very texture" that it "could not be eradicated without destroying the essential values of the book." Woolsey, who made it clear from the start which side he favored, peppered Coleman with questions, at one point asking him to define *obscenity*. Coleman said he thought material was obscene when it had a tendency to "corrupt youth," even if it was nonsexual. Shaking his head, Woolsey offered a narrower view—something was obscene when its primary purpose was to "excite sexual feeling."[73]

Throughout the hearing, Woolsey talked freely and animatedly from the bench. "This isn't an easy case to decide," he said, drawing smoke through a long ivory cigarette holder. "I think things ought to take their chances in the marketplace. My own feeling is against censorship. I know that as soon as you suppress anything the bootlegger goes to work. The people see about as much of the prohibited article as they otherwise would and the profits go into illegal channels."[74]

Woolsey confessed his struggle to get through *Ulysses*, which greatly amused the crowd. Trying to get through Joyce's book, he said candidly, was like "walking around without your feet on the ground." He admitted, "Some of it was so obscure and unintelligible that it was difficult to understand it at all." When Woolsey further admitted his "shocking surprise" that he had "perfectly understood" the passages alleged to be obscene, the audience chuckled. "Parts of it are pretty rough, really, but other parts are swell. There are passages of moving literary beauty, passages of worth and power."[75]

Ernst then stood and made his memorable argument, pleading for more than an hour.

* * *

He began as he often did in obscenity cases, attacking the government's arguments about the purported harms of erotic literature. Officials always claimed that dirty books caused depravity, but Ernst had never seen a single instance where a book actually led to a "crime of passion."

Would Ernst feel comfortable having a "girl of 18 or 20 read the soliloquy of Marion [Molly] Bloom?" Woolsey asked. "Wouldn't it be apt to corrupt her?"

"I don't think that's the standard we should go by," Ernst replied. The "law does not require that adult literature be reduced to mush for infants."[76]

Ernst's main theme was the arbitrariness of words. Deploying his familiar tactic of "educating" the court, Ernst gave Woolsey a "lesson" in language. Ernst explained to the judge how irrational it was to fear "dirty words," mere letters arranged in random order. He pointed out the absurdity of using euphemisms and veiled terms to describe facts of life that everyone knew. As a boy, he recalled, signs read "Water Closet." They were later changed to "WC," then to "Toilets," then "Men's Lounge." None of these, of course, had anything to do with "what [a toilet] really is."[77]

Continuing, Ernst began his famous meditation on the word *fuck*. With Maggie's help, he researched *fuck*'s origins. There was nothing inherently dirty about *fuck*—indeed, it once had a much different meaning:

> ERNST: Judge, as to the word "fuck," one etymological dictionary gives its derivation as from *facere*: "to make—the farmer. . . . fucked the seed into the soil."

In its contemporary usage, *fuck* was "cleaner and less revolting" than paraphrases of it, Ernst explained. He told Woolsey that he liked the word *fuck*, although he didn't use it in polite company. It had "strength and integrity," he asserted, "more integrity than a euphemism used every day in every modern novel to describe precisely the same event."[78]

> WOOLSEY: For example. . . . ?
> ERNST: "They slept together." It means the same thing.
> WOOLSEY: (*smiling*) But, Counselor, that isn't even usually the truth![79]

* * *

Ernst went on to explain Joyce's stream-of-consciousness style. *Ulysses* was Joyce's "dramatic incisive attempt to record those thoughts and desires which all mortals carry within themselves," he told Woolsey.[80]

Woolsey noted that *Ulysses* left him "bothered, stirred, and troubled." "I think that is exactly the effect of *Ulysses*," Ernst replied. "You have not used the adjectives 'shocked' or 'revolted.' You have used the adjectives 'bothered,' 'troubled.'" Ernst expounded, "I think that peculiarly is the power of this book. It is an adventure not in action or in the deeds of men, but it is a weird epitome of what is going on in a human mind."[81]

The "greatest hurdle" in the argument, Ernst recalled, came when Woolsey asked whether Ernst himself had read *Ulysses* cover to cover. Ernst feared Woolsey was implying that "if it's this tough reading what harm will there be if the public is denied it?"

> ERNST: Yes, Judge. I tried to read *Ulysses* in 1923 or 1924 but couldn't get through it. This was before glossaries and instructional aids had been published. But in preparation for this trial I was trying again when an odd event made the reading easy. I was invited to speak at the Unitarian Church in Nantucket last summer on the bank holiday, the Federal Reserve System and the function of the New York State Banking Board of which I was a member.

"What's this got to do with *Ulysses*?" Woolsey asked impatiently. Ernst continued:

> I talked with true concern about our banking system and when I sat down I remembered, Judge, that while I was talking about banks I was at the same time thinking about the long windows on the sides, the clock in the rear, the old gray woman in the front row, the baby in the rear and a myriad of items unrelated to banks or my conscious mind. . . .
>
> This is *Ulysses*, and now in court while I thought I was thinking only about Joyce and *Ulysses* and my argument in defense of the book, I must tell you that I have also been thinking—if that's the word for it—about the gold ring around your tie, how your gown is slipping off your left shoulder, and about the picture of George Washington hanging up behind the bench. That, Judge, is the essence of *Ulysses*.

For a moment, Ernst was nervous, unsure whether he had made the point of "two streams in one mind at the same time."

But then Woolsey turned to him, nodding approvingly. "I understand your argument," he said. "In fact, I have been much worried about the last 50 pages or so of the volume. But now although I have listened as intently to the argument I must confess that all the time you were discussing the book I was also thinking about the Hepplewhite chair in back of you."

Ernst recalled of that triumphant moment, "This *was* the book. This *was* my case."

For the next ten minutes, they chatted about the judge's interest in antique furniture, and it was on that note that the argument closed.[82]

* * *

Two weeks later, on December 6, 1933, Judge Woolsey issued his opinion in *United States v. One Book Called "Ulysses."* In typical Woolsey style, the opinion was witty and erudite but short on legal reasoning and analysis. Much of the opinion consisted of Woolsey's personal reactions to *Ulysses*; the technical legal standards of obscenity were only obliquely addressed. Many likened the opinion to an eloquent book review rather than a judicial ruling.[83]

Woolsey's opinion was nonetheless historic, a major victory for Ernst and Lindey and a landmark in the law. Adopting most if not all of Ernst and Lindey's positions, Woolsey declared that a literary work must be judged as a whole, and assessed for its effects on the average adult, according to contemporary standards. The intent of the author was important, and literary merit mattered. Woolsey denied that the assessments of critics were irrelevant in determining whether a book was obscene. To Woolsey, expert opinion was critical to understanding whether descriptions of sex in novels were genuinely literary or merely gratuitous.

* * *

In his brief three-page opinion, Woolsey walked carefully through the steps he took to reach his conclusion that *Ulysses* was not obscene. He read through the entire book once, he explained, and the passages the government complained of several times, taking great care because of the book's significance and reputation in the literary world.

Woolsey's first inquiry was to ascertain the intent of the work—

whether Joyce wrote *Ulysses* the way he did for a serious purpose or a "pornographic" one. Woolsey concluded that the frank discussion of sex was not meant to "satisfy the leer of the sensualist" but was rather an integral part of Joyce's "technique," his stream-of-consciousness style:

> Joyce has attempted—it seems to me, with astonishing success—to show how the screen of consciousness with its ever-shifting kaleidoscopic impressions carries, as it were on a plastic palimpsest, not only what is in the focus of each man's observation of the actual things about him, but also in a penumbral zone residua of past impressions, some recent and some drawn up by association from the domain of the subconscious. He shows how each of these impressions affect the life and behavior of the character which he is describing. . . . What he seeks to get is not unlike the result of a double or, if that is possible, a multiple exposure on a cinema film, which would give a clear foreground with a background visible but somewhat blurred and out of focus in varying degrees.

If Joyce did not portray the candid thoughts and desires of his characters, he would be "unfaithful to his chosen technique," Woolsey wrote:

> It is because Joyce has been loyal to his technique . . . [because he has] honestly attempted to tell fully what his characters think about, that he has been the subject of so many attacks and that his purpose has been so often misunderstood and misrepresented. For his attempt sincerely and honestly to realize his objective has required him incidentally to use certain words which are generally considered dirty words and has led at times to what many think is a too poignant preoccupation with sex in the thoughts of his characters. . . . The words which are criticized as dirty are old Saxon words known to almost all men and, I venture, to many women, and are such words as would be naturally and habitually used, I believe, by the types of folk whose life, physical and mental, Joyce is seeking to describe. In respect of

> the recurrent emergence of the theme of sex in the minds of his characters, it must always be remembered that his locale was Celtic and his season spring.

Accordingly, Woolsey concluded, "I hold that *Ulysses* is a sincere and honest book, and I think that the criticisms of it are entirely disposed of by its rationale."[84]

But the question of whether *Ulysses* was obscene depended on more than the author's intent. It also required the application of a "more objective standard" to determine how the work would affect the average reader, according to Woolsey.

Woolsey determined that the legal meaning of *obscene* was "tending to stir the sex impulses or to lead to sexually impure and lustful thoughts." He stated, "Whether a particular book would tend to excite such impulses and thoughts must be tested by the court's opinion as to its effect on a person with average sex instincts—what the French would call *l'homme moyen sensuel*." Gracefully, Woolsey had repudiated *Hicklin*. "It is only with the normal person that the law is concerned," the judge declared.[85]

Woolsey conceded the danger of using a "reasonable man" test in obscenity cases. A judge, "however fair he might be," could very well substitute his own tastes and idiosyncrasies for those of the "reasonable man." To avoid this, Woolsey said, he checked his impressions of *Ulysses* with two friends. Though he did not reveal their names in the opinion, they were Henry Seidel Canby, editor of the *Saturday Review of Literature*, and Charles E. Merrill Jr., a publisher of textbooks.[86] Both agreed with Woolsey "that reading *Ulysses* in its entirety, as a book must be read on such a test as this, did not tend to excite sexual impulses or lustful thoughts." Rather, "Its net effect on them was only that of a somewhat tragic and very powerful commentary on the inner lives of men and women."[87]

The judge concluded, "I am quite aware that owing to some of its scenes *Ulysses* is a rather strong draught to ask some sensitive, though normal, persons to take. But my considered opinion, after long reflection, is that, whilst in many places the effect of *Ulysses* on the reader undoubtedly is somewhat emetic, nowhere does it tend to be an aphrodisiac. *Ulysses* may, therefore, be admitted into the United States."[88]

Published in the foreword to the first Random House edition of *Ulysses,* Woolsey's eminently quotable opinion became one of the most celebrated and widely read judicial opinions in American history. Random House used it as the preface to *Ulysses* for half a century, and it was read by more than half a million people.

* * *

Woolsey's ruling and the ensuing publication of *Ulysses* led to a media frenzy. Newspapers were preoccupied with the decision for weeks, and the opinion was endlessly reprinted.[89] In his column, Heywood Broun praised the "young lawyer who beat a pathway for *Ulysses.*" Lewis Gannett, in the *New York Herald Tribune*, lauded the *Ulysses* case as the culmination of an "amazing series of amazing victories for Morris Ernst."[90] The *March of Time* newsreel even reenacted part of Ernst's courtroom argument.[91]

Ernst issued his own statement to the press. "The new deal in the law of letters is here," he announced.[92] "The decision means more than that a great prose work has been made available for the general reading public. . . . It means that authors, writing with integrity concerning common aspects of daily life, need no longer seek refuge in euphemisms. It means the good old Anglo-Saxon words known to any child may now be read by adults."

Prohibition had been repealed the day before, prompting Ernst to declare:

> The first week of December 1933 will go down in history for two repeals, that of Prohibition and that of squeamishness in literature. . . . We may now imbibe freely of the contents of bottles and forthright books. It may well be that in the future the repeal of the sex taboo in letters, inherent in Judge Woolsey's decision, will prove to be of the greater importance. Perhaps the intolerance which closed our breweries was the intolerance which decreed that basic human functions had to be treated in books in a furtive, leering, hypocritical manner.[93]

Ernst's statement, slightly rewritten by Lindey, was later included in the foreword to *Ulysses* and has remained in every edition since 1934.[94]

On January 25, 1934, Random House published *Ulysses* with a first printing of 10,000 copies, which had been sold in advance. A month and five more printings later, 35,000 copies were in circulation. With his 5 percent royalty on every copy sold, Ernst was profiting from the decision in more ways than one.[95]

* * *

For a few months, it seemed as though the celebrated case was over. Sam Coleman told the press he thought Woolsey's ruling was fair—a "masterpiece and thoroughly wholesome"—and that he would recommend to the US Attorney that the government not appeal the decision.[96] Coleman said he felt much as Woolsey did about *Ulysses* and that "the reason for the action was that there had been so much adverse criticism of the book and such adulation of it . . . that the government felt that there should be an authoritative ruling at this time as to whether or not the book was obscene."[97]

But Coleman's was not the last word. On December 26, 1933, three weeks after Woolsey's opinion, a new United States attorney named Martin Conboy took office. Conboy, a devout Catholic, was an officer of the New York Society for the Suppression of Vice and had represented the society as its lawyer. On March 13, 1934, Conboy announced that the government would appeal the *Ulysses* decision and that he himself would argue it.[98] The case would come up before the Second Circuit Court of Appeals.

The *Ulysses* appeal was argued on May 16, 1934, before an "unusually large number of male spectators" in the federal court building.[99] Hearing the appeal were Martin Manton, chief judge of the Circuit Court, the eminently respected Learned Hand, and his cousin Augustus Hand, who had written the opinion in the *Dennett* case. Although Ernst and Lindey had no hand in the selection of the panel, the assignment could not have been more fortuitous. Learned Hand, in particular, was a renowned liberal, noted for his advocacy of freedom of speech.

"Blushing, stammering, [and] rocking nervously on his heels," Conboy read in a shocked and indignant voice the passages of *Ulysses* the government deemed obscene.[100] "This book is filthy, offensive to modesty, subversive of decency, therefore it complies with all the definitions of obscenity which I have read."[101] "All vices and all licentious thoughts are set forth without restraint . . . sexual practices, normal and abnormal, are dealt with, as is the use of contraceptives. A large part of the book is taken up with minute descriptions of performances and conversations in a brothel."[102] Conboy ended his oration with an impassioned reading of Molly Bloom's soliloquy. "It is obscene! It is obscene!" he cried, waving a damning finger at the book. When Conboy "filled the room with some pretty husky Anglo-Saxon verbiage," one of the two young women in the audience dashed for the door. The other stayed for the rest of the proceeding.[103]

For an hour, the judges heard Ernst praise *Ulysses* as a great work of fiction and Joyce as a "majestic genius."[104] He reminded the court that *Ulysses* was taught in English courses at Harvard and sought by numerous libraries. Although the legal definition of *obscenity* had remained largely the same since the days of Comstock, the standards of the time had changed towards greater liberty, Ernst explained. "We can't bind the masses by the rules that actuated the saints."[105] The book had been written for noble purposes, "to present a study of the human mind and emotions in certain phases," Ernst contended. "It has not been hawked about in a coarse, grasping sense. Those shouting loudest for censorship are the big business fellows who tell dirty stories in Pullman cars."[106]

When the judges convened after the argument, it was clear there was no hope for a unanimous opinion. Manton, who believed that *Hicklin* was the appropriate standard, and who was morally outraged by *Ulysses*, wanted to overturn—and denounce—Woolsey in a righteous opinion. "Who can doubt the obscenity of this book after a reading of the pages referred to, which are too indecent to add as a footnote to this opinion?" Manton wrote in dissent. "Congress passed this statute against obscenity for the protection of the great mass of our people." He asked, "Are we to refuse to enforce the statute Congress has enacted because of the argument that 'obscenity is only the superstition of the day—the modern counterpart of ancient witchcraft?'"[107]

Both Hands agreed with Woolsey but were critical of his "literary" opinion. Learned Hand thought Woolsey was a "show-off" and had a weakness for using language that "was not perfectly apt."[108] He resented the idea of judicial opinions being "performances in a publicity circus." Neither of the Hands wanted Random House to be able to use their opinion to sell the book, as it had with Woolsey's, and therefore decided that the opinion upholding Woolsey should be dry and technical. As a consequence, Augustus was assigned to write it instead of Learned, whose writing tended to be more controversial and flamboyant.

Augustus Hand's opinion—which turned out to be eloquent and quotable—upheld Woolsey on every point. Works must be assessed as a whole; the adult's reaction, not the child's, must serve as the test of obscenity; the effect must be judged against community standards; the work's merit and intent are relevant, and expert opinion should be considered in determining whether a work was obscene. In back of these points was a deep concern with free expression:

> It is settled, at least so far as this court is concerned, that works of physiology, medicine, science, and sex instruction are not within the (obscenity) statute, though to some extent and among some persons they may tend to promote lustful thoughts. We think the same immunity should apply to literature as to science, where the presentation, when viewed objectively, is sincere, and the erotic matter is not introduced to promote lust and does not furnish the dominant note of the publication. The question in each case is whether a publication taken as a whole has a libidinous effect. The book before us has such portentous length, is written with such evident truthfulness in its depiction of certain types of humanity, and is so little erotic in its result, that it does not fall within the forbidden class. . . .
>
> We think that *Ulysses* is a book of originality and sincerity of treatment and that it has not the effect of promoting lust. Accordingly

> it does not fall within the statute, even though it justly may offend many.[109]

Though not all courts accepted the Second Circuit's position, the opinion had major impact. It was cited in more than three hundred subsequent cases and established the foundation for later Supreme Court decisions that formally rejected *Hicklin* and adopted the "community mores" test and "work as a whole" standard in literary obscenity cases.[110] In the opinion of the *Harvard Law Review*, the *Ulysses* decisions were the most important in the three-hundred-year-long Anglo-American struggle against legal restrictions on writings about sex.[111]

* * *

Immediately after the Second Circuit's decision, an outraged Conboy wrote to the solicitor general of the United States requesting that an application for a writ of certiorari be made to the US Supreme Court.[112] The solicitor general refused permission.[113] In November 1934, the *Ulysses* case officially closed—"finally, definitely, and conclusively, "and may I say happily," Lindey wrote to Cerf.[114] When it was certain that the government would not appeal, Cerf donated the imported, dog-eared copy of the book to the Columbia University Library.[115]

Joyce had followed the legal developments but had no idea that Ernst was his lawyer. When he found out, he sent Ernst a copy of *Ulysses* with "a few words inscribed which are a very meager return for the great service you have done to me and it." This was after Ernst met Joyce at a cocktail party in Paris in 1937. "Until I had the pleasure of meeting Mrs. Ernst and yourself here, I had no idea that you were 'my' lawyer, that is, enlisted almost voluntarily and from conviction for the general and particular causes you sustained so brilliantly. Evidently I was in error, and I hasten to repair my *bevue*."[116]

13

THE IMPORTANCE OF BEING ERNST

Ulysses was the moment. Though Morris Ernst never believed that the case was as significant as *The Sex Side of Life*, *The Well of Loneliness*, and *Married Love* cases in reforming the law of obscenity, he could not deny that it transformed his career. With *Ulysses*, Ernst became a cultural icon; he was celebrated as one of the "leading liberal lawyers of America" and the "the ablest of the progressive leaders of the American bar."[1] This recognition stoked his ego to alarming proportions. Ernst was consulted, quoted, featured, interviewed, and—in a true testament to his notoriety—lampooned and caricatured. Described as a "famous barrister," Ernst was a character in a 1935 detective story titled *The Smiling Corpse*.[2] Peggy Bacon, a well-known satirist, did a cartoon sketch of Ernst with accompanying verse for her 1934 book *Off With Their Heads!*

> Head hard nut to crack. Face yanked up at left in uncanny grin. Deep wide laughing Punch-mouth. Wiggly hair. Eyebrows like the devil. Eyes deepset black buttons, twisted askance. Nose long, sinewy with eel ripple. . . . Hungry, fiery, dancing mind, glitteringly unoriginal. Wits dart like a waterbug.[3]

The *New Yorker*'s James Thurber sketched a cartoon showing a dozen people, of motley variety, waiting to get into Ernst's office. The *New Yorker* rejected publishing it on the ground that it would be appreciated only by those who knew Ernst. He hung it on the wall in his law office. The caption read: "There's been some mix-up or other; we're waiting for Morris Ernst."[4]

* * *

Indeed, there were many people waiting to see Ernst, and the 1930s were his best and most fruitful years. He maintained "one of the most human and luscious law practices on Manhattan," in the words of one journalist, with a large and eclectic roster of clients ranging from Wall Street banking houses to unions, writers, artists, and all manner of liberal groups.[5] A typical daily calendar showed appointments with leaders of the City Club, the Garland Fund, the State Insurance Board, the Banking Board, the Dramatists Guild, the Newspaper Guild, and the *Nation*, along with such illustrious individuals as Margaret Sanger, Art Sulzberger, Edna Ferber, and Heywood Broun, among others. Ernst met his clients in his suite on the twenty-second floor of a fancy building at Madison Avenue and Fortieth Street. His private corner office, set off by frosted glass doors, was cluttered with inscribed photographs, knickknacks, mementos, and books, including bound records of the important cases he argued. On the wall were photos of his mother, his daughters, Heywood Broun, and Judge Woolsey. Directly behind his desk hung an autographed picture of Justice Louis Brandeis.[6]

His energy was prodigious, and his slate of activities enormous. "Unpopular causes . . . gather around his door like flies around a honey barrel," recalled his friend Ernest Cuneo.[7] Ernst worked quickly, in intense bursts. He never labored hard in the traditional sense of being a practicing lawyer, studying law books and plotting strategy; instead he provided ideas, calling on others to provide the practical tools that made his plans useful.[8] Much of the day-to-day leg work on his cases was conducted by his young and admiring assistants at the firm.

Uninhibited and conversational, Ernst was "kind and warm to a degree that most men, particularly harassed New York lawyers, are not," noted one interviewer. Though Ernst loved to talk about himself, he was famous for listening to people and practicing "amateur psychoanalysis" on them to solve their troubles. Ernst called everyone by their first names, even if they'd just met. Colleagues in the

ACLU recalled an incident where there was fierce dispute and historical incidents were brought up to prove points. One concerned an event that took place in James Madison's administration. Before it was over, Morris was referring to the fourth president as "Jimmie."[9]

* * *

By the time of *Ulysses*, Ernst was a part of New Deal circles. The New Deal was very much a "lawyers' deal," needing the service of lawyers to administer programs, to draft laws, and to become administrative law judges to settle disputes arising under new regulations. A "plague of young lawyers" descended on Washington, DC, to staff President Franklin D. Roosevelt's agencies, and Ernst became acquainted with many of them.[10]

Ernst's entrée into the New Deal community was facilitated, in part, by his friend Felix Frankfurter, a longtime member of the ACLU Board of Directors. Frankfurter advised President Roosevelt informally and helped fill prominent New Deal positions with his Harvard students. Frankfurter saw the president weekly, even daily, and functioned as a kind of "freelance troubleshooter" around Washington, a role that Ernst himself would envy and emulate.

Ernst and Frankfurter's friendship dated back to the 1920s, when Frankfurter established himself as a leading liberal. A cofounder of the ACLU, Frankfurter was an expert on labor injunctions, wrote for the *New Republic*, and was involved with the NAACP. He came to world attention with his article in the *Atlantic Monthly* analyzing the evidence in the Sacco and Vanzetti case and declaring the trial a miscarriage of justice. Frankfurter was the first Jew to teach at Harvard Law School, though he was not religious. Bursting with joy and wit, Frankfurter had enormous presence, despite being only five feet tall. He was always eager to exchange gossip or to debate; biographer Matthew Josephson wrote, "wherever Frankfurter is, there is no boredom."[11] Frankfurter and Ernst were drawn together in the early years of the Great Depression by their mutual interest in banking reform and their admiration of Brandeis; Frankfurter was a Brandeis disciple.

Frankfurter's top students from Harvard, nicknamed the "Happy

Hot Dogs," took positions in myriad New Deal agencies such as the Reconstruction Finance Corporation, the Tennessee Valley Authority, and the Agricultural Adjustment Administration. "Frankfurter men" included Thomas Corcoran, Benjamin Cohen, David Lilienthal, Gardner Jackson, Charles Wyzanski, and Jerome Frank, all Ernst acquaintances. "I have seen quite a bit of your men in Washington," he wrote to Frankfurter in 1934. "They are all swell . . . all told your boys in Washington are doing you proud."[12]

Ernst and Frankfurter maintained spirited correspondence in the 1930s. Much as he was a Brandeis hanger-on, Ernst also was a Frankfurter hanger-on. How he loved big names! Read one of his typical, fawning missives to "Felix": "You don't know what a joy your letter was. It made me feel nearly as intimate as if I were one of your boys—that is, one of the bunch that sat at your feet and worshipped."[13] Ernst was much fonder of Frankfurter than Frankfurter was of Ernst.

Other New Deal contacts included Ernest Gruening of the Department of the Interior; Herman Oliphant, general counsel to the secretary of the treasury; Henry Wallace, secretary of agriculture; James Lawrence Fly, general counsel for the Tennessee Valley Authority; and Harold Ickes, a progressive Chicago attorney and ACLU member who was Interior secretary and head of the Public Works Administration. In the early 1930s Ernst became especially close with Jerome Frank, a corporate lawyer, leading light of the legal realist movement, and former Yale law professor who became general counsel of the Agricultural Adjustment Administration and later a federal judge. Ernst and Frank were intellectual sparring partners; over the two and a half decades of their friendship, they critiqued each other's writings, shared mutual interests in the sociology of law, and aggressively promoted each other's careers. Frank worked briefly for Ernst's law firm in the 1930s. Ernst described Frank as "having the keenest, most exciting legal mind I've ever met," with "an intuitive feel for the solution of social problems."[14]

Behind them all was the mythic figure of Roosevelt—"the Boss," Ernst called him—whom he worshipped like a god.

Generous and eager to help, Ernst barraged his friends in the administration with gossip, advice, and offers of assistance: "Do you need anything? Is there anything I can do? Can I help?"

* * *

Ulysses transformed Ernst's aspirations. With Ernst achieving public figure status, and with the ascendance of his liberal friends in government, he began to glimpse the possibility that he, too, could be a political player and insider. From time to time he confided to Frankfurter his restlessness at being "on the sidelines." "Every once in a while, when I go down there [to Washington], I wish I were really in the swing," Ernst confessed. "I am quite bored with being what you most favorably call a private public servant."[15]

Over the next several years, friends and admirers attempted to get Ernst appointed or elected to public positions. In 1933,supporters tried to convince him to run for mayor on the ticket of the Fusion Party, which brought together Democrats and Republicans opposed to the machine politics of Tammany Hall. Ernst's supporters worried that the major problem with his candidacy was that he had represented birth control advocates, which would negate votes from Catholics.[16] The mayoral campaign ultimately never materialized; Ernst also rejected suggestions that he run for Congress. Ernst confided to a colleague that he knew he would "hate like hell being a congressman."[17]

Ernst also began to be mentioned for political appointments, including a position on the Federal Reserve Board, a position on the National Labor Relations Board, and governor of Puerto Rico. He was one of three names that figured prominently as a candidate for American ambassador to Russia, a position he truly wanted. He confided to Drew Pearson, "I know that I would love to go to Russia."[18] Ernst's friends hired a publicist to come up with a strategy to get him favorable press "either for the Russia opportunity or for the federal reserve"—"to cash in on him for the public good as a social force, a leader, instead of a private adviser."[19] For unknown reasons, this project was abandoned.

Ernst was considered for US Attorney for the Southern District of New York, in the position vacated by Martin Conboy, who had argued the government's case in *Ulysses*. In the spring of 1935, Attorney General Homer Cummings submitted a list of approved candidates for the job to Roosevelt. According to the New York *Daily News*, Ernst was high on the president's list.[20]

In conjunction with the potential appointment, FBI Director J. Edgar Hoover directed agents to conduct a "discreet" investigation. Although the report contained the usual iterations of allegedly "communistic" ACLU and other left-wing activity, it found Ernst's character and reputation to be impeccable. Agents looked into Ernst's record at Williams and discovered that he was one of the college's most distinguished alumni. Leading members of the New York bar regarded Ernst "outstanding in ability and integrity." The New York Bar Association called him "one of New York's most prominent lawyers," rated highly for character and reputation. One New York Bar Association member said that Ernst was "fearless and honest and has the reputation for faithfully performing any task which he sets out to do." When Ernst "made up his mind to follow a certain procedure he has the courage to proceed even against all obstacles."[21]

Ernst's supporters wrote to Cummings urging the appointment, but this effort also fizzled. In the end, it seems, Ernst's friends, and Ernst himself, recognized that his restlessness, whimsicality, quirkiness, and independence made him ill suited to serve in a public position that required stability, allegiance, and deference.

Ernst would never serve in public office. Instead, he exerted influence on public affairs by performing "off-the-record chores," as he called them, for New Deal administrators, New York Mayor Fiorello La Guardia, and President Roosevelt himself. Over the next ten years Ernst would work as a negotiator and "fixer," making deals, gathering information, and papering over conflicts. Working with government officials and putting his imprint on policy by "pulling wires from behind the scenes," Ernst built bridges between the ACLU and the Roosevelt administration, brought civil liberties issues to the agendas of New Deal leaders, helped the ACLU achieve many of its policy goals, and brought the ACLU further into the cultural and political mainstream.

* * *

In November 1933, Fiorello La Guardia was elected mayor of New York City by a coalition of Fusion and Republican Parties. The "Little Flower" took office determined to revitalize New York. This project was enabled by the federal government's willingness to spend on employment programs, as well as La Guardia's close ties to Roosevelt.

Ernst had campaigned for La Guardia, a longtime friend and ACLU ally.[22] Ernst's relationship with La Guardia dated back to his earliest years in law practice, when La Guardia was a lawyer representing poor immigrants and labor unions. La Guardia was elected to the US Senate in 1919 as a progressive Republican from a working-class Italian and Jewish district in East Harlem. A loud, blustering, hyperenergetic man whose voice would ascend into falsetto when he was excited, La Guardia was infamously temperamental and mercurial, oscillating between kindness and rage.

Ernst served as La Guardia's personal lawyer for a while in the 1930s. The two strong-willed men often clashed, which resulted in an eventual falling-out in 1942. "He and I fought and made up, only to fight again. He was one of the most attractive men I have known. I enjoyed him when he did not irritate me; he was impossible to work for or with," Ernst recalled.[23] Ernst refused to take compensation from La Guardia. "If I had accepted a farthing, Fiorello would have thought he owned me, and all too much he loved owning other men."[24]

After the 1934 election, La Guardia called on Ernst to do "chores" for him, including arbitrating various public crises and labor disputes. Two significant tasks included mediating a bitter taxi strike in the winter of 1934 and working on an interracial commission to improve conditions in poverty-ridden Harlem, site of a brutal race riot in 1935.

* * *

The Depression hit the taxi industry hard. If reduced fares weren't devastating enough, the city had imposed a nickel-per-ride tax on cabs in 1933. Cabbies complained that the tax was hurting their already decimated business. A month after it began, the state Supreme Court ruled the tax illegal. The sum of $250,000 was given to the drivers, with no instructions as to how to divide it. Tensions over the unallocated funds, as well as union organization attempts, led twelve thousand cabdrivers to strike in February 1934. Drivers marched through Times Square, slashed tires, and set vehicles on fire.[25] Ernst had dropped by the mayor's office to chat about something, and La Guardia said, "What are you doing this afternoon?" He appointed him to settle the dispute, and Ernst didn't get home for four days.[26]

On the afternoon of February 3, 1934, Ernst entered into conferences at New York City Hall with delegations from the striking cabbies and their employers. After four and a half hours, he announced that four employees' organizations, representing about thirty thousand drivers, had agreed on a joint committee of thirteen members to meet with the representatives of the cab owners and nonunion drivers of the large companies.

After an eleven-hour conference the following day, Ernst announced that a compromise had been reached by unanimous consent of the operators and a majority vote of the drivers' delegates. The compromise called for equal division of the impounded tax money between the operators and the drivers, and the setting aside of three successive Mondays, "Taxicab Mondays," on which the public could ride in cabs at two-thirds the usual cost.[27] The bargain rate was expected to increase the use of cabs. The drivers would also get 40 percent of a new fare increase of five cents. The settlement was announced in Ernst's office. Ernst wrote to his pal Charles "Barnesie" Barnes, "I have just spent four days and nights on the taxicab matter."[28]

But the settlement didn't stick, and unrest resumed in March. The Communist Party, which had been trying to organize the drivers, had played a critical role in the strike. The party denounced La Guardia's plans for distributing the nickels and for the fare holiday as a "sell-out," and it accused Ernst of putting cops in cabs to trick and arrest strikers.[29]

* * *

Harlem, where Ernst had grown up, was poor, predominantly black, and one of the most densely populated sections of the city. It was devastated by the Depression. The unemployment rate was more than twice that of other neighborhoods. Rents were extortionate, and goods of all kinds were sold at discriminatory prices. Festering racial and economic tensions led to a riot in March 1935.[30]

The incident took place at the W. H. Kress five-and-dime store, which was noted for refusing to hire black clerks. The manager of the store saw a black Puerto Rican teenager stealing a knife and dragged him through the store to turn him over to a policeman. This incident triggered a rumor that the police were beating up the man, and several black shoppers began shouting. A huge crowd assembled, including members of the Communist Party, who were actively organizing the unemployed in Harlem. The Communists decided to stage a militant protest against the Kress management, which turned violent. In the fight, three people died, hundreds were injured, and there was an estimated $2 million in property damage.[31]

Mayor La Guardia commissioned an interracial citizens' committee of noted liberals to look into the causes of the riot. His Mayor's Commission on Conditions in Harlem was headed by African American sociologist E. Franklin Frazer, with members including Ernst, white lawyer and ACLU cofounder Art Hays, white *Washington Post* editor and civil rights activist Oswald Garrison Villard, and black labor leader A. Philip Randolph. The commission divided its work among six subcommittees dealing with problems in Harlem: crime and police; health and hospitals; housing and recreation; education; discrimination in employment; and discrimination in relief. Ernst was head of the housing committee.[32] The commission held twenty-five hearings and collected testimony from 160 witnesses. Several hundred Communist Party members descended on the hearings, detailing discrimination against Harlem residents and interrupting the testimony with shouts and hooting.[33]

During the hearing on housing, witnesses told of poor living conditions and abnormally high rents.[34] Ernst personally believed that the Kress incident had not been a race riot but "was really a housing riot."[35] Ernst's committee concluded that rentals in Harlem ran up to 40 percent of average income, out of line with the rest of the city. "These high rentals require Negro families to surrender an exorbitantly large part of their meager income for the privilege of living in dwellings, many of which are unsanitary and dilapidated, and some totally unfit for human habitation," read the committee's report. "That the landlords of Harlem are able to exercise such autocratic power over the lives of 200,000 people is due to the fact that Negroes cannot move about freely in the city and live where they please."[36]

After a year of deliberations, the Mayor's Commission issued its report, *The Negro in Harlem: A Report on Social and Economic Conditions Responsible for the Outbreak of March 19, 1935*, which identified "injustices of discrimination in employment, the aggressions of the police, and racial segregation" as conditions that led to rioting. The commission described the riot as Harlem's response to racism and unemployment and called for municipal action to combat job discrimination, improve healthcare, create more schools and parks, build decent affordable housing, and address the problem of crime and insensitive police. Its suggestions also included the creation of an interracial commission to hear complaints of police misconduct.[37]

Ernst's housing committee recommended, among its proposals, that the Housing Authority condemn dwellings unfit for habitation and that the tenants of Harlem organize and protest against exorbitant rents. Ernst urged Governor Herbert Lehman and Mayor La Guardia to back emergency legislation "making it unlawful for any owner of real estate to refuse to rent to colored people." He acknowledged that the passage of the antidiscrimination proposal was unlikely. "I would rather have us be foolishly brave than normally timid," he wrote to his friend Langdon Post, then serving as tenement house commissioner.[38] "My . . . fear is that unless something is done by the legislature to indicate at least an inclination to meet the restlessness of the neighborhood, more trouble will ensue. . . . A year from now, unless there is another riot, we all will have forgotten the stinking conditions in Harlem."[39] The legislation never went forward, and because the commission's report was so critical of the police and La Guardia's most trusted commissioners, it never left the mayor's office.[40]

* * *

Red-baiters spun the facts surrounding the Harlem riots to link Hays, Ernst, and the ACLU to the Communist Party. Harold Lord Varney, a well-known anti-Communist, accused Hays and Ernst of subverting the Mayor's Commission's inquiry from Communists in Harlem, who were widely accused of fomenting the riot, to the actions of the police. "The radical role in the Harlem unrest was waved aside, and the Communists, instead of being the accused, were invited into the prosecution box," he wrote in "Liberalism à La Moscow," published in the *American Mercury*. Varney went on to describe the ACLU as the "organization which is doing the most fruitful work to advance the so-called Class War in America today."[41]

Such allegations flourished in the mid-1930s, when a conservative backlash swept the nation. Professional patriots, antiunion businessmen, and other traditionalists tried to stop the wave of radicalism that started with the onset of the Depression, encouraged by the liberalism of the New Deal.[42] Congress was flooded with bills to curb free speech; state legislatures enacted sedition statutes, and radical teachers were dismissed for their views. The ACLU's annual report declared 1935 to be the "toughest" in its history. "Not in years have the principles of civil liberty been so under fire as they are today in the attempt to outlaw by federal and state legislation . . . the Communist Party, all anti-capitalist organizations, and militant labor and farmer movements."[43] "Never before in the fifteen years of our existence were these forces so united, so determined and so powerful."[44]

The conservative William Randolph Hearst press published a garish editorial on its newspapers' front pages titled "Unmasked," which represented the ACLU as a Communist organization. Elizabeth Dilling, a right-wing crackpot, published *The Red Network: A "Who's Who" and Handbook of Radicalism for Patriots*, which became the bible of the traditionalists. Drawing on the reports of the Lusk and

Fish Committees, Dilling described the ACLU as "directed by Communist and Socialist revolutionary leaders and their sympathizers, . . . work[ing] untiringly to further and legally protect the interests of the Red movement."[45] Several ACLU leaders were singled out for mention, including Ernst, described as "co-author with William Seagle of a sex book . . . recommended by the atheist Free Thought Club."[46] Ernst encouraged Roger Baldwin to bring a libel suit against Dilling on behalf of the ACLU, and Baldwin sued the *American Mercury* for $50,000 over the Varney article.[47]

* * *

Though the ACLU was never a Communist-affiliated organization, by the mid-1930s an increasing number of leftist groups did have ties to the Communist Party. Communism was becoming a significant force on the left, in the labor movement, and in public life more generally. At a time of hopelessness and despair, the party was responding to the Depression with action, not just rhetoric, by organizing unemployed workers, conducting marches for relief, and forming militant unions. Although the core of active Communist Party membership was only around fifty thousand at its peak in the late 1930s, through aggressive publicity and organizing, it was able to mobilize large numbers of non-Communists.[48]

The primary instrument for Communist recruiting was the "front organization." In the early 1930s the Communists had supported the thesis of the Communist International (Comintern) that world capitalism had entered its final crisis and the Communists must be militant and uncompromising. In 1935, however, the Seventh Comintern Congress reversed positions and adopted a Popular Front or United Front against fascism. The Soviet leadership feared being isolated and vulnerable to Nazi Germany under Adolf Hitler. The protection of the Soviet Union would be accomplished through an antifascist coalition with other Socialist and left-wing organizations. The Communist Party expanded its influence by shedding its radical image and deemphasizing its Marxist ideology to form coalitions with other liberal democratic antifascist forces. It set up hundreds of so-called front organizations, dubbed "fronts" because they fronted for the Communist Party, disguising party affiliation behind titles such as the Civil Rights Congress and the International Workers' Order.[49]

Roger Baldwin, although not a Communist, had been involved in several Popular Front groups, which gave the impression that the ACLU was "red-tinged." From time to time, Baldwin's careless words also conveyed as much. In his thirtieth anniversary Harvard yearbook he wrote, "I seek social ownership of property, the abolition of the propertied class and sole control by those who produce wealth. Communism is the goal." The statement was not typical of Baldwin, but it haunted him for decades.[50] There was also the troublesome fact that Harry Ward chaired both the ACLU and the American League for Peace and Democracy, a well-known Popular Front organization formed by the Communist Party in 1933.

Despite its seemingly red image, the ACLU's relationship with the Communist Party continued to be tense.[51] Socialists Norman Thomas and John Haynes Holmes were outspoken critics of the Communist Party and the front tactic. An incident in 1934 furthered the anti-Communist sentiment of many ACLU leaders. The Socialist Party had held a rally at Madison Square Garden to protest the Nazi coup in Vienna. Communist members came to the meeting and demanded that their leaders be allowed to speak. When one of the leaders mounted the platform trying to speak, he was beaten up by the Socialists and ejected.

The ACLU Board appointed a commission to look into the riot. Their report condemned the Communists, stating that "it is undisputed that the Communists participated in the Madison Square Garden meeting for the announced purpose of preventing two speakers from being heard and of demanding places for two of their own speakers on the program."[52] At the same time, the report criticized the Socialists for assaulting the would-be speaker. Thomas was outraged over this seeming attack on the Socialists and claimed that the report had been put out by Communist sympathizers on the ACLU Board. He commenced an effort to purge Communists from the ACLU. Baldwin convinced him that there were no Communists in positions of influence in the organization, and Thomas dropped the matter.[53]

The ACLU's work with Communists in legal defense matters was also a source of friction. Communists had taken the lead on the defense of the Scottsboro Boys, the nine young black men from Alabama wrongly convicted of the rape of two white women that became a liberal cause célèbre. The ACLU had cooperated with the Communist Party's legal wing, the International Labor Defense, in a joint defense, as it had in other cases. Ernst played an influential role on the Scottsboro Defense Committee, collecting funds for the defense and serving as liaison between the committee and the Scottsboro Boys' attorney, Samuel Leibowitz.[54] Ernst collected thousands of dollars but never received any accounting of the funds; he believed that the Communists "siphon[ed] off Scottsboro nickels and dimes" to fund its publicity activities and its publication the *Daily Worker*.[55]

By that time, Ernst was at odds with the Communists and anxious about the increasing presence of Communist Party members in liberal organizations. Ernst saw the Communists as untrustworthy, insidious tools of Moscow. By 1936, the revelation of the wide-scale use of repression and political murder in the Soviet Union—in particular, the Moscow show trials in which Joseph Stalin's former colleagues confessed their crimes before being executed—convinced many liberals that the Soviet Union was as oppressive as Nazi Germany and renewed doubts about American Communists, who defended Stalin's actions absolutely.[56] Ernst was outraged by the seeming hypocrisy of liberals who professed to stand for democracy and civil liberties yet refused to condemn Soviet repression.

Before long, Ernst had joined the growing ranks of liberal anti-Communists who rejected Communism as a philosophy incompatible with individual liberty.[57] Ernst was convinced that Communists were doing irreparable damage to the liberal movement by undermining its integrity, subverting its goals, tarnishing its image, and leaving it vulnerable to attacks from the right wing.[58] If liberals did not act swiftly to purge their organizations of Communist influence, he believed, everything he had worked for would be compromised.

14

DEFENDING THE NEW DEAL

> Constitutional law is not made in the abstract but stems from the realities of life.[1]

From the start of the New Deal, observers anticipated a clash between the administration and the US Supreme Court.[2] President Franklin D. Roosevelt knew that the Court's conservative justices, dubbed the "Four Horsemen," would vote to invalidate almost all of his recovery program. Indeed, starting in 1935, the Supreme Court struck down most of the New Deal's foundations. Morris Ernst dove into the ensuing national debate and constitutional crisis with his trademark vigor. He reveled in the opportunity to defend the New Deal and "the Boss," and for two years, it became for Ernst a near-religious crusade.

* * *

In May 1935, in *Schechter Poultry Corp. v. United States*, the famous "dead chicken" case involving a kosher poultry shop in Brooklyn, the Supreme Court invalidated the National Industrial Recovery Act (NIRA). The Court held that Congress had delegated excessive authority to the president and improperly involved the federal government in regulating intrastate commerce. Most of the federal government's authority over the economy stemmed from the clause in the US Constitution empowering Congress to regulate interstate commerce. The Supreme Court, however, construed *interstate commerce* so narrowly that not even an industry such as coal mining was within the commerce power.[3] With *Schechter*, the justices destroyed Roosevelt's industrial program and threatened the rest of the New Deal. At a press conference, Roosevelt called the implications of the ruling more important than the Dred Scott case and said that the nation had been relegated to the "horse and buggy definition of interstate commerce."[4]

The following year, in *United States v. Butler*, the Supreme Court struck down the Agricultural Adjustment Act. The decision was highly unpopular, and Roosevelt was urged to take action. His advisers favored a constitutional amendment to curb the power of the Court. In Congress, some members wanted to make constitutional grants of power to Congress more explicit; other proposals included requiring a supermajority vote for the Court to strike down acts of Congress, increasing the Court's membership, and amending the Constitution to prohibit judicial review. With Roosevelt's encouragement, Attorney General Homer Cummings sought to come up with a plan to generate a more favorable response from the Court. The President recognized that he had to move carefully because most Americans believed the Supreme Court to be sacred.[5]

"The courts have and will continue to mucker up . . . any program along the lines of a planned economy," Ernst announced in an April 1935 radio address. "Look what the courts have done to the TV [Tennessee Valley] project, the NRA [National Recovery Administration] and practically all of Roosevelt's program. . . . I want the [Supreme Court's] decisions to be in line with my own prejudices. In any event, don't you think . . . that it is about time that the prejudices of the courts change because the old prejudices certainly have put this nation into the soup. . . . If you look over most of the New Deal legislation you will find that it was written previously in one form or another over the last 30 years and was consistently thrown out by the United States Supreme Court."[6]

Like many New Dealers, Ernst advocated a constitutional amendment that would restrict or eliminate judicial review. He told Felix Frankfurter, "I do feel . . . that the American people will not stand for general talk of constitutional revision, but will never be much scared by any proposed single amendment."[7] In his column, Heywood Broun asserted that the power of the Supreme Court "can be readily whittled down by constitutional amendment." He pointed out, "I am not speaking on my own authority but by advice of counsel Morris Ernst, the lawyer whom I retained at the usual fee of spending a nickel to get him on the telephone."[8]

It was during the Supreme Court controversy that Ernst began corresponding with FDR, pursuing a "scant relationship" he had with him when Roosevelt was governor. Invariably the letters started "Dear Governor." In the summer of 1935, Ernst began sending memos to Roosevelt, which he called "tidbits." In a line or two Ernst would set out a suggestion for the president or a bit of gossip. Each point was numbered to save him time in his answers. Read the first "tidbit":

> My Dear Governor,
>
> In regard to the fantastic attacks made upon you because of your comment on the necessity of constitutional changes, I thought you might be interested in re-reading President Jackson's veto message on the banking bill where he indicated that the court ought not to control the coordinate branches of this government. He went as far as to state that the Congress, the Executive, and the Court "must each for itself be guided by its opinion of the Constitution." . . . If I can be helpful in getting any of this material, do not hesitate to let me know.[9]

This was the real beginning of their relationship, which blossomed into regular correspondence and occasional White House visits. Ernst's relationship with the president inflated his vanity and sense of self-importance. Ernst kept his correspondence to Roosevelt in bound volumes in his office, considering them one of his prized possessions. He carried letters from FDR around in his jacket pocket, showing them to his friends with a quick peek to verify their authorship.

FDR thanked Ernst for his "tidbit." The president wrote back, "Last year somebody in the State Department—Judge Moore, I think—gave me a brief on Jackson and his messages and statements. He was a grand old fellow! We will hear more of him in the days to come."[10] According to Ernst, FDR's letters inspired him to write a book advocating a constitutional amendment to curb the high court. He wrote to Frankfurter, "I am in the throes of doing a book on the Founding Fathers, the Supreme Court, et al. Your pal, FDR, without knowing it got me interested in doing this job through two or three letters which he sent me."[11] Shortly after, Ernst contracted with Simon and Schuster for a book to be titled *The Ultimate Power*.

* * *

A week after the *Schechter* decision, the American Newspaper Guild met for its second annual convention. By that time, the loss in the code battle, the lack of improvement in journalists' working conditions, and the invalidation of the NIRA made it clear to guild members that if they wanted to make gains, they needed to become a union and take part in collective bargaining.[12]

Meanwhile, the National Labor Relations Act, also known as the Wagner Act, passed in July 1935. The act guaranteed the right of all employees under its jurisdiction "to self-organization, to form, join, or assist labor organizations, to bargain collectively through representatives of their own choosing, and to engage in concerted activities, for the purpose of collective bargaining or other mutual aid or protection." Employers were prohibited from interfering with these activities through restraint, coercion, discrimination, or dismissal, which would be designated "unfair labor practices." The bill contained the teeth that the NIRA had lacked in the form of an enforcement arm, the National Labor Relations Board (NLRB), a three-member panel appointed by the president to issue complaints, arbitrate disputes, hold hearings, and issue cease and desist orders.[13] The power of the federal government was for the first time in American history placed on the side of workers. With the Wagner Act, there now existed the prospect of unionizing unorganized industrial workers, long excluded by the American Federation of Labor's craft unions. In 1935, John L. Lewis would organize the Committee for Industrial Organization to "promote organization of workers in the mass production and unorganized industries of the nation."[14] The CIO chartered unions in the automobile, glass, radio, rubber, and steel industries. By the end of 1937, it would have two million members.[15]

The Newspaper Guild members saw the passage of the Wagner Act as an opportunity.[16] Before they could take advantage of it, they needed to be certain it would withstand constitutional challenge. The guild asked Ernst, who agreed to serve as its counsel, to explore a test case. The Wagner Act had jurisdiction over all interstate commerce; the dispute over its merits would involve the definition of *interstate commerce*. Ernst and the guild leaders determined that a test case involving a daily newspaper would not implicate interstate commerce, but one involving a wire service such as the Associated Press would. The AP was the largest collector, compiler, and distributor of domestic news in the United States, with 1,300 member newspapers across the nation, indisputably engaged in interstate commerce.[17]

In mid-September 1935, Ernst conferred with Morris Watson, the lead Newspaper Guild organizer, in New York's AP office. Watson was one of the AP's star reporters, but he had been transferred to the night shift and assigned to menial work as punishment for his union activities.[18] Ernst then went to Washington, DC, to meet with NLRB lawyers, who were ready to find good cases in which to start proceedings in accordance with their "master plan" for testing the Wagner Act's constitutionality.[19]

Somewhat serendipitously, a few days later, the Associated Press revoked the five-day workweek they had recently instituted as a concession to reporters in return for suspending efforts at collective bargaining.[20] Broun, acting as president of the guild, sent a letter to AP head Kent Cooper calling for a meeting to begin collective bargaining. The next day, Watson was fired. Watson submitted a report to the National Executive Board of the Newspaper Guild describing the events leading to his dismissal, noting that he had experienced reprisals for his union activity despite his reputation for excellent work. He concluded, "It is my firm belief I was not fired for incompetence." The guild board subsequently passed a resolution declaring that it would "pledge its full resources" to working for Watson's reinstatement and battling the AP for its unfair labor practices.[21]

The guild board resolved that Watson's case be given to Ernst and taken before the NLRB. On November 7, the Newspaper Guild filed two complaints with the NLRB regional office in New York, one for the dismissal of Watson and the other in the event that AP refused to collectively bargain.[22] Ernst instructed his associates to begin collecting data on the AP's setup and corporate structure to illustrate that it was engaged in interstate commerce despite its claim to be a nonprofit organization.[23] He believed that the case could be historic and had his "heart set on this as the pet case of more than twenty years of practice."[24] In late November 1936, NLRB regional director Elinor Herrick, in her investigation of the AP's records, found a memorandum in Watson's file stating that "he is an agitator and disturbs morale of staff at a time when we need especially their loyalty and best performance," evidence that he had been fired for his organizing work. The NLRB scheduled a hearing for January 1936.[25]

* * *

From the outset, the government's lawyers recognized that the case would be contentious and had to be handled carefully. The AP had retained John W. Davis as counsel. Former solicitor general in the Wilson administration and Democratic presidential candidate in 1924, Davis was an erudite Wall Street lawyer who represented many of the nation's largest corporations in challenges to federal and state regulation and appeared before the Supreme Court more than one hundred times. Davis was counsel for the American Liberty League, a political organization formed in 1934, comprised of wealthy business elites opposed to the New Deal. The powerful American Newspaper Publishers Association was attacking the Wagner Act as a violation of freedom of the press and was expected to support the AP on the issue.[26]

Davis's first move was to bring an injunction suit to halt the hearing. He alleged that the AP would suffer irreparable damage if forced to participate in a hearing, that the AP was not engaged in interstate commerce, and that the Wagner Act was "null and void in toto."[27] Ernst retorted that the news AP generated was a commodity sent to profit-making businesses nationwide and that without the labor of its editorial workers, the flow of interstate commerce would be interrupted. "The question," Ernst asked, "is who shall bear the risk of irreparable damage, the employer who under the law must make a clear and convincing showing of threatened, imminent, irreparable injury, or the employees whose feeble attempt to live a better life is sought to be crushed."[28]

The case was heard by Judge William Bondy in federal district court. Davis maintained that the Wagner Act was unconstitutional. NLRB lawyer David Moscowitz argued that there was no question of the law's constitutionality and that "men like Watson are entitled to protection under the Constitution just as well as corporate interests like the Associated Press." The Newspaper Guild injected itself dramatically into the case when Broun, who was present in the courtroom, asked to be permitted to speak to the court following formal arguments, which the judge denied. During an interchange Broun nonetheless read to the court his statement, "John W. Davis is asking you for permission for the Associated Press to run a yellow-dog shop." The judge struck it from the record.[29]

Bondy took his time deciding the case. As the delay lengthened past two months, the government's lawyers became impatient. Broun wrote an extraordinary letter to the judge pointing out that the delay presented the AP with "an easement, a kind of legal laxative which works while you sleep."[30] Bondy finally allowed hearings to go forward.[31] The NLRB then called a hearing before Trial Examiner Charles Clark, dean of the Yale Law School. The AP moved immediately for dismissal on grounds that the Wagner Act was invalid under the Fifth and First Amendments and an invalid exercise of the commerce power. Clark denied the motion, reserving a ruling on the issue of interstate commerce until evidence regarding the nature of AP's operations was presented.[32] The first day of the hearing was taken up with the testimony of Lloyd Stratton, assistant general manager of the AP. Ernst asked Stratton whether it was correct that bonds were issued to obtain capital for the expansion of the

AP's operations, whether the largest and wealthiest publishers had purchased the most bonds, and whether the amount held in bonds correlated with voting power, which meant that the most powerful profit-making publishers in the country controlled the association.[33]

Clark filed his report concluding that the AP had engaged in unfair labor practices and ordered Watson's reinstatement with back pay.[34] The AP appealed to the Second Circuit Court of Appeals. Before that court, Davis insisted that the organization was not run for profit and then ingeniously argued that the AP was only engaged in manufacturing and not in interstate commerce. Editorial employees were like factory workers who reworked the news and prepared it for distribution. The actual transmission of the news, like the shipment of goods, was a separate function. "News is manufactured over editorial cables, while Bessemer Steel may be manufactured by the open-hearth process. News comes in as raw material and is put in final shape by editorial employees, and then only does its interstate transmission begin." Ernst's associate Callman Gottesman quipped, "Many readers of the Associated Press have doubtless long suspected them of manufacturing news, but never expected the company's learned attorney to so admit in open court."[35] A unanimous three-judge panel rejected AP's argument, stating that the federal power to regulate interstate communication had been established as interstate commerce in previous cases. The AP appealed to the US Supreme Court.

On Cooper's suggestion, Davis's Supreme Court brief included an extensive First Amendment argument. Davis claimed that "freedom of the press" exempted the AP from any interference with its business operations and that the accuracy and objectivity of the news would be compromised if newspapers were forced to hire union members, who would inject prolabor biases into their writing. "The National Labor Relations Act . . . destroys the independence of the press in this country. Can freedom and independence of the press be maintained if a federal Bureau may dictate to American newspapers the persons they employ to prepare their news reports? . . . How can accuracy, independence and impartiality survive a deliberate attempt by the government to impose upon the Associated Press a requirement that its news editors be union men?"[36] Broun noted that "if the Supreme Court upholds his contention, freedom of the press will be a very scorpion to beat the life out of all social legislation. If Mr. Davis has his way, the newspapers of the nation will become absolutely lawless, since no statute will be able to touch them . . . and the way for any local Hitler to get a start will not be to hang paper but to buy one."[37]

Ernst's brief focused on the necessity of the Wagner Act in light of labor unrest gripping the nation. With employers resisting unionization activities in major industrial plants, the winter of 1936–37 witnessed a massive wave of sit-down strikes. Workers seized a General Motors plant in Flint, Michigan, and held it for six weeks to enforce demands for union recognition. From September 1936 to May 1937, more than 450,000 workers engaged in sit-down strikes that closed plants employing over one million workers.

The United States is "within the throes of a second Civil War," he wrote. "Armed strife continues to rock the nation, leaving in its wake lives lost and property devastated." Must the federal government "wait to intervene until an epidemic of violence and waste has broken out, or may it adopt the technique of preventive medicine and prescribe an industrial vaccine?" He also asked, "Do the words of the Constitution permit Congress to safeguard the free flow of interstate commerce by protecting the rights of employees to organize and bargain collectively . . . or do the words of the Constitution compel Congress to stand by powerless to prevent the waste, suffering, and bloodshed which, experience has shown, will inevitably follow if the workers of the land may not have a forum to guarantee against unlawful interference with those rights?"[38]

Ernst rejected the idea that ordinary labor legislation violated the First Amendment. Far from violating freedom of speech, he argued, the protection of labor's right to organize furthered the circulation of ideas. Conflicts between newspaper employers and employees had threatened to shut down newspaper operations. "They have precipitated newspapers into receiverships; they have caused newspaper plants to be shut down for extensive periods. And it cannot be doubted that interruption of the operations of press associations would seriously affect virtually every newspaper in the land." The state was justified in taking affirmative steps to create the economic and labor conditions that would facilitate freedom of expression, Ernst argued, because "Congress is forbidden to abridge the freedom of the press. It is not commanded to remain inert before an evil [that] threatens . . . to nullify that freedom."[39]

Moreover, the Wagner Act did not prohibit employers from firing reporters who failed in their duties; it only prohibited them from discharging them for their union activities, Ernst pointed out. The AP's argument that Wagner Act impeded objectivity and "integrity of the news" was ludicrous. The Constitution did not guarantee "objectivity of the press," nor was objectivity even possible in a subjective world. "The question really raised by petitioner is not whether news shall be unprejudiced but rather whose prejudices shall color the news," Ernst said. Here he took a crack at the publishers, stating in no uncertain terms that their probusiness bias distorted the news.[40]

Ernst was enormously proud of the brief, believing that it outdid the original "Brandeis brief" in marshaling social facts. He noted to Frankfurter, "Enclosed find our brief in the AP case. You won't like it because it even outdoes the L.D.B. brief in the Oregon case."[41]

* * *

The Ultimate Power was originally intended to be tied in with the 1936 presidential campaign, but when Ernst couldn't complete the manuscript in time, Simon and Schuster dropped it. He went to the publisher Doubleday Doran and got a contract.[42]

Ernst threw himself into Roosevelt's second-term campaign. In the summer of 1936 he joined the American Labor Party (ALP), a New York third party founded that year by the New York State branch of Labor's Nonpartisan League, comprised of liberal Democrats, labor activists, and Socialists who wanted to reelect Roosevelt. Roosevelt had recommended to New Deal labor leaders the formation of a New York labor party as a device for liberals to vote for Roosevelt without stamping themselves with the Tammany Democratic label. The party polled more than 270,000 votes for Roosevelt, and it helped reelect La Guardia as mayor the following year.[43] "We have all been grumbling for years that we wanted a new political lineup. The American Labor Party is IT," Ernst wrote to a friend.[44] Communists soon became central to the ALP, and Ernst would eventually resign in 1940, protesting that the party had been "captured" by Communists.

In January 1937 *The Ultimate Power* was published. Ernst believed it was the best of his works and could become a best seller. He dedicated it to "Heywood Broun, who asked for it."[45] In it he contended:

> The . . . more than three hundred judicial vetoes of state and sixty-seven of congressional legislation are no doubt one of the main causes of our economic depression. The [US Supreme] Court has enforced continued inequality of opportunity among our people and prevented practically every attempt to reduce the miseries of unemployment, old age, disease, and accident. It has put its foot down on industrial nationalism. It does not allow the governmental machinery to be brought up to date, to be in tune with the new industrialism. It compels employers to destroy each other. . . . It condemns the nation to a laissez-faire policy never intended by the vital Founding Fathers.[46]

It was Ernst's main argument that the Supreme Court had "subverted" the Constitution and the intention of the framers, which was to permit federal regulation of economic affairs. The book described the post-Revolutionary "spectacle" of economic disparity and commercial jealousy among the states and argued that the motivating purpose of the framers was to provide security that only uniform regulation of the national economy could ensure, through such provisions as the taxing power, the power to coin money, and the power to regulate interstate and foreign commerce. The protection of civil liberties was only inserted in the Constitution, he claimed, because without it, ratification proved impossible.

The Constitution must be amended "so that Congress has the power to override any decision of the Supreme Court," he argued. Congress should have the power to override a decision on constitutional matters by a two-thirds vote of both houses. This proposal, he alleged, had actually been made by James Madison at the Constitutional Convention. In case both the president and the Supreme Court vetoed an act, a three-fourths vote would be required to override dual vetoes. "This would be real democracy, throwing the question of a law's constitutionality back to the representatives of the people. Then the court would be a real part of our system of checks and balances, for today it is merely a check, without a balance," Ernst asserted. "The frustration of congressional action by judicial interpretation requires Congress to choose between surrender and leadership," he concluded.[47]

Written hastily, based on research conducted by Ernst's family and law associates, the "quickie" book suffered from the usual defects of his works. Although endorsed by Broun, John L. Lewis, and other liberal notables, it was panned in the press. The University of Chicago's law journal attacked its "slapdash style, frequent historical inaccuracies, and coloring of historical detail."[48] "Considered from the point of view of serious scholarship there is little to commend Mr. Ernst's effort," noted the *Harvard Law Review*. "Standing on [a] shaky base he balances inaccuracy on misinterpretation and does it all with the confident gusto of a vaudeville artist."[49] "Mr. Ernst's style is almost as jumbled as one of those scissors and paste opinions of which McReynolds puts out when he's too lazy to sound off in his own words. I've no doubt that Ernst is quite brilliant as a lawyer. . . . But as a writer?" asked a *Scribner's Magazine* writer. "His book sounds as if it were dictated at odd moments between cases or between swimming and late afternoon cocktails at Nantucket."[50]

The *New York Times* review of the book was unforgiving. "Mr. Ernst is a brilliant if somewhat slap-dash and haphazard writer and a crusading lawyer who has been engaged by the administration to defend the Wagner Labor Bill before the Supreme Court," critic John Corbin wrote. Corbin played out in detail many of the embarrassing inaccuracies in the book. "As historian of the era of the Constitutional Convention and interpreter of the thought of the Fathers, Mr. Ernst leaves something to be desired. A few of his many slips will sufficiently warn us against slap-dash brilliancy." Corbin went on,

"Reading the Constitution, [Ernst says,] one will find no mention of the right to habeas corpus. This crusading constitutional lawyer is respectfully referred to Article I, Section 9." Ernst represented James Wilson as opposing, at the Constitutional Convention, the election of the president by the people, yet according to Corbin, the convention's records showed that Wilson was the foremost proponent of popular election. Madison's proposal of a collaboration between the Supreme Court and Congress was explicitly urged to strengthen the Court against Congress.[51] In an unsigned article several days later, the *New York Times* added, "Whether trivial or not, such errors, and there are many of them, show in my judgment a slipshod reading of both the debates in the convention and the instrument as signed and ratified—which instrument Mr. Ernst now proposes to amend fundamentally and drastically. Surely, the greater the scope of the author's work, the more important it is that it should be founded on exact knowledge."[52]

Outraged, Ernst prevailed on the *Times* to publish a correction. "I have read John Corbin's review of my book. . . . I must ask you to correct the probably unintentional but completely false statement made by [Corbin] . . . that I have been engaged by the administration to defend the Wagner Labor Bill before the United States Supreme Court. . . . I make no mention of the equally unfair and inaccurate statements made elsewhere by Mr. Corbin in the review of the book."[53]

Publisher Art Sulzberger personally responded that he was "more unhappy than I can tell you about the whole thing" and ordered the immediate publishing of a correction and apology.[54] The following day a notice appeared in the *Times* stating that the book was not an expression of official New Deal views and that "of four errors of fact cited by the reviewer in his criticism of Mr. Ernst's book, two have to do with matters that appear debatable and two with matters that seem trivial in comparison with the scope of the author's work. Mr. Ernst, by his long and successful record defending freedom of expression, has demonstrated that he would prefer the reader to appraise his book, rather than attempt to influence a critic's pen. However, the *Times*, in fairness to Mr. Ernst, regrets the misstatement of fact."[55]

This gesture meant little; the criticism of his masterpiece was devastating to him. Ernst wrote to friends denouncing the review as a "vicious anti-New Deal article in the book section purporting to be a review." He urged Doubleday to publish an advertisement signed by his prominent friends stating that "we enjoyed the book; we are not bound to the conclusions reached which are controversial but we recommend it to the American public."[56]

Ernst maintained great hopes for the book, believing it could win a Pulitzer Prize. He wrote to his brother George, "I think this is the best job I have ever done. . . . I do hope it goes."[57] Ernst sent a copy to FDR with an accompanying note stating, "I am sending you a copy of the Ultimate Power which you may find of some interest in connection with the infinite number of constitutional amendments which your various lawyer friends are proposing."[58] The book came out just days before FDR announced his court-packing plan.

* * *

On February 5, 1937, FDR shocked the nation when he proposed that the nine-member Supreme Court be expanded. Roosevelt asked Congress to empower him to appoint an additional justice for any justice over seventy years of age who did not retire. The president wanted to appoint as many as six additional justices, which would be plenty, as he had consistently been losing by a 5–4 margin. He justified this request by saying that a shortage of judges had caused federal dockets to become congested, creating delays for litigants.

Roosevelt's message touched off intense debate. The president was said to have been surprised by the strength of the opposition to court packing. For 168 days the controversy dominated headlines. Roosevelt's foes likened him to Hitler, Mussolini, and Stalin.[59]

Ernst disliked the plan, which he felt failed to do the president justice because of its deceptiveness about its obvious motivations.[60] "It is only temporary relief," he told the press.[61] Ernst and other like-minded New Dealers set to work behind the scenes to get a substitute proposal accepted. FDR was shocked when friends who could be counted on joined the opposition's ranks.[62] Ernst continued to advocate his proposed "Madison amendment." Eventually he came around and defended Roosevelt's plan. "We can't wait for an amendment. Let's go forward with the president," he said in lectures and speeches.[63] "We are either going to get out of this mess by a change in the court or with machine guns on street corners." He was hissed and booed.[64]

* * *

The Associated Press case came up before the Supreme Court on February 9, 1937. It was one of five Wagner Act cases heard that day.[65] Ernst was determined to argue the case, even though the Newspaper Guild was only amicus curiae and technically not a party. He had petitioned the Department of Justice to make the argument. The issue was not resolved before the day of the hearing, and Ernst appeared at the Court with Solicitor General Stanley Reed. He took the podium to plead for twenty minutes to speak for the guild as the "real party of interest" in the case. "The working people of the country will never really understand why they are denied an opportunity to be heard in the Supreme Court," he protested.[66]

Chief Justice Charles Evans Hughes, taken by surprise, hesitated for several seconds, his face reddening. He concluded that the Court would not object if the government gave Ernst some of its time. When Reed declined, Ernst bowed and sat down.[67] Many observers thought Ernst would have done as well as the government's lawyers. Noted one news report, Ernst "had to chafe at the sidelines like a spectator, feeling that the government's legal representatives were passing up points they should have scored."[68]

In the long weeks of waiting for the Supreme Court's decision, Justice Owen Roberts unexpectedly switched his position on the New Deal. In a 5–4 decision in *West Coast Hotel Company v. Parrish* in March 1937, the Court validated a Washington state minimum wage law. This "switch in time" would save the New Deal and the Supreme Court. The court-packing debate was now moot, and in July 1937, the US Senate tabled the proposal for good.

* * *

In a Supreme Court opinion by Justices Roberts, Hughes, Brandeis, Cardozo, and Stone, issued in April 1937, a majority declared that the Associated Press had engaged in unfair labor practices affecting interstate commerce and upheld the constitutionality of the Wagner Act. To the AP's contention that editorial employees were not engaged in interstate commerce, the majority replied that it was obvious that the AP's operations involved the constant use of channels of interstate and foreign communication and that strikes would have a direct effect on its activities. It proceeded to dismiss the AP's First Amendment argument:

> The business of the Associated Press is not immune from regulation because it is an agency of the press. The publisher of a newspaper has no special immunity from the application of general laws. . . . The regulation here in question has no relation whatever to the impartial distribution of news. . . . [The Associated Press] is free at any time to discharge Watson or any editorial employee who fails to comply with the policies it may adopt.[69]

The Supreme Court also upheld the Wagner Act in 5–4 opinions in the other four cases. In each, the majority declared that if labor disputes interrupted the free flow of the products of manufacturing in interstate commerce, then Congress had the power to pass and enforce legislation to end labor disputes. The Court that had held in 1936 that coal mining did not constitute interstate commerce now read the Constitution so broadly that it justified intervention by the federal government in the labor practices of one Virginia clothing factory. Nearly every lawyer agreed that in one afternoon, the interstate commerce clause had been entirely rewritten.[70]

After the decision came down, Ernst had a drink at the Carleton Hotel in Washington, DC, with John Davis. "This casual and pleasant meeting was interpreted by the Communist leaders who had infiltrated the Guild as a betrayal of my client," Ernst later recalled.[71] As Ernst put it, the Communists had "captured" major parts of the

Newspaper Guild.[72] Shortly after, Ernst withdrew as Newspaper Guild counsel.[73]

* * *

The ACLU Board of Directors, with its traditional antistatism, had opposed the Wagner Act, describing it as a "dangerous fascist intrusion by the government into unions." On the board, only Art Hays and Ernst were in favor of the act. Hays admitted that the ACLU had usually taken the position that government power resulted in the denial of workers' rights but that the Wagner Act gave labor opportunities to protect its rights.[74] Ernst said he knew of no procedures other than those contained in the bill "by which labor may be aided in its battle for organization in order to develop a strength which may possibly defeat fascistic movements."[75] They convinced the board to poll the National Committee and the ACLU affiliates, which supported the measure.[76] The ACLU ultimately went on record in support of the act.[77] The Wagner Act transformed the ACLU's work. Recalled Roger Baldwin, "no single decision in my experience more largely affected civil liberties in the one major area where they had been most grossly violated." The struggle for the rights of labor "was almost overnight changed from local violence and repression to the conference table."[78]

Baldwin, who had initially worried about the increasing power of government under the New Deal, had come around to seeing the usefulness of working with the Roosevelt administration.[79] In part through Ernst's connections, the ACLU had won many friends in Washington. Many active members of the ACLU held high office in the administration. Felix Frankfurter was appointed to the Supreme Court in 1939, Adolf Berle was with the State Department, and Harold Ickes headed the Interior Department. "They were civil liberty minded; they were for the most part our friends, many of them former or present members of the Union," Baldwin recalled. "Access to the president was simple; his secretaries were of our persuasion. . . . We basked in the light of understanding as never before."[80]

Indeed, the two years after Roosevelt's reelection saw rapid implementation of many of the ACLU's goals.[81] Congress defeated every gag bill before it.[82] No new prosecutions for opinion under the sedition or criminal syndicalism laws were instituted, and the number of political prisoners declined. Radical aliens were permitted to enter the country. Mob violence, use of troops against strikers, and vigilantism were rare.[83] In *Herndon v. Lowry* (1937), a case involving a black Communist organizer in Georgia punished under an old statute forbidding "insurrection," the Supreme Court at last accepted the speech-protective "clear and present danger" standard as the First Amendment rule. *DeJonge v. Oregon* (1937), jointly defended by the ACLU and the International Labor Defense, invalidated the conviction of Communist organizers under a criminal syndicalism law for holding political meetings. In *Palko v. Connecticut* (1937), Justice Cardozo stated that Americans had a handful of fundamental rights that were the very essence of a "scheme of ordered liberty," including freedom of speech and press. The Court announced that laws that impinged on freedom of expression would be reviewed with heightened scrutiny by the courts; with a "thumb on the scale" for speech.[84] Writes one historian of the ACLU, "ideas that [the ACLU] had championed virtually alone in 1920 were now established law and public policy."[85]

The new, more liberal social, legal, and political climate was attributed to a degree of economic recovery, the FDR administration, the diverse New Deal coalition, the rise of fascism in Europe, and the steady influence of the ACLU, which increased the public's commitment to democracy and personal freedom as American ideals.[86] "Faith and hope burned more brightly than it had in many years," observed ACLU secretary Lucille Milner. "The Bill of Rights was now the concern of the United States government and the impact of that was felt right down the line to the most insignificant sheriff in the smallest county."[87] Civil liberties were becoming mainstream. In Baldwin's words, "We were making hay in the New Deal sun."[88]

15

THE CHAMPION OF FREEDOM

> I cannot help feeling that liberty is not any one big thing but is a combination of little freedoms which have to be fought for day by day.[1]

Despite his many involvements in New Deal politics, Morris Ernst remained active in the birth control movement. Ernst assumed the position of chief counsel for Margaret Sanger's American Birth Control League in 1934. He continued to seek test cases, confident that the courts would "nullify" the Comstock laws to the point of irrelevance.[2] Sanger meanwhile focused on legislative change, establishing the National Committee on Federal Legislation for Birth Control in 1930 to lobby Congress to amend the Comstock laws. "Margaret, don't try to change the law, get it reinterpreted," Ernst advised her.[3]

Developments in the early 1930s convinced Ernst that "judicial nullification" of the Comstock laws was close at hand. Judge John Woolsey's 1931 decision in the *Contraception* book case limited the Tariff Act's prohibition on importing information about contraception. Another important decision, *Youngs Rubber Corporation v. C. I. Lee, Inc.* (1930), involved the distribution of contraceptives through the mails. In that case, a manufacturer of condoms tried to enjoin a competitor who had stolen the firm's trademark. The injunction was denied in the lower federal court because the mailing of condoms was said to be banned by the Comstock law—it was illegal to send articles "intended for preventing conception." But the Second Circuit Court of Appeals granted the injunction, concluding that condoms did not fall under the Comstock law's proscriptions because they were used for the prevention of disease as well as for birth control. The court held that for an article to come under the ban, it must be exclusively intended for the prevention of birth, and that if it had any other lawful purpose, it could be sent through the mails, at least to doctors and their agents.[4]

Sanger often ordered contraceptive devices and literature from other countries for use and testing at her clinic. In the fall of 1931, Dr. Sakae Koyama of Osaka, Japan, sent Sanger a *pessary*, or diaphragm, made of soft rubber in a cone shape, which he marketed as the Koyama Suction Pessary. Sanger asked for additional pessaries to test on women at her clinic.[5]

Customs officials promptly seized Koyama's shipment. Ernst contacted the Customs Bureau and had the devices returned to Japan. He knew he would have a hard time contesting the seizure with Sanger, a person with no medical degree, as the recipient of the package. Sanger later arranged for more of Koyama's pessaries to be sent to clinic doctor Hannah Stone. In January 1933, the customs office informed Stone that it had detained the devices under Section 305 of the Tariff Act.[6]

Sanger asked Ernst if he would defend the clinic. Alexander Lindey advised Sanger's secretary Florence Rose that the firm of Greenbaum, Wolff, and Ernst would be happy to do so and that they had a good chance of winning, based on *Youngs v. Lee*. "The Circuit Court of the United States for the Second Circuit gave legal recognition to the fact that a condom was entitled to the facilities of the United States mails because it could be used for a legal purpose as well as an illegal one. The Customs authorities have consistently refused to accept this view. We feel confident that if the issue were tested out in the courts our contention would prevail. The Clinic may desire to make this a test case, as a victory may tear the Tariff Act wide open," Lindey wrote.[7] Sanger secured a promise from Ethel Clyde, a devoted wealthy supporter, to pay Ernst's legal fees.[8]

The case was heard by Judge Grover Moscowitz in the federal district court in 1935. The government argued that *Youngs v. Lee* was inapplicable and that the prohibitions of the Tariff Act were absolute.[9] Ernst countered that a reasonable construction of the Tariff Act exempted shipments intended for lawful use, and he cited recent cases requiring the government to prove that contraceptives were imported for an illicit use and not a health use. He told the judge that "what I am concerned with, in addition to the proper course of jurisprudence, is the horrible effect on the medical profession in case you fail to hold that the government must so plead. In other words, if the government does not have to plead the intended illegal use, then every doctor is at the mercy [of the law] every time he uses one of these articles."[10]

Ernst called prominent doctors to testify that they prescribed contraception for the lawful purpose of keeping mothers healthy and free from disease. Gynecologist Frederick Holden testified that he advocated birth control for women who suffered health problems. Neurologist Foster Kennedy and clinic doctor Hannah Stone followed with similar statements.[11] The government's one witness was an eminent surgeon, Frederic Wolcott Bancroft. His testimony actually supported Ernst's case. Bancroft admitted that he prescribed diaphragms to address medical conditions and that he endorsed child spacing for health reasons. Florence Rose noted that Bancroft was "so helpful to our side that one wondered whose witness he really was!!"[12]

"This is an unusual case," Ernst summarized in his closing argument:

> It is the people of the United States against a little bit of an object. . . . It is the people of the United States against this box. It is not against a human being, but that doesn't mean it is not punitive because if the government wins, this is destroyed. . . . .The defense of this article . . . is far more important than the defense of any human being because there is not any human being in the world who can relieve as much misery and add as much to the health of the population as this article.[13]

In his groundbreaking decision, Judge Moscowitz issued another victory for the birth control movement. He agreed that the language in question in the Tariff Act could not be taken literally but must be given "reasonable construction." Since the confiscated articles were imported for "experimental purposes to determine their reliability and usefulness as contraceptives to cure or prevent disease, a lawful purpose, it must be held that the . . . articles do not come within the condemnation of the statute." Further, "Taken literally, the language of the statute would seem to forbid the importation of any article for the prevention of conception, even though the article might be capable of legitimate uses and the importer intended that it would be so used. Such a construction would prevent the importation by physicians of any article for the prevention of conception even though the physician desires to use it for the purpose of saving a human life. As the Circuit Court of Appeals said in *Youngs Rubber* . . . the intention to prevent such a proper medical use 'is not lightly to be ascribed to Congress.'"[14]

The government appealed the decision. In the fall of 1936, the case came before the Second Circuit Court of Appeals. In preparing for the appeal, Ernst worked with Harriet Pilpel, one of the firm's first female associates. A Jewish Vassar graduate who was married and had two children, Pilpel joined Greenbaum, Wolff, and Ernst after graduating from Columbia Law School. After reading about Ernst in the papers, Pilpel was set on working for his firm. Ernst prided himself on his willingness to hire women lawyers. "Because most lawyers won't hire women, we get the cream of the crop," he recalled. "But one thing I insist on—they have to stay feminine! As soon as they start dressing like me, they're fired. A lawyer has to learn to strut his stuff—and that goes double for women!"[15] Under Ernst's mentorship, Pilpel would become one of the most important lawyers in the birth control movement.

The *One Package* case was argued before a familiar lineup: Judges Learned Hand, Augustus Hand, and Thomas Swan. Ernst's brief mobilized medical and sociological evidence to demonstrate the necessity of birth control for health reasons. Ernst maintained that the history of the statute demonstrated that it was passed to prevent the spread of immorality and was never meant to apply to articles used by physicians in legitimate practice.

The appellate court upheld the ruling. Augustus Hand characterized all the federal prohibitions that originated from the Comstock Act as "part of a continuous scheme to suppress immoral articles and obscene literature and should so far as possible be construed together and consistently. If this is done, the articles here in question ought not to be forfeited when not intended for an immoral purpose." Relying on *Youngs Rubber*, Hand wrote that the design of the Comstock Act was "not to prevent the importation, sale, or carriage by mail of things which might intelligently be employed by conscientious and competent physicians for the purpose of saving life or promoting the well-being of their patients."[16]

Ernst and Pilpel called Hand's opinion the medical profession's "Bill of Rights" in the field of birth control. "The Court's decision marks the successful termination of a 60-year-struggle to make clear that the federal obscenity laws do not apply to the legitimate activities of physicians," they wrote in the *Journal of Contraception*.[17] Ernst noted that "nowhere in its opinion did the Court specifically state under what circumstances a doctor was free to prescribe a contraceptive. The inference was clear that the medical profession was to be sole judge of the propriety of a prescription in a given case, and that as long as a physician exercised his discretion in good faith the legality of his action was not to be questioned."[18]

The attorney general announced in January 1937 that he would not appeal the case to the Supreme Court. The Customs Office then sent out a circular stating that in light of the decision, imported contraceptive devices would not be detained if the consignee was a reputable physician and the devices were to be used to protect the health of patients. The Post Office Department promulgated a similar ruling.[19] Ernst concluded that "for all practical purposes, federal statutes do not bar from the mails or interstate shipment or importation . . . any contraceptive articles or literature intended for lawful medical use."[20] Ernst believed that the state courts, though not legally bound to do so, could be expected to follow the lead of the federal government. Indeed, the Comstock laws remained on the books, but officials and courts in most states, except Connecticut and Massachusetts, did not enforce them. The *Columbia Law Review* observed that "it is difficult to escape the conclusion that the Comstock Act . . . has been almost emasculated by judicial nullification."[21]

Sanger told supporters triumphantly that "the birth control movement is *free*" and shut down her lobbying organization. "You must know how I feel about you . . . you are a 'swell guy' and we all love you," she wrote to Ernst.[22] She dedicated her 1937 volume on birth control "to Morris L. Ernst, who more than any one man has fought successfully for clarification of the laws on birth control in the United States."[23]

* * *

By that time, "fear of sex was on the wane," as Ernst put it. The activities of John Sumner and the New York Society for the Suppression of Vice had practically ceased.[24] Belatedly, the sexual revolution of the 1920s was being incorporated into the law. After *Ulysses*, Ernst's law firm and the ACLU's National Council on Freedom from Censorship (NCFC) dealt with few book censorship cases. One of Ernst's last literary censorship cases against the NYSSV involved Gustave Flaubert's novel *November*, seized by Sumner in 1935. Ernst represented Herman Miller, the bookseller. Citing the decisions in the *Casanova's Homecoming*, *Well of Loneliness*, *Sex Side of Life*, and *Married Love* cases, Ernst's brief pointed out "that in recent years there has not been a single instance where a book, openly dealt with by the book trade, and generally accepted by the press, literary critics, the reading public, and the community at large . . . was ultimately condemned by the courts." The court threw out Sumner's suit.[25]

The NCFC remained active in its work against censorship, especially in film and theater, which had become the main battlegrounds of the censorship fight. Greenbaum, Wolff, and Ernst, effectively the law firm for the NCFC, was one of the premiere anticensorship organizations in the nation. Alexander Lindey, in particular, was a major force in the movement, doing pioneering work for which he received almost no credit. Lindey authored most of a well-reviewed book on censorship titled *The Censor Marches On* (1940), which bore both Ernst's and Lindey's names. Lindey and Pilpel consulted Ernst for advice on censorship cases they worked on, and Ernst was occasionally called in to argue cases on appeal. Ernst and Lindey successfully argued several cases involving newsdealers and authors arrested for publishing and selling nudist magazines.[26] Ernst represented New York burlesque houses in their efforts against the city's commissioner of licenses, Paul Moss, who suspended the licenses of several theaters for "obscene" performances, and was also involved in the continuing battle against the Post Office Department, lobbying for the defeat of a proposed postal censorship bill that would have rendered not only senders but recipients of purportedly obscene materials subject to prosecution.[27]

One of the last major censorship cases in which Ernst was directly involved concerned the public health film *The Birth of a Baby*. The forward-looking quasi documentary, which featured images of a live childbirth, had been produced in 1938 under the auspices of several medical organizations, including the American Association of Obstetricians, Gynecologists, and Abdominal Surgeons, and the Children's Bureau of the U.S. Department of Labor. An issue of *Life* magazine was banned across the country for publishing still photographs from the film. Pressured by Roman Catholic groups, several states and municipalities declared the movie and *Life*'s pictures of it to be obscene. In Bronx County, the district attorney confiscated the magazines, and obscenity charges were made against three newsdealers who sold it.[28]

Recalled Ernst, "I looked at the defendants. I found three newsdealers, arrested without warning, pounced on by police." As he saw it, "Here was the battle line—a great religious army versus three impecunious newsboys. . . . I became interested in the 'three boys.' None of them had seen the magazine before it was dumped from a delivery truck on their stands. If they had read the issue they would have been unable to test the legality of the pictures. And above all, it was absurd to think that these boys could afford to engage counsel."[29] Ernst went to the office of *Life* and met with managing editor Roy Larsen, who agreed to submit to arrest and trial in a test case. Larsen sold a copy of *Life* to a detective, and the following day a complaint was filed against him for violating Section 1141 of the Penal Code.[30]

Ernst presented the case in the Court of Special Sessions, using the testimony of twenty-one experts in medicine, education, religion, and social welfare. The witnesses described the pictures from the film as "valuable, constructive, dignified, and decent," asserting that the photographs would "allay fears of expectant parents and help disperse ignorance."[31] Ernst asserted that objections to the photos came from "petty people who worry about dirt but not about death."[32]

In a unanimous decision, the three judges ruled that the pictures were not indecent. It was the court's opinion that "the picture story, because of the manner in which it was presented, does not fall within the forbidden class. . . . There is no nudity or unnecessary disclosure. The subject has been treated with delicacy." The court concluded, "Conceptions of what is decent or indecent are not constant. . . . Recent cases illustrate the caution with which courts have proceeded in this branch of the law to avoid interference with a justifiable freedom of expression," citing Ernst's cases, including *Ulysses*.[33]

Ernst hailed the decision. "This means there will be no more of this nonsense in this country where petty police chiefs set themselves up as censors of the nation's reading."[34]

* * *

With obscenity prosecutions on the decline, Ernst represented the book industry in other matters. Doubleday Doran, the nation's largest mail-order bookdealer, was publisher of Ernst's books. In 1935, Ernst brought suit on behalf of Doubleday Doran against Macy's for price-cutting on Doubleday books. Macy's practiced "loss leader" selling, luring general customers through their doors by selling books far below the regular retail price in the hope that customers would continue shopping and buy additional items in the store at full price. Doubleday sought an injunction under the Feld-Crawford Fair Trade Act, recently passed by the New York Legislature, which permitted the manufacturer of a trademarked article to fix the resale price of its product.[35]

Macy's challenged the law's constitutionality. Its lawyer argued that Macy's was being deprived of property without due process of law. Ernst cited his idol Louis Brandeis in his briefs. Ernst argued, "It is essential to the sound economic life of the nation that there be competition not only for the purpose of curbing excessive prices but also to encourage individual effort, ingenuity, and initiative. By killing off competition, price cutting may have the effect of converting us from a nation of alert resourceful independent businessman to a nation of subservient clerks. This is not an exaggerated view; it was adverted to many years ago by Justice Brandeis."[36] The New York Court of Appeals held that the Fair Trade Act was unconstitutional as an unauthorized restriction upon the disposition of one's own property.[37] In 1937, however, the law was upheld when the Court of Appeals reviewed it in light of recent Supreme Court rulings.

Ernst was a great supporter of the book trade, arguing that book publishing and selling constituted "the most important industry in America." Unlike the biased and highly partisan press, he believed, books were the real venue for freedom of expression "because books are the only medium through which liberal thought can be spread." Radio, as a "matter of mathematics," must have some measure of government censorship. "We can't hope for a free press from newspapers, whose vast aggregations of capital necessarily influence their policies."[38]

Chatting one evening with Nelson Doubleday, Ernst came up with an idea that would not only increase the "marketplace of ideas" through the publication and circulation of books but also accrue to his friend Doubleday's fortunes. At the time, books were charged the same postal rate as first-class mail. Newspapers and periodicals could be sent for a second-class rate. Ernst believed he had a good argument to lobby for the extension of second-class postal rates to books and that he could convince his friends in the administration to support the measure.

Ernst assigned the research to Pilpel, who found that the president had the power to modify book postage rates by proclamation. Ernst dashed off a letter to Roosevelt.[39] It read, "I am sending you two presents with no request for a commitment as to which you enjoy most. In the package you will find three Holy Bibles weighing about five pounds. If you mail those to some spiritually needy person on the [West] Coast, it will cost you sixty-five cents. You will also find in the package twelve spicy magazines. If [the Postmaster

FIGURE 3. Morris Ernst (*center, holding out closed book*) defends Gustave Flaubert's novel *November* in 1935. Courtesy of Harry Ransom Center, University of Texas at Austin.

General] lets these go through the mails, it will cost you eight cents to mail them to some other spiritually needy friend."[40] He argued that the discrimination against books had been responsible for the lowest ratio of book reading to literacy of any country in the world.[41]

On October 31, 1938, at a ceremony at which Ernst had brought representatives of adult educational groups, librarians, and outstanding authors, the president signed a proclamation to make charges for the mailing of books the same as that for magazines and newspapers.[42] While signing the proclamation, Roosevelt announced, "The more they burn books in Germany, the cheaper we should make them here."[43] The following spring Ernst wrote to FDR, "The first great fruits of the Postal Rate proclamation are coming to life. Your order is responsible for the vast social change in the distribution of books. Rental libraries by mail are being established. People will be able to get any book for no more than twenty cents a week and no matter where they are located in the United States. . . . Historically this may prove more important to the life and culture of America than even an agency such as the S.E.C. which deals with money instead of ideas."[44]

The rate reduction was for an experimental period of one year. In July 1939 Roosevelt signed a new proclamation extending the rate for two years.[45] Later he told Ernst, "You had better not rely on the whim of a President. Go to Congress for statutory relief." Senator James Mead of New York sponsored a bill, and Ernst and Pilpel created an organization, the National Committee to Abolish Postal Discrimination Against Books, to lobby for it. The law was passed in June 1942, and ever since, books have been mailed at second-class rates.[46]

16
THE NATIONAL LAWYERS GUILD

From the start of his career, Morris Ernst had been an outspoken critic of the legal profession. He became progressively disenchanted as opportunities for lawyers declined during the Great Depression, and conservative lawyers did everything in their power to block the New Deal.

A legal realist, Ernst rejected the notion that there was anything rational, logical, or scientific about or judging or the practice of law. "The law is nothing more or less than the pressure of public opinion at any particular time on particular judges," he would often remark. "There is only one way I know of by which a judge can act, and that is to make up his own mind on the basis of what his nurse or his mother told him, and on his economic background and prejudices, and come to his own conclusion, and then he goes to the old law books of 1878 or 1802 in order to justify the conclusion which he has reached in his prior thinking."[1] "The decisions of the courts have nothing to do with justice," he said. "They are merely the interpretations of the individual prejudices of the individual judges."[2]

Litigation was a "game," a "matching of wits" that had "very little to do with" rightness or justice, Ernst believed. He attacked "stuffed shirt" lawyers who fought for corporate interests at the expense of the public good, damning their self-interest, hypocrisy, and efforts to bolster their status by "mystifying" the public. "When the lawyers want to bewilder the public they bring in 'certiorari' and 'demurrer' and similar words," he complained. "Lawyers rely heavily on gobbledygook, and . . . no attempt has been made by the bar to bridge the legal profession and the non-lawyers of our society."[3]

Ernst had long been opposed to the American Bar Association, with its elitism, racism, conservatism, and concern with property rights over civil rights. A sort of social club for white gentleman lawyers, most of its members were affiliated with the corporate bar. The ABA had attacked the growth of administrative law and consistently opposed New Deal programs. It was notoriously indifferent to social and economic realities of the time and rejected the idea that law should be a pragmatic tool to address social problems.

"The legal profession is a vast army, retained in the main by those who have wealth to resist any social change," Ernst told an audience of the New York County Lawyers Association in 1934. "The rights of minorities and the interests of those of smaller wealth are of little value, if each pauper has to plead his own case through his own attorney."[4] In a skit at the annual dinner of the New York Bar Association in 1936, he pretended to enact a telephone conversation between John W. Davis and a potential client. "No, I'm sorry but I can't take your case," Davis said, according to Ernst's hilarious take-off. "No, I can't do anything about it. You'd better see Leibowitz at the Civil Liberties Union, he might do something for you. . . . Oh well, that's different. Why didn't you tell me you had robbed a bank? I thought you had only robbed a grocery store. Come right over."[5]

* * *

During the Depression, many lawyers were unable to support themselves. Solo practitioners and those in small partnerships had resorted to driving cabs and working in the subway to make ends meet. These conditions prompted the formation of an organization called the Lawyers' Security League. The league lobbied the Works Progress Administration to create public employment opportunities for lawyers. At the same time, a group of progressive lawyers were trying to bring together attorneys who were defending unpopular causes and encountering ostracism for doing so. A Detroit lawyer named Maurice Sugar, later counsel for the United Auto Workers, had visited New York in 1935 to meet with lawyers, some affiliated with the Communist Party, to discuss the formation of a national organization that would provide "support to lawyers subject to oppression in the pursuit of their labor, progressive, and liberal activities."[6]

In the fall of 1936, leaders of the Lawyers' Security League heard about a speech Ernst had given expressing interest in creating a "democratic, socially-conscious lawyers guild."[7] For years, Ernst had wanted to unify progressive lawyers in a force that could counter the American Bar Association (ABA).[8] Representatives of the league subsequently conferred with Ernst. Mortimer Riemer, a Communist Party member, and a few of his friends gathered at Ernst's house, and they agreed to ask the league to end its plans for a proposed conference in favor of a meeting Ernst would arrange with prominent New Dealers. Ernst convinced them that an organization that could pose a meaningful challenge to the ABA needed to attract well-known liberals who might not be concerned with public employment for lawyers but were interested in civil liberties and labor legislation.[9]

Ernst sent an appeal to well-placed friends, asking them to join the new organization. "A Call to American Lawyers" pulled no punches. "In recent times . . . certain groups within the legal profession have done much to block progress and to befuddle the legislative processes," read the invitation. "The profession has become popularly characterized by that minority proportion of its membership which has consistently taken a hostile stand towards proposals and legislation of a forward-looking character. The position of that minority on such vital issues as child labor, reasonable business regulation, security, and labor legislation is too well known to require comment. Its concern for liberty has been secondary to its concern for property." It suggested that the group discuss the formation of an organization of "a national association of American lawyers which will be a truly progressive force in the life of the nation."[10]

Twenty-five lawyers met at the City Club on December 1, 1936, to discuss the new association. The meeting brought together attorneys from a variety of backgrounds. Many New Dealers were present, including Jerome Frank; Henry T. Hunt, general counsel for the Public Works Administration; and noted progressive lawyer Frank P. Walsh, chairman of the New York Power Commission, who was elected president of the group. There were also young, radical lawyers who were interested in broader issues of free speech, labor rights, opposition to rising fascism in Germany, Italy and Spain, and generally pushing the Roosevelt program to the left.[11] Shortly after, Walsh announced to the press the new organization, the National Lawyers Guild. The guild seeks to be a "progressive force in the life of the nation," he said. "We are living in a time of great economic distress. The civil rights of the American people are under widespread attack. Never before has the need been greater for genuinely true leadership."[12] Temporary headquarters were established in Ernst's office. Within two weeks, chapters had been organized in several cities, and more than 2,500 lawyers expressed interest.[13] Riemer was chosen national secretary, and he became the connection between Ernst and the radicals.[14]

In late December Riemer and Ernst traveled to Washington, DC, in an effort to enlist influential government lawyers in the National Lawyers Guild. Ernst sought the endorsement of the president himself. "My dear Governor," he wrote in January 1937, "The National Lawyers' Guild is well underway with Frank Walsh as President. . . . This is the first national answer to the Liberty League and the ABA. . . . If you take the resolutions of the ABA for a decade and put them in reverse, you will come fairly close to the program which the NLG will . . . promulgate."[15] He visited the White House in early February and asked Roosevelt to open the upcoming national convention, suggesting that the president "might want to use this occasion in respect to the Constitutional fight."[16] After the Supreme Court expansion proposal emerged, Roosevelt's secretary Stephen Early informed Ernst of the president's feeling "that it is best for him to hold himself completely apart from any organization or any efforts on the part of organizations which have to do with the judicial reform plan which he has submitted to the Congress. This does not, of course, indicate any lack of interest whatever in the purpose of the Lawyers' Guild. On the contrary, I can assure you that the President is interested in and is appreciative of the Guild for support and assistance."[17]

On February 19, 1937, more than six hundred lawyers from around the country met in the Rose Room of the old Hotel Washington in the capital for the founding convention of the National Lawyers Guild. In a welcoming letter to the group, Roosevelt said, "It is a time for progressive thinking, and I have every confidence that your deliberations will affect the welfare of your own profession and the well-being of the country at large."[18] The convention approved Roosevelt's judiciary program as the only proposal "immediately available to make possible progressive legislation now imperatively needed."[19] It endorsed, in addition, a constitutional amendment to restrict judicial review, the Child Labor Amendment, wider employment opportunities for lawyers, antilynching legislation, more public defenders, and a new code of legal ethics acknowledging the responsibilities of the lawyer to society. The first elected president of the guild was John Devaney, chief justice of the Minnesota Supreme Court. Key speakers included assistant Attorney General Robert Jackson, a guild member who denounced the ABA for its resistance to the New Deal. The executive board, "a who's who of liberalism in Washington," included eminent New Deal lawyers and judges, as well as counsel of the American Federation of Labor, chief litigator of the NAACP, and prominent lawyers for the ACLU.[20]

The guild faced difficulties from the start. One problem was that many of its members, coming from the nonelite sectors of the profession, were unable to pay their dues. The organization was also torn apart by politics. When four hundred New York lawyers convened to launch a local chapter, the result was described in the *New York Times* as "an uproar." A slate of officers suggested by Ernst and Walsh was rejected with protests that the guild was not to be "steamrollered" in the manner of the American Bar Association.[21] Paul J. Kern, a twenty-nine-year-old political assistant to New York Mayor Fiorello La Guardia, was elected president of the chapter. In Washington, Thomas Emerson, assistant general counsel to the Social Security Board, representing a new wave of radical activist lawyers, was elected over Henry Hunt, a well-known but aging civil liberties lawyer. The guild's volatility and the presence of radicals in the leadership concerned Ernst, who feared that the organization would not present an appealing image to the thousands of liberal lawyers he wanted to attract.[22]

Before long, Ernst was complaining about the obstructive tactics of "extremists" in the leadership. This dissatisfaction crested with the controversy over the Roosevelt administration's policy on the

Spanish Civil War.[23] In November 1937 leftists on the guild's Committee on International Relations compiled a report criticizing Roosevelt for his implementation of a boycott on arms sales to the loyalists fighting the fascists in Spain. The report was printed in the NLG's publication, the *National Lawyers Guild Quarterly*. Ernst felt the report was beyond the legitimate concerns of the guild and insisted that the controversial report would only "confirm the opinion entertained by many that the Guild is a small body of left-wing lawyers, not representative even of the liberal part of the American bar."[24] Like many liberals in 1937, Ernst did not favor American involvement in emerging European conflicts. He wrote to several guild leaders expressing fears that the antiadministration position would cause loss of membership and support. Ernst then circulated a statement signed by thirteen NLG leaders to counteract the negative publicity that he believed had been brought about by the report. "It would be inimical to the future usefulness of the Guild," his statement said, "if a pseudo-legal report—one purporting to be dealing with legal issues but in fact based on considerations of policy—were to be sponsored or endorsed by the Guild."[25]

Ernst blamed the report on the organization's relatively small but vocal Communist-oriented minority. He wrote to Riemer, "Dear Morty, I am tremendously shocked and embarrassed at the way in which the Spanish report appears in the National Lawyers' Guild Quarterly. I thought it was distinctly understood that it was inadvisable for chapters to take any position on international affairs. The headnote encourages them to do so. How in hell can we build up a national organization if chapters are to act even on international affairs? You will wreck the organization by such strategy."[26]

Ernst considered withdrawing from the NLG for as long as "the present Riemer policies" prevailed. "I hope you agree with me," he wrote to Thurman Arnold, "that the Lawyers' Guild should be concerned with clearing up problems that affect American lawyers before they start curing China, Japan, Roumania, and Spain."[27] Indeed, he found that when the guild sought to increase membership among government lawyers, it was confronted with "allegations of radicalism within the ranks of the Guild." The guild's active Communist or Communist-inclined minority was mentioned as a deterrent to potential joiners. Ernst despaired that Communists, "posing as liberals," were "taking over control of the important offices" and giving the group "a *Daily Worker* tone."[28] Quietly, he vowed to take action to diminish their influence.

"We were asleep. I was chiefly at fault. The Communists sneaked in, never saying 'Here we are—the Commies,'" he recalled. "Their tactics of wreck or rule became evident after the first convention. . . . All too late we saw what was happening. A lawyers' guild—dealing, we thought, with problems of our craft—was being converted into a mouthpiece for American Communists."[29]

* * *

Similar tensions were playing out in the ACLU. Libertarian liberals on the board, including Ernst, Art Hays, and John Haynes Holmes, opposed a left-wing, prolabor faction led by Elizabeth Gurley Flynn, a Communist Party member, and "fellow travelers" Harry Ward, Mary Van Kleeck, Nathan Greene, Robert Dunn, and Abraham Isserman, who seemed to decide civil liberties issues with a mind toward what was best for labor.[30] The rift was brought into the open with the 1938 controversy over Henry Ford.

The United Auto Workers of America, emboldened by the passage of the Wagner Act, targeted the Ford Motor Company for its unionization drive. Henry Ford was an unabashed foe of organized labor. Ford fought a vicious campaign against the UAW that involved, in part, issuing pamphlets and public statements designed to discourage workers from voting in favor of union representation. In February 1938, the National Labor Relations Board issued an order requiring the Ford Motor Company to cease those activities. The ACLU's committee on the rights of labor endorsed the NLRB's order on the ground that any speech directed by an employer to an employee implied the threat of coercion and was beyond the protections of free speech.[31]

This endorsement set off a major dispute on the ACLU Board of Directors. To Ernst, Hays, and other ACLU libertarians, the NLRB's actions clearly violated Ford's freedom of speech. The labor-oriented minority argued that labor's rights had been consistently abridged by employers and that Ford's opinions on unionism would deter union organizing. The libertarians contended that an injunction was unconstitutional unless Ford's speech was followed by actions.[32] Hays wrote a memo suggesting that the ACLU would defend "the expression of [employers'] opinion which does not amount to a direct threat or an act of coercion."[33] At a special meeting at Ernst's home, the board adopted Hays's proposal.[34] Ernst was "strongly in favor of the Hays statement" but was reluctant to attack the NLRB and believed the ACLU should not have gotten into the issue in the first place.[35]

Roger Baldwin considered the Ford incident "the greatest controversy we have had ever of free speech in the organization."[36] The divisions escalated into bitter feuds, and after the incident the board had difficulty functioning. "The Union had never intended upon conformity to any particular conception of free speech. But now the question—not so much of what we should do but of what we believed—was raised continually," Hays recalled.[37]

The Ford controversy seemed to confirm the libertarians' concern that the prolabor faction was subordinating the cause of civil liberties to the agendas of its friends on the far left. In Holmes's assessment, "we [the ACLU] are allowing ourselves to become mere advocates of the rights of labor to the denial of those rights as exercised by those who are against labor. . . . More reluctantly than I dare confess, I find myself believing that our enemies have good reason for charging us with being partisan in the labor struggle, and using the civil liberties principle as a means of fighting labor's battles and the cause of radicalism generally."[38] Ernst himself had become convinced that the Communist sympathizers on the board, led by chairman Harry Ward, had given up protection of the civil liberties of other groups.[39] He wrote in a letter that "the disturbing factor in the Union lies in the fact that Harry Ward and some others do not believe in civil liberties as an end. They look on it only as a means. In other words, they defend the absence of civil liberties in some other lands. . . . Some of the outstanding members of the Union would forego all civil liberties tomorrow if they could have their kind of dictatorship."[40]

The growing split on the board also reflected concerns that the public was beginning to see the ACLU as little more than a Communist front. Baldwin, who was becoming more centrist, was increasingly sensitive to charges of Communist influence in the ACLU. By 1938, he had severed his connections to Popular Front groups and was recruiting conservatives to balance the ACLU's far-left faction.[41]

* * *

One of the biggest attacks on the ACLU came from the House Committee for the Investigation of Un-American Activities (often called the House Un-American Activities Committee, or HUAC). In the spring of 1938, HUAC had been created by a House resolution instructing the Speaker to appoint a special committee to conduct an investigation into "the extent, character, and objectives of un-American propaganda activities in the United States."[42] Though the stated goal of the committee was to investigate "all organizations or groups existing in the United States which are directed, controlled, or subsidized by foreign governments or agencies and which seek to change the policies and form of government of the United States in accordance with the wishes of such foreign governments," chairman Martin Dies, an ambitious Texas Democrat who had broken with the New Deal when it began to adopt a more liberal tone, set up the hearings to grind a political axe. Through the hearings, Dies hoped to discredit the Roosevelt administration by convincing Americans that Communists controlled much of the liberal movement and the New Deal programs he despised.[43]

The initial hearings established the methods that HUAC would use throughout its history. Dies permitted witnesses to make fantastic, unsupported charges and rarely accorded the accused the right to reply.[44] All testimony was accepted into the public record without attempts at verification.[45] "Communism" encompassed the broadest range of activities, including affiliation with organized labor and an array of New Deal and leftist organizations.[46] The National Labor

Relations Board was accused of harboring Communists on its staff. Liberal politicians were accused of catering to the Communists. Hundreds of organizations, ranging from the Camp Fire Girls to the American League for Peace and Democracy, were labeled Communist fronts. The hearings outraged the liberal community. Liberals condemned Dies for "interfering in local political contests" and allowing right-wing elements a platform from which to destroy the New Deal.[47]

The ACLU, with its long history of purported Communist ties, was an easy target for HUAC. Walter Steele, managing editor of the conservative monthly the *National Republic*, provided the first mention of the ACLU during HUAC's hearings. On August 16, 1938, he accused the ACLU of being affiliated with the Communist Party.[48] Dies then delivered a radio broadcast in which he alleged that the ACLU was Communist controlled and "carrying on the work of the Communist Party under the guise of democracy." The ACLU was accused of Communist affiliation six times before the committee in 1938, with each mention announced in national headlines.[49]

The ACLU launched a campaign to end the Dies committee. In December 1938, Gardner "Pat" Jackson, the chairman of the ACLU's Washington, DC, affiliate, contacted leaders of liberal organizations for assistance in forming a nonpublicized committee to coordinate an anti-Dies campaign. The group wanted to discredit the Dies committee through an analysis of its public hearings, including an investigation of HUAC's right-wing witnesses for criminal records or evidence of mental illness.[50] Characterizing the conduct of the Dies committee as a "public scandal," the ACLU called on the incoming House to end HUAC's "unsavory career."[51] ACLU leaders set out to convince two of HUAC's more liberal members to issue a statement criticizing Dies's conduct. The efforts came to naught.[52]

Robert Stripling, the secretary of HUAC, requested that the ACLU submit an affidavit denying charges of Communist affiliation, which he promised would be included in HUAC's report. In late December 1938, Baldwin, Holmes, and Ben Huebsch submitted affidavits stating that the ACLU was not a Communist front.[53] HUAC ignored this evidence. In January 1939, HUAC urged that the

ACLU be investigated, presenting a report that allegedly linked the ACLU to the Communist Party.[54] Hays wrote Dies that the accusations were false, challenged Dies to produce evidence, and offered to appear before the committee.[55] HUAC gave only tacit acknowledgment to Hays's letter.[56]

Dies asked the House for an extension of his investigation and lobbied for HUAC's renewal. The ACLU sent out a plea to its members, calling on them to write their representatives: "The Dies Committee Must Die!" Baldwin and Ernst made radio addresses condemning Dies's procedures.[57] Despite the opposition, the reauthorization measure, which received bipartisan support, passed by a vote of 344–35.[58]

* * *

Ernst's dinner parties, now written up in gossip columns such as Drew Pearson's syndicated column "Washington Merry-Go-Round," were dotted with eminent names in politics, law, banking, and publishing. Thanks in large part to the silent and tireless efforts of wife Maggie, who coordinated all their events, Morris Ernst was a renowned social host. New Dealers were present at the soirees, as were writers such as Marc Connelly, Edna Ferber, and H. G. Wells, and stage and screen actors, including Katherine Cornell, Groucho Marx, and Lynn Fontanne. Big-name journalists and publishers such as Time-Life publisher Henry Luce, celebrated reporters John Gunther and Dorothy Thompson, and columnist Walter Winchell always had a place at the table. Most of his friends were on the left, but Ernst, believing that true enrichment came from communication between opposing points of view, was always sure to have at least one conservative present.

There were old, beloved acquaintances in attendance—Ferber, Heywood Broun, Art Sulzberger, Felix Frankfurter, Governor Herbert Lehman, Mayor La Guardia—and new ones too. One of Ernst's closest confidantes was Russell Leffingwell, one of the leaders of the J. P. Morgan Company, the nation's foremost investment banking institution. Ten years older than Ernst, Leffingwell was renowned as a specialist in corporate finance. Leffingwell served as assistant secretary of the Treasury during the First World War and engineered wartime financial policies. He developed the Liberty Loan organization, supervised vast bond issues, and negotiated loans to the European allies. After the war, Leffingwell joined J. P. Morgan and quickly established himself as a leader in the firm. Cultured and widely read, Leffingwell was considered a business intellectual and was said to have the keenest mind among the Morgan partners. Six feet tall and trim, with a prominent nose and a piercing gaze, he was genteel, courtly, and articulate.[59] Ernst and Leffingwell, who had first met in 1933, conferred regularly until Leffingwell's death in 1960 to discuss the "finance problems of our nation." Ernst treasured the brilliant Leffingwell as an intellectual sparring partner, an "intellectual needler," like his friend Jerome Frank.

"I wish I could be more like Russell but I can't," Ernst opined. "It's background, glands—probably many intangibles. His wisdom and sureness about even his unsureness, his conscious disciplined reach for truth and fairness act as a refresher to me on many occasions. . . . It's a source of constant wonderment that Russell and I click so well."[60] Leffingwell was one of Ernst's "idols," one of the four men he considered most influential in his life, along with Brandeis, Broun, and Ted Lewis.[61]

Another frequent guest at Ernst's parties was John L. Lewis, head of the United Mine Workers and the Committee for Industrial Organization. Ernst had met Lewis through his work on the Pennsylvania Anthracite Coal Commission, to which Governor Howard Earle had appointed Ernst in 1937. When the anthracite industry was severely injured during the Depression, bootlegging—the illegal mining of anthracite—skyrocketed. Earle said that bootlegging was "the greatest conflict between moral and legal rights" and called for an investigation commission. Until 1940, when Lewis turned against Roosevelt, Ernst had a friendly relationship with the labor leader, whom he described as a table-pounding, "keen, self-educated, humorless" man.[62]

Many of Ernst's parties were simply gabfests; others involved discussion of "constructive solutions" to social problems. In some of the sessions, Ernst introduced New Dealers to his friends in banking and the press and gathered information for Roosevelt informally. Ernst remained renowned for his ability to mediate diverse interests. At one party in 1939, John Lewis, Henry Luce, Wendell Willkie (corporate attorney and Republican presidential candidate of 1940), and FDR economic adviser Leon Henderson discussed "an immediate program for putting men back to work."[63] Ernst subsequently wrote to FDR, "I think that it might be worthwhile for me to report to you the gist of the conversation, because when Willkie, Lewis and Henderson agree, there must be an inviting possibility."[64] FDR replied, "I read about your famous dinner party in the Merry-Go-Round or some similar column. Keep up the good work."[65] At another earlier soiree, Lewis and Leffingwell got together when the steel strike of 1937 was on and Leffingwell and Lewis were enemies. "The whiskey was good, the wine was good, and before the evening was over, Leffingwell and Lewis went out arm in arm and in a few days the steel strike ended," it was recounted, and Ernst took credit for this.[66]

At one soiree, reported in the "Washington Merry-Go-Round" column, H. G. Wells, John L. Lewis, Edna Ferber, and Jerome Frank engaged in a "cat and dog fight." They argued about Henry Ford, literature, and "almost everything under the sun." They found that they agreed on one point. At the end of the day, they sent a birthday telegram to Louis Brandeis that read, "We have all agreed that you are a swell guy."[67]

17
ERNST VS. HAGUE

In 1938, Morris Ernst was at the peak of his powers. As fascism spread overseas and democracy witnessed one of its sorriest hours, Ernst had become, in the minds of many liberals, an icon of democracy, freedom, and hope. The "prophetic, mythical image" that Ernst projected "helped to shape me and many of my generation who sought a model of hope in a world that was going mad," recalled one young lawyer.[1]

That year Ernst was the subject of news articles, profiles, and celebratory features. *Scribner's Magazine* ran a feature article on him in the lead position, written by Pulitzer Prize winner Marquis James.[2] "Morris Ernst works for nothing—to fight for your right to worship as you please. For a free press, for free speech, free assembly, and against persecution of anybody," wrote Walter Winchell in his syndicated column.[3] Drew Pearson and Robert Allen did a tribute in their "Washington Merry-Go-Round" column that was practically penned by Ernst himself: "Morris Ernst . . . is the greatest crusader for the Bill of Rights since the younger days of Louis D. Brandeis. There is hardly a case of suppressed civil liberties anywhere in the country that he has not championed, yet he also represents some of the biggest firms on Wall Street. He has amassed a considerable fortune, yet he dips into his own pocket to finance most of the human rights cases which he champions."[4]

These paeans came in the midst of Ernst and the ACLU's fight to free Jersey City, New Jersey, from the autocratic rule of Mayor Frank Hague, who suppressed union organizing and quashed free speech and assembly. The fight against Hague was the ACLU's last "all out case," its last major use of direct-action tactics, with press releases, provocative speakers, dramatic incidents, and large-scale publicity. Norman Thomas was egged and arrested, Art Hays made a speech on top of a car, and Hague threatened to throw Ernst in jail. The ACLU's efforts resulted in a US Supreme Court ruling declaring streets, parks, and public squares to be constitutionally protected spaces, "public forums," where the public discussion of public issues was shielded from state interference. *Hague v. Committee for Industrial Organization* represented one of the most significant rulings of the decade on freedom of speech and assembly.

* * *

Mayor Hague, nicknamed the Hitler of Hudson County, ran an autocratic, old-school political machine. First elected in 1917, he was the perpetual "boss" of Jersey City. Hague stayed in power by stealing votes, intimidating opponents, wiretapping, and making false arrests to silence his critics. Inhabitants of insane asylums and people on their deathbeds were on Hague's voter lists. In 1932, Hague delivered New Jersey to FDR; the president named him vice chairman of the Democratic National Committee.[5] Ignoring Hague's scandals, Roosevelt allowed him to add hundreds of thousands of federal jobs and millions of dollars to his corrupt machine.[6]

Few observers doubted Hague's infamous words, uttered in a 1937 speech, that "I am the law in Jersey City." "Our law is the nightstick and we use it," he said.[7] Guided by Hague's slogan of "No Vice, No Crime, No Racketeering," his heavy-handed police eliminated street crime and enforced his puritanical views. Even after the repeal of Prohibition, women were forbidden to be in establishments where alcohol was served. Police stopped automobiles they considered "suspicious," forced occupants out, and banished them from the city.[8]

Hague attracted business to Jersey City by suppressing unions. Billboards announced, "Jersey City Has Everything for Industry." Jersey City was known as the "sweatshop center" for attracting runaway shops fleeing union contracts in other cities.[9] To ensure that no organizing efforts would take place, Hague's police strictly enforced ordinances regulating the distribution of circulars and requiring permits to conduct public meetings.[10] A city ordinance provided that the police chief, after investigation, could deny a permit "for the purpose of preventing riots, disturbances or disorderly assemblage."[11] If the Committee for Industrial Organization (CIO) or the Socialists announced a meeting and Hague's supporters threatened to break it up, cops would forbid it in the interests of "law and order."[12] Jersey City police often "transported" union organizers beyond the city limits, a practice Hague defended on the ground that the police were protecting them from the wrath of the citizenry. Hague believed that when a police officer put such "undesirables" in a car and took them "somewhere not the police station," he was "doing them a favor."[13]

Hague was tall and erect, with a full face, cold eyes, a shiny bald head, and the imposing physique of a prizefighter. Though dapper and well-groomed, he was at heart an uncultured thug who still talked in the language of the Horseshoe, the tough neighborhood where he grew up. Hague was infamous for his garbled syntax, for statements like "I have went" and for using singular subjects with plural verbs. He orated pompously and jabbed his finger into his listener's chest to emphasize his points, emphasizing his favorite phrase, "You know I'm right about that!"[14]

The mayor latched onto Communism as symbol of threats to "Americanism" and "law and order." He described efforts to unionize Jersey City as a "red invasion." "As long as I am Mayor of this city the great industries of the city are secure," he said. "We hear about constitutional rights, free speech and the free press. Every time I hear these words I say to myself, 'that man is a Red, that man is a Communist.' You never heard a real American talk in that manner."[15]

* * *

The CIO began its efforts to organize unskilled workers in Jersey City in 1937. Its affiliate, the United Shoe Workers of America, set up an office. On the morning of November 29, a group of unionists met at the headquarters to organize workers in three shoe factories. Carrying handbills announcing a meeting, they marched through the early dawn streets.[16]

The "red invaders" were confronted by policemen who searched them and confiscated their handbills. Some were herded onto a ferry bound for Manhattan; others were driven off in police cars to a remote marshland where they were released. Police officers assigned to the rail station attempted to turn back incoming unionists. Thirteen organizers were arrested and prosecuted, and seven were found guilty of violating the city's ordinance against distributing circulars without a permit.[17]

John L. Lewis asked Ernst to serve as counsel for the CIO and to investigate the matter. Ernst reported to Lewis, "Civil liberties have been wiped out for the CIO organizers and other citizens who chance to disagree with Mayor Hague's social or economic ideas. I have seen situations in rough and tumble areas of America but in my opinion there has been no attack on basic civil liberties as insidious and threatening as the one of Mayor Hague. . . . His Chief of Police testifies under oath that the police have the right to eject people from the town. . . . Your organizers are barred from renting halls for meetings. . . . The tactic of Mayor Hague is a departure in the American scene." Hague's regime "has only one tendency—that of a local dictatorship. . . . The issue is whether civil liberties shall prevail in Jersey City, or whether Hague shall be permitted to make a Calcutta black hole of suppression out of one metropolis in this country."[18]

Ernst told Lewis that he intended to take the case to federal court. "We are going to proceed with a federal action and have really doped out a good one," he wrote. Lee Pressman, one of the radicals in the National Lawyers Guild with Communist ties, was general counsel for the CIO.[19] Communists had been drawn to the CIO, with its program of industrial unionism, and Lewis, who needed talented and aggressive organizers, welcomed Communists into his movement. Communists played a key role in building such CIO affiliates as the United Auto Workers and the United Electrical, Radio, and Machine Workers of America.[20] Many CIO-affiliated unions had significant Communist membership, although Communists were secretive about their party affiliation.[21] Pressman disliked Ernst but agreed to have him work on the case. The ACLU later joined in and Spaulding Frazer, dean of the Newark Law School, was also retained as associate counsel.

Ernst brought all of his showman's skills to bear on the matter. Massive, dramatic publicity was the key to his strategy to "free" Jersey City. Before filing suit, Ernst attempted to organize opposition to Hague in Congress.[22] In early December he met with a group of Democratic congressmen and described conditions in Jersey City. "If you allow this Mayor to get away with this, other Mayors will follow his example and you will have in the United States a pattern for European dictatorship," he asserted.[23] Twenty-six congressmen signed a letter calling for an immediate investigation of the treatment of union organizers in Jersey City.[24]

The centerpiece of Ernst's efforts to "take the CIO's case before the public" was a "30-week campaign" involving his friends in the New Deal and in the press.[25] Harold Ickes was instructed to denounce Hague at a banquet of the National Lawyers Guild. "I have arranged for radio time on three occasions," Ernst wrote to ACLU colleague Gardner "Pat" Jackson. "I have other tactics in mind and it is all a matter now of timing these blows so that they pepper the situation from time to time."[26] He envisioned broadcasts from trucks stationed in Jersey City, regular newspaper coverage, and daily "parades" of automobiles bearing CIO stickers throughout the city. Well-known liberal journalists such as Heywood Broun, Dorothy Thompson, Walter Lippmann, and Hugh Johnson were asked to comment on the events. Ernst engineered extensive newspaper publicity, arranged for ministers to go on a picket line in Jersey City, and had newsreels made.[27]

In late December, Ernst formed the Committee on Civil Liberties in Jersey City, consisting of sixty-four notables from the theater, religion, law, journalism, and academia.[28] Ernst was determined to make the Jersey City fight "respectable" by dissociating it from the radical CIO and associating it with what was then seen as the more "mainstream" cause of civil liberties. The new committee's founding statement announced that it "does not intend to concern itself with questions of organized and unorganized labor, or of industrial versus craft unionism, because the real issue in Jersey City is democracy versus dictatorship."[29]

Hague retaliated, singling out Ernst for attack. He denounced

Ernst as an "associate of the leading communists of the country" and the "chief lieutenant of Roger Baldwin, head of the American Civil Liberties Union, which is the Communist Party under another name." Hague charged, "Every word on this record spells 'radicalism' and demonstrates that Morris L. Ernst is one of its important leaders."[30]

"The CIO is determined to keep after Jersey City," Ernst retorted. "We are going to keep on until we open that territory to the Bill of Rights and make it again a part of the United States."[31] The fight in Jersey City was "more important than anything else in the labor movement," Ernst said, as reported in the *New York Times*. "You can write all the statutes you please and if a mayor like Hague can tear them up you have just got to develop a new technique."[32] Hague threatened that if Ernst repeated those remarks in Jersey City, "I will guarantee that his friends will not see him for a long time."[33]

The ACLU, the CIO, and Roger Baldwin applied for permits to hold outdoor meetings. Hague's police chief Daniel Casey wrote to Ernst informing him that he was considering the applications. Meanwhile, an "Important Notice," labeled "Message from the Mayor's Office," was circulated among several thousand veterans calling for attendance at a rally. The meeting was held and resulted, not surprisingly, in an antiradical "protest," which Casey used to justify denying the permits.[34]

* * *

After the New Year's holiday, Hague renewed his attack in 1938 with an anti-Ernst, anti-CIO "monster meeting" in the Jersey City Armory. More than twenty thousand Hague supporters attended the "Americanization Day" event, including veterans and civil service employees who had been bused to the Armory by Hague's henchmen. Hague announced:

> I promised that I would expose the close tie-up between the head of the ACLU and the leaders of the Communist Party of this country. I have already proven that the ACLU . . . is nothing else than the Communist Party of the United States under another name. I have

> also proven beyond question that . . . "Roger N. Baldwin, alias John Moscow" is behind the whole CIO movement in this country, which proof establishes the common identity of the CIO organization and the Communist Party.
>
> Morris L. Ernst, who is the general counsel for the ACLU, is also counsel for the CIO, and he is second in command to Baldwin in the ACLU. . . . Ernst . . . is treasurer of the Garland Fund and connected with numerous organizations identified with communism and Soviet Russia. . . . He prides himself on organizing 5000 lawyers in the Lawyers' Guild. He has induced thousands of men to join the CIO and organized newspaper men into communism to control the editorial and field men of newspaper work.[35]

Observed Heywood Broun later:

> The Mayor's grammar was not good, but his sentiments were even worse. Seemingly he has not kept up . . . with current affairs. He was back talking about the Garland Fund [which by that time was nearly defunct]. . . . Roger Baldwin and Morris Ernst were identified as the twin dictators of the radical movement, which I think might well be a surprise to many, including Baldwin and Ernst.
>
> It was all very comical and very silly. But it will not do merely to laugh Hague off. In the beginning people in Germany thought that Hitler was too preposterous ever to come into power. The fact that Hague is a . . . man of meager intelligence does not shove him out of the picture as an actual menace to our democracy.[36]

* * *

Ernst listened to the radio broadcast of Hague's talk from the studio of station WOR in New York and then spoke extemporaneously over the air. Many observers believed it was Ernst's finest moment.

> I want to get one issue out of the way first. During the last half hour of words and words, you have heard a lot of talk about the word "communism." As counsel for the CIO and also for the American Civil Liberties Union, I am authorized to say tonight that I represent

> those great communist leaders of the nation, General Hugh Johnson, Dorothy Thompson, Walter Lippmann . . . and hundreds of other dangerous reds.
>
> Frank when you said I am the law, you meant only one thing. You meant that you have torn up the statute books of the State of New Jersey, . . . you have ripped up the Bill of Rights . . .
>
> I don't care how many people you have at the mass meeting in Jersey City because I know how you got them there. You got them there by orders through district clubs, through coercion, by duress, by postal cards, by bands, by mail, in busses, by distribution of leaflets in the streets of your city. . . .
>
> A year ago it was the AFL [American Federation of Labor] that you were suppressing. Now it happens to be the CIO. I am interested in protecting the rights of minorities. I have appeared in the City of New York to defend the rights of the Nazis, whom I detest, to hold a meeting in this city. You are a danger to the American nation because you are the basic radical of our day, radical in the sense that you are going back on the Founding Fathers and our Bill of Rights . . .
>
> The American public that believes that the wealth of this nation depends on the development of the human mind, that there must be free trade in ideas . . . No man is big enough in the United States to announce with assurance that he is the law. Frank Hague, you are not the law. The Constitution of the United States, you will find out shortly, is the law of the land.
>
> Mayor Hague, the fight goes on. We are not going to stop until that town is open to the traditions and folklore of the American people. . . . How do you answer that, Frankie?[37]

* * *

Communist CIO leaders were livid over Ernst's handling of the case. Some denounced Ernst as a "fascist" because he secured support from prominent liberals. Not long after the radio speech, Neil Brant, the chief lawyer of the Communist-dominated United Electrical, Radio, and Machine Workers of America wrote to Ernst, complaining, "Your answer . . . was entirely unsatisfactory. . . . You calling Frank Hague the 'greatest radical' may be cute but in my opinion it only tends to confuse the people and . . . is a bit of red-baiting because it holds up the word 'radical' to contempt . . . Your use of such personages as Dorothy Thompson and General Hugh Johnson, both outspoken enemies of the CIO, is no credit to our drive in Jersey City. This is but another attempt to clothe our cause in respectability which seems to be an obsession with you. . . . Your manner of delivery did not have the dignity that the occasion deserved. I did not know that you were so chummy with the Dictator of Jersey City that you could call him Frank."[38]

The CIO eventually decided to take over its own public relations, resulting in the case dropping out of the headlines. Ernst wrote angrily to Pressman about the "disastrous effects of your present tactics." Squabbling between Ernst and Pressman over publicity, strategy, and fees continued throughout the case.[39] Pressman complained about Ernst's "spectacular and dramatic" tactics and threatened that the CIO would withdraw from the litigation.[40]

These exchanges heightened Ernst's animus toward the Communists. "The Communist line was to attack the strategy of the litigation at every possible angle," Ernst recalled. "One of the lawyers most used in Jersey City by the Communists attacked us in writing as fascist because we welcomed the support of Walter Lippmann, Hugh Johnson and Dorothy Thompson. Unbelievable as it seems, that is literally the truth. . . . The Communists didn't want the case to be won. They really don't want civil liberty—they much prefer any occasion to protest and raise hell."[41]

* * *

On January 7, 1938, the day after the radio address, Spaulding Frazer, Ernst, and several young associates from Ernst's office commenced a lawsuit in federal court. The main issue was the validity of the Jersey City ordinance giving an official unfettered discretion to ban street meetings. The complaint alleged that Hague and his officers illegally forbade all meetings organized for the purpose of discussing the work of the CIO, that they enforced a "censorship on the owners of meeting halls in Jersey City, and have implemented these allegedly unconstitutional acts by teeth-bearing penalties in the form of imprisonment and fines," in violation of the First and Fourteenth Amendments.[42] The plaintiffs argued for the issuance of an omnibus injunction restraining the Jersey City authorities from further interference with constitutional rights in the CIO organizational drive, "to preserve the principles of liberty and freedom inherent in American democracy and to prevent the Jersey City example from leading to dictatorship on a national scale in the United States." Ernst asked that Hague be compelled to set aside "Hyde Parks" in Jersey City where anyone could express their views, with full police protection.[43]

One problem Ernst's team faced was that such laws had been generally upheld as constitutional. "The whole trend of the law before the *Hague* case," observed eminent First Amendment scholar Zechariah Chafee, had run "toward giving city authorities virtually complete control of open-air meetings."[44] There was also a jurisdictional problem. To avoid the lenient state judiciary, filled with Hague allies, Ernst's team filed in federal court. To do this, they made use of an antiquated, barely used post–Civil War civil rights statute, the Civil Rights Act of 1871, known as the Ku Klux Klan Act, that had been written to enforce the Fourteenth Amendment against violations of civil rights by state officials.[45]

The prospect of litigation didn't faze Hague, and police harassment in Jersey City continued. That spring, Congressman Jerry O'Connell of Montana, a CIO ally, attempted to address a crowd in Jersey City's Journal Square and was ushered away by police. Art Hays protested on top of a car and was roughed up by cops. Norman Thomas, who had been denied a meeting permit, attempted to speak at a May Day rally and was "deported"—picked up by police, placed in a car, and delivered to the waterfront and put on a ferryboat. Thomas retained Arthur Vanderbilt, president of the American Bar Association, to bring suit against Hague. Vanderbilt chose to litigate in the New Jersey courts. With Ernst in federal court and Vanderbilt in the New Jersey courts, they "joined forces in a pincer movement."[46]

* * *

Hague v. Committee for Industrial Organization went to trial in June 1938 before District Judge William Clark. An eccentric man, Clark had achieved brief notoriety by holding that the Prohibition amendment was invalid because it was ratified by the states rather than issued from a constitutional convention. Before trial, Hague's lawyers revealed their line of defense, which relied in part on a 1902 New Jersey antianarchy statute that prohibited illegal organizations seeking to overthrow the government from receiving the protections of the Constitution. Hague charged that membership in the CIO and ACLU automatically made one a Communist and that Ernst himself was a Communist. To "prove" this, Hague's lawyers subpoenaed the files of the CIO, the ACLU, and the Garland Fund, as well as Ernst's papers, including notes on several books he had written.[47]

Casey, Hague's police chief, was Ernst and Frazer's first witness. Evasive in his responses, he finally admitted that he denied permits on the grounds that granting them would lead to riots or disorder. Ernst and Frazer got Casey to testify that his "investigation" of applications consisted of waiting for orders from Hague, who claimed to have gotten his information about speakers from reading newspaper articles "between the lines."[48]

Ernst and Frazer then took the unusual step of calling Hague as a witness to prove their case in chief.[49] Technically, Hague was testifying against himself. Ernst and Frazer were certain that the mayor would damn himself, that proof of his suppression of constitutional rights would flow freely from his lips once he started to talk. On this point, Hague did not disappoint. What emerged from the record was a truly extraordinary exposé of Jersey City's tinhorn dictatorship.[50]

Hague was calm and composed, sitting back in the witness chair relaxed. He was candid and eager to talk, on occasion imperiously overruling his own counsel John A. Matthews and insisting on answering questions to which he had objected. He referred to himself in the third person, saying "Mayor Hague" did this or that.[51]

Hague not only assumed responsibility for the deportations of citizens and other violations of civil rights but also justified them.

He insisted that he had a right to deport people from Jersey City—to "put undesirable persons out of the city for the sake of their own personal safety." Asked if a man who did not commit any overt act should have a right to peacefully advocate revolution, Hague replied that it depended on who the person was. Individuals had this right, he said, if they are "high class citizens" and met in a peaceful manner, but if they previously urged the overthrow of the government, "I don't assume they have any rights."[52]

Frazer questioned Hague during the first two days of trial. On the third day, Ernst began his interrogation. The Ernst-Hague fireworks made headlines. Although Hague had been respectful of Frazer, he was abusive of Ernst, whom he insisted on calling "Mr. Ernest." Noted the *New York Times*, "the event took on the aspect of a Donnybrook Fair," with Hague and Ernst shouting at each other and Hague's lawyers yelling at the top of their voices "in a bedlam through which nothing could be clearly heard." Ernst walked quickly up and down in front of the witness stand, hammering in questions. Hague leaned forward in the chair and seemed almost on the point of jumping out of the box at his antagonist, "Mr. Ernest." At one point Hague charged that Ernst was trying to "browbeat" him and asked for the "protection" of Judge Clark.[53]

Hague's lawyer, Matthews, was even worse, calling Ernst "cattle," "stuff," and "that piece of humanity." At one point he used Hebrew words in a crude anti-Semitic attack.[54] When Morris said that Attorney General Frank Murphy was a guest of his in Nantucket, Matthews replied, "I didn't know you could go to Nantucket."

ERNST: I shall not stoop to his level, no matter how he behaves.

MATTHEWS: If you did, you would have to get up near the ceiling. I am picking you out of the gutter, continually.

ERNST: This is a court of law.

MATTHEWS: You have made it a circus.[55]

* * *

"We are going to prove," Hague announced—"he has got a subpoena in his hand, Mr. Ernest has now—we are going to prove that he is treasurer of the Garland Fund . . . that they supply all the funds to the known communist groups in this country. Now, if that isn't exposing Mr. Ernest as a known communist, I would like to know what is."[56]

"All over the State of New York, all over the State of New Jersey. . . . on street corners. . . . and clubs and restaurants [it's] common talk, [that] you are posing as the great [Communist] power," Hague said, his voice rising, pointing at Ernst.[57]

"In your investigation of me, do you know that I was denied the right to enter Russia?" Ernst asked. (Morris and Maggie had tried to go to Russia in 1937 but were denied a visa, which Morris attributed to his support of civil liberties.)

"Don't insult my intelligence. This is an act you're putting on. You weren't denied a visa to Russia. You know very well it is an act you and your side partner are putting on." The mayor identified the "side partner" as "Arthur Baldwin," conflating Roger Baldwin and Arthur Garfield Hays.

At one point Hague called reporters into a room in the back of the court and dictated a statement charging Ernst with having stopped the McNaboe legislative committee investigation into Communism in New York public schools. He said, "When Communist leaders sway that type of influence the American people better be on guard. He is the master mind, going about the country telling about his influence." Ernst asked Clark to hold Hague in contempt. The mayor sheepishly told the judge, "I done it with no intention of offending the court."[58]

* * *

For his work on the *Hague* case, Ernst received more fan letters, as well as hate mail, than for any other case in his career. Wrote "A Loyal Patriotic American," a letter writer not courageous enough to sign a real name, "just a few lines to let you know that the ship bound for Moscow, Russia, will set sail in a few weeks and there will be room for you and Spaulding Frazer aboard." The correspondent concluded, "Your examination of the Honorable Mayor Frank Hague of Jersey City proves beyond a doubt that you are a contemptible Red trying to hide behind the guise of 'liberalism.'"[59]

As he did after almost all of his big civil liberties cases, Ernst received anti-Semitic mail, as exemplified by the same anonymous letter writer, who threatened, "If you damned Jews don't cease your un-American, un-Christian agitation, you'll get the same medicine you are getting in Germany and other parts of the world." This "Loyal Patriotic American" spewed, "You are a son-of-a-bitch trying to bore from within, but we're wise to you and your kind, you dirty little kike."[60]

Prominent Jewish leaders urged Ernst to step down from the case. According to the *Nation*, some opined that Ernst had hurt Jews in the United States by "identifying a Jew with subversive and disreputable ideas."[61] "As an American Jew who is interested in the welfare of his co-religionists I believe it imperative that you disassociate yourself from the present litigation and the publicity attendant therewith," wrote Maurice Tishman, a wealthy New York merchant, to Ernst. "Unfortunately, Judaism is being linked with radicalism throughout the world."[62]

Ernst wrote to Brandeis in despair, "In my attempt to battle down some intolerance in Jersey City, I am receiving a mass of letters from rich Jewish people begging me to withdraw from the matter. . . . I thought you would be interested in this observation and possibly you might have time to drop me a line giving me any suggestions you have as to the tactics of handling the rich Jewish front that wants now to live an underground life negating the concept of a unified people in this nation."[63]

Brandeis replied, "Morris, if you ever decide to accept a [case] or decline one because of the popularity of the client, I suggest you first resign from the bar. Maybe, if that happens, you should even resign from the human race."[64]

* * *

The unpredictable Judge Clark shocked Hague and his cronies by issuing an injunction against interfering with organizers, the distribution of their literature, and their holding of public meetings. Clark's quirky fifteen-thousand-word opinion, which invoked the Fourteenth Amendment as well as excerpts from various legal and nonlegal sources ranging from Socrates to Mussolini, was arranged under the titles of "Liberty of the Person" and "Liberty of the Mind." The judgment enjoined city officials from excluding or deporting unionists except in connection with a lawful search or seizure and from interfering with their rights to distribute leaflets or carry placards. It forbade the city from denying permits for open-air meetings, unless the designated time or place for the meeting would interfere with the public recreational purpose of the city's property, and required the city to actively protect speakers against interference by hostile spectators.[65] Hague appealed to the Third Circuit Court of Appeals. In a sweeping majority decision in which Hague and his associates were accused of having "troubled the waters in order to fish in them," the Third Circuit upheld Clark's ruling, declaring the meeting ordinance unconstitutional and placing even greater restrictions on Jersey City officials.[66] Ernst hailed the ruling as a great victory for the rights of free speech and free assemblage.[67]

With speed shown only in cases of the greatest importance, the US Supreme Court agreed to hear the case on February 27, 1939. Ernst presented the facts before the Court and Frazer argued the law. Ernst's argument was less than stellar; it faltered in part due to the bad manners of Justice James McReynolds, who expressed his disgust by turning around in his chair and presenting his back to counsel the whole time. Ernst recalled, "I was heckled to death and could not get to first base."[68]

On June 5, 1939, the Supreme Court issued its 5–2 decision upholding the injunction. Five opinions were needed to settle the case. Justices Owen Roberts and Hugo Black joined in one ruling, Justices Harlan Stone and Stanley Reed shared another on different grounds, and Chief Justice Charles Evans Hughes tersely concurred in the general result. The only dissenters were McReynolds and Pierce Butler. The remaining two justices, Felix Frankfurter and William O. Douglas, did not participate in the case. The plurality held that the right to peaceably assemble and communicate about matters growing out of national legislation is protected by the Privileges and Immunities Clause of the Fourteenth Amendment. The public had an affirmative right to access streets and parks, "public forums," which are "held in trust for the use of the public and, time out of mind . . . used for purposes of assembly, communicating thoughts between citizens, and discussing public questions." The Court declared, "Such use of the streets and public places has, from ancient times, been a part of the privileges, immunities, rights and liberties of citizens. The privilege of a citizen of the United States to use the streets and parks for communication of views on national questions may be regulated in the interest of all; it is not absolute but relative, and must be exercised in subordination to the general comfort and convenience, and in consonance with peace and good order; but it must not, in the guise of regulation, be abridged or denied."[69] The ruling had major implications for labor organizing as well as freedom of speech and assembly more broadly. Commenting on the decision from Nantucket, Ernst told the *New York Times*, "the next time any tin-hat Hitler wants to run his bailiwick like a czar he'll have to think twice about it."[70]

Not long after the ruling, Hague called Ernst and asked him to "draw up the best free speech ordinance in the country." He drafted a utopian document, which went through the city council in five minutes. Ten days later, Norman Thomas returned to Hague's town to speak in a mass rally celebrating free speech in Jersey City.

Thomas wrote to Ernst:

> I know that you must feel gratified that all the good work you put into the case has resulted in more than just another court decision. . . . It was really a fine meeting that was held Monday night; better, I think, than any of the newspapers described it. The crowd was very sympathetic. There were a few lone hoots but that was all from the crowd of seven or eight thousand who packed the Square. It was a wondrous sight to behold; all those heads close together and not a nightstick coming down on any one of them.
>
> The police called on us to make arrangements. When I got to Journal Square, Dan Casey asked if there was anything he could do and I asked him to have the buses moved. He said, "Right away." . . . He later asked me if everything was alright and I told him I thought it was. Then he said, "Ernst would be pleased." I agreed with him

FIGURE 4. Morris Ernst delivers his extemporaneous on-air response to Jersey City mayor Frank Hague at radio station WOR in New York City, January 6, 1938. Courtesy of Stephanie Begen.

FIGURE 5. Morris Ernst (*center*) in 1939, not long after his victory in *Hague v. Committee for Industrial Organization*. Courtesy of Library of Congress.

> and wished against hope that somehow or other you would show up at the meeting because it really was your meeting. . . . I asked that three cheers be given for you as the attorney who had really made the show possible. They were given and the cheers, I am sure, were a little cheering to all of us who knew how much you had put into this.[71]

* * *

"Keep an eye on Morris Ernst as a candidate for mayor of New York City," Drew Pearson and Robert Allen wrote in their "Washington Merry-Go-Round" column shortly after the Hague affair. "He is the hard-hitting lawyer who forced Mayor Hague to accept the CIO in Jersey City."[72] Two months later, Walter Winchell reported that Ernst was in line for a federal court judgeship.[73]

Ernst was deluged with letters and phone calls after Winchell's column. He told Winchell that he was "not at all interested in becoming a judge. I'm having a good time as it is and I really believe I can be more effective in the defense of the liberties of the common people as a mere advocate at the bar before the judges of the land."[74] Ernst wrote directly to "the Boss" himself, telling FDR that "I am not interested in becoming a judge. I would probably have as little fun at it as you would and, in fact, I desire no political post of any kind. I am content if I can continue to perform anonymous chores in your behalf."[75]

Roosevelt replied, "You are a man after my own heart! Why either you or I should want to become a Judge is wholly beyond 'our' comprehension. In continuing as you are, you are infinitely more valuable to the common cause of a liberal democracy."[76] Ernst so cherished this letter that he framed it and put it on his bookshelf, where it remained for the rest of his life.

18

CONTROVERSY IN THE ACLU

By 1939, Morris Ernst had become a "red-baiter"—in his words, "frankly a baiter of the Communists and the Nazis and of all those who are opposed to our Bill of Rights."[1]

Several forces contributed to Ernst's increasingly fierce anti-Communism. Even before the Nazi-Soviet pact of August 1939, Ernst maintained that Communists were a dire threat to democracy and civil liberties. Joseph Stalin's purges and show trials had made clear that the Soviet Union was a totalitarian regime on par with Nazi Germany. Ernst's bitterness toward the Communists was also the result of his personal experiences, as we've seen. The slights and indignities he experienced at the hands of Communists and their sympathizers, who edged him out of organizations and challenged his leadership, hurt his fragile ego. Ernst had become convinced that Communists were destroying worthy liberal organizations such as the Newspaper Guild, the National Lawyers Guild (NLG), and the ACLU by fomenting internal divisions, pushing liberals out of leadership positions, disrupting their work, and tarnishing their image. Liberal organizations needed to become explicitly anti-Communist, he believed, to preserve their integrity and defend themselves against the attacks of Martin Dies and his ilk.[2]

For the next two decades, Ernst would attempt to reconcile his hatred of the Communists with his belief in free speech and civil liberties. This internal struggle led him to convoluted positions, odd alliances, and diminishing credibility in liberal circles, not to mention the loss of lifelong friendships. It marked a new phase in his life, a long phase, and not a good one.

* * *

Ernst remained concerned with the image of the National Lawyers Guild, which had not flourished as he expected. The reason for this, he was sure, was the guild's far-left minority, which projected the image that the group was a Communist front. When he traveled the country stumping for the guild, he found that there was no city where the guild was not viewed with suspicion because it was "not frank" in its opposition to both Communism and fascism.[3]

At the end of 1938, Ernst began a campaign to "purge" the National Lawyers Guild of its radical members. He presented a resolution to the NLG Executive Committee to amend its constitution to condemn "dictatorships of both left and right," making clear that "we are for democracy and the Bill of Rights, and we are opposed to Communism, fascism, and Nazism." Ernst reasoned that Communist sympathizers would never endorse such a statement and would leave the organization when asked to do so. No one could object to his proposal "other than persons who believe in dictatorship." Thousands of lawyers were ready to join the guild as soon "as we make this pronouncement," he believed.[4] Such "Communazi" resolutions, as they were dubbed, barring members of the Communist Party or fascist groups from joining or holding office, would become a commonly used tactic for distancing liberals from Communists and were adopted by dozens of organizations and unions in this era.[5] The NLG Executive Committee expressed concerns about "red-baiting," and the motion was voted down.[6] Ernst and a friend, New York state judge Ferdinand Pecora, subsequently met with several New Deal attorneys to assure them of the guild's "political respectability."[7]

At the National Lawyers Guild's third annual convention in Chicago in February 1939, Ernst revisited the proposal.[8] On the first day of the convention, he told board members that he had come to the conclusion that the greatest obstacle to the growth of the guild was the fact that the public misunderstood its position, and he again put forward the amendment. There was intense discussion, but the board members deferred taking action so they could attend the convention banquet.[9]

At the banquet that evening, Pecora, as retiring president, gave an unexpected speech that showed that he and Ernst were of one mind. "Let no lawyer who does not unreservedly and wholeheartedly believe in the full spirit of American democracy—who is not prepared to battle for its preservation—join our ranks," he announced. "We oppose any and all ideologies or political philosophies which challenge our democratic institutions, whether from the right or from the left. Communism, Fascism, Naziism—any ism, be it of native or alien origin—which seeks to supplant our democracy, is a target for our attack."[10]

When the twenty-nine members of the board reconvened later that night, they were eager to reach a consensus before the so-called Ernst issue disrupted the whole convention.[11] Alexander Frey of the University of Pennsylvania Law School opposed Ernst's motion, stating that any change in the NLG constitution would suggest that there was justification for the charge that it had been favoring a "dictatorship from the Left."[12] Osmond Fraenkel of the ACLU, Malcolm Sharp of the University of Chicago, New Dealer Felix Cohen, and others spoke out against a blanket denunciation of Communism, arguing that any such position would play into the hands of the guild's opponents. The debate was lengthy and acrimonious. Ernst's friend Ernest Cuneo introduced a resolution giving unqualified approval to Pecora's speech, which was defeated. Sharp proposed that the board thank Pecora for his address, record their general agreement, and ask the editors of the *National Lawyers Guild Quarterly* to print the address with an expression of sympathy. The board eventually adopted this motion.[13] Ernst and his allies threatened to resign over the board's unwillingness to take a strong anti-Communist stance. The showdown at the convention made him "heartsick," Ernst wrote to the incoming guild president, John Gutknecht of Chicago.[14]

By the time of the following year's convention, many New Dealers—including Ernst, Pecora, Jerome Frank, Thomas Corcoran, Nathan Margold, Adolf Berle, and Robert Jackson—had left the National Lawyers Guild over the issue.[15] When the guild's anti-Communist luminaries resigned, they took from the organization the respectability it once had from counting among its members the

US Attorney General as well as a constellation of federal and state judges, law professors, and government officials.[16]

Shortly after the 1939 guild convention, Ernst's reappointment to the state Banking Board was held up, ironically, on charges that he was a Communist.[17] Ernst was attacked in the New York State Senate by the notorious red-baiter Senator John T. McNaboe, who linked him with the ACLU and declared that it was the "front organization to the Communist movement in the United States."[18] Quipped the Communist *Daily Worker*, "Only a few days after Morris Ernst led a red-baiting drive within and against the NLG, he now wakes up to find himself the victim of the same sort of unscrupulous campaign." It concluded, "The obvious lesson is, don't engage in red-baiting."[19] Ernst replied to McNaboe that "anyone who knows my record knows that I am opposed to communism and fascism, and opposed to dictatorship by the left, right, or middle, and that I am an addict to the Bill of Rights. I want us to have the right to complain against our rulers on the street corners or in the press, which can't be done in Berlin, Moscow, or Rome."[20] Ernst was finally confirmed on March 22, 1939, by a vote of 37 to 5.[21]

* * *

Ernst continued to publicly attack the Dies committee. In a radio speech on NBC's *America's Town Meeting of the Air*, he decried the "great disservice" done to democracy by Dies. The committee "did not try to define what it thought to be subversive. To that committee all change is subversive. . . . Mr. Dies promised at the opening of the hearings to prevent character assassination. He went completely sour on this pledge. Persons attacked were given no opportunity to answer. The record is replete with the wildest kinds of inferences as to people and organizations."[22] Yet Ernst believed that, its disgraceful procedures notwithstanding, the House Un-American Activities Committee (HUAC) led by Dies had in fact performed a useful function in exposing the existence and membership lists of underground Communist groups.

In January 1939, Ernst wrote his first proposal for "disclosure," an idea that would obsess him for the next decade. In the proposal's initial iteration, Ernst advocated the creation of a government "Social Exchange Commission," akin to the Securities and Exchange Commission, with authority to expose the origins and sources of funding of "all propaganda for the destruction of the Bill of Rights." He believed that public disclosure of the funding sources of anonymous propaganda pamphlets put out by isolationists, anti-Semites, and fascist and Communist groups, bearing such titles as "Vote American," "Buy Christian," or "Kill the Catholics," would cause those organizations to fold up. When the public learned the sources of their funding, they would refuse to support them. Additionally, he believed, "disclosure" would forestall the enactment of proposed legislation to outlaw the Communist Party. Ernst didn't want to outlaw the Communists, only to "expose" them—"smok[e] them out and not driv[e] them further underground."[23] He described his proposal thus:

> Two large world movements—communism and fascism—believing that the end justifies the means, are working underground with anonymity and stealth, at times simulating a belief in the Bill of Rights. . . . Democracy must insist on full and open declarations. The best way to fight ideas is with other ideas, but we must promptly, without any controls or limitations, insist that the proponents of ideas be ready to stand up and be counted . . .
>
> We have ample powers under the Interstate Commerce and other clauses of the Constitution to provide that if a man prints words on a piece of paper known as a certificate of stock, that there be a full declaration as to officers and directors in back of the statement . . .
>
> A social exchange commission bill will contain the following provisions—all organizations that print and disseminate material in printed form or . . . [in] the radio, movies, or other means of disseminating ideas, shall file with some authority the following information . . . names of officers; names of directors; names of contributors, with specific provisions against pseudonyms and anonymity; statement of methods used for distribution of material and of obtaining income; affiliation with any other organizations; copies of all printed material . . .

> In view of the fact that the Bill of Rights is our outstanding contribution to the civilization of the world, and that communists and fascists are opposed to it, it might not be unreasonable for a democracy to ask . . . that a statement be made as to whether the organization favors the Bill of Rights and the free market of thought and is opposed to the communist and fascist philosophy on this point.[24]

There was no First Amendment problem, he posited, because "disclosure" was adding more information to the "marketplace of ideas" to help the public make informed decisions. Ernst apparently never considered that disclosure might have a chilling effect insofar as it inhibited anonymous speech.

Ernst sent the proposal to well-placed friends, including Harold Ickes, Louis Brandeis, Art Sulzberger, Adolf Berle, Jerome Frank, Norman Thomas, and Franklin and Eleanor Roosevelt. In May 1939, Ernst had joined the Committee for Cultural Freedom, an organization of prominent anti-Communist liberals headed by John Dewey and Sidney Hook, whose manifesto insisted that Communism and fascism were morally equivalent as variants of totalitarianism. The CCF approved Ernst's "disclosure" proposal and printed it in its bulletin.[25]

Ernst continued to forward the proposal in the summer and fall of 1939. With the Nazi-Soviet Pact in late August, the outbreak of war in Europe, and the Communist Party's switching from advocacy of American action to resist fascism in Europe to endorsement of isolationism, the need to expose and eliminate Communist and fascist groups seemed even more urgent.[26] Believing that endorsement from the ACLU would quell potential civil liberties objections, in October 1939 Ernst presented a lengthy, detailed position paper on "disclosure" titled "Possible Methods of Defeating Legislation in Derogation of the Bill of Rights" that he encouraged the ACLU to adopt.

"Present-day public temper is likely to produce an avalanche of legislation in derogation of the Bill of Rights," Ernst had written, referring to dozens of bills against aliens, Communists, and Nazis then pending in Congress. "With the temper of the public, repressive steps will be taken against such groups, and in time tend to smother all of us." He argued that public support for such measures stemmed from "a valid bewilderment because of the inability to find out who is back of what movement."[27]

Ernst proposed that the ACLU support a measure that would require any organization seeking postal privileges to provide the Post Office Department with the names of its officers, members, and donors, as well as copies of its constitution, bylaws, budget and printed material:

> There is no basic right of anonymity. The mail pouches should be open to all printed matter but the market place of thought, to be a fair market, should not be deluged as at present with thousands of pamphlets financed by cowardly undisclosed persons. There is no need for any suppression or censorship. There is immediate need for the light of day on all those selling ideas to our public. The Bill of Rights negates the need of anonymity.[28]

Roger Baldwin denounced Ernst's scheme as "quack idea." Hays feared that it would "prevent little men from expressing themselves." A disclosure law would "no doubt be followed by requirements of registration. Certainly civil liberties are not promoted by restrictions." The ACLU Board of Directors concluded that it would inhibit minority groups that depended on anonymous speech to forward unpopular ideas and resoundingly rejected "disclosure."[29]

* * *

Just as he had sought to eliminate Communists from the National Lawyers Guild, Ernst sought to "purge" the ACLU. This effort, commenced in early 1939, precipitated one of the most corrosive and controversial episodes in the organization's history.

At one of the first board meetings that year, Ernst introduced a resolution declaring that the ACLU opposed "all totalitarian governments—fascist, Nazi, or communist." The timing was planned; January was a month of vacations, so meetings were not well attended.[30] On January 23, 1939, the ACLU Board of Directors passed the measure by a vote of eight to four. Several on the board protested, arguing that the sole purpose of the ACLU was to defend civil liberties in the United States and that it should not be concerned with civil liberties in other countries. At a meeting at Ernst's home on March 6, by a vote of seventeen to six, the board rescinded the resolution.[31] Agitated, Ernst and his allies continued to bring up the "communist issue" again "week after week, month after month," recalled philosopher Corliss Lamont, a Socialist who was one of Ernst's opponents on the ACLU Board. "It embittered our work and made it almost impossible at times."[32]

Meanwhile, Dies continued to attack the ACLU. In August 1939, Dies had written to the Department of Justice requesting that criminal charges be brought against the Communist Party and other organizations, including the ACLU, for their failure to register with the State Department as agents of foreign governments. In October, he told the press that many of the organizations sponsoring the national conference on "Civil Liberties in the Present Emergency," put on by the ACLU, were Communist fronts. The threat to the ACLU loomed further when Dies announced his intention to investigate the American League for Peace and Democracy, which was the largest and most important Popular Front organization. Harry Ward, chairman of the ALPD, was to testify before the Dies committee on October 23. This investigation figured ominously because Ward was also chairman of the ACLU.[33]

At the HUAC hearing, Ward testified that the Communist Party had given financial support to the ALPD, said there was no dictatorship in the Soviet Union, and declined to bracket Communism with Nazism as an imperialistic movement. Unexpectedly, toward the end of Ward's testimony, Dies declared, "This Committee found last year, in its reports, that there was not any evidence that the American Civil Liberties Union was a Communist organization. That being true, I do not see why we would be justified going into it."[34]

* * *

Why did Dies suddenly change his mind about the ACLU? According to legend, Dies's about-face on the ACLU resulted from a nefarious "secret meeting" between Dies, Ernst, and Hays that had been orchestrated by Ernst.

The day before Ward's testimony, Ernst had given a cocktail party for Dies in Washington, DC, at the Hay-Adams Hotel with Hays, Jerome Frank, Assistant Secretary of State Adolf Berle, and Jerry Voorhis, a New Deal Congressman from California. Ernst had approached Dies to seek his support for his "disclosure" program. Ernst also used the opportunity to try to convince Dies that the ACLU was not in Communist hands and to try to get a hearing for the ACLU before HUAC. Whether anything else happened remains a matter of dispute.[35]

Dies published his own account of the meeting in the January 27, 1940, issue of *Liberty* magazine in which he reported that "Morris Ernst . . . came to see me in my office in Washington and discussed with me a proposed bill to require publicity in connection with the activities of organizations in the United States. . . . He asked me if I would meet with Congressman Jerry Voorhis, a group of New Dealers, [and Art] Hays . . . for the purpose of discussing proposed legislation. We met . . . and the conversation not only dealt with proposed legislation but principally Communism and the work of the committee. Jerome Frank and Adolf Berle agreed with me that the real liberals of the country should take a definite stand against communism and that in the interest of democracy the administration should cooperate with the committee."[36]

According to the Communist *Daily Worker*, Ernst and Hays made an "unholy deal" at a "convivial cocktail party held in Washington," agreeing that if Dies would "clear" the ACLU before HUAC, the board would remove Ward as chairman and purge the ACLU of Communists:

> Dies was told in plain language that liberals like Ernst, Hays, Frank, and Voorhis would be willing to work with him if he went after the Communists and left them alone.
>
> Specifically at issue was the case of the Civil Liberties Union. In its first report to Congress, the Dies Committee had been quite hostile in its attitude towards the ACLU. The liberals at the cocktail party

> were anxious for a clean bill of health for the ACLU in the next committee report to Congress.
>
> Dies was willing to declare the ACLU free from even a pinkish hue on one condition—that his liberal friends give him real cooperation in his fight against the Communist Party and such progressive organizations as the American League for Peace and Democracy. That was fine with all persons concerned and the agreement was arrived at. . . .
>
> But the big coup of the Dies-Ernst axis is still to come off. This is to be the removal, or resignation, of Dr. Ward as chairman of the ACLU. Ernst is working feverishly behind the scenes to achieve this end.[37]

Influential ACLU members wrote to Baldwin, fearful that Ernst and Hays had "sold out" the ACLU.[38] Baldwin rejected the story. "There was no deal," he insisted. "The purpose of the meeting was to get Dies to put representatives of the ACLU on the stand to refute the slanderous charges against us," Baldwin wrote to an ACLU member in Boston. "Dies promised, but he has never delivered. . . . Conviviality among gentlemen was apparently made to appear as a political deal—but no such statement has been made in print by any responsible person."[39] ACLU insiders attacked Ernst for his attempts to "play ball with Martin Dies."[40]

Ernst maintained that all he had done was to convince Dies to stop hounding the ACLU. He wrote to Baldwin, "As you know Harry Ward was about to testify that there was no personal dictatorship in Russia. . . . If the ACLU had been tied up with such nonsense by Ward being examined in behalf of the ACLU as a believer in the Bill of Rights and the incongruity between that belief and a statement that there was no personal dictatorship in Russia, very few people would deny but that the ACLU would have been terrifically injured." He asserted, "I am thoroughly convinced that I was successful in preventing the hearing from wrapping Ward's testimony, as head of the League, around the neck of the ACLU. In my own way I still think I did the ACLU a very valuable service by preventing the organization from being tarred with such personal dictatorship nonsense talk."[41]

It's unclear whether there really was a "secret deal." As scholars of the ACLU have noted, such an agreement would have been inconsistent with the character of Hays, who was principled, not prone to backroom maneuvering, and opposed to ideological purges. It was consistent with Ernst's character, however. A likely possibility was that there was no explicit quid pro quo, but that Ernst and Hays used the meeting to try to convince Dies that the ACLU was not a Communist front, that Ward's connection to the ALPD did not bind the ACLU, and that the anti-Communists on the ACLU Board were trying to curb the influence of Ward and other Communist sympathizers.[42] Whether or not the "deal" really happened, the story plagued the ACLU for decades.

Ernst was on friendly terms with Dies and wrote to him that he was proud to have been deemed by the *Daily Worker* "red-baiter number two." At the same time, Ernst opposed HUAC's procedures. "Much as an investigation is needed, the way he goes about it does more harm than good," Ernst wrote to his friend Jacob Wilk.[43] "I gave a cocktail party for Martin Dies recently and I certainly think he needs help."[44] "I trust you don't mind my continuing to be frank," Ernst wrote to Dies. "Cutting under all questions of motives, I should imagine that technically the method of procedure is not only ineffective but at times inevitably leads to public wilderment or disgust. . . . If you don't want to get these stern words from me once in a while don't hesitate to tell me."[45] Ernst told friends that he was trying to get his clients to sue Dies for libel and that he was interested in doing a "Hague job" on Dies.

* * *

Another source of infighting on the ACLU Board of Directors was its report on the Dies committee. In the fall of 1939, the ACLU sought to build its campaign against HUAC around a position paper outlining its threat to civil liberties.[46] That November, the board created a special subcommittee to compile the report. Because Harry Ward failed to attend the meeting, the acting chairman, John Haynes Holmes, appointed the members. Holmes packed the subcommittee with anti-Communists, including Ernst, Roger William Riis, Florina Lasker, and Raymond Wise, who served as chair. The subcommittee members believed it was their responsibility to produce a "middle-of-the-road" report that would help bring the ACLU to a position of "pragmatic realism" toward Dies's work.[47] After thirty days of work, the subcommittee presented its report to the board.[48]

Ernst's hand was apparent in the report. The Wise report, as it was called, began by praising "congressional investigations properly conducted" as "one of the admirable attributes of our democracy" and endorsing "exposure" as "the only defense of a democracy against movements which use the 'Bill of Rights' in order to destroy the 'Bill of Rights.'" It praised the Dies committee for performing a useful and important service, asserting that HUAC "has usefully revealed much propaganda and many activities by those who desire to destroy or suppress American principles and democratic institutions and who would set up in their place some form of dictatorship whether of the right or the left."[49]

Yet Dies had failed in this task because his committee's procedures were flawed, the report claimed. It condemned HUAC's reliance on hearsay evidence from unreliable witnesses, its failure to cross-examine witnesses, its unwillingness to permit those accused of Communism an opportunity to rebut, and for assuming guilt by association. HUAC failed to offer the public the true picture of subversive activities that it needed, the report contended, because the "public has been confused as to the real nature and extent of Communism and led to believe that many worthy, important, and even vital liberal and progressive movements, organizations, and individuals should be suspect."[50]

The Wise report caused a firestorm on the ACLU Board. Board member Osmond Fraenkel called it "an unworthy attempt to curry favor with Mr. Dies." Others indicated shock and dismay. Ultimately a compromise was arranged that retained much of Ernst's endorsement of "exposure" but eliminated the document's overt praise of Dies.[51]

* * *

By the end of 1939, the controversy over Harry Ward and the Wise report led Baldwin to seek a desperate solution to keep the fragmenting ACLU Board together.

Ernst, Thomas, and Holmes continued to insist that the ACLU must be purged of Communists and fellow travelers. Baldwin was sympathetic to this call. He recalled that "after the Nazi-Soviet pact we could have kicked God himself out [of the ACLU]. The inconsistency between what we believed and the Nazi-Soviet pact was so great that you couldn't tolerate anybody then who was a Communist. Because a Communist was no longer just a Communist after the pact. A Communist was an agent of the Soviet Union."[52] Ernst, Thomas, and Holmes started a movement to force the resignation of Ward.

Norman Thomas, one of the board's most fervent anti-Communists, published an article in the *Call*, the publication of the Socialist Party, calling for a purge of Communists on the ACLU Board. Thomas argued that the credibility and effectiveness of the ACLU were impaired by the presence of Communists who seemed to use a double standard with regard to civil liberties violations by Communists. In a meeting in Hays's home in January 1940, the board refused to take any action on Thomas's article and rejected the idea of ousting Ward. "Members of the Union differ sharply in their economic and political views and all are free to express them without involving the Union," it announced.[53] The anti-Communists pressured Baldwin to act, exploiting his fears about the ACLU's reputation and the consequences if well-placed persons resigned. In January 1940, Baldwin and Ernst drew up an antitotalitarian resolution:

> The National Committee of the American Civil Liberties Union regards it inappropriate for any person to serve on the governing committees of the Union who is a member of any organization which supports totalitarian dictatorship in any country or who by his public declarations and connections indicates his support to such a principle. Within this category we include organizations in the United States supporting totalitarian governments of the Soviet Union and of the Fascist and Nazi countries such as the Communist Party, the German American Bund, and other organizations with . . . antidemocratic objectives such as the Ku Klux Klan, the Christian Front and others.[54]

Baldwin provided the statement to the Nominating Committee, which mailed out the resolution to the National Committee for approval in preparation for the annual election of officers at the ACLU's national convention in February. This was apparently in violation of the bylaws, which held that the National Committee could pass only on matters that had first been acted upon by the ACLU Board.[55]

On January 18, 1940, the ACLU Board voted that the Nominating Committee had exceeded its authority. It defeated the resolution and opted for one that read, "It is the sense of the Board that there is no occasion to adopt the resolution setting up standards of qualifications for membership on the National Committee or Board of Directors and the National Committee should be so notified."[56] Ernst was in Washington, DC, and voted against the motion by letter. But this vote was not binding; the ultimate test was to be at the February convention. Ernst wrote to Eleanor Roosevelt, "Monday the 5th, annual meeting of the ACLU, may bring to a head the issue of the future of the ACLU based on the question of whether believers in dictatorships should be allowed on the Directors Board of the Union, which is fighting for the Bill of Rights."[57]

After a stormy three-hour debate, on February 5, 1940, the National Committee and the ACLU Board passed the following resolution:

> While the American Civil Liberties Union does not make any test of opinion on political or economic questions a condition of membership, and makes no distinction in defending the right to hold and utter any opinions, the personnel of its governing committees and staff is properly subject to the test of consistency in the defense of civil liberties in all aspects and all places.
>
> That consistency is inevitably compromised by persons who champion civil liberties in the United States and yet who justify or tolerate the denial of civil liberties by dictatorships abroad. Such a dual position in these days, when issues are far sharper and more profound, makes it desirable that the Civil Liberties Union makes its position unmistakably clear.[58]

The resolution received significant and favorable newspaper publicity. It won the ACLU "respectability" in business and political circles, but it tore apart the organization. More than forty members resigned. Dissenters issued a sharply worded statement declaring that the resolution not only set up a "loyalty oath for officers but also definitely involves the ACLU in issues properly outside its field." It embroils "the Union in the heated ideological battles going on all over the world."[59] Lamont believed that the resolution was "a major turning point in the retrogression of civil liberties in America" that became a model for other organizations and helped sow the seeds for the postwar Red Scare. In a letter to Margaret DeSilver, he described Ernst as the "evil genius behind the whole business of wrecking the regular work of the Union."[60]

Ward subsequently resigned from the ACLU Board and was replaced as chairman by John Haynes Holmes. "In . . . penalizing opinion, the Union is doing in its own sphere what it has always opposed the government for doing in law or administration," Ward announced in a public statement. "What kind of civil liberties is this? It is certainly not the kind which has been proclaimed in all our printed matter from the beginning."[61]

The ACLU was not yet out of the woods. Many observers wanted to know whether the resolution was merely public relations or if the organization intended to back it up by expelling its openly Communist member, Elizabeth Gurley Flynn. Recalled Lucille Milner, "I think it can be safely said that this was the most critical time in the Civil Liberties Union's existence."[62]

* * *

Elizabeth Gurley Flynn had been an early leader of the Industrial Workers of the World and a charter member of the ACLU. As a young woman in the early twentieth century, she was famous for her rousing speeches at labor rallies where she stirred audiences to a high pitch. Many admirers saw her as a living legend.[63] Flynn had served on the National Committee and Board of Directors of the ACLU since 1920. When Flynn joined the Communist Party in 1937, she immediately informed the ACLU Board. Because she was so revered, they told her that it made no difference, and in 1939 she was unanimously reelected to the board for a three-year term.

On March 4, 1940, the ACLU Board of Directors passed a resolution requesting Flynn to resign in view of the decision to exclude Communists.[64] She refused and demanded a hearing, written charges, and the right to counsel. Flynn made a lively defense of her position in an article in the Communist *New Masses* entitled "Why I Won't Resign from the ACLU" and another in the *Daily Worker,* "I Am Expelled from the Civil Liberties Union!" Her language was inflammatory and contributed to the feelings against her. Proceedings were immediately instituted for her removal.

The board made three charges against Flynn. One was based on her Communist Party membership; another was that Flynn was disqualified from serving on the board because she made inappropriate remarks in the *New Masses,* and another was based on her comments in the *Daily Worker*. Baldwin selected Dorothy Dunbar Bromley, a board member who wrote for the Scripps-Howard newspapers, to move to terminate Flynn's membership.[65]

John Haynes Holmes wrote to Ernst that "we must do our utmost to see this Flynn matter through. There can be no turning back now if we are to avoid complete disaster. . . . The ACLU could never survive the failure at this point to act upon the full consequences of our resolution. . . . I am counting on your being present . . . at the special meeting . . . and meanwhile I hope you will use your utmost endeavor to see to it that other members of the Board are present and ready to act forthrightly on the Flynn charges."[66] Ernst replied, "I am with you 100% in this fight, and I think the turning point will come when you call on Roger at the meeting to state his position."[67]

* * *

On the evening of May 7, 1940, the Board of Directors, including many who had come together to form the ACLU twenty years earlier, met at the City Club on West Forty-fourth Street to "try" Elizabeth Gurley Flynn. "I can still clearly visualize the scene which made me want to laugh and cry at once," recalled Milner. "All around one felt the clash of old traditions with the personal bitterness which had grown out of living feuds and prejudices. . . . I remember the sober faces of those men and women, many of whom were not altogether sure of themselves or of their case against Elizabeth."[68]

As the board's counsel, Hays began his cross-examination of Flynn. The trial was not to be governed by rules of evidence, he announced, and there were no limitations on questions. Most of the questions posed by the board had to do with the relationship of the Communist Party to Moscow. To the critical question of whether her allegiance to Communism would get in the way of her concern for civil liberties, Flynn answered that there had never been any conflict between her civil liberties work and her obligations to the Communist Party.[69]

The hearing lasted from 8:00 that evening until 2:20 in the morning. Ernst was silent, piping up only at the end with a comment that he "heartily disapproved" of Flynn's attacks on Baldwin. The vote on the first charge was 9–9, with two abstentions and Wise having gone home. Flynn was not allowed to vote. Holmes, as chair, cast the tenth vote for expulsion.[70] The counts on the second and third charges were both 12–8. Ernst voted yes on all three charges. The National Office polled members of the National Committee, which voted 27–13 to uphold the board's action.[71]

The Flynn affair, summarizes historian Geoffrey Perrett, "was the kind of hearing that the ACLU had denounced elsewhere." The techniques used by the ACLU "would appear again, in a more public forum, almost exactly a decade later, presided over by a Senator from Wisconsin."[72] Observes historian Ellen Schrecker, with the Flynn purge, "the nation's most important liberal organization had officially signed onto the anticommunist crusade."[73]

* * *

Around this time, Ernst had a new pal—J. Edgar Hoover. Ernst had begun corresponding with the FBI director in 1938. For the next twenty years, Ernst would write to Hoover much as he did to FDR, sending "tidbits" of advice, gossip, and suggestions. Ernst's relationship with Hoover, like his relationship with Roosevelt, Brandeis, and Frankfurter, was fawning. He "loved" Hoover, he would say.

It's unclear how Ernst and Hoover met. FDR may have been responsible for introducing them; Ernst's daughter Connie may have also brought them together. After graduating from Bennington College, Connie worked as a radio producer for CBS in New York. Connie was charming and glamorous and a fixture of the nightclub scene, with a slew of eminent suitors. She seemed to know everyone in New York and Washington, DC. "If you are coming up to New York shortly, let me know," Morris wrote to Hoover in the summer of 1938. "I would like nothing better than to throw a gentle party for you. As a matter of fact, if I do not arrange it, I will be in dutch with my daughter who, to my amazement, turns out to be one of your great feminine boosters in the district."[74]

Ernst and Hoover met that year, and their relationship soon became more personal. In the spring of 1939, he wrote, "Dear J. Edgar, will you be in New York . . . I'm throwing a small party without blonds or brunettes. Let me know if you will join us and I will let you know the time and place later."[75] By the end of the year, he was seen socializing with the FBI director at the Stork Club and the 21 Club, where Ernst had his own regular table.[76]

A major topic of their correspondence was wiretapping. In 1938, a bill had been introduced to the US Senate intended to amend the Communications Act of 1934, which had created broad prohibitions on wiretapping. Under the Communications Act, "No person not being authorized by the sender shall intercept any communication and divulge or publish the existence, contents, substance, purport, effect or meaning of such intercepted communication to any person." The proposed new law would authorize "the interception of radio and wire communications under certain circumstances . . . to equip law-enforcement officers . . . with a much-needed and practical method of combating organized crime." It authorized interception "where the head of [a] particular department or establishment concerned 'reasonably believes' that a criminal law has been or is being violated by two or more persons." It also provided that "where intercepted communications disclose the commission of crimes, other than those under investigation and by persons other than the named suspects, the evidence obtained will be available for use in prosecutions for such crimes."[77]

The ACLU was concerned with the civil liberties implications of the bill, and at a meeting in early 1938, the board raised the question of whether they should oppose it. Ernst supported the restriction of wiretapping by local police but believed the FBI should have a free hand to conduct wiretapping in national security (espionage and Communism) cases. He wrote to Hoover, his new acquaintance: "My dear Hoover: I am anxious to get your personal judgment as to the proper social way of handling the proposed new legislation in regard to wiretapping. . . . My own feeling is that whereas I might trust you for a short time to have the right to tap wires on some certification without an application resembling the application for a warrant, and without the necessity of making public, after a certain time, all of the certifications granted by all department heads, I am damned certain that there are few people in the government whom I would trust with the power."[78]

Hoover opposed the legislation, or at least publicly said he did. In the 1920s Hoover had cooperated with Attorney General Harlan Fiske Stone's ban on political surveillance. At the urging of President Roosevelt and Attorney General Homer Cummings, however, FBI spying to investigate domestic fascists and Communists started again in 1936.[79] In 1937, in the *Nardone v. United States* decision, the Supreme Court had interpreted the Communications Act to prohibit wiretapped information from being used as evidence in criminal trials. The FBI continued to wiretap; Hoover believed the law did not apply to the FBI as long as it did not disclose information gained by wiretapping or provide it to prosecutors. Hoover nonetheless stated publicly that he was concerned with the broad sweep of the 1938 bill and its implications for civil liberties, and he made comments to the effect that the FBI would only back new wiretapping legislation if it was "written by liberal lawyers such as Judge Pecora or Morris Ernst."[80]

When Ernst found out about this recommendation, he was impressed with Hoover's apparent concern with civil liberties, and this set the tone for their relationship. "I started with suspicions" about the FBI, Ernst recalled. "I listened to the blank, indiscriminate attacks on [Hoover] by my civil liberties friends. . . . But after listening to repeated assaults on the FBI at meetings of liberals, I took the time to look into the facts." Ernst allegedly investigated the FBI's record and claimed that he had found no instances of violations of civil liberties; "no duress, no holding incommunicado, no rubber hose, no third degree."[81] He believed that the FBI had the "most remarkable record" of any police department in the nation in terms of civil liberties.[82] Ernst became convinced that whatever "rumors and gossip and suspicions" swirled around the FBI, Hoover respected civil liberties and that the FBI must be defended against accusations of impropriety. Ernst, in his celebrity worship, was being duped by Hoover.

19

THE TURNING TIDE

The 1940s were a time of change, marked by the loss of old and cherished relationships. By 1941, Heywood Broun and Louis Brandeis were dead. Morris Ernst's connections to the ACLU were fading. Though he remained general counsel, he grew distant from the ACLU Board of Directors over disputes about Communism and "disclosure." Ernst's civil liberties work declined; he was involved in no major free speech cases after *Hague v. CIO*. Meanwhile, Ernst grew closer to President Franklin D. Roosevelt and FBI director J. Edgar Hoover, seeing himself as a "fixer" for his two "Bosses," as he called them. These were his preoccupations for the next half decade. Ernst's 1945 autobiography was titled *The Best Is Yet*, but by that point his best years and most significant contributions were behind him.

* * *

In 1939, Ernst lost his best friend. Just before his death, Heywood Broun had been at the lowest point in his life, in the midst of personal and professional crises. Broun had remarried, and his new wife had asked him to convert to Roman Catholicism. During his soul-searching, he turned to Ernst, as he usually did. At the 21 Club, Broun passed Ernst a slip of paper. It read, "I need you for no less than two hours and no more than 20." They spent the next day and a half together. Broun, an agnostic, wanted Ernst's advice as to whether he should join the church. Ernst recalled, "We talked that night of Heywood's life. . . . He was upset and serious. I kidded and suggested that he might become a Jew. Why not join our boys? We were being beaten all over the world and Heywood was a star masochist."[1]

Roy Howard of the *World-Telegram* fired Broun from the paper because of his work on the Newspaper Guild. At the same time, the Communists on the guild were edging Broun out of the guild because of his position on the Nazi-Soviet pact. Broun retreated to Ernst's office in despair.[2] Eager to help, Ernst acted as Broun's unpaid employment agent and turned up an offer from the *New York Post*.[3]

Ernst offered to throw a party to cheer him up. He hired the top floor of the posh restaurant Sardi's for midnight on January 8, 1940, and invited a list of notables to attend. The party never happened because Broun died of pneumonia in December 1939 at the age of fifty-three.[4]

Nearly ten thousand people attended a memorial service. FDR sent a letter to be read at the event: "The cause of true liberalism suffered irreparable loss with the passing of Heywood Broun. . . . In him the underprivileged always found a steadfast friend."[5] It was one of the only times Ernst cried in public. "Immortality is only a matter of tense," he wrote. "He is still my best friend."[6]

* * *

By the time of the 1940 presidential campaign, Ernst's relationship with FDR had deepened. His visits to the White House were about once a month instead of three times a year, and they often lasted an entire weekend. "Every so often [in] a few minutes at the White House" FDR would "load me up with additional chores," he recalled. "It filled a kind of niche, and I took great pride and joy in it."[7] His correspondence with the president increased as well; "tidbits" reached Roosevelt's desk every three or four days.[8]

Ernst immersed himself in the campaign, which pitted the Democratic FDR against Republican candidate Wendell Willkie. Ernst served as chairman of the American Labor Party's "Citizens' Committee for the Election of Roosevelt" and enlisted his literary, artistic, and journalistic friends in the cause.[9] After FDR won a comfortable victory in November, Roosevelt, recognizing Ernst's efforts in the campaign, rewarded him with more White House visits and "chores." According to Harold Ickes, Roosevelt was considering Ernst for the position of counselor of the Department of State because Ernst had been "of material aid financially and otherwise in the recent campaign." Ickes recalled that "lately Ernst has become quite a favorite of the President and he is at the White House a lot."[10] Ernst was later suggested for a position on the Supreme Court, which went to Robert Jackson.

Ernst's affection for FDR was sincere, affectionate, and noninstrumental. He wanted and took nothing from the Boss—no payment or title—other than the pleasure of "helping out." During Roosevelt's third term, Ernst began a tradition of giving Christmas gifts to Roosevelt's personal staff. He sent to Edwin "Pa" Watson, FDR's secretary, an annual check to be disbursed to "people carrying the burden at the White House of telephone, stenography and the like," the "doorman, butler, chauffeur, maids, housekeeper, [and] usher." He told Watson, "I have a warm spot for these anonymous and tireless workers who are close to the president and must be of constant aid and comfort to him." But he noted, "There is only one condition that I must insist upon and that is that my name be not known."[11]

Ernst's relationship to the president, he recalled, "created one of the richest episodes of my life."[12]

* * *

On the eve of World War II, the First Amendment was in the ascendant. Never before had freedom of speech been so prized and protected. The results in the *Hague* case had met with enormous popular approval. In 1939, Attorney General Frank Murphy created a special Civil Liberties Unit in the Department of Justice. Against the backdrop of international fascism, the United States Supreme Court extended exceptional protection to free speech, freedom of religion, and freedom of conscience. The protection of the "intellect and spirit" from government control was the "purpose" of the First Amendment, Justice Jackson wrote in the majority opinion in *West Virginia Board of Education v. Barnette*, striking down a compelled flag salute law.[13] Roosevelt declared freedom of speech and worship to be among the "four freedoms" essential to democracy, "inherent in the right of free choice by free men and women."[14] The administration's tolerance of free speech during the Second World War contrasted starkly with the repression of the previous war. The ACLU concluded in 1941 that "liberty in the United States has never rested on firmer legal foundations."[15]

Despite their victories in the civil liberties field, the ACLU Board of Directors remained fraught in the wake of the Elizabeth Gurley Flynn expulsion. When Ernst, disgusted with the board's politics, backed away from involvement in the early 1940s, Art Hays and Osmond Fraenkel took over most of the legal work. Fraenkel was a distinguished constitutional lawyer but Ernst's ideological opposite; Ernst opposed him because of his isolationism and because Ernst believed he was a Communist sympathizer who followed "straight totalitarian lines."[16]

By the early 1940s, Ernst had become convinced that the ACLU was stuck in an outmoded view of its role as a civil liberties organization. It had always adopted a defensive position, coming to the aid of the persecuted, but never sought to shape policy. Ernst believed that the ACLU needed to become "affirmative," an active agent in engineering public policy and shaping public opinion, and he began a long campaign, unsuccessful at least in the short term, to refashion it in that image.[17] Ernst had also come to believe that the ACLU's negative libertarian stance failed to address the two most pressing free speech issues of the time—problems raised by secret, "underground" groups, as well as those posed by the concentration of the media industry in large corporations, which created "bottlenecks" in the marketplace of ideas. In vain, he tried to get the ACLU to take up these causes, which he dubbed "disclosure" and "diversity."

* * *

"Disclosure" was Ernst's main cause in the early 1940s, and he never missed an opportunity to preach the importance of exposing the backers of Communist, fascist, isolationist, and other "subversive" groups. "The Fifth Column can only live in darkness," he argued on the *American Forum of the Air* radio show in February 1941. "Disclosure, rather than suppression, is the way to get them out of the caves and into the daylight, where we can count their teeth."[18] A few months later he wrote, "I am coming to the conclusion more and more that, faced as we are with two underground totalitarian movements, we will be forced to adopt measures of suppression if we do not go exactly to the other extreme—namely, requiring disclosure as to all groups that are operating vis-a-vis the public."[19]

He continued to press his idea on New Deal officials, and it appeared to be having influence. Attorney General Francis Biddle, a friend of Ernst's, declared in a public lecture in the spring of 1941 that the greatest problem facing the Department of Justice was not espionage but propaganda. Propaganda, he said, could be met whenever it could be brought out into the open. When driven underground, it was dangerous. A possible measure worth considering, he suggested, was "governmental scrutiny of second-class mail to ferret out anonymous propaganda to expose its source and its adherents." He said his suggestion had come from Ernst.[20]

Shortly after, with Roosevelt's blessing, Ernst urged Secretary of the Treasury Henry Morgenthau to support a change in Internal Revenue Service regulations that would require tax-exempt corporations to file annual reports giving the names of their officers and directors and an accounting of the sources and expenditures of their funds.[21] His memorandum to Morgenthau, a longtime friend and client, was "predicated on the hope that ultimately, through these tax returns, we [will] make known to the public all of the facts in regard to underground groups, particularly the bigotry, fascist, and communist groups." Morgenthau responded to Ernst stating that he thought "disclosure" was useless, that it would not produce significant revenue nor would it be feasible to make any distinction between illegitimate and bona fide organizations.[22] Roosevelt ultimately forced Morgenthau's hand, and the regulations were issued in 1942. In March, the Treasury Department began collecting detailed information on tax-exempt organizations.[23] "For the first time the government will receive . . . information as to who was back of [the isolationist group] America First, . . . the [anti-Semitic] Coughlin groups, Gerald Smith et al," Ernst wrote.[24]

Ernst encouraged FDR to issue an executive order making the information available to the Department of Justice to use in criminal prosecutions.[25] "If Biddle goes after the disclosure and tax end, he won't have to do any prosecuting or indicting for sedition," he wrote to Roosevelt.[26] Ernst advised J. Edgar Hoover, "Why don't you talk to Biddle and see if he cannot work out some way of vitalizing the information from these returns? There is no civil liberty in anonymity for anyone who throws himself out into the marketplace."[27] Hoover told Ernst that he was speaking to the US Attorney General with the goal of "trying to have some sort of an order issued so that the information in these returns may be made available to the Department of Justice. It seems to me to be a most fertile field for exploration and inquiry and may unearth some rather 'smelly' situations."[28]

In the end, Treasury and Justice Department officials were unenthusiastic about developing criminal cases from the tax return information. By 1942, the attack on Pearl Harbor of the previous December had led to declarations of loyalty from former isolationists, and it had become evident to Morgenthau that investigating the political connections of White House enemies would raise demands for similar disclosures about some of the administration's more dubious allies.[29] The scheme produced no results. Ernst nonetheless refused to give up on "disclosure."

* * *

Ernst's other major cause was "diversity," as he called it. From the start of his civil liberties career, Ernst had maintained that freedom of speech was not only a negative concept. Freedom of expression and thought could not be protected solely by the government keeping its "hands off." Speech was not "free" if individuals and groups could not effectively reach an audience in the "marketplace of ideas." Speech was also unfree when the public was limited in its ability to "see, read, and hear" a diverse range of expressions and thoughts. Ernst believed that it was the responsibility of the government to create the conditions under which the speech marketplace could flourish, in part, by limiting the voices of powerful speakers such as corporate media entities that "drowned out" less privileged speakers. Just as the government during the New Deal had intervened in the economy to ensure more equitable distribution of wealth, it must correct imperfections and inequalities in the speech marketplace. "It does little good to permit everybody to speak his mind if one man has sole access to the only amplifier which will enable others to hear him," Ernst wrote.[30] "Only if they may hear a diversity of views have they that opportunity for choice which is the essence of freedom."[31]

Although most on the ACLU Board were not sympathetic to this view, the Federal Communications Commission embraced it. During the 1930s and '40s, under the leadership of James Lawrence Fly, the FCC, bringing a Brandeisian perspective to the regulation of the news media, broke up radio chains, limited ownership of radio stations by newspapers, and curbed the power of news syndicates such as the Associated Press.[32] The FCC's desire to dismantle media chains also stemmed from the administration's long-standing war with the press. Major publishers of conservative bent, including Robert McCormick of the *Chicago Tribune*, had viciously attacked the president. Roosevelt was hesitant to publicly chastise them, but members of his administration felt free to do so. Harold Ickes made several speeches before the National Lawyers Guild stating that he felt it was a "pity" that many newspapers "persist in representing a class interest, a money interest, instead of the public interest" and regularly "color news, distort news, suppress news and invent 'news' in favor of those with whom they are allied financially and socially, and with whose objectives they are in sympathy." Ickes urged that newspaper publishers not be permitted to own radio stations. If radio was to "survive as an independent instrument of communication," Ickes argued, "it must not become a handmaiden of the press."[33]

As press support of Roosevelt declined further during his third term, the administration increasingly believed that radio was the only outlet through which the public could be informed of the administration's work. This sentiment was responsible, in part, for a government investigation of newspaper ownership of radio stations in October 1941. Ernst testified at the FCC hearings in his individual capacity and was the "star witness" who asserted the most direct version of the policies that Roosevelt and Fly supported.[34] Ernst recommended that the FCC adopt a "broad philosophical rule" prohibiting newspaper ownership of radio stations. He reiterated the importance of "keeping the pipelines open to the marketplace of thought" and stated that "we can't maintain our democratic way of life if the pipelines to public thought become fewer and fewer." He carried his theory to the extreme, going as far as to assert that if there was no other applicant for a radio license in a small town, he would not grant it to a newspaper. Ernst was on the stand for the entire seven-hour session.[35]

Ernst attempted to engage the ACLU in the cause, believing that it was the organization's chance to "do a job on the offense instead of merely the defense."[36] He argued to the board that the ACLU should shift the organization's emphasis from legal cases and make the fight against media monopoly its major concern.[37] After the FCC hearing, he prepared a memorandum for the ACLU Board on why the "concept of the four freedoms must today be regarded as a dynamic concept":

> The Civil Liberties Union has been valiantly engaged in the defense of civil liberties, but they conceive of the defense, and therefore of the liberties in static 1787 times. The Union resists every effort to cut in on what is generally regarded to be freedom but it has done almost nothing to round out the contours of the concepts of freedom in terms of maintaining the freest possible market place in this nation at this time. . . .
>
> Freedom of speech and thought and press in 1941 must be defined in terms of the world of 1941 as it exists . . . if we examine the meaning of the rights of free speech and free press and the terms of what those freedoms can and should mean in the twentieth century we see that there are two major effective barriers to the realistic expansion of those freedoms. . . . They can be summed up under the twin headings of disclosure and diversity. . . .

> I believe that our market place in thought only has vitality and a chance of serving as an arena in which truth can win out if many diverse currents of thought flow into the marketplace as is mechanically and physically possible. . . . The number of newspapers are shrinking. New services such as the AP, etc. prevent new newspapers from coming into being. They have consistently attempted to bottle up the news by preventing its flow over the radio. . . . Chain newspapers bottle up the market still further. The increase of syndicates . . . lessens diversity of opinion. Meanwhile the bottleneck gets tighter. We should examine the relationship of the government subsidy of 95 million dollars to the press in the form of second-class mailing rates to its effect on aiding the giant newspapers to close up the small ones. We should consider the desirability of affording more encouragement to small than to large newspapers. . . .
>
> I could go with the scores of additional danger direction signs . . . I know the ACLU is not emotionally equipped to go forward on the wide campaign that appeals to me.[38]

Hays opposed Ernst, arguing that the extension of the ACLU into the fields Ernst described would undermine the organization's purpose, which was to "secure the guarantees of liberty expressed in the Bill of Rights" without considerations of "our economic and political system." It was not the place of the ACLU "to take a stand on such matters as the enforcement of antitrust laws, [and] contractual relations that lead to monopolistic practices" and other such matters.[39] "Civil liberties must be distinguished from economic issues," he wrote to Roger Baldwin. "Morris has them badly confused and . . . before he gets through he would have us devoting most of our time to trying to change our economic system."[40]

When the Department of Justice sought to break up the news-gathering monopoly of the Associated Press under the Sherman Antitrust Act, Ernst urged the ACLU to back the government's case. "You will recall that my general thesis was that it is silly to talk of free speech in the abstract, that we must relate it to the marketplace, and that to the extent the people could not get into the marketplace, free speech was throttled," he told Baldwin.[41] The government breakup of monopolies in the news industry would not be "government encroachment" but merely "the injection of the government in order to prevent private encroachment on freedom of the press."[42]

Judge Learned Hand of the Second Circuit issued a famous opinion in favor of the government in *United States v. Associated Press* (1943). The newspaper "industry serves one of the most vital of all general interests: the dissemination of news from as many different sources and with as many different facets and colors as is possible. That interest is closely akin to . . . the interest protected by the First Amendment; it presupposes that right conclusions are more likely to be gathered out of a multitude of tongues, than through any kind of authoritative selection," Hand had written.[43] Ernst believed that it was "the most important pronouncement on freedom of speech. . . . The idea of looking to the realities of the marketplace and the listeners, and the idea that freedom can be lost by inaction as well as action, should have a profound effect on our law in this field in the future."[44]

After the Hand opinion, "no longer should the [ACLU] Board continue to say that a case like the AP case does not involve freedom of the press," Ernst wrote to John Haynes Holmes. "We cannot take the position that if the court deems a matter to involve freedom of the press that we still disagree and therefore remain silent."[45] The board nonetheless refused to undertake Ernst's program, maintaining that however alluring other fields of action seemed to be, as Hays put it, "the American Civil Liberties Union should hold onto its accustomed business."[46]

* * *

Justice Brandeis remained a vivid presence in Ernst's life. Ernst continued to see the judge at his summer home in Chatham, Massachusetts. After one of Ernst's visits, Brandeis dropped him a note suggesting that he write a book on the "economic factors of excessive size in business and government and cities."[47] Ernst cherished this note and immediately began work on the book.

In February 1939 Ernst received a contract from Atlantic Monthly Press, an imprint of Little, Brown, for a work tentatively to be titled

"The Perils of Monopoly," subtitled "The Brandeis Philosophy."[48] The publisher, Robert Lamont, offered him an advance "so big that it shocks me," Ernst told Felix Frankfurter.[49] The royalty was a lavish 15 percent. Lamont was determined to get an endorsement or foreword from Brandeis. He wrote to Ernst, "from a cold-blooded business standpoint, the success of this book is going to depend to a considerable extent" on a "tie-up" with Brandeis.[50]

Ten days after the contract was signed, Brandeis resigned from the Supreme Court. Ernst solicited his assistance on the book, "now that you have no daily job to do for the government."[51] Ernst assured Lamont that Brandeis "will really go to town for me."[52] But Brandeis was reluctant to get involved and never lent his name to the book or wrote a foreword.

Ernst continued to labor on the project throughout 1939. In July, he sent fifty thousand words of the draft to Brandeis and his daughter Elizabeth, a noted economist, for comments. Later, he sailed to Chatham to discuss the book with them. Brandeis looked over drafts from time to time and warned Ernst that "that the book must be free from inaccuracies."[53]

The manuscript dragged on into the fall. In December, Ernst wrote to Lamont, "I am to finish the goddamn book."[54] Possible titles included "A Preface to Moderation," "The Measure of Man's Minds," "On the Road to Colossus," "The Reign of Bigness," "The Bane of Bigness," "Gargantua Threatens," "The Burden of Bigness," "No Place for Giants," "Too Big for Use," and "Beyond Control."[55] They finally decided on *Too Big*, the title reminiscent of Edna Ferber's prizewinning novel *So Big*. "This is the best title because the big fat O and the big fat B are luscious tidbits for the human eye," Ernst concluded.[56] Brandeis commented, "Edna Ferber has given you a good title."[57]

The book was Ernst's own interpretation of the Brandeis position. It consisted of case studies in coal, steel, oil, insurance, movies, and retail merchandising in support of the fundamental proposition that "bigness" in industry, government, and culture was inefficient and undemocratic. Ernst argued that there was a point at which mass production increased instead of reduced the cost of each individual item, raising the price to the customer as sales increased. Similarly, there was a point at which the affairs of a sprawling enterprise became so vast that the leaders were bewildered and unable to comprehend the problems facing them. Ernst also wrote that "giantism destroys will and ambition." The concentration of industry in a few large corporations was breeding a "race of clerks" who were "devoid of initiative, stripped of individuality and barren of imagination." *Too Big* argued against bigness in culture, the "concentration of cultural forces in New York City." Ernst proposed the limitation of land holdings, the vigorous use of antitrust enforcement, fair trade laws, and taxation as ways to lift the "curse of bigness."[58]

When Brandeis died in October 1941, it was a tremendous blow to Ernst. Though Ernst was not usually sentimental, he prevailed on Brandeis's daughter Elizabeth to obtain the lamps that the judge had used on his Supreme Court desk and on his desk at home. He believed that the lamps should be owned by "somebody who really loved [Brandeis]."

When Ernst found out that the lamps were Court property and couldn't be given to him, he begged Justice Frankfurter to broker a deal. Ernst would receive Brandeis's lamps in exchange for two replacement lamps. He sent two ugly goose-necked fluorescent lamps to the Supreme Court marshal, and the trade was made. "Dear Morrie—who says the law ain't wonderful!" Frankfurter quipped.[59] Ernst kept one of the lamps on his desk for years. "It was a lawyer's Aladdin's lamp or Diogenes' lantern," he wrote. "Not much of a mystic, I nevertheless touch it once in a while with my finger tips as if the spirit of Louis Dembitz Brandeis might be transmitted."[60]

* * *

During World War II, the ACLU lost some of its credibility as a defender of civil liberties. In some circles, its epitaph was "Born in the First World War—Died in the Second." The ACLU had been much bolder in the defense of civil liberties during World War I. This had to do, in part, with the fact that Roger Baldwin, like many of the top ACLU leaders, had grown older and more conservative. It was also because many ACLU members believed that the second war had a strong moral justification. As such, during World War II the ACLU was reluctant to take cases involving alleged sedition or other issues of national security.[61]

The ACLU Board of Directors was badly split on the issue of civil liberties during the second war. Several on the board, including John Haynes Holmes, were pacifists. Libertarian absolutists, including Hays and Fraenkel, were in favor of civil liberties at all costs. Others who were more relativist in their views, including Ernst, Roger Riis, Elmer Rice, and Raymond Wise, believed that the ACLU should support Roosevelt and the war effort.[62] Ernst opposed ACLU efforts to challenge the administration and was accused of pushing the board to adopt "a militant pro-war policy."[63] At board meetings, Ernst insisted that the ACLU must take an "affirmative position" on the government's side to win respect and popular support.[64]

The ACLU's position on Japanese American internment would be regarded as a great moral lapse. Though it eventually condemned the internment as one of the worst civil rights violations in American history, the ACLU Board initially failed to act. A 52–26 majority of the National Committee accepted President Roosevelt's order in principle, conceding that the government had a right to establish military zones and to remove persons from the zones, both citizens and aliens, when their presence endangered national security. It was not until several weeks after the internment order that the board expressed to the president grave concerns with the civil liberties implications of the order and urged that individual hearings be held. Ernst and four others refused to sign the letter to Roosevelt; Ernst told Baldwin that he did not see "any possible constitutional question if there is military necessity," adding somewhat sarcastically, "and I assume the ACLU does not pretend to know anything about military necessities."[65] Ernst would later conclude that the internment of Japanese American citizens was unconstitutional as well as racist and by 1943 was encouraging Roosevelt to release citizens from the camps.[66]

The ongoing disputes over wartime policy, free speech, and the ACLU's role fueled acrimony between Ernst and the board. Though he did not yet resign as ACLU counsel, Ernst wrote several times to

John Haynes Holmes about the possibility of quitting the position, which he found "embarrassing and limiting":

> I have declined to go into quite a number of important civil liberties situations, particularly with respect to contractual controls of the press, the air, and the radio. You know how deeply I feel on such matters but I have consistently declined to become associated as counsel in any such cases for fear that confusion would be created in a field where I differ violently from the Civil Liberties Union position.[67]

> I've come to the conclusion that I had better spend more of my civil liberty time in avenues other than the ACLU. I'm bored with endless legalisms and substitute motions and its. The mere passage of a resolution of protest, the filing of an amicus brief, or on occasion press releases are puerile spit balls and it is silly how our leading parliamentarians still think that such gestures are the equivalent of action.[68]

> I think the work we are doing at the moment is only of the slightest significance. But there is no reason, if we appreciate our own infirmities, and adjust our tactics, why the officials of the ACLU, with 20 years of experience, should not be the first persons called upon by the government for advice in all matters on which our experience has touched.[69]

* * *

Other than attention from Roosevelt, nothing pleased Ernst more than praise from J. Edgar Hoover. Egged on by Hoover and one of his top aides Louis B. Nichols, who exploited Ernst's pathetic wish to feel close to the important and powerful, Ernst continued to volunteer his "help" to the FBI.

Ernst's assistance consisted primarily of image management. Hoover was notorious for his obsession with the FBI's image and his mastery of public relations. In particular, Hoover sought to cultivate liberal support by having his PR men present the FBI as a progressive, professional law enforcement organization with respect for civil liberties and individual rights.[70] Ernst became useful to Hoover in this project. Whenever a critical article about the FBI appeared in the press, Ernst wrote angry letters to the publishers "educating" them on "the true facts" about the FBI. "I would be less than frank if I did not say that for many years I looked at John Edgar Hoover with high suspicion . . . because he represented the 'constable' in life," Ernst wrote to publisher Joseph Patterson of the anti-Roosevelt New York *Daily News*. "I made an intensive study of the FBI. I can assure you that I have not found a single instance of violation of civil liberties in any case handled by Hoover's boys."[71] The FBI had the "most remarkable police record of the nation," Ernst asserted.[72]

Ernst would inform Hoover when a negative article was coming out, gave Hoover advice on how to respond, and sometimes tried to quash the piece. When the *New Republic* in 1941 published an article criticizing the FBI for allegedly failing to uncover the plan to attack Pearl Harbor, Ernst complained to Hoover, "This nonsense is getting under my skin" and promised to "crack down on it."[73] When Ernst found out that the *New Republic* was going to run a critical article on the FBI written by Roger Baldwin, Ernst wrote to Hoover, "I understand that the *New Republic* is getting an article written about the FBI. The editor will send it to me and I intend to send it to you. I should think that you would want to then and there answer whatever criticism there is, and in this connection I would be honored if you would let me write you a letter containing parts of the answer, to the end that you could incorporate parts of my letter in your answer. . . . I am convinced that [Baldwin] has got nothing in the way of factual evidence to rely on."[74] Shortly after, he met with FBI assistant director Percy Foxworth and offered public relations advice, mentioning that "I'm countering several critical articles." He outlined possible responses to press attacks on the FBI, noting that in each case he was a friend of the writer or publisher and could persuade them to cancel or rewrite the piece.[75]

In the summer of 1943, a pseudonymous civil service employee, "Mr. XXX," writing in an article called "Washington Gestapo" in the *Nation*, revealed that FBI agents had asked him, as part of the screening process under the federal loyalty program, whether colleagues had "ever agitated for labor unions," "mix[ed] with Negroes," seemed to have "too many Jewish friends," or supported the Newspaper Guild. These questions, the author suggested, served "no other purpose" than to push "anti-fascists and liberals out of the government." With its reliance on hearsay and guilt by association, the FBI operated as the United States' own "Gestapo."[76]

Outraged by this indictment, Hoover wrote to Ernst expressing his fear that "sincere readers . . . may absorb some of this venomous poisin [*sic*] which The Nation is disseminating about the FBI."[77] Ernst took some of Hoover's language and used it to form a public response in the form of a letter to the editor. "Dear Freda, I am writing because I feel that a high injustice has been done by the author of 'Washington Gestapo' and in consequence by the *Nation*. . . . I believe [the FBI's] protection of personal liberty is one of the outstanding contributions to civil liberties in my time in the United States."[78] "I have yet to hear a single proved case of violation of the basic civil liberties. This is close to a miracle." The *Nation*'s I. F. Stone quipped that "like most miracles, this does not stand up too well under examination."[79]

When ACLU members questioned FBI wiretapping policies, Hoover asked Ernst to help get the ACLU off his back. Hoover expressed disgust that in spite of his purported respect for due process, "the American Civil Liberties Union, or at least segments of it, have consistently tried to find some excuse for criticizing the FBI."[80] In a disturbing betrayal of his colleagues, Ernst alerted Hoover when the ACLU was planning to publicly criticize the FBI and provided Hoover with ACLU reports and minutes of board meetings.

Ernst never revealed any truly confidential information about the ACLU, and his letters to Hoover never resulted in the compilation of dossiers. Ernst did not "spy" on ACLU members and never "named names," at least as far as his ACLU colleagues were concerned. Ernst nonetheless damaged the cause of civil liberties by facilitating the FBI's long-standing surveillance of the ACLU and persuading some of his friends on the left that the FBI posed no threat to civil liberties. Indeed, the ACLU's criticism of the FBI was meek during the 1940s and '50s; it looked the other way when it came to the FBI and refused to pursue allegations of FBI violations.[81] In part due to Ernst's efforts, the organization that had the prestige and independence to investigate and expose the illegalities of the FBI took a disturbingly passive route.

* * *

"Let me know if there are any chores you want me to do," Ernst wrote to FDR in early 1942.[82] "I am doing plenty of chores for your boys in Washington, but I am in your army 24 hours a day—or more if you want me."[83] Ernst had become so well known as a "fixer" for the president, so efficient in addressing "unsolved problems, bottlenecks, and near-scandals" that Jerome Frank advised Roosevelt to hire him in a permanent "troubleshooter" position with a staff of assistants. For a while, Roosevelt seriously considered the idea.[84]

Even in his unofficial capacity, Ernst was valuable to Roosevelt, especially when it came to dealing with the press. As he did with Hoover, Ernst used his ties to the publishing world to get information for Roosevelt, to find out what was about to be published and alert Roosevelt and his advisers. Ernst also used his influence with the press to "soften up" Roosevelt detractors and to change the image of officials who were "taking a beating" in the papers. In the words of historian Richard Steele, Ernst was a "two-way conduit" whose home functioned both as a "polling place" where influential people registered opinions with the White House and a venue where the president's views were informally disseminated.[85]

Ernst set up a series of dinner parties for cabinet officials so they could meet influential members of the press. "I'm arranging a series of quiet evenings for Leon [Henderson], Donald Nelson and a few of your top boys to meet with [Raymond Gram] Swing, [William] Shirer, [John] Gunther, Helen Reid [of the *New York Tribune*], Charlie Merz [of the *New York Times*] and others. I think . . . these news and radio people can really get a new grasp of the situation if they sit for an evening with each of your top men," he wrote to Roosevelt in 1942.[86] Ernst described his parties as "the affirmative way of beating inaccurate columns," asserting that "I know of no better way of dispelling ignorance and misunderstanding on the part of commentators than having responsible officials sit around chewing the rag with them."[87] He was certain that his "hair-down" parties had effectively countered antiadministration sentiment in the press.[88]

During the war, Ernst also pursued "chores" for Roosevelt overseas, making three trips to London, or "missionettes," as he called them. In November 1942, Ernst traveled as a consultant for the War Production Board, assigned to study the effect of British paper restrictions in anticipation of similar restrictions in the United States.[89] Ernst returned to London in late 1943 to do government business and also to represent J. Arthur Rank, a British entertainment conglomerate owner interested in marketing British films in the United States.[90]

In January 1944, Roosevelt established the War Refugee Board, tasked with the "immediate rescue and relief of the Jews of Europe and other victims of enemy persecution." In February, Ernst invited John Pehle, head of the WRB, to come to his house to meet his "gang" of friends, including Russell Leffingwell, Dorothy Thompson, Helen Reid, journalists Quincy Howe and Samuel Grafton, and author George Fielding Eliot.[91] Ernst collected $100,000 from his friends to be used in aid of Pehle's efforts and was handling the funds in a personal bank account.[92] "I am advised that if there is valid occasion for the use of additional funds a total sum of up to $500,000 will be turned over to me for such purposes," he wrote Pehle.[93] This "secret money" never appeared on any of the WRB's accounting logs.[94] Ernst told Pehle he could draw on the money anytime and advised him that he was "at the moment not in the least concerned with anything but saving life."[95] Some of Ernst's money was used to pay the salary of Ira Hirschmann, the WRB's European representative, and to assist with refugee transportation.[96]

During this time, in an episode that is shrouded in mystery, the evidence of which has been almost entirely cleansed from Ernst's files, Ernst appears to have assisted in smuggling newsprint to the French resistance. The details of this "missionette" are unknown. Ernst claimed that only Roosevelt and one other person knew of it. Ernst's actions led to his receipt of the French Legion of Honor in 1951, awarded to those who contributed to France and its ideals, as "a token of gratitude for eminent services you rendered to the Allied cause during the war."[97] For the rest of his life he wore in his left lapel proudly the little red ribbon signifying the Legion of Honor.

* * *

In the 1940s, Ernst argued two cases before the US Supreme Court. Neither were successful, but they established the groundwork for later landmark decisions in free speech and reproductive rights, Ernst's dearest civil liberties causes.

The first was a libel case. Drew Pearson and Robert Allen had been sued by Senator Martin Sweeney for accusing him in their "Washington Merry-Go-Round" column of being anti-Semitic. Sweeney sued, in addition to Pearson and Allen, fifty newspapers in which their column appeared, in a so-called chain libel suit. Ernst was not originally associated with the cases but was asked to argue in the Supreme Court that throttling such comment was unconstitutional. Ernst argued that it was the right to criticize political leaders that distinguished democracy from dictatorship. Immunity from libel, he added, served as protection for minority groups, who should retain their right to "slug back against bigots in verbal terms." Ernst argued, "To allow libel law to restrict criticism of antidemocratic bigotry would only cause it to become a tool in the hands of bigots and the merchants of hate." The Court came down with a 4–4 tie vote, with one abstention for reasons unknown.[98] Ernst's arguments about the potentially chilling effect of libel law on free speech and the democratic process helped establish the rationales for decisions under the later Earl Warren–led Court expanding free speech protections in libel law, including *New York Times v. Sullivan* (1964).[99]

Ernst remained active in the birth control movement as counsel for the American Birth Control League, renamed Planned Parenthood in 1941. Ernst was a controversial figure in the movement; some activists viewed him as bold and innovative, while others saw him as quirky and impractical. In 1940, Ernst and local birth control activists, on the basis of the *One Package* ruling, successfully defended a law authorizing government-run birth control clinics in Puerto Rico, a victory that Ernst hoped would clear the way for the federal government to provide birth control services in the mainland United States.[100]

Massachusetts and Connecticut, where the Comstock laws were enforced vigorously, were the main battlegrounds in the birth control fight. In 1937, reacting to *One Package*, police raided a clinic in Salem that had been operated by the Birth Control League of Massachusetts under medical supervision. A doctor and two nurses were found guilty, and the conviction was upheld by the state's highest court, which ignored the trend of federal law and held that doctors could not prescribe contraceptives even to save their patients' lives.[101] The US Supreme Court refused to hear the appeal. Ernst subsequently proposed to the Massachusetts Birth Control League two test cases, one based on the sale of a medical book to a physician and another on what he described as a "perfect case" where a mother's life was threatened if she had another baby. "By means of these cases, an intensive effort will be initiated to have Massachusetts reinterpret the law judicially, and to clarify the issue in the public mind," Ernst wrote in his proposal, which the league never pursued.[102]

Ernst made a similar proposal following *Commonwealth v. Nelson*, involving the arrest of two doctors and a nurse under Connecticut's Comstock law, which was upheld by the state's highest court in 1940. In *Nelson*, the court did not hold that birth control was illegal; it said only that it could not be prescribed to address a general health interest. Ernst proposed that Connecticut's Birth Control League announce that all the Connecticut clinics would be reopened at once, along with new ones attached to churches, which would limit the dispensation of birth control to cases where a woman's life was in jeopardy. The Connecticut attorneys did not agree with the plan and refused to consider both it and Ernst's later suggestion to bring a test case where a birth control publication was suppressed.[103]

Connecticut birth control lawyers pinned their hopes on *Tileston v. Ullman*, a test case involving a respected physician, Wilder Tileston, who was barred by the Comstock law from prescribing contraceptives to married women even when pregnancy entailed health hazards. The lawyers sought a declaratory judgment asserting

FIGURE 6. Morris Ernst on his beloved Nantucket, circa 1940. Courtesy of Harry Ransom Center, University of Texas at Austin.

that the law was unconstitutional under the Fourteenth Amendment as "an unwarranted invasion of personal liberty." The case failed before the state's Supreme Court. Ernst was called in to "salvage" the case and win it on appeal to the US Supreme Court.[104]

The state's lawyer, Abraham Ullman, was quick to point out the defects in Ernst's case. The doctor's life, health, and liberty were not at issue—the risk was to the doctor's patients, but they were not on the record as parties to the case. As such, Ullman argued, Dr. Tileston did not have standing to raise the issue, and he urged the US Supreme Court to dismiss the case on jurisdictional grounds.[105]

The case was called for oral argument late in the afternoon of January 13, 1943. Ernst alleged that Connecticut and Massachusetts were "unique among the 48 states and the federal government in outlawing birth control where doctors agree that life and health make it mandatory."[106] Ernst had barely begun his argument when the chief justice questioned his assumption that the US Supreme Court had jurisdiction over the case. "Is Dr. Tileston's 'life' at issue here?" he asked. Ernst recalled, "The Supreme Court went medieval on us. They picked on the most technical points in the original pleadings and refused to hear the case on the merits."[107]

On February 1, 1943, the Supreme Court dismissed Tileston's appeal in a short, unsigned per curiam opinion. Ernst was angered and embarrassed by his failure.[108] His humiliating defeat was highlighted in a full-length profile in *Life* magazine by one of his most ardent detractors, Fred Rodell.

20

ERNST AT HIS WORST

In early 1944, Yale law professor and occasional journalist Fred Rodell approached Morris Ernst about doing a biographical article on him for *Life* magazine. *Life*'s editor, Roy Larsen, had commissioned Rodell to do a write-up. In January, Rodell and Ernst met at the 21 Club for an interview. Rodell, who despised Franklin D. Roosevelt, warned Ernst that he would "slam the little group around the President in the course of the piece."[1] Ernst was not alarmed by this and continued talking.

Shortly after, Rodell complained to Ernst about the difficulties he was having writing the article. "Frankly you're a hell of a guy to write up and I am going nearly crazy in the attempt," he explained. "There are too many facets, too many angles, and I keep floundering around simply trying to decide which one to grab at next."[2]

"I don't know why you are puzzled about me," Ernst replied. "I seem like a rather simple guy who has not hurt anybody in twenty years and who has a hell of a lot of fun. Don't worry about me. You can be as tough as you think justified. I can dish it out and I can take it."[3] Of course, that wasn't true.

* * *

The article appeared in February 1944, titled "Morris Ernst: New York's Unlawyerlike Liberal Lawyer Is the Censor's Enemy, the President's Friend."

> Morris Ernst's friends range from Franklin Roosevelt to Frank Costello. They include . . . Henry Wallace, Fiorello LaGuardia, Henry

> Morgenthau, Harold Ickes, Herbert Lehman, Sumner Welles, Donald Nelson, Dorothy Thompson, Walter Lippmann, Morgan-partner [Russell] Leffingwell, New York *Times* publisher Arthur Sulzberger, Leon Henderson, John Gunther, William Shirer, Raymond Gram Swing, Thurman Arnold, Jerome Frank, Edna Ferber, Maurice Evans, Katherine Cornell, and Sally Rand—to name a few. Many of these are, or have been, Ernst's clients. All of them, save the President, he speaks of by their first names. With the possible exception of Harold Laski, the British Socialist gadfly, no living man can compete with Ernst when it comes to first-naming the famous.

Rodell described Ernst as a "smallish, darkish man whose birdlike eyes and manner belie . . . his seeming physical solidity, a man with a Dagwood-style bow tie and incongruous steel-rimmed glasses," the neckwear comment a reference to a character in a popular newspaper comic strip. "The probable reason why Ernst is not better-known outside the circle of celebrities who know him well is simply that his interests are so catholic, his energies so diversified, that the average man cannot keep up with this jumping-jack-of-all trades."

Rodell claimed that it had been rumored—"bruited about"—that Ernst was devoted increasingly to the role of "'fixer,' 'operator,' [and] confidential odd-jobber for his good friend Franklin Roosevelt." Rodell noted that Ernst was spending less time on book writing and had argued almost no civil liberties cases in recent years. But Ernst was "no fixer for Franklin Roosevelt." Rather, he was a "court jester—and today one of the President's favorites." Ernst is "typical of the men around the president in that he . . . offers diversion and entertainment. He is temperamentally very like the President. The constitutional optimism, the quick-smiling charm . . . the bright, encyclopedic, and often superficial, mind, the fluency and cleverness with words—all these are characteristic of both."

Rodell proceeded to "psychoanalyze" Ernst:

> His most obvious surface characteristic is the constant mouthing of well-known names, the anxiety lest his listener not know in what

> select circles he moves. Here is clearly indicated some innate sense of insecurity, some feeling of inferiority turned inside out for self-protection. Perhaps it comes from his being a Jew in a civilization not always kind to Jews. Perhaps his insecurity is based on the fact that his family moved hither and yon when he was young so that he never had a place he could permanently think of as home. . . . He is gnawed, too, by the knowledge that he did not attend, as did his partners, a first-class law school, that he never made Phi Beta Kappa in college, that he was never much of a muchness until he was over 30. He has driven himself to make up for it since.

Ernst was preoccupied with sex, Rodell noted. "His office bookcases are crammed with sex literature, far beyond the number of books he has saved from suppression."

> This strong intellectual sex streak in Ernst may well have had its source in a typically unfortunate sex education in his youth. Certainly neither it nor a mild and middle-aged tendency towards bottom-pinching can spring from an off-beat marriage relationship, for Ernst's is normal and happy. . . . More probably the sex stuff, like the famous-name stuff, is a form of exhibitionism. . . . His exhibitionism betrays, in inverted form, a sense of inferiority.[4]

* * *

Rodell's unflattering article was remarkably astute, down to the "psychoanalysis" and detailed exposition of Ernst's obsessions and insecurities. Ernst raged at this highly public assault on his vanity and ego. He professed—disingenuously—to be unbothered by the portrayal of him but instead irate at the attacks on Roosevelt. Ernst complained to Eleanor Roosevelt that the article was "just another attempt to snipe at the President. . . . written by the most bitter anti-FDR liberal I know."[5] The purpose of the article was to "attack the administration and spoil my relationship with my friends in Washington," he told his daughter Connie. "This they failed in doing—thank God."[6]

"Dear Mr. Larsen, formerly known to me as Roy," read Ernst's hate letter to Larsen. "I thought you might want to know that there is a frightening number of factual errors in the anti-Roosevelt piece in this week's issue." His father was not wealthy, he wrote, and he was not a classmate of Heywood Broun, as the article claimed. "I think I would be less than frank if I did not say that the indecent and remote sniping at Roosevelt, Hopkins, Frankfurter, et al is exactly what I knew would happen. . . . [Rodell is] one of the most articulate and bitter writers against Roosevelt . . . [and therefore] he should have been disqualified. I write this because I really think that in the long run journalism suffers if the extreme bias of a reporter and a piece like this is not disclosed to the publisher and public."[7]

His friends turned out in a gracious show of support. Edna Ferber wrote that "the Life piece . . . was a shocking thing, deliberate, distractive, vicious . . . intended as a knife into Roosevelt." The article "was not only a political barb; it was anti-Semitic, and the more so because it was written by a Jew who doesn't like being a Jew."[8] Rodell had been born Alfred Rodelheim. Ernst latched onto this. He wrote to friends, "as to Rodell, may I merely say that I think his difficulty arises from the fact that he is a Jew who is a little ashamed of being a Jew. I don't object to people changing their names except if they do it out of cowardice."[9]

"I was distressed for you by the Life article," Russell Leffingwell wrote. "It will be forgotten in a day or two. Let it go to sleep. Don't let it change you. You are yourself. I am myself. That is perhaps fundamentally the reason why different as we are, we like each other as friends. So don't change any at all because of Life."[10] Ernst replied, "I'm happy that so many of my friends have written to Life. I just don't like injustice particularly if it is due to distortion effects . . . I have learned more from you than from life with a big L can ever teach me."[11]

Ernst tried to get Rodell banned from writing any more articles for *Life*. Rodell lashed back in an article in the *Progressive* magazine, titled "Ernst at His Worst." "He is our worst best civil liberties lawyer," Rodell wrote. "A great little guy if a touch on the touchy side. A game little game-cock, a cut on the cocky side."[12]

* * *

But Ernst had the last word. In 1945, he published his autobiography. He had written it in Nantucket over the summer, on legal pads with his favorite Parker 51 fountain pen. Ernst wrote to Ferber, "For the first time in my life, I have done some hard work on a book."[13]

The book consisted of forty-eight short chapters, written in Ernst's uninhibited, conversational style. There were chapters on Nantucket, censorship, banking reform, his childhood, and his children, as well as several devoted to quack theories and "scientific observations" about such phenomena as birdsongs, eyebrows, and sneezing. It was a hodgepodge of buzzing, random thoughts, an apt reflection of Ernst. It was titled *The Best Is Yet*, after a line in Robert Browning's poem "Rabbi Ben Ezra"—"grow old along with me! The best is yet to be." Its original title, more descriptive, was "Autobiography of an Irrepressible Man."

Chapters praised Leffingwell, Hoover, and the Roosevelts. Morris had Eleanor prescreen the sections on FDR to "let me know if you think it is in bad taste, hurtful, or whether it would in any way offend the President."[14] Hoover reviewed and edited the section on the FBI. "Hoover is a great constable," Ernst gushed. "He knew Holmes and Brandeis and their philosophic interpretations of the value of the Bill of Rights." Further, Ernst asserted, "The assaults on Hoover . . . do not stand up in the eyes of anyone desirous of looking at the complete record."[15]

The publisher, Harper and Brothers, touted the book as "the story of one of New York's most famous lawyers, friend of many of the great, even the greatest, such as the Roosevelts, LaGuardia and other big men galore in the political, social, literary, and last, but not least—law world." One reviewer noted that in addition to smartness and quick thought, Ernst also "possesses a precious treasure of humanity accompanied by tenacity and an unusual skill in working for the good of Mr. John Doe, American. Few people realize that the freedom from censorship, low postal rates for books and other vital public benefits are his doings."[16] Wrote Bruce Bliven in the *New Republic*, "there is a small garden carnivore whose life tension is so high that it must consume its own body weight in food every 24 hours to survive; Morris Ernst, whose basal metabolism must be at least plus 150, has somewhat the same problem."[17]

The Best Is Yet was an unexpected hit, selling out its first two editions. It was on the *New York Times* best seller list and topped the best seller list at Brentano's bookstore in New York for two weeks. It was Ernst's first truly successful book.

* * *

When *The Best Is Yet* came out, Ernst was in the midst of outlining another book. More than ever, he was convinced that "bottlenecks into the marketplace of thought" were the greatest threat to freedom of speech. The increasing concentration of ownership and control of the media, he was certain, was decreasing the number of voices in the marketplace of ideas, with dangerous implications for democracy and freedom. Ernst hired a research staff of four, including his cousin Eleanor Timberg, to gather information showing "the frightening concentration in fewer and fewer hands of the control of movies, radio, and the press."[18] "We are truly in bad shape," he wrote an acquaintance. "Four companies are so big that they own practically all of the important radio time; five movie companies own 70% of the movie market, and the newspapers are shrinking at a frightening pace."[19]

The First Freedom came out in 1946, a time of intense public criticism of large, powerful media conglomerates. Concentration of ownership and decreased competition had created widespread distrust of the press. The need for press reform was a matter of public consensus, and criticism of newspapers had become a kind of "public sport."[20]

Ernst maintained that the government was no longer the greatest obstacle to freedom of thought; the primary threat came from concentrated economic power, which limited public debate and reduced the public sphere to an expression of the interests of "a narrowing group of owners and clients." These limitations in the marketplace of thought could lead to totalitarianism, with a handful of corporations "dictating the mind of America."[21] Most of the book was made up of data on the growth of chains and oligopolies in the media industries. In ten states there was not one city with competing daily newspapers. In twenty-two states, there was no competition among Sunday newspapers. Twenty-five percent of the total daily newspaper circulation was controlled by eighteen papers owned by fourteen companies. One news company owned more than three thousand weekly newspapers. There were 117 cities in the country where competing dailies still survived. One-third of all regular radio stations were interlocked with newspapers. Five companies dominated the movie industry, controlling 2,800 movie theaters.[22]

The cure to this problem of "bigness," Ernst argued in Brandeisian fashion, was to restore competition. Ownership of radio and press must be divorced, he insisted. Movie companies should be prohibited from owning interests in radio and television. Chains should be kept out of the movie production business, and production companies should be forced to sell all their theaters. Networks should be required to make network programs available on equal terms to all stations and should not be permitted to own multiple radio stations. Media monopolies should be broken up through antitrust enforcement. Ernst appealed to Congress to help him with his "Crusade Magnificent," to undertake an investigation of the American "marketplace of thought" which "would concern itself not with the governmental restrictions [on] content, but rather with the economic factors which are at present limiting the market."[23]

Ernst's publisher pitched it as "the most controversial book of the year."[24] Indeed, many reviewers believed that *The First Freedom* was "the most significant work on freedom of speech and expression that has appeared in many a moon."[25] Ernst "made a major contribution toward thinking through a problem all too often and too gladly ignored by press, radio, and screen."[26] *The First Freedom* generated an investigation by the Senate's Small Business Committee on the decline of small-town newspapers in which Ernst participated as an expert witness, claiming that the "small newspapers of the nation" were "the boys having their brains beaten out by the inequities of the marketplace."[27]

Ernst was among the first critics to sound the alarm at the trend toward monopoly of media ownership and to predict dire results. For decades, *The First Freedom* was the main text cited by advocates arguing for the breakup of media monopolies in the interest of diversity in the marketplace of ideas. In the 1970s, taking a page from Ernst's work, media critic Ben Bagdikian lamented "fewer and fewer people controlling more and more of our public intelligence," with "fewer than 100 corporate executives hav[ing] ultimate control of the majority of each medium in the United States."[28] The issue is still unresolved, and similar critiques of media monopoly along the lines of Ernst's continue to this day. *The First Freedom* remains the most enduring and significant of Ernst's books.

* * *

Ernst's last "tidbit" to FDR was on March 12, 1945. Roosevelt died in April. It was the end of an era. With the death of Roosevelt, "out go[es] the White House palace guard of the New Deal Era, including former Judge Samuel I. Rosenman, Roosevelt's one-time ghostwriter Broadway playwright Robert . . . Sherwood, and White House intimate Morris Ernst, Manhattan attorney," noted columnist John O'Donnell.[29] "I don't know Truman very well," Ernst confessed to Eleanor Roosevelt. "I think I could be of service to him in a feeble, minor way, doing anonymous chores such as I enjoyed doing for FDR."[30]

Ernst forwarded notes and suggestions to Truman, as he would to every subsequent president in his lifetime. In 1948, Ernst campaigned for Truman under the auspices of a new third party, the Liberal Party, made up of the "right wing" of the American Labor Party that had left the ALP over the Communist issue. Ernst developed a personal relationship with Truman, although their relations were formal and distanced. He made regular White House visits to meet with the president but was never again an intimate adviser as he had been in the era of Roosevelt.

After Roosevelt's death, with no more "tidbits" to pen, Ernst became an especially prolific writer of books. In 1948 Ernst published his second autobiography, titled *So Far So Good*, a sequel to *The Best Is Yet*. Shortly after, he found a coauthor in journalist David Loth, with whom he wrote seven lightweight, "quickie" books. *American Sexual Behavior and the Kinsey Report* (1948) was an attempt to translate the conclusions of the Kinsey Report to a lay audience and to promote Alfred Kinsey, a friend and client of Ernst's.[31] Ernst considered the Kinsey Report the "greatest contribution of science to the rule-making part of the law in my lifetime" and was certain that the scientific discoveries in the report, documenting the prevalence of "taboo" practices such as masturbation and homosexuality among the male populace, could lead to the decriminalization of consensual sexual acts; "laws touching on sexual drives" would be viewed with "more than shame or feigned self-righteousness, with more of an eye toward cure than reprisal."[32] On human relations more generally, Ernst and Loth's *For Better or for Worse* (1951) resulted from interviewing one hundred of Ernst's divorce clients about their "current situation and how the divorce action had affected it."[33]

The People Know Best: The Ballots vs. the Polls (1949), also coauthored with Loth, dissected the mistakes of the press in the 1948 election; in particular, the missteps that led papers to famously announce, "Dewey Defeats Truman." The book argued that the press had lost touch with the people, hence freedom of the press was in jeopardy. "The presidential election of 1948 has given us the most dramatic, the most significant example of the hazards which our basic concept [of a free press] is facing," they predicted.[34] "If you hadn't written this book, I'd have written it myself," Truman reportedly told Ernst when he visited the White House. "It just had to be done."[35]

* * *

Ernst remained active in his law firm's practice, working in an array of fields ranging from estates, trusts, banking, and insurance to divorce and copyright. He continued to serve prominent and colorful clients, including the Racket King, gangster Frank Costello. Ernst had represented Costello since the early 1940s, when Costello was hassled by federal authorities for income tax evasion. In 1947, Ernst negotiated a deal with the IRS in which Costello would pay a certain percentage of claims for income tax arrears and would be given a clean slate in return.[36] For the rest of his life, Ernst had a cordial relationship with Costello, who gave him generous annual gifts including Tiffany watches, fine champagne, and cash. Ernst cherished Costello as one of his "controversial" friends.

In the 1940s, Ernst's firm litigated high-profile media and publishing lawsuits that resulted in significant freedom of the press precedents. Ernst was tangentially involved with some of these, though most of the work was done by the firm's young associates. Notable cases included *Sidis v. F.R. Publishing* (1940) and *Koussevitsky v. Allen, Towne, and Heath* (1947), limiting the liability of the press in right to privacy cases.[37] In 1947, the firm litigated the case that freed the racy novel *Forever Amber* from a ban in Massachusetts. Ernst had long complained that the ACLU was "squeamish" with respect to sexual matters, always ready to defend political speech but less eager when it came to obscenity.[38] To Ernst's delight, the ACLU began an "all-out" campaign against literary censorship after the war. Ernst contributed to ACLU amicus briefs in *Hannegan v. Esquire* (1946), in which the Supreme Court struck down Post Office Department restrictions on "immoral" magazines, and *Winters v. New York* (1948), invalidating a vague New York obscenity statute that prohibited depictions of "bloodshed, lust, and crime."[39]

Ernst remained interested and active in the fight against film censorship. In the 1940s, presaging the Supreme Court's eventual ruling on the matter in 1952, Ernst argued that under First Amendment precedents, prior restraints on film could be struck down as unconstitutional if the major Hollywood producers had the temerity to bring a test case.[40] He chided Metro-Goldwyn-Mayer's chief publicist, "What is the use of words about a free country and the Bill of Rights if companies like Metro-Goldwyn-Mayer are more interested in profit rather than principle[?] . . . Victory is a cinch for you if only your boys have courage."[41]

* * *

After the war, Ernst's two main preoccupations were "disclosure" and defending the FBI. In many ways this was a continuation of his earlier efforts. But there was a new, frightening intensity to it. Ernst was aging and becoming increasingly conservative. The Red Scare was intensifying. His relationship with Hoover became obsessive, almost childlike, in many ways replacing the one he had with FDR. Ernst always needed a "Boss," someone powerful in his life, an authority figure to admire and please. It had been Roosevelt and now it was Hoover.

* * *

Ernst maintained a chummy correspondence with Hoover—chummy at least from Ernst's point of view. "You are a grand guy," he would often write to Hoover, "and I am in your Army."[42] Hoover aide Louis B. Nichols and Hoover encouraged Ernst's efforts as self-appointed defender of the FBI. "Do not ever hesitate to call day or night when you get in a controversy involving us and you need the ammunition," Nichols urged Ernst.[43]

Though Hoover and Nichols responded to Ernst cordially, privately they viewed him as little more than a toady. Hoover never reacted well to Ernst's gratuitous advice or patronizing tone. Ernst frequently lectured Hoover, which irritated the arrogant, humorless FBI director. Hoover and Nichols pretended to give Ernst's suggestions serious consideration but would usually file and forget them.[44]

Ernst sent hundreds of letters to Hoover and made countless telephone calls and innumerable personal visits. Whenever he went overseas, he asked if there were any "chores" he could undertake for "your boys." In 1945, when Ernst's daughter Connie married Simon Michael Bessie, a major figure in the book publishing world, Ernst included Hoover on the mailing list for Connie's wedding announcement. Ernst regularly invited Hoover to his soirees and dinner parties. Ernst wrote to Hoover in inviting him to one such occasion, "I would like nothing better than to sit with you or some of your brain trust and try to help dope out some new approach to attack the underground boys, communist, bigots, etc."[45] Hoover claimed that he was too busy to attend but commented privately to Nichols that he feared Ernst had ulterior motives—ego-boosting and self-aggrandizement.[46]

As revelations of FBI violations of civil liberties became increasingly public after the war, including wiretapping and the presence of hearsay and gossip in FBI dossiers, criticism mounted in liberal circles.[47] Hoover relied on Ernst to "fix" his growing public relations problems. In 1946, *Time* magazine published a mocking piece portraying Hoover "as being drunk and disorderly in a fantasy which would take place in the event the United States should ever lose a war and its officials tried such as those of the German government have been tried at Nurnberg."[48] Hoover wanted to sue *Time* for libel—it is "inexcusably in bad taste and I believe libelous"—and wrote to Ernst for advice.[49] Ernst was able to secure an apology that ran in the magazine; *Time* also published Ernst's letter to the editor. "As friend and attorney for Mr. Hoover I write to say that your crack could have no result but to undermine the standing of J. Edgar Hoover as a unique law-enforcing official who has impressed on our folkways a concept of law and order while still preserving full civil liberties even for law violators," he wrote.[50] Ernst wasn't really "Hoover's lawyer" but often claimed to be. Ernst missed no opportunity to publicize his friendship with "the Boss," and his relationship with Hoover and the FBI was well known among the ACLU and in liberal circles.

Defending the FBI became Ernst's main crusade. He injected himself into every public controversy surrounding the FBI and was always ready to provide public relations advice to Hoover. Hoover had gotten in the habit of writing letters to the editor in response to his critics. Ernst advised him not to "apologize too much."[51] "If you don't mind my being impertinent, may I suggest that I think you are getting a little thin-skinned, and I think you are probably writing too many letters making corrections of attacks on the FBI," he told Hoover.[52] "I don't like your denying that the FBI is a Gestapo. . . . It is a bad association of ideas to ever have the word 'Gestapo' and FBI in the same paragraph."[53] When the *New York Star* published a series of critical pieces, Ernst wrote to Hoover's assistant Clyde Tolson, "Dear Clyde, can I do anything to help you and Edgar on this stinking series of articles appearing in the *Star*?"[54]

Ernst advocated that Hoover go on the offensive against critics who charged the FBI with conducting a "witch hunt" under the federal loyalty program. In 1947, intimidated by the Republican Congress, the Democratic President Truman had announced that the government would assess the loyalty of all federal employees. The government could deny employment to anyone when "reasonable grounds exist for the belief that the person involved is disloyal to the government of the United States." Evidence of disloyalty included "membership in, affiliation with or sympathetic association with any foreign or domestic organization, communist, or subversive." Ernst wrote to the *New York Herald Tribune*, the *New York Star*, the *Saturday Review*, and other publications with statistics purportedly showing the "admirable" record of the FBI in "handling its responsibility under the loyalty program [which] completely dispels the hysteria," noting in particular that only a small percentage of federal employees had been investigated by the FBI and a miniscule number dismissed.[55] Ernst continued to forward Hoover copies of letters he received from such FBI critics as journalist I. F. Stone, the columnist Max Lerner, Congressman Wayne Morse, and former FCC chairman James Lawrence Fly, an ACLU Board member who had long opposed FBI wiretapping. Ernst noted that in forwarding the letters to Hoover, he was "double-crossing" his friends but insisted that it was for "justified motives."[56]

As to "naming names," Ernst was not an extensive name-dropper, but he did occasionally suggest to Hoover that certain individuals were Communists. In 1945, Ernst gave Hoover the names of four associates of William Remington, who had been convicted on perjury charges growing out of allegations made against him by Elizabeth Bentley, the so-called Red Spy Queen. In 1948, Ernst asked to see Hoover about a woman whose brother was an important Communist Party official. He later sought to give Hoover information about a man whom Truman was considering as secretary of labor, alleging that the man's wife had been a Communist.[57]

In 1949 FBI agents arrested Judith Coplon, a Justice Department employee, on charges of delivering FBI reports to the Soviets. In her trials, defense attorneys revealed a pattern of FBI wiretapping. As Hoover complained to Ernst, this represented a substantial public relations "setback" for the FBI.[58] James Fly responded to the revelations with an attack on wiretapping in *Look* magazine. Fly asked the

ACLU to advocate a congressional investigation of FBI wiretapping and called for a federal antiwiretapping law.[59]

Ernst urged the ACLU Board to condemn Fly's criticism and issue a statement supporting the FBI. He advised members of the ACLU to "stop sniping" at the FBI and to be thankful that someone fair and nonpolitical like Hoover was heading the FBI, and not "the New York City Chief of Police, or a Tom Dewey type."[60] Intense debate on the board ensued, with Art Hays and other libertarians joining Fly's call for a federal law, and Ernst maintaining that wiretapping was justified in cases involving national security.[61] Fly wrote a letter to Ernst expressing a sentiment felt by many of Ernst's colleagues at the time: "Your own close personal relation to Mr. Hoover has blinded you to the fairness of the fair critics. You appear long since to have lost your judicial poise on any issue involving this one agency. . . . I am wondering if even you do not have your stomach turned by the recent exposures of various illegal activities of the FBI."[62] Ernst was so irate by Fly's criticism that he sent to Hoover the draft of letters he received from Fly and drafts of his personal replies. Hoover called Fly "a stinker and a liar."[63]

Ernst believed he was Hoover's confidante and "secret adviser" on public relations matters. He wrote proudly to Hoover, "I am fast becoming known as the person to pick a fight in relation to the FBI. . . . Of course a lot of people think I am just a stooge for you which I take as a high compliment. There are few people I would rather publicly support."[64] He occasionally called the FBI office to tell Hoover that he "loved him."[65] Again and again he asked: "Can I help? What can I do?"

* * *

On December 5, 1946, Truman issued Executive Order 9808 establishing the President's Commission on Civil Rights. The commission was formed in the wake of postwar racial violence to make recommendations for legislation to strengthen the federal government's hand in dealing with racial discrimination.[66] The group was a collection of prominent citizens from diverse backgrounds, including African Americans, Jews, labor leaders, and conservatives, all with admirable records of public service.[67] To serve as chair of the fifteen-member body, Truman appointed Charlie Wilson, president of the General Electric Company. Ernst was appointed to the commission as part of "Subcommittee Three," which was to consider the work of private organizations whose activities affected civil rights.[68] Others on this subcommittee were African American civil rights activist Sadie Alexander, lawyer Franklin Delano Roosevelt Jr., and Boris Shishkin, head of the AFL-CIO Department of Civil Rights. Of his many appointments, Ernst considered this one his highest honor. One historian described Ernst as the most outspoken, "aggressive and intellectually formidable contributor" to the commission.[69]

One of the first things Ernst did was to press upon the committee's director, Robert K. Carr, his "disclosure" idea. Ernst fought hard to secure the commission's endorsement of a general disclosure program. Ernst was clear that the program must be aimed at exposing all secret groups, including anti-Semitic and racist groups, and he opposed singling out Communists for special treatment. "Any attempt to try to define or limit the groups which would be called upon to make disclosure," he explained, would lead inevitably to "the basic evil of the Dies concept."[70] Hearings were held on the "disclosure" proposal in April, when Ernst was hospitalized with a serious gallbladder infection. Many witnesses who testified before the committee, including Post Office and Justice Department officials, spoke about the administrative difficulties in implementing disclosure, as well as the potential misuses of the program in terms of government suppression of speech and thought. Ernst received reports of the hearing from Shishkin and wrote from his sickbed that he believed the witnesses were wrongly "thinking in terms of a government Gestapo." Ernst insisted that the government must remain neutral when disclosing information about groups and that no civil liberties issues were involved.[71]

The commission's deliberations were heated, especially after Ernst began reattending meetings in June. About half the committee was in favor of moderate approaches to desegregation, but Ernst and a few others pushed a more liberal line.[72] Members fought, in particular, over a recommendation to condition federal grants-in-aid to educational institutions on the elimination of discrimination. The southerners on the committee opposed this frontal attack on segregation. Ernst was the leader of a minority that supported the proposal, arguing vehemently that to fail to protest when government funds were given to segregated school systems was to "endorse segregation by default."[73] Ernst believed that this was the most important issue under the committee's purview and that a strong antisegregation position might stimulate a national discussion to "raise the sights of the American people."[74]

Ernst also raised hell over a section of the draft report that was highly critical of the FBI. He was supported by Hoover, who had been sent, by Ernst, a copy of that section of the report.[75] After lobbying by Ernst, the committee agreed to change the tenor of the report to "constructive criticism." Instead of charging the FBI with "superficial and unintelligent work" in the civil rights field, the revised report noted that "upon occasion investigations in this very difficult and highly specialized area have not measured up to the Bureau's high standard in the handling of other types of cases."[76] Ernst told Hoover that he had personally eliminated from the report all derogatory references to the FBI and that this had taken some "pushing" on his part.[77]

The final, 148-page report, titled *To Secure These Rights*, was presented to Truman on October 30, 1947. It was compared to Magna Carta or the Bill of Rights in the field of civil rights. The report attacked racial discrimination and segregation and called for the federal government to protect the nation's civil rights. Despite the initial negative comments on disclosure, resulting from a lengthy disquisition by Ernst, the report ultimately endorsed disclosure as "the appropriate way to deal with those who would subvert our democracy by revolution" and called on the government "to provide a source of reference where private citizens and groups may find accurate information about the activities, sponsorship, and background of those who are active in the market place of public opinion." Such "disclosure" would include a statement about the names of officers, sources of financial contributions, disbursements, and the purpose of the organization. The report also advocated Ernst's idea of making tax returns of organizations public and amending postal laws to make disclosure required for those using both first- and second-class mail.[78]

This ringing endorsement of "disclosure" convinced Ernst that he could now successfully press for the adoption of a general disclosure law. A few weeks later, he started a public campaign for it. On December 8, 1947, Ernst urged in a public address that all "subversive" groups be "forced out into the open." He contended, "The only danger to freedom in the United States comes from the attacks of underground movements. The Klan, the Communists, the bigots, the vigilantes cannot operate in the United States in the open. The position of the Hollywood magnates urging that we drive the Communists underground is exactly the wrong proposal."[79]

For the first time, Ernst's proposal received national publicity and widespread support. The *Washington Post*, *Christian Science Monitor, Baltimore Sun, Boston Globe*, and the *New York Herald Tribune* did favorable write-ups. Robert Bendiner in *Commentary* magazine praised Ernst's ideas at length, arguing that disclosure would make unnecessary more repressive measures—it would deprive the House Un-American Activities Committee (HUAC) of the chance to harass individuals for the sake of publicity, eliminate the need for loyalty oaths and government "lists" of subversive organizations, and protect innocent individuals from joining front groups. The Bar Association of the City of New York went on record supporting the proposal.[80] Walter White, head of the NAACP, supported Ernst's idea as a method of exposing the Ku Klux Klan. "Ever since I made the proposal publicly, my telephone has been ringing," Ernst told reporters proudly.[81]

Ernst's campaign elicited protests from the *Daily Worker*, his longtime antagonist, which had been running a years-long campaign against Ernst as a "professional red-baiter." The *Daily Worker* branded "disclosure" as "cold fascism," calling it "a police measure intended to bring drastic economic and social punishment down on the heads of those American citizens whose political views clash with that of the Truman government."[82] For three years in a row, the ACLU Board voted against disclosure.[83] Art Hays remained disclosure's most outspoken opponent. "Legislation that would strip from political and economic organizations the right to operate anonymously would hinder democracy by discouraging freedom of expression," he told a newspaper reporter. "If a man were forced to put his opinions on the public record, it would mean that it might be dangerous to hold unpopular opinions."[84] He argued in the *Nation* that "we are now asked to do something to protect people from 'bad' ideas, thus drawing the distinction between 'bad' and 'good' ideas. . . . But freedom includes the right to be corrupted and contaminated in the realm of ideas."[85]

* * *

With the emerging Cold War, rumors of espionage, and intense suspicion of domestic Communists, the Red Scare was in full swing. HUAC conducted heavily publicized hearings seeking out Communists in the movie industry, in government service, and in private associations. Approximately two million federal employees were screened under Truman's loyalty program by 1948. Ernst considered the loyalty program "unfortunate but necessary," both important to protect national security and "an important and valuable stop-gap to prevent disastrous hysterical legislation contemplated by Republicans," he reported to the ACLU Board.[86] When US Attorney General Tom Clark, at Truman's direction, drew up a list of subversive organizations, Ernst defended the list on the grounds that none of the proscribed organizations engaged in disclosure. The attorney general was justified in taking the position that "an anonymous organization is a suspect organization." Ernst urged that there be a presumption that any member of a "secret organization" was a security risk.[87]

The ACLU spoke out against the anti-Communist hysteria, yet at the same time, because there was a strong anti-Communist faction on the board, the ACLU kept a low profile. The ACLU wrote the 1940 "purge resolution" into its constitution and began including a statement opposing Communism in all its briefs.[88] Its criticism of HUAC and public and private loyalty programs was tepid, and it refused to denounce the government's list of "subversive" organizations.[89] Ernst, not surprisingly, was a strong voice on the board discouraging the ACLU from challenging the government's anti-Communist efforts.

Most of the ACLU Board opposed HUAC, but rather than call for its abolition, which they knew would be futile, they campaigned to reform the committee's procedures. Ernst, who believed that the purpose of the committee was sound and that much of its power should be preserved, drew up proposed procedural guidelines. He believed witnesses should have the right to an attorney and to file additional statements but not to cross-examine accusers.[90] Ernst pressed these ideas on his new acquaintance, Congressman Richard Nixon, a member of HUAC who was gaining a name as an aggressive anti-Communist.[91] Hays and others on the ACLU Board argued that the accused should have a full hearing and fair publicity. Ernst confided to federal judge Charles Wyzanski, "I just don't happen to be one of the obstructionist boys."[92]

The Mundt-Nixon bill of 1948, also known as the Subversive Activities Control Act, would have required all members of the Communist Party to register with the attorney general and barred them from government employment. The ACLU joined other liberals in opposing the bill as "unconstitutional and dangerous."[93] Ernst opposed Mundt-Nixon's registration provision for "sing[ling] out one group by name," although he noted that it wisely adopted the "basic philosophy of publicity and disclosure."[94] Nixon asked several liberals, including Ernst and Hays, to testify on the bill at a HUAC hearing in February 1948.

Prior to the hearing, Ernst informed Nixon that he approved of HUAC's purposes but that he thought the committee needed to reform its procedures to "help you in preventing the kind of horrible public clamor which tends to cut down the right of Congress to conduct inquiries in the public interest." He cautioned, "It is a shame to let the dictatorship boys get the Committee in a spot because of the Committee's procedural methods."[95] Ernst used his testimony to condemn legislation singling out a particular group for outlawing and advocated a general theory of "disclosure" because "it will improve the market place of thought, because the public will be better able to appraise what comes into the market place for appraisal by the American mind."[96] After the hearing, Ernst continued to chastise Nixon for naively assuming that the Mundt-Nixon bill would solve the Communist problem and pushed for a general "disclosure" law. He wrote in a letter to Nixon, "I have examined the bill with some care. I would be less than frank if I did not say . . . what I thought I had made clear in my testimony, that sanctions proposed in the legislation just won't work. The trouble with you people is that you have not dealt long enough with underground rats. . . . The bill gives the Communists all kinds of chances to squirm out. . . . I only wish that you had stuck to [a] simple disclosure plan for all groups."[97]

Over the next year Ernst continued to speak out against Mundt-Nixon and sought support for his own measure. He sent drafts of his proposal to Nixon, the Senate Judiciary Committee, and the liberal anti-Communist Americans for Democratic Action, of which Ernst was a member. Congress ultimately incorporated the basic elements of the Mundt-Nixon bill in the McCarran Internal Security Act of 1950 and never considered Ernst's disclosure law.[98]

* * *

When twelve top Communist Party leaders were indicted in 1948 under the Smith Act, which outlawed advocating the overthrow of the government by force or violence, Ernst supported the charges against the Communists and warned Hoover that the government would face a challenge in its prosecution because of the "clear and present danger" rule.[99] Ernst proceeded to draw up an elaborate theory reinterpreting "clear and present danger" to exclude anonymous or "secret speech" from the First Amendment's protections and formed a Clear and Present Danger Committee on the ACLU in the hopes of getting the board to put forward a policy declaration stating that "secret advocacy" does not come within the First Amendment.[100] Ernst justified his position based on what he believed was the Brandeis interpretation of "clear and present danger," which, in Ernst's view, proscribed the suppression of speech only when there was enough time to debate it in the marketplace of ideas.

FIGURE 7. Morris Ernst works on a carpentry project in 1945. Courtesy of Stephanie Begen.

Ernst argued that since there was no opportunity to subject "secret speech" to public discussion, it could be quashed without constitutional difficulty.[101]

Ernst likened the speech of underground Communist groups to a "conspiracy to rob a bank," writing in the *Saturday Review*, "The Communist conspiracy can be likened to a conspiracy by a group of bank robbers who sit in a secret meeting to plan and advocate . . . the subversion of a bank."[102] However, he pointed out in a letter, "Our society does not have to wait until the robbers are at the door of the bank."[103] He told the *New York Herald Tribune*, "We are in danger of having this trial discussed and reported as if it had any relation to the protections provided in the First Amendment." Yet the indicted

Communists, it was widely known, had not committed any overt acts in furtherance of revolution or even discussed plans for revolution; their "advocacy" of overthrow of the government consisted only of teaching the abstract doctrines of Marxism. Ernst's analysis was deeply flawed. Roger Baldwin retorted in the *New Republic*, "In spite of Morris Ernst's novel principle, the only fair acid test I can conceive would continue to be 'clear and present danger.' Ideas alone should not be punished as incitements in the absence of acts or the immediate danger of them."[104]

Ernst continued to advocate his questionable theory, even going so far as to forward them to the presiding judge in the trials, Harold Medina.[105] Observes historian Jerold Simmons, by 1950 Ernst's anti-Communism had carried him to extreme positions, beyond "disclosure" toward a defense of even more repressive government actions, including prosecution of Communist leaders under the Smith Act and the FBI's antiradical program.[106] And still, there was more to come.

21
DESPERATE MOVES

In the thirty years since the ACLU's founding, freedom of speech had revolutionized. By 1950, there was a well-developed body of First Amendment law where none had existed two decades earlier. The speech-protective "clear and present danger" standard was the rule under Supreme Court jurisprudence. Suppression of speech on the basis of viewpoint was generally proscribed under the First Amendment, and Communists, fascists, Jehovah's Witnesses, labor unionists, and other unpopular groups could express their ideas with relative freedom. Taking language practically from the ACLU's briefs, the Court declared free and robust "public discussion" to be the basis of the democratic process and a core purpose of the First Amendment. Prior restraints were in the main unconstitutional. Freedom of speech was deemed to be in a "preferred position" in the scheme of constitutional liberties, subject to the highest degree of judicial solicitude.[1] Both cause and consequence of these legal changes, social norms had moved in the direction of greater tolerance of unorthodox views. As Roger Baldwin summarized in 1950, "Our country has moved from an era of force and violence to an era of reasonable progress by law. . . . Our Supreme Court has affirmed in a long series of decisions those rights and liberties recognized . . . only in the dissents of Justices Holmes and Brandeis."[2]

Censorship of literature was on the decline, practically limited in the realm of book publishing to outright pornography. The New York Society for the Suppression of Vice (NYSSV) closed its doors in 1947. With the exception of two states (Connecticut and Massachusetts), the dissemination of birth control was effectively legalized. Even prior restraints on film were on the verge of being declared unconstitutional. By 1960, the entire structure of literary and artistic censorship had practically crumbled.

Morris Ernst played a central role in these developments, as we've seen. Through his advocacy, writings, and legal cases, Ernst spurred changes both in the formal jurisprudence of free speech and in popular thinking about freedom of expression. His later-life anti-Communism notwithstanding, Ernst had forcefully advocated many of the ACLU's positions on free speech, such as viewpoint neutrality and "freedom for the thought that we hate." At the same time, he often went beyond the ACLU, offering forward-looking views that influenced and sometimes presaged initiatives that the organization would later pursue. In the 1920s and '30s, as discussed in earlier chapters, Ernst spurred the ACLU to take up the issue of literary and artistic censorship, which became important to its mission. Ernst advocated not only the right to speak as a First Amendment right but also the right to "see, read, and hear," which the ACLU adopted as a slogan in the 1940s and '50s. In his work on media monopoly, Ernst went beyond the ACLU's negative, libertarian conception of the First Amendment to suggest that free speech could be enhanced by government initiatives to create the economic and technological conditions in which the "idea marketplace" could flourish, a position the ACLU has on occasion taken since Ernst's time.[3] Ernst and his law firm colleague Harriet Pilpel were ahead of the ACLU when they argued for reproductive rights as a civil liberty, a cause that the organization would pursue starting in the 1950s.[4]

In part due to Ernst's efforts, the ACLU had gone from a persecuted fringe group to a respected, even mainstream institution. By the end of World War II, the ACLU, and the cause of civil liberties more generally, were no longer regarded as "un-American." A majority of the populace had come to regard civil liberties as the core of the American democratic ideal, as ACLU publicity had long preached. In 1945, the organization marked its twenty-fifth anniversary with a lavish dinner at the Biltmore Hotel in New York City. President Harry Truman sent a telegram, and Governor Thomas Dewey praised the ACLU.[5] A staff of twenty worked in the ACLU's headquarters, and there were more than eight hundred volunteer attorneys. Although "case work" remained the backbone of the ACLU's endeavors, much of the national ACLU's day-to-day efforts now involved close collaboration with government administrators and legislators, with the precedent for such activities set by Ernst. Baldwin told the press that "we have moved from a position of suspected subversion to one of unexpected respectability. The times have caught up with us." ACLU general counsel Arthur Garfield Hays said that it "was a far cry from the lonely days of 1920 when free speech was a suspect idea," recalling how "in the old days we used to go into the coal fields of New Jersey and hold test meetings and get ourselves locked up. Now we file a brief. Governors speak at our dinners." Observed ACLU special counsel Clifford Forster, "The Union began outside the legal system and in opposition to the government. But in recent years it has become assimilated into both."[6]

Baldwin resigned as ACLU head in 1950 and Hays resigned as general counsel the following year. Though Ernst and Hays disagreed on much, they respected each other greatly. "You and I have had many differences, and I am glad to know that you feel as I do, that each of us recognizes the sincerity of the other fellow," Hays wrote to Ernst upon his resignation.[7] Hays died in 1954. Ernst resigned as general counsel that year.[8] New talent in the ACLU would further develop the strategies and ideals that their forebears had so brilliantly devised.

* * *

In his sixties and seventies, Ernst remained indefatigable. Despite declining esteem in liberal circles over his red-baiting, Ernst was characteristically cheerful and confident, comfortable with himself and convinced of the rightness of his efforts. He continued at his law firm of Greenbaum, Wolff, and Ernst, though he scaled back on his paid work and spent more time at his home on Nantucket. Ernst gave dozens of lectures at colleges, wrote books with Dave Loth, and traveled the globe in pursuit of "world peace," universal literacy, and other grand, humanitarian schemes. He mailed a seemingly endless stream of correspondence, filled with critiques, inspirations, and suggestions—"tidbits"—to presidents, Congressmen, and world leaders.

No amount of letter writing, book writing, and globetrotting, however, could make up for the inescapable fact that his influence was fading. The opinions of Morris Ernst meant less, attracted less attention. This disturbed him deeply.

* * *

The Holocaust, the wartime experiences of African American soldiers in a segregated military, and a series of race riots after the war had provoked unprecedented civil rights consciousness. Ernst's crusade against racism and "bigotry," as he called it, gained increasing public support and became one of the most precious causes in his life.

Ernst maintained the importance of state and federal antidiscrimination legislation but insisted that racial equality could not be achieved through censorship or suppression of speech. The postwar years saw a resurgence of efforts to ban hate speech, and Ernst continued to oppose them, maintaining that punishing speech on the basis of unpopular viewpoints was unconstitutional and undemocratic. On behalf of the ACLU, he testified before the House Post Office Committee opposing a bill that would ban from the mails false and defamatory statements about religious and racial groups.[9] "I explained at the hearing that I wanted for myself the right to hold up to contempt the Baptists when they outlawed the teaching of evolution, the Catholics of Boston when they fight freedom for birth control, the Jehovah's Witnesses groups in their un-American attacks on Catholicism, or"—Ernst had always opposed Zionism—"the Zionists when they urge the political Jewish state." The measure "wouldn't be effective. Falsity is a vague concept. What does 'tend' mean? As a prior restraint on freedom of the press it was unconstitutional. It would set a dangerous precedent."[10]

Ernst similarly opposed campaigns by civil rights groups to ban literature and films with racial and religious stereotypes. The 1948 film *Oliver Twist* contained stereotyped portrayals of a Jewish character, and Jewish organizations called for a ban. "This is the United States and not Russia," Ernst insisted. "The people have a right to decide their literary and movie diets."[11] Ernst lashed out at minority "pressure groups" trying to advance the laudable aim of antidiscrimination through the unconscionable means of censorship.[12] Rather than attempt to suppress anti-Semitic material, Jewish leaders should focus on fighting back—"We'll take it and we'll answer back and truth will win out," Ernst said in a radio broadcast.[13]

Ironically, it was in this period that Morris experienced anti-Semitism in a way that truly hurt him, for one of the first times in his life. Throughout his career Ernst had encountered anti-Semitism but had always managed to deflect it, telling others—and himself—that he was only "nominally a Jew."

In 1950, when the kids were grown, Morris and Maggie Ernst sold the brownstone on West Eleventh Street. Roger was married and in the foreign service, and Connie was married and living in New York. Joan had graduated from college, was working in theatrical set design, and was soon to be married.

Morris and Maggie wanted to get an apartment in Greenwich Village and applied to several buildings. The owner of a posh apartment at 40 Fifth Avenue, talking with Maggie, remarked that the building was restricted against Jews. He didn't know she was Jewish. She told him that they were Jews and that was the end of the conversation.[14]

Ernst dashed off letters to his friends: "I am having quite an experience. I have had a life of joy in part because of a glandular defect which makes me resent seeing people being pushed around."[15] "As you know, I have spent a good bit of my life helping Jews, Catholics, Protestants, Negroes, and other groups when they were unduly pushed around because of race, creed, or color."[16] "With a kind of historic justice I now find that for the first time in my life I am being pushed around."[17]

As if he were trying an obscenity case, Ernst solicited letters of endorsement from Russell Leffingwell, Helen Reid, Edna Ferber, and other big names, which he forwarded to the apartment owner. At the same time, Morris and Maggie told him they didn't want to live in a "bigot house." Morris wrote, "We don't like bigots; we don't like agents for a bigot house and we do not think that bigots are good enough for us or our children."[18]

They ultimately moved to a modest two-bedroom apartment in a newly constructed, twenty-story building at 2 Fifth Avenue, across the street from the Washington Square Arch. The apartment was on the fourth floor—Morris had a superstition that one should never live above the sixth floor, so as not to "lose connection with your roots."[19]

* * *

In November 1955, Ernst resigned from the ACLU Board of Directors after twenty-eight years on the board and twenty-six years as general counsel. He became vice chairman of the board, basically an inactive position. The main reason for his retirement was his age; of course, his resignation followed a decade of serious tensions with the board. One of Ernst's last acts was to support, with Norman Thomas and James Lawrence Fly, a militant denunciation of the Communist Party, after the staunchly anti-Communist US Senator Joseph McCarthy, a Republican from Wisconsin, declared the ACLU a Communist organization.[20] Ernst claimed to be weary of the ACLU's respectability and easy victories, writing that "I want to live in the mood of 30 years ago when a sense of urgency existed on the Board and at every meeting there was a cry to arms—who will take on [NYSSV leader John] Sumner?"[21]

Both for the ACLU and on his own behalf, Ernst continued to fight against what remained of artistic and literary censorship. After World War II, there was a resurgence of efforts to impose book censorship, spearheaded by such Roman Catholic "pressure groups" as the National Organization for Decent Literature. During the "comic book panic" of the early 1950s, concerned citizens feared that violent comic books were corrupting children, and New York passed a comic book censorship bill. Ernst went on the warpath, describing it as "the kind of legislation which a Stalin or a Hitler might have invoked."[22] Ernst and his law firm remained active in the film censorship issue, filing amicus briefs in cases that went before the US Supreme Court, including *Superior Films v. Ohio*, involving Ohio's censorship of the racy French film *La Ronde*.[23]

The 1950s saw a surge of interest in obscenity law. The question of the law's role in regulating sexually explicit content had become especially acute with the increase in pornographic and sexually themed media during and after the war. A generation of young attorneys and scholars picked up Ernst's legal strategies and analyses. Several obscenity test cases were litigated, and Ernst's *To the Pure* was often cited. The issue of the First Amendment's relationship to obscenity was finally brought before the Supreme Court in *Roth v. United States* in 1957.

Ernst and Pilpel considered taking the case of Samuel Roth, the notorious pornographer, but feared that their relationship with Jerome Frank, now a judge on the Second Circuit Court of Appeals hearing the matter, would backfire if it caused Frank to recuse himself from the case.[24] Frank joined the majority ruling against Roth, but only in deference to the US Supreme Court. Frank's concurrence drew on Ernst's writings to suggest that obscenity laws violated the First Amendment and that the Supreme Court should reconsider the issue. The Court should no longer allow suppression of material that provoked "undesirable sexual thoughts, feelings, or desires" but had not been proven to create a "clear and present danger." A footnote of his opinion read, "Everyone interested in obscenity legislation owes a deep debt to many writings on the subject by Morris Ernst."[25] Feeling strongly about carrying forward the ground that Frank "brilliantly . . . laid in his opinion," Ernst filed an amicus brief when the case went on to the Supreme Court.[26] He argued what was by then the ACLU's position on obscenity: that obscenity could not be defined with precision, that that the "clear and present danger" test should be applied to obscenity law, and that there was no scientifically proven connection between obscenity and antisocial conduct.[27]

The Supreme Court in *Roth* rejected Ernst's propositions, declaring obscenity to be outside the protections of the First Amendment. It nonetheless adopted a more speech-friendly standard, rejecting the *Hicklin* test as incompatible with free speech. The Court defined *obscene* material as that whose "dominant theme taken as a whole appeals to [the] prurient interest" of the "average person, applying contemporary community standards."[28] *Roth* was the beginning of a series of cases over the next ten years in which the Supreme Court steadily expanded the terrain of constitutionally protected, sexually themed material, representing the culmination of one of Ernst's most important lines of work.

Ernst remained active in the birth control fight in Connecticut and Massachusetts, encouraging Planned Parenthood in both states to pursue test cases. In the 1950s Harriet Pilpel took primary responsibility for Planned Parenthood's legal work in Connecticut. The head of Connecticut's Planned Parenthood decided that Ernst, who was disliked for his anti-Communism and known to be difficult to work with, should have nothing to do with any Connecticut test cases.[29] Pilpel and Ernst filed an amicus brief on behalf of Planned Parenthood in *Poe v. Ullman*, a challenge to Connecticut's Comstock law that went up to the Supreme Court in 1961. The Court dismissed *Poe* for lack of jurisdiction, just as it had *Tileston v. Ullman*. *Poe* was the direct precursor to *Griswold v. Connecticut* (1965), in which Ernst and Pilpel also filed a brief, in which the Court finally invalidated Connecticut's Comstock law banning contraceptives, as a violation of the "right to privacy" safeguarded by the Fourteenth Amendment.[30]

* * *

As he aged, Ernst became more zealous about representing "unpopular causes." Ernst's unpopular causes were once civil liberties and free speech; they now included defending anti-Communism and the FBI, both unpopular causes on the left.

In the early 1950s Ernst and FBI director J. Edgar Hoover's relationship was at its peak. Ernst was on Hoover's "Special Correspondents" list; persons of this rank received special replies signed by Hoover. Ernst continued to work actively with Hoover, his aide Louis B. Nichols, and other FBI officials to shape the FBI's public image.[31] Ernst believed that films and television shows on the

FBI would enhance the bureau's stature and offered to pressure his media clients to make such an intervention.[32] In 1951 Ernst urged his friend and client, CBS broadcast journalist Ed Murrow, to produce a documentary depicting "the FBI's critical role in American society," which would take the FBI out of the realm of "cops and robbers" and reveal its real activities—"who its agents are, the extensive training they receive, and why the FBI is not a Gestapo."[33]

Ernst continued to forward to Hoover minutes of ACLU meetings. In January 1952 Ernst sent Hoover ACLU meeting minutes and updated the FBI on the ACLU's proposed program on blacklisting in the media and its intent to file a complaint with the Federal Communications Commission. Later Ernst informed Nichols about an ACLU Board meeting in which James Lawrence Fly had criticized the FBI's practice of including a section in all loyalty reports detailing instances where attorneys defended Communists, a "derogatory information" section. Hoover sent Ernst a list of talking points defending the FBI's practices for Ernst's use against the ACLU critics.[34]

Whenever Ernst heard that an anti-FBI article was coming out in the press, he would pressure the editors to send advance copies to him and to Hoover for "censoring" and prescreening. Ernst wrote several pro-FBI articles for popular magazines, including a piece in *Look* magazine titled "Let's Help People Quit Being Reds" and an article in the *American Scholar* defending the FBI's involvement in the loyalty program. Perhaps the most egregious of Ernst's FBI defenses was his article titled "Why I No Longer Fear the FBI," which appeared in *Reader's Digest* in December 1950. *Reader's Digest* announced, "A noted liberal examines the record of the FBI and finds a 'fervid insistence on protecting the rights of individuals.'"[35]

The idea of a *Reader's Digest* article endorsing the FBI as a protector of civil liberties came from Nichols in October 1949, after the public relations problem posed by the Coplon decision and the article on wiretapping by Fly. Hoover agreed with Ernst that the FBI needed to engage in damage control. Nichols met with Ernst to strategize a response. *Reader's Digest* editor Fulton Oursler, a friend of Hoover's, and publisher DeWitt Wallace made arrangements to pay Ernst $1,000 to "tell the story of the FBI to the American public." Hoover directed FBI officials to assist Ernst, and the FBI Crime Records Division became deeply involved in "the Ernst projects" by forwarding material from FBI files. The main concept of Ernst's article was that of a "famous liberal who viewed the FBI with great suspicion and some fear, investigated it for himself, and emerged as one of its most enthusiastic champions." Oursler rejected Ernst's initial version of the article, finding it too pedantic. Nichols offered to revise Ernst's text and brighten the narrative with examples and anecdotes.[36] The final version of the article was produced in the fall of 1950.

Another crisis for the FBI had surfaced in the summer of 1950 when *Publishers Weekly* announced that a book by longtime FBI foe Max Lowenthal, titled *The Federal Bureau of Investigation*, would be published. Hoover engaged Ernst to contact the publisher, William Sloane Associates, and urge that the book be canceled.[37] Ernst recommended against direct intervention, arguing that it could backfire. He then began telling friends in the media that the book was inaccurate, "vicious and thoroughly unfair." Ernst proposed to Hoover that the FBI release a booklet titled *The Federal Bureau of Investigation* and register it with the Library of Congress to confuse the issue.[38] Ernst believed the Lowenthal book was part of the "smear campaign" against the FBI.

The *Reader's Digest* article, which Ernst hoped would neutralize the Fly and Lowenthal critiques, appeared in December 1950. In the article, Ernst recalled his own "conversion story"—how he had heard criticisms that the FBI was made up of "witchhunters" and then conducted his own investigations to find "a remarkable absence" of fault.

> In my study of the FBI it soon became clear that lies were being spread against it. For example, it has been said and printed repeatedly that agents in loyalty investigations demand to know whether a suspect reads certain magazines of leftist tinge. This charge is a lie. . . . Directives to FBI agents forbid such questions, unless the reading

> matter is published by the Communist Party. . . . I have personally checked about 100 complaints and I have yet to find one piece of evidence of improper questioning by agents.
>
> A real "smear" campaign has been carried on against Hoover's work. Those who feared the Bureau—as I once did—will be glad to know the facts. The FBI is unique in the history of national police. It has a magnificent record of respect for individual freedom . . . [and] it has zealously tried to prevent itself from violating the democratic process.[39]

Hoover was enormously pleased with article. The FBI mailed 375 reprints to opinion leaders including journalists, members of Congress, police officials, and clergy members.[40] At the time, the *Reader's Digest* had the largest circulation of any magazine in the world. Hoover lauded Ernst, stating in a letter to him, "You have indeed set forth in a clear, concise, and factual fashion some of the problems which confront my associates and me. Your words coming as they are from the pen of a most competent practicing attorney . . . do much to clarify our position in the minds of the few doubting Thomases."[41]

Another of Ernst's insidious efforts to promote the FBI was his 1952 book *Report on the American Communist,* coauthored with Dave Loth. The treatise, originally titled "The Nature of the Enemy," proposed how to "end the Communist Party in America." Employing a popular trope of the time, the book was a pseudo-Freudian explanation of why people became Communists and were allegedly unable to leave the party. Several of Ernst's friends—broadcaster Edward R. Murrow, Democratic Senator Hubert Humphrey of Minnesota, and Republican Senator Karl Mundt of South Dakota—as well as the FBI's Nichols assisted in arranging interviews with three hundred ex-Communists.[42] Nichols arranged to have several FBI field offices assist Ernst with his research. The FBI's assistant director William Sullivan reviewed a draft copy of the manuscript and offered suggestions for revision.[43]

In the book, Ernst and Loth pronounced sweeping judgments.

Communists were "more or less neurotic people" who joined the Communist Party primarily for psychological rather than political or economic reasons. Communism in the United States had little, if any, economic base, they argued. Instead, Communists were driven to party membership by a need for "emotional satisfaction," escaping family rejection by substituting "comradeship" for family ties. *Report on the American Communist* abounded with psychobabble—"father complexes," "mother fixations," "sense of guilt," and "need for group approval." Incidents that they claimed caused people to join the Communist Party included rejection by or hostility to their parents, the influence of a sexual partner, frustration arising from a physical or emotional handicap, or even the "mistaken ardor of youth." According to Ernst and Loth, "All or most" Communists possessed "a sense of personal inadequacy" as well as a lack of "humor and optimism."[44]

Ernst and Loth's premise was that a major factor preventing Communists from leaving the party was the stigma of having been an ex-Communist—fear of being "exposed, smeared and discriminated against."[45] They asserted that 90 percent of Communists would leave the party "if they knew they would be accepted by free society." Ernst encouraged forgiveness for ex-Communists and the creation of a government commission consisting of clergy and psychologists to "prevent new membership and siphon the present membership."[46] The five thousand "hard-core" Communist Party members, he asserted, should be left to the FBI.

The book received faint praise from a few reviewers but was mostly attacked by critics across the political spectrum. Ernst was touchy about criticism, as usual. The right-wing American Legion wrote a blistering review, saying of Ernst and Loth, "They claim to have interviewed some 300 ex-communists but all remain nameless. . . . And all of them talk just like Ernst! . . . Even to parroting his clichés and absurd fallacies . . . a completely worthless book."[47] Ernst demanded a retraction.[48] A small, liberal anti-Communist publication, the *New Leader*, was set to publish a "roast-review" of the book. When he found out about it, Ernst contacted the editors and told them that if they printed it, he could prove in court that it was written by a personal enemy. The magazine's editors decided to not risk being sued.[49]

* * *

Ernst and Loth's book would also come to have a connection to the infamous Rosenberg case. In March 1951, Julius and Ethel Rosenberg were convicted of conspiracy to commit espionage by transmitting nuclear weapon designs to the Soviets and were sentenced to death in the electric chair. The ACLU had taken the official position that the Rosenberg trial raised no civil liberties issues and that it therefore should not intervene. With the execution looming at the end of 1952, the couple's relatives were desperate.[50]

Julius Rosenberg's brother and sister tried to find prominent figures to support them in a call for clemency. One of the people they called on was Eleanor Roosevelt. The former First Lady told them she did not think she could sign a petition for clemency because if she did, it would suggest that she believed the courts were wrong. Instead, she suggested that they see Ernst, whom she called a "great civil rights lawyer." Ernst met with the Rosenberg family in December 1952. According to Julius Rosenberg's sister, Ethel Goldberg, the meeting was short and unpleasant, consisting mostly of "lectures on communism" by Ernst. He had a copy of *Report on the American Communist* on his desk and pushed it toward them to read. Ernst offered to see their attorney, Manny Bloch, claiming that he had an angle that could save the couple's lives.[51]

Ernst called Nichols at the FBI to say that he had been in touch with the Rosenberg family, that they wanted him to intercede, and that he thought there was a "good chance" that he would enter the case. He said that he would get involved only if he could "make some contribution" to the FBI. According to an FBI memo, Ernst stated that he was willing to get into the case "solely for the purpose of being able to talk to the Rosenbergs and possibly get them to talk." Ernst reportedly told Nichols, "If [Julius] Rosenberg breaks and tells all he knows, this would be a terrific story and would probably be most helpful to the Bureau." Ernst asked Nichols for FBI information on the Rosenbergs but was advised that they could give him nothing. Nichols told Ernst that the case was now "out of our hands" and that the FBI "simply could not under any circumstances become involved."[52]

A week later, Ernst reported to Eleanor Roosevelt that he had done a "psychological analysis" of the Rosenbergs—pseudopsychological, to be sure—and was persuaded that because of "interesting psychological factors," their lives could be saved by "penance and confession."[53] Ernst's theory was that "Mrs. Rosenberg is the master and Mr. Rosenberg the servant in the relationship. As a matter of fact, the dominance of Mrs. Rosenberg seems so clear to me that my mind went back to the tragic Leopold and Loeb story. I recall that Clarence Darrow told how, when the slave in that relationship had discovered that the master was less than perfect, the slave became a free man, confessed all and was on the way to self-redemption."[54] Ernst also reported this "study" to Nichols and Hoover. According to Joyce Milton and Ronald Radosh, authors of a study of the Rosenberg case published in 1983, government officials seized on this theory because it gave some justification for going ahead with the execution of Ethel Rosenberg. Ernst's "psychological study" would later appear in official reports, in statements by the attorney general, and eventually in President Dwight D. Eisenhower's personal correspondence as a reason for not granting clemency at least to Mrs. Rosenberg.[55]

Ernst believed that the Rosenberg family had been enthusiastic about his offer to help, but their attorney, Bloch, never contacted him. Ernst complained to Roosevelt that "the behavior of the attorney is, to say the least, enigmatic. I am at a total loss to understand his failure to see me as he promised he would."[56] Ernst told Nichols that he thought Bloch preferred that the Rosenbergs be executed—that they were more valuable to the Communists as martyrs.[57] Both Rosenbergs were executed in June 1953.

In their book *The Rosenberg File*, Milton and Radosh conclude that the FBI records painted "a shocking picture" of a lawyer offering to represent clients "only with the FBI's permission, and then, in effect, only to act as the Bureau's servant."[58] Another writer, Richard

Harris, observes, "The offer was probably a disbarable act and was certainly a disgraceful one."[59] Wrote lawyer Alan Dershowitz in a *New York Times* review of the Milton and Radosh book, "Ernst, who died in 1976, cannot respond to these serious charges of perfidy, the legal analogue of espionage and treason. It is, of course, possible that the FBI memorandums do not accurately reflect his motivations . . . possibly he was using unorthodox measures in a desperate effort to save the Rosenbergs' lives. Perhaps some rebuttal or explanation will be forthcoming from his legion of friends and admirers. If not, this revelation will require some reassessment of Ernst's important place in the history of American civil liberties."[60]

Did Ernst seek to join the Rosenbergs' defense team for the purpose of assisting the FBI? Yes and no. As was the case with many of Ernst's efforts, especially in this period of his life, his motives were mixed. Ernst genuinely wanted to save the Rosenbergs' lives, which he believed he could accomplish with his pseudopsychological explanation. At the same time, he wanted to score points with Hoover and to help the government fight the Communist menace. His genuinely humanitarian instincts coexisted with his befuddled beliefs about the FBI and his hatred for the Communists. Ernst's ham-handed and disturbing efforts to intervene in the Rosenberg case reflect his state of mind at the time—arrogant, overconfident, enmeshed in his own quack theories, infatuated with authority, and at the same time still possessed of a kernel of good, always willing to "help."

* * *

Ernst's old friends were dying, growing old and sick, drifting apart. Laurie Greenbaum died in 1951. Jerome Frank passed away in 1957. Roger Baldwin was still alive but had split with Ernst over politics. Some of Ernst's main companions in the 1950s were the younger members of the firm, especially Arthur Joel Katz and Alan Schwartz, recent law graduates. Ernst was famous for his guidance and mentorship of the "youngsters," offering them cobilling on his books and briefs and giving them use of his sailboat. Malcolm Hoffmann, who had worked in the antitrust division of the Department of Justice and joined the firm in 1955, became Ernst's best friend during the last two decades of Ernst's life. Ernst and Hoffmann sparred intellectually and started a social club, called the Discourse Club, devoted to animated discussion of social issues under the proposition that "reasonable men should defend their civilization as well as improve it."[61]

Ernst's children remained a source of love and cheer, as did his five grandchildren. Connie and Roger each had two children. Joan, the severely hearing-impaired daughter who had married a man who was deaf, had a daughter of her own, Stephanie, who was a delight to Morris. Morris was impressed by the spunk and resourcefulness of "Steffie," who could hear. At three or four she learned to answer the phone and could use sign language to communicate effectively with her parents. She would become one of the most important persons to him in the last years of his life.[62]

Marie Jahoda was a Austrian Jewish sociologist who had immigrated to the United States in 1945 after living in England as a refugee during the war. A professor at New York University, Jahoda was renowned for her work theorizing the psychology of racial prejudice. Ernst and Jahoda met in the late 1940s and developed a strong emotional and intellectual bond. Jahoda lived nearby and made the Ernsts' home her "coffee shop" during afternoons. Ernst delighted in his lively conversations with Jahoda, describing her as "my great needler and invigorator" and "my most significant adult teacher," and even dedicating a book to her.[63]

It has been suggested that they had an affair.[64] There is no direct evidence of this, although Ernst's correspondence with Jahoda did have an intimate tone. When Jahoda went to England in 1958 and married a British politician, Ernst was lonely and depressed. "My dear Marie," he wrote to her, "I miss you more than anybody."[65]

* * *

In 1955, Ernst published one of his most unusual books, *Utopia 1976*. It was a prediction of American life twenty years in the future, by a "glandular optimist who has carried on a lifelong love affair with the United States." Based on "extrapolation of known facts," Ernst envisioned a wondrous "Utopia" where citizens enjoyed more leisure time, better health, and expanded educational and cultural opportunities, facilitated by new technologies and sources of energy. Ernst foresaw "trucks propelled on special highways without drivers, climate regulated by man, global travel without passports, . . . fish farms to help feed larger and healthier populations," and "elimination of the common cold."[66] "Since I believe that dreams make history," he proclaimed in a letter to an acquaintance, "I am not ashamed to ask people to spread my Utopia 1976."[67]

Ernst appeared on Murrow's television show *Person to Person* to promote the book. The half-hour show featured Morris and Maggie Ernst in their apartment. Maggie was visibly nervous, but Morris, who loved television and became a regular on the talk show circuit, was gregarious and in his element.[68]

Ernst enjoyed such trips before the spotlight, but they were increasingly few and far between. By the mid-1950s it was clear that he was becoming a relic of times gone by. No longer being important, relevant, or desired was intolerable to him, and it led him to make a desperate move.

* * *

On March 12, 1956, a forty-two-year-old named Jesus de Galindez, a doctoral student at Columbia University, disappeared without a trace from a New York subway station. Galindez was a quiet, scholarly man who had been exiled from Spain in 1939 and then went to France, where he stayed until the Nazi invasion prompted him to take refuge in the Dominican Republic, where he lived until 1946, when he came to the United States. Galindez was an opponent of the Dominican dictator General Rafael Trujillo and had written a doctoral dissertation exposing the violence and corruption of the Trujillo regime, including more than 140 political assassinations. Galindez was seeking a publisher when he disappeared.

Soon after his disappearance, police and reporters turned up evidence that he had been kidnapped by Trujillo's agents and flown to the Dominican Republic in a light plane piloted by a young man named Gerald Murphy. The plane had taken off from a commercial airport at Amityville, on New York's Long Island. In February 1957, *Life* magazine published an article purporting to track the Murphy plane to the Dominican Republic, where Galindez was allegedly murdered after a dramatic confrontation with Trujillo. *Life* reported that Murphy was subsequently killed in the Dominican Republic because of his knowledge of the kidnapping.[69]

Coincidentally, around the same time as the *Life* article came out, Ernst was in the Dominican Republic. The visit was part of a personal crusade he undertook in the 1950s to travel the world and promote literacy through the use of television and radio.[70] He spent "two valuable days in Santo Domingo," he had written to his friend Franklin D. Roosevelt Jr. With Roosevelt's encouragement, Ernst had met Trujillo to seek support for his "universal literacy" mission.[71] Ernst did not deny that Trujillo was a dictator but believed that Trujillo's regime was not as bad as it had been portrayed in the American press. He wrote to the Dominican ambassador, "I am at a loss to find the reason why your republic should be so much more unpopular with our government and among our people than are other Central and South American governments operating under a one-party system."[72]

Sydney Baron, a New York publicist, handled public relations for Trujillo. After the *Life* article, Baron asked Ernst if he would undertake an independent inquiry of the Galindez matter for Trujillo. Ernst accepted Baron's proposal and was offered a retainer of $100,000 from Trujillo via Baron.[73]

Ernst's decision to get involved was met with astonishment. Five prominent liberals sent a letter to Ernst questioning his wisdom. His friends professed utter disbelief that he should have anything to do with Trujillo. Roger Baldwin wrote a strongly worded letter to Ernst's law firm partner Eddie Greenbaum saying that he was "shocked and troubled by Morris' acceptance of a case so foreign to his record and reputation. . . . You will appreciate, Eddie, my concern not only for an old and treasured friendship . . . but also my fear that his usefulness to the cause we have so long shared may be irrevocably compromised."[74] Greenbaum and fellow partner Herbert Wolff asked Ernst to decline the retainer and told him that the firm would have nothing to do with the matter. Ernst subsequently set up an independent investigative agency and commissioned William Munson, a retired

New York Supreme Court justice, as well as Ernst's young law partner, Alan Schwartz. Ernst warned Schwartz, "You are going to get your ears slapped. But that is what ears are for."[75]

Why Ernst decided to take the case is not totally clear. He told news outlets that it was because "too many lawyers will not take unpopular clients." He also said he wanted to fight back against "trial by press." Ernst claimed that because the press had produced evidence that Trujillo was implicated in Galindez's disappearance, it was important that he make an "independent inquiry" to establish the truth.[76]

There is also some evidence that Ernst had real humanitarian motives and believed he could achieve them by getting involved with the case. This line of reasoning is perverse but not inconsistent with Ernst's thinking at the time. In his acceptance letter to Baron, he said his involvement could improve relations between the United States and the Dominican Republic, which would aid the "furtherance of democratic institutions in the latter."[77] Ernst also apparently thought that if he cooperated with Trujillo, he might be able to obtain funding from the dictator to develop literacy programs in Latin America.[78] Ernst planned to use the funds he received for the job to commission the writing and publication of books about "techniques for transition from dictatorships to democracy."[79] However, it seems most likely that Ernst's hunger for the spotlight was the main motivation for his involvement in this debacle.

Ernst claimed he had been told by "fast friends" at the White House, the FBI, and the Department of Justice that the government would welcome his going into the case and would work with him; that he "checked in with the FBI, Justice Department, and White House" and got "green lights all over the place."[80] He soon found that they had no interest in cooperation. "As you know, I have been treated like a leper," he complained to Baron.[81] Attorney General Herbert Brownell reminded Ernst of his duty as an American citizen—if he had information about a crime, he should bring it forward and not expect the Justice Department to tell him the evidence it had.[82] Ernst wrote to Hoover attempting to engage him in a quid pro quo, telling him that he would share with Hoover what he found in his investigation if the FBI turned over its material. Hoover refused, confiding to Nichols that he believed Ernst was "maneuvering in his own interest," and advised the attorney general against any cooperation with Ernst.[83] Hoover was also reluctant to take part because Galindez was an informant who had been paid since the 1940s by the FBI to monitor Communist and other radical groups in New York.[84]

Ernst also asked the CIA to get involved, not knowing that there had been a Galindez-CIA connection for more than a decade. Since the early 1940s, the CIA had been funding an anti-Franco, Basque espionage network for which Galindez had been a trustee. The CIA turned over more than a million dollars to Galindez to finance it. The CIA wanted to prevent this connection from being revealed. The CIA sent an agent to Ernst's office, purportedly to assist Ernst and Schwartz, but they soon found that the agent was there to divert them. The agent led them on a wild-goose chase; accompanied by the agent, Schwartz traveled to Cuba to inspect airport logs and interview Cuban secret police on the theory that Murphy had flown Galindez to Cuba.[85] Ernst and Schwartz believed that the CIA's purpose was to "block any attempt by us to find the real answer to the puzzle."[86]

Ernst and his team spent ten months on the investigation. Ernst's report, titled *Report and Opinion in the Matter of Galindez*, an obvious attempt to exonerate Trujillo, found "not a scintilla of evidence" to connect the disappearance of Galindez to Trujillo. The document stated that "no accusation connecting the Dominican Republic or any of its officials with the disappearance of Galindez is supported by any evidence."[87]

Ernst's principal argument was based on Murphy's flight schedule. Ernst argued that it was impossible for Murphy to have made a round trip to the Dominican Republic on the night Galindez was kidnapped. Ernst alleged to have tracked the Murphy plane and concluded it had gone to Havana. Even after the Justice Department made public documents in Murphy's handwriting including the log of a flight similar to the one he had purportedly made with Galindez, Ernst insisted that there was no link between Galindez and Murphy's plane. The report further suggested that Murphy was a shady character, a freelance pilot with a temptation to smuggle guns and drugs, and that Galindez was alive in Spain and a tax evader who used his position as a registered agent for the anti-Franco Basque government-in-exile to profit from and then engineer his own disappearance.[88]

A major part of the report dealt with the Basque fund Galindez had handled. Ernst figured out that it had been provided by the CIA. He and Schwartz had lunched in Washington with chief of the CIA's Western Hemisphere Division, who told him that if the agency connection were revealed, hundreds of lives would be endangered. Ernst made no mention of the CIA connection in the report, claiming that he did not want to embarrass the government with any of his findings.[89]

When Ernst and his associates released their report, the explosion in liberal circles was extraordinary. *Life* ran an article titled "Costly Whitewash of Black Charges," which described the investigation as having "its main purpose to refute a story that appeared, more than a year ago, in *Life*."[90] ACLU members resigned over the matter. The ACLU worked swiftly to distance itself from Ernst, publicizing the fact that the ACLU was not involved in Ernst's investigation and that apart from the Galindez case, Ernst had made notable contributions to the defense of civil liberties.[91] Representative Charles Porter of Oregon, who had been goading the government to conduct an investigation, indicted Ernst in a *New Leader* article for assassinating the characters of Galindez and Murphy and for writing a "lawyers' brief, and not a very good job at that, and not worthy of Morris Ernst." Porter asked, "What happened to Morris Ernst? Where is the great liberal and keen lawyer of yesteryear? Why did he prostitute his talents for Trujillo?"[92]

"Attorney Morris Ernst was the liberals' liberal," observed *Newsweek* after the report was issued. "Last week, however, there wasn't an old-time liberal in the U.S. with a good word for Morris Ernst." One distinguished champion of civil rights said bluntly, "Ernst is a publicity hound." Ernst had exhibited an "absence of a judicial spirit and a capacity for logical analysis" charged Norman Thomas, who concluded, "The whole proceeding has been anything but judicial."[93] Wrote an anonymous "old friend" to Ernst, "There is a trace of senility in this whole performance. I tell you this as an old friend and with the hope that you can extract yourself from what increasingly looks like the ruins of a carefully built-up legend of a liberal."[94] Longtime adversary Fred Rodell summarized his thoughts in a postcard that read "No comment," addressed to "Morris Faust, Nantucket, Mass."[95]

Ernst was unfazed. He insisted that the report was true and that he had been courageous in his defense of an "unpopular cause." The real villain in the episode, he told friends, was the government, which attempted to suppress the CIA connection, and the press, which had not seriously commented on the source of the money and "in fact they are not interested in solving the problem."[96]

"The Galindez barrage continues," he confided to Marie Jahoda in the summer of 1958. "I feel comfortable because I have the truth even though the *Times* and the press won't print it."[97] To Bernard Knollenberg he wrote, "Isn't everybody entitled to a lawyer? Does this apply only in a courtroom? What about an appearance before a Senate committee, and above all, what about the terrible destruction of truth and reputations by the undisciplined mass media?"[98] He believed that the "affair Galindez" had been reduced by Congressmen from a "sober, thoughtful discussion" to "an attack on me."[99]

Two months after the report was released, Ernst wanted the inquiry to be reopened. He told friends that he felt that he had made a mistake in not mentioning the connection to the CIA, which was beginning to be discussed in the press.[100] In June 1959 Ernst appeared, at his own request, before a subcommittee of the Senate Judiciary Committee in executive session to press for a full-scale congressional investigation.[101] It was a crass effort to exonerate himself by focusing attention on the CIA's involvement, which was far removed from the kidnap-murder issue. His request was denied, and the case was never reopened. After the assassination of Trujillo in May 1961, the government of the Dominican Republic opened its files on the

Galindez affair. The account that emerged left no doubt that Galindez had been kidnapped and flown to the Dominican Republic by Murphy, as reporters originally surmised.[102]

* * *

To Ernst, the most problematic consequence of the Galindez affair was not damage to his reputation but the breakdown of his relationship with Hoover. By the time of the Galindez matter, his relations with "the Boss" were already on the decline. Hoover had become increasingly discontented with Ernst's arrogance and patronizing tone. In 1954, Ralph Toledano of *Newsweek* reported to Clyde Tolson, Hoover's top deputy, that Ernst had been "very careless about references he had made to the Bureau" and that Ernst was attempting to use the FBI as a "private police." Ernst was well known for using his FBI contacts to attempt to get assistance for his private clients, some of whom were "cleared" by the FBI on Ernst's request.[103] In addition, Toledano said, Ernst was going on radio shows and boasting about how close he was to Hoover.[104] This irritated Hoover, as did Ernst's unsolicited advice the following year. Ernst wrote to Hoover that he had heard rumors that "some silly Republicans" wanted Hoover to run for president. Ernst advised him against it, telling "the Boss" that "I like you as head of the FBI but not as President or even a candidate for it." Hoover's replies subsequently became chilly.[105]

The real falling-out came over Alger Hiss. In 1957, Ernst had given an endorsement to the publisher of the book *In the Court of Public Opinion*, written by Hiss, the State Department official convicted of perjury in 1950 after accusations that he had been a Soviet spy. Ernst said that although he had not read the trial record, he was "now inclined to believe that Hiss was not guilty. . . . I have a hunch that the validity of the court processes in the Hiss case may one day be profoundly re-examined." Ernst implied that the FBI manufactured the typewriter that had been a key piece of evidence in the Hiss trial.[106]

Shortly after, Ernst informed Nichols that he had been hired in the Galindez matter. Hoover wrote to Nichols, "I am surprised that [Ernst] would come near FBI after [stating] that the FBI fabricated the typewriter in the Hiss trial."[107] When Nichols relayed to Ernst that Hoover would have no dealings with Ernst because of his review of the book, Ernst was devastated. "My dear Lou," Ernst wrote Nichols. "I was bewildered and shocked by the message you sent me from Edgar. I have never found any persuasiveness in the manufactured typewriter story. In any event, you must know by now, if you ever will learn, my profound and publicly stated admiration and faith in the FBI."[108] Hoover scribbled on Nichols's memo: "He is a liar and I want no explanations from him. I will not allow any FBI contact with him."[109] Ernst had been cut off, and his name was erased from the list of Hoover's Special Correspondents.[110] After Ernst submitted the Galindez report, he offered to come to Washington, DC, to see Hoover at any time, but there was no reply.[111]

For the next ten years, Ernst continued to reach out to Hoover, in vain. He wrote to Nichols, "As you know, I have been more deeply hurt by Edgar than by any person in the last decades."[112] In 1960, Ernst asked Hoover to have dinner so they could get "back into our old relationship of trust and confidence and communication."[113] The following year, Ernst dropped by the office to tell FBI Assistant Director C. D. DeLoach that he believed the FBI was "in difficulty" and that he wanted to write another article for *Reader's Digest* "protecting the FBI." Hoover replied to DeLoach, "Ernst, of course, is the last one that we would want to write an article for us."[114]

* * *

A year after Ernst's death, in 1977, a Freedom of Information Act request by the ACLU brought to light Ernst's correspondence with Hoover. The ACLU retrieved 45,000 pages of FBI files, including some of Ernst's letters to Hoover. The ACLU asked a *New York Times* journalist, Anthony Marro, to go through all the files and to write an article. Marro's story, headlined "FBI Files Disclose '50s Tie to ACLU," appeared on the front page of the *Times* on August 4, 1977.

The *Times* reported that Ernst passed information to the FBI. The documents showed, according to the *Times,* that Ernst "alerted the FBI to the anti-FBI sentiment of some union members and to plans of some ACLU members to attack the Bureau."[115] Other newspapers picked up the story. The *Baltimore Sun* reported that Ernst aided the FBI in surveillance of the ACLU, and the *Chicago Daily News* wrote that files showed that "Ernst secretly established a personal relationship with FBI Director Hoover" and that "Morris Ernst passed inside information on American Civil Liberties Union activities to the FBI from 1942 to 1964."[116] The articles further noted that another ACLU leader, Irving Ferman, head of the ACLU's Washington office from 1952 to 1959, sent the FBI names of persons in state ACLU affiliates who were purportedly Communist Party members or engaged in "subversive" activities. Ferman's activities were far more insidious than Ernst's; Ferman was truly an informer. According to one historian of the FBI, "had he known of Ferman's actions, even Morris Ernst would have been appalled."[117] When the press accounts of the ACLU files appeared, most of the focus was on Ernst, however, since he was better known.[118]

The ACLU appointed a special commission to review the FBI files. The committee singled out Ferman as having engaged in spying but exonerated Ernst of any "overt improprieties," though it acknowledged that he had maintained a "friendly and somewhat clubby relationship" with Hoover.[119] Aryeh Neier, then executive director of the ACLU, told the press, "the harshest judgment about Morris Ernst I can make on the basis of the files is twofold: He valued the company of people such as J. Edgar Hoover and he helped ward off ACLU criticism of the FBI . . . by openly defending Bureau practices which to me seem indefensible." Neier concluded, "Wrongheaded, yes, but a spy, no."[120] Ernst was again an embarrassment to the ACLU when the Milton and Radosh book on the Rosenbergs appeared in 1983. Norman Dorsen and Ira Glasser, president and executive director of the ACLU, respectively, wrote a sharply worded letter to the *New York Times* distancing the organization from Ernst's activities described in the book, stating that "if Ernst did what is alleged, it was . . . certainly not in the ACLU's behalf."[121]

A 1984 *Nation* article titled "The Strange Correspondence of Morris Ernst and John Edgar Hoover, 1939–1964" illuminated the Ernst-

FIGURE 8. Margaret and Morris Ernst sailing off Nantucket, circa 1950s. Courtesy of Debbie Nicholson.

Hoover relationship in disturbing detail. The piece was written by Harrison Salisbury, a former *New York Times* journalist whom Ernst had considered a friend and confidante. Salisbury reported in detail Ernst's involvement in the Rosenberg case, the Galindez affair, and Ernst's "secret, unauthorized sharing of letters from third parties."[122]

The *Nation* advertised the Salisbury piece as demonstrating how the FBI "manipulated and abused the confidence of a leading civil libertarian and in so doing compromised the ACLU."[123] This characterization is incorrect. Ernst was not a victim. He instigated the connection with Hoover and used it for his own ends, just as Hoover and his assistants used Ernst for their purposes. Ernst, like Hoover, was fully a coconspirator.

22

UTOPIA 1976

Ernst denied that he was getting old. "I celebrated my 70th birthday," he told friends in 1958. "I realized that the greatest killer on earth, greater even than cancer, is the Biblical myth about three score and ten and the resulting psychology of borrowed time."[1] He believed old people should walk quickly and erect and not assume the postures of old age; he proudly went up two stairs at a time. "I run away from people my age and seek company among youngsters, which I have always found exciting," he told a friend in 1962, when he was seventy-four.[2]

Ernst pursued his "crusades" until the end of his life—reproductive rights, "antibigotry," anticensorship, and expanding the marketplace of ideas through literacy and education. Ernst's main enemy was no longer the Communist Party, which had been effectively quashed by the Red Scare, or the censors, largely vanquished by changing cultural norms and Supreme Court decisions, but the mass media—in particular, the television networks, which he believed dominated the channels of communication, interfered with the free exchange of ideas, distorted the truth, and degraded public morals. "The whole moral tone of our communications media is at a low ebb and too much power to control what people read, see, and think resides in too few hands," he asserted.[3] The news media had become an "evil influence" in society.[4]

He worried, too, about the moral tenor of the times. Ernst, who in his old age became increasingly conservative, decried the proliferation of sexually explicit material, believing that freedom of speech and moral permissiveness had gone too far. "I deeply resent the idea that the lowest common denominator, the most tawdry magazine pandering for profit . . . should be able to compete in the marketplace with no restraints," he told the press in 1970.[5] In a turn that many observers found surprising, this champion of freedom and "grand old man of civil liberties" spent his last years pessimistic about the cultural and legal changes he had set in motion.

* * *

With no civil liberties cases and relatively little work at the law firm, Ernst turned to "scribbling"—copious writing of books. He began keeping diaries; a true exhibitionist, he not only wrote but also published them. The diary of his seventieth year was published in 1960 as *Touch Wood*. In it, he described how he carried on his law practice, consulted with federal officials in Washington, traveled the globe, and puttered around Nantucket. The book moved from the making of chopped chicken liver (one of his favorite foods) to his "scientific" experiments with a dead seagull, to a report on ulcers in monkeys and the Viennese telephone service. One reviewer described it as a "breathless book, crowded with encounters and chunks of a busy, alert, energetic man."[6]

Ernst's second diary, *Untitled: The Diary of My 72nd Year*, published in 1962, was somewhat less upbeat. By then, his "glandular optimism" was waning. He lost some of his hearing and had to be fitted for a hearing aid. His and Maggie's "parties" now consisted of one or two guests at dinner. He confessed a loss of direction: "I'm low because I'm in doubt, constantly questioning what to do with the tail end of my life."[7] He missed the intellectual excitement of his glory years, lamenting that "I'm lonely for men or women of the mind. . . . As I have reached my elder years, I've lost my intellectual stimulators—LDB [Louis D. Brandeis], Heywood [Broun], Jerry [Frank], and others. . . . . I want a player . . . to bat an idea back and forth." Russell Leffingwell, one of his remaining interlocutors, died in 1960. "He was precious to me—one of the few who deeply influenced my attitudes and desires," Ernst recalled. "Not since Heywood's death have I wept."[8]

That year Ernst made a trip to the South for a book tour. He returned to Uniontown for the first time since 1890. It was an "odd emotional experience," he wrote. Two "gracious bureaucrats" from the mayor's office met him and gave him pictures of his birth home, which stood elegant and sturdy.[9] He went on to Austin, where he met with Harry Ransom, president of the University of Texas, and agreed to sell his massive collection of archival papers to the university, principally for tax deductions. He later sold his trove of "banned books" to the University of California at Santa Barbara.

The year of *Untitled* he withdrew altogether from the ACLU and began contemplating his mortality. "How many more days and nights will . . . Maggie and I have in good health together?" he wondered.[10] He predicted, incorrectly, the date of his death—April 2, 1968.[11]

* * *

By the early 1960s, both Morris's and Maggie's health were in decline. Ernst underwent two ear operations, which restored much of his hearing. In March 1962, he was diagnosed with a polyp in his throat and had an operation that caused him to lose his voice temporarily. He wrote to his son Roger, "Just out of hospital and muted for several weeks to the joy of friends and foes."[12]

Maggie's condition was more serious. She had a heart attack in the summer of 1962 but recovered and was well enough to go to England in September. The following summer, her heart stopped beating. She was revived and told she would have to live the rest of her life on medication. Again, she miraculously recovered. To pass time when she was recuperating, Morris and Maggie started a company called "M&M Books."[13] They conceived of ideas for books, outlined tables of contents, and found authors and publishers. Their topics were eclectic, including geophysics, post offices, icebergs, and "30 Lawsuits That Could Not Have Happened 30 Years Ago."[14]

In the summer of 1964, Maggie was in great shape, sailing and swimming in Nantucket. They made their annual trip to England in November. But the strain was too much. Not long after they returned to New York, Maggie had a massive left-sided cerebral hemorrhage and died on December 2, 1964, the day before her seventieth birthday.[15] Morris's famed stoicism failed him this time. A testament to the depth of his suffering, he stayed out of his law office for weeks.

According to his secretary Paula Gross, he seemed "to miss Margaret more and more as the days go on."[16]

"For some reason since Maggie's death I can't feel close to anyone—no matter how much I try," he wrote in his personal, unpublished diary.

> For years we ran to—together. And now I run away—and all alone. No one's hand to touch. No snuggling every morning. I fix my breakfast alone, rather than on our two trays every day for 40 years—or was it 100, or was it only one.
>
> Maggie, I've tried, as you instructed me, to find someone to fuss over, someone who might enjoy my little court cases and might need me a little—not as you and I needed each other.[17]

With Maggie's death, Ernst's heart broke—literally. He was hospitalized with heart trouble and later had a massive coronary that almost killed him. Friends advised him to slow down, but he characteristically defied them. "Walked up three flights of stairs today—mainly because the doctors and all my friends are making a cripple out of me," he wrote in his diary. "I must live and not listen to all those loving bastards—all full of 'don't do that.'" He vowed, "I have firmly decided that I shall not live as a vegetable. I'd rather live X days more at my desired pace than a thousand X as a cripple partial human."[18] Once, after going to lunch with Malcolm Hoffmann at the Harvard Club, Ernst fainted on sidewalk. "I don't find it amusing to live on the edge of death," he wrote. He was less concerned with the possibility of dying than "nuisancing Connie, Mal [Malcolm Hoffmann], Herb [Wolff], and others."[19]

With his debility, Ernst's depression deepened. In 1966, he sold his home in Nantucket because "I got no pleasure in living in great and happy memories."[20] His social life dwindled.[21] Ernst wrote to his old friend Marie Jahoda, "I miss you and I have never found a substitute with whom I can solve the world over a drink or a dinner."[22] To a friend named Jean he wrote, "I have no one to share my life with and no one to whom I can say, "Good Morning," or "What's new?"[23]

Ernst became convinced he was a failure. He confessed to his diary, "I'm such a fraud. People have thought and still think I'm strong and have no tear glands. Every once in a while with shame I let Connie know I'm nothing, weak and miserable. No hopes. . . . I've failed with life."[24]

Ernst became fascinated with suicide. He talked about it, wrote about it, and collected articles on it. Ernst was convinced that suicide rates, which he believed correlated to "frustrated ambition," were an index to the level of civilization in a society. "Frustration can occur only if you have a dream, an ambition. Since only people who have enough to eat have time to dream, the same 15 countries that have the highest income and eat the most calories also have the highest rate of suicide. I call it the 'ambition index.' People who dream also despair."[25] Suicide was both an academic interest and, increasingly, a personal possibility. He wrote in his diary, "It would be wise and rational to end it all."[26]

* * *

But Ernst didn't end his life, nor his scheming and crusading. He continued his whimsical plans and projects. In addition to writing articles for periodicals such as *Film Comment* and *Variety*, he continued to issue at least one book a year, most with coauthors. For Macmillan, which was doing a series on "law in the vernacular" to "bridge the gap between lawyers and non-lawyers," Ernst and Alan Schwartz wrote *Privacy: The Right to Be Let Alone* (1962) and *Censorship: The Search for the Obscene* (1964). In the same vein were Ernst's *How High Is Up: Modern Law for Modern Man*, coauthored with David Loth (1964), *Lawyers and What They Do*, coauthored with Schwartz (1964), and *The Great Reversals: Tales of the Supreme Court*, written solo (1973). In 1968 he published his third autobiography, *Love Affair with the Law*. The publisher described it as "the Horatio Alger story of a pushcart peddler's son whose enduring love for liberty and the law made him one of the foremost defenders of freedom in the land." Ernst went on a TV "book tour," appearing on *Today* and other talk shows to promote it. Not long after, he chartered a boat with his son Roger to cruise the Greek Isles. After he returned to New York, he found out that a law journal had referred to him as the "late Mr. Ernst."[27]

Some of Ernst's ideas were frankly crackpot. After representing as a client Eileen Garrett, an Irish medium and parapsychologist who was the primary exponent of extrasensory perception in the United States, he became a believer in paranormal psychology, writing that "I am a strong adherent of much of modern paranormal psychology, and the adventures of man in the areas of post-hypnotic controls, pre-cognition, and telepathy."[28] He began writing literary "hoaxes," including a work that purported to be the diary of *Alice in Wonderland* author Charles Dodgson. He published it in 1965 under the title *Pandect of C.L.D.* and fooled two book review editors.[29] For a while, he was immersed in a book project on the culture of Iceland. He wondered, "why has Iceland an income three times that of formerly great Greece and more than three times the income of luxuriant Jamaica? Why is it near the top of all nations in terms of kilowatt hours, per capita calories, literacy, and those other factors that man throughout the planet holds in high esteem?"[30] In 1966 he traveled to Iceland on an "adventure of the mind" to find the answers. His friend Edna Ferber warned him that the trip was a "boondoggle."[31] The expedition never resulted in a book.

Another outlet for Ernst's energies was the civic life of Greenwich Village. Ernst was proud of his longtime neighborhood and concerned about its apparent degradation, with skyrocketing crime rates and the presence of "hippies" in the 1960s. He told them when they asked him for handouts, "I'll give you money but first, for your own pride, you must do some work—like helping clean up a patch of this park."[32] When the Washington Square Arch was defaced with graffiti, Ernst hired a team of young hippies to clean it. Outraged by the playing of bongos in Washington Square Park, Ernst circulated an "antibongo petition" among residents. The city put up a sign near the fountain that read NO BONGO PLAYING.[33]

Other of Ernst's ideas and projects included "Operation Girlfriend," a plan to reform male juvenile delinquents by having their girlfriends set good examples for them, and the installation of "anti-anxiety committees" in apartment buildings to ease stress for old people living alone.[34] The weekly column Ernst wrote for a Greenwich Village newspaper, the *Villager*, served as a platform for his plans. In classic Ernst fashion, the column's title was "I Have a Concern."

* * *

With surging interest in James Joyce in the 1950s and '60s, there was renewed fascination with the *Ulysses* case. Joyce scholars and fans wrote to Ernst in 1958, the twenty-fifth anniversary of the *Ulysses* decision. Ernst was prodded into writing the story of the trial by a professor at the University of Buffalo, which had one of the great Joyce collections in its library. "I seem to have been in error as to the importance of the *Ulysses* case," he wrote. "*Ulysses* did in fact open the minds of writers and readers to seemingly new skills."[35] He took the opportunity to attack the major media outlets:

> But long after *Ulysses*, its publisher Random House, and Judge Woolsey have long been put in their proper place in history—man will still have to consider aspects of culture that fall outside of *judicial* controls. I refer to TASTE. Our mass media, within the law, is producing a tawdry, vulgar, and tasteless people. . . . In a world of newspapers and TV when only bad news is news, the people of our Republic must lower their visions, and lose insight into the mysteries, joys, and gaieties of the loveliness of life, and the gaiety of sexual relationship turns into a bit of vulgar gymnastics.[36]

Ernst's campaign to reform the mass media—in particular, television—was the last crusade of his life. By then, television was the most powerful and influential of the mass media; the three major television networks ABC, CBS, and NBC attracted larger audiences than radio, print, and film. Ernst lamented television's domination of the "channels of communication" and attributed the social chaos of the 1960s, with its bullet-scarred politics, riots, and protests, to "Paley and Sarnoff" (the heads of CBS and NBC, respectively). In its crass search for profit, TV was promoting vulgarity and fomenting "violence, bitterness, and hate," he believed, "breeding the next generation which believes that sadism is normal."[37] He accused the press of stooping lower and lower to get the biggest audience and attested that he was more concerned with the tawdriness in the press, with its lurid accounts of murders and violence, than any sort of fictional obscenity.

The "communications industry is engaged in a tacit campaign to present only bad news about life in America," he wrote to an acquaintance in 1966. "My friends . . . Paley [and] Sarnoff . . . should be shamed because they displayed 10,000 murders last year in prime time when in fact we only had 8000 murders in our nation."[38] As always, he was not shy about expressing his views publicly as well. "We have been given this picture by Paley and Sarnoff and we are lucky we haven't matched the violence one for one," Ernst opined in 1968 in *Variety*. "We're getting murdered by tv, not by the guns."[39] In a *Publishers' Auxiliary* contribution that same year, he asserted, "We have become a people condoning violence. We have given up our faith in the use of quiet courtrooms to employ thoughtful reason to seek truth."[40]

Ernst embarked on what he called a "good news" campaign and went on all of the major talk shows to promote it. "The press, the radio, and the movies . . . predominately report the dregs of the glass, the sordid and the painful . . . emphasizing fear and cynicism," he alleged.[41] If the mass media reported good news, "this would give courage," he wrote to Mississippi governor Paul Johnson. "Only by good news can the people of our Republic move forward with hope rather than cynicism. The virtual suppression of good news results from an irresponsible desire to sell papers."[42] He tried to entice all the major networks and newspapers, including the *New York Times*, to feature a "good news" section, which he proposed to write.

Ernst attributed what he saw as the irresponsibility of the press—both its bad taste and its increasing challenges to the government—to concentration of media ownership, as well as to recent Supreme Court rulings, including *New York Times v. Sullivan*. The much-heralded 1964 *Sullivan* decision, which greatly limited the liability of the news media for libels about public officials, was the "greatest single danger to the First Amendment in the last decades," he believed.[43] The actions of leakers and news publishers during the Pentagon Papers and Watergate affairs of the early 1970s convinced Ernst that the press was "destroying the basic values of the First Amendment"—civility, open-mindedness, and the search for truth.[44] He confided to civil rights lawyer Whitney North Seymour, "I think the biggest scars on freedom of the press are now being generated by the best of our mass media, which in the main is on a rampage in favor of purloining documents, thievery, and betrayal of agreements."[45] The First Amendment, he believed, was imperiled like never before.

* * *

The "new morality" of the 1960s also disturbed him greatly. Though Ernst had always been forward-looking on sexual matters, he never advocated complete liberty and believed that sexual freedom had gone too far. "Having happily fought our governmental censors for more than half a century, I recall with fondness that such success as I had was no doubt due to the fact that I made clear that I was opposed to utter freedom. Utter freedom bespeaks a culture without the pleasures of privacy," he wrote in *Variety* in 1970.[46] "My . . . liberal friends are confounded when I ask them if they would revoke the license of a tv station that showed hours of nude sodomy every afternoon," he wrote in correspondence the following year.[47] Ernst maintained that government censorship was unconstitutional in most every case and that producers and publishers should bear the main responsibility for policing media content. Yet he supported government restraints on what he called "hard-core" material. Ernst corresponded with Supreme Court Justice William Brennan, an acquaintance from Nantucket, as the Court heard a series of obscenity cases in the late 1960s. Reversing his decades-long stance on the relation between sexual images and actions, Ernst urged Brennan to take a hard line in obscenity cases involving "sadist" movies and literature because doctors and psychologists were now in "virtual agreement as to the causal relation between pictures and words and concomitant human behavior."[48]

In 1970 Ernst appeared on a television talk program titled *New York Closeup* to discuss the subject, "Shall We Restore Censorship?" Since Ernst was often assumed to be a free speech absolutist, his opinions surprised many viewers. Recalling his defense of *Ulysses*, he said, "Whereas I defended the book and legitimatized a four-letter word, that doesn't mean that the four-letter word, out of context, should be spread and used—or sodomy on the stage or masturbation in the public arena here and the world over." His pronouncements, printed in the *New York Times*, made news throughout the nation.[49] "Perhaps no American alive today has been deeper in the fight for civil liberties and against overheavy censorship than Morris Ernst," observed the *Christian Science Monitor*. "Thus when Mr. Ernst, after an almost unique experience in this field, states that he would not wish 'to live in a society without limits to freedom,' and that unbridled immorality on the stage and in literature is wrong, these are not the words of a 'blue-nose.' They are the judgments of a man whose long career has taught him that a life worth living demands certain restraints."[50] Ernst's statements appeared prominently in newspapers and were used by the judge in the 1972 trial of the notorious film *Deep Throat* to justify his decision condemning the film as obscene.[51]

* * *

Ernst became an advocate for the elderly and urged senior citizens to assert their "old power." He set the example himself, following a regime that would have exhausted younger men.[52] In May 1970, at the age of eighty-one, Ernst entered politics for the first time, running unsuccessfully for a seat on the Democratic State Committee from a district on Manhattan's West Side. Ernst received endorsements of both "senior citizens" and young Democrats, who called him "Mr. Gap," in reference to the generation gap he spanned with ease.[53] In 1973 he made another failed election bid, this time for the New York City Council. In typical Ernst fashion, he promised a program of "100 items" so as "to restore New York to its former status as the greatest city in the world."[54]

Only at the very end did he slow down, and even then, not so much. Ernst stopped traveling in September 1972 but went to his office every day. One of his young friends wrote to the president of Williams College in 1973, recommending Ernst for an honorary degree. "Morris is 85 now. His mind allows him no leisure. He is in his office daily, and currently writing another book even though the *Taming of Technology* was published just last fall."[55]

Ernst's heart and legs were getting weak. Even more difficult for Ernst was his increasing unimportance. Ernst conferred with a spate of potential biographers, urging them to write, but none of them did, concluding that a biography of Ernst, with his massive papers and multiple crusades, would take up too much time. He sent annual entries to *Who's Who*, each year embellishing the "facts" about his life a little more. At one point he claimed to have been "one of the founders with Roger Baldwin of the ACLU in 1920."[56] Truman's Civil Rights Commission came into being because of a single conversation he had with the president, he asserted. Ernst even claimed responsibility for the desegregation of New York restaurants and hotels. Was this poor memory? Senility? (Ernst does appear to have been senile in the last half decade of his life). Or was he still deeply insecure, feeling still like the lonely boy with a tubercular mother, the sole Jew at an elite WASP college, an outsider at the bar, needing to prove that he was better than others? Did he feel, in his extraordinary life, that he had still not done enough?

He continued to go to his usual restaurants, cherishing the words of friends: "Mr. Ernst, it's so good to see you." Those outings were the highlights of long days filled with crossword puzzles, cups of coffee, and yellow pads on which he turned out ideas for books, *Villager* columns, and copious letters to public figures in Washington, which almost always went unanswered. Sometimes he felt well enough to go out for a walk, using his expensive cane, in Washington Square Park near his apartment. Much of his time was spent wearing his favorite bathrobe and relaxing in his big recliner chair.[57]

Malcolm Hoffmann saw Ernst in mid-May 1976. Ernst was obviously dying. Hoffmann had taken in a "mock-heroic way" to calling Ernst "Great Man." He admitted that it sounded "a little bit nauseating but I used to gaily put that thought into conversation because I thought he needed to be reminded of the fact that he was." The last time Hoffmann saw him, Ernst said he needed help to get to his bed from where he was seated. A nurse escorted him to his bed. Holding Hoffmann's hand, he said, "this is the way great men die."[58]

The previous winter, Williams College informed Ernst that he would receive an honorary doctoral degree at the following year's commencement, in June 1976. He was thrilled. But that spring, his health condition became dire. One of his young friends tried to keep him upbeat. "Sure, you are going to make it. Absolutely!" she told him on the afternoon of May 20. He was propped up in his chair with his big bathrobe around him. "Now Morris, you only have a couple of weeks before this big trip to Williams College," she said. He replied, "Oh yes, it is going to be wonderful." He said, "It's about time Williams gave me the degree."[59]

He died the next day, May 21, at the age of eighty-seven, in his utopia year of 1976.

* * *

He never got that degree. Williams had strict requirements; to receive an honorary degree, the awardee had to be present. The president of the college made a statement at commencement in Ernst's honor, stating that "He fought throughout his life against censorship and other restraints on publication and expression. He had a great zest for life and for the many causes that he served. He delighted in friendships and was loyal towards the individuals and institutions that were dearest to him."[60] That summer was the first in fifty years in which Monomoy, Nantucket, did not see Morris Ernst.

Obituaries appeared in the *New York Times* and nearly a hundred other newspapers. "Morris Ernst, 'Ulysses' Case Lawyer Dies," read the *Times*'s lengthy obituary, which described him as a "witty, tweedy, bow-tied man whose friends included judges and jockeys,

FIGURE 9. Margaret and Morris Ernst on Nantucket, early 1960s. Courtesy of Stephanie Begen.

bankers and barristers, Presidents and precinct politicians." The *Times* noted, in addition to *Ulysses* and his other book censorship cases, Ernst's work in the Associated Press case and *Hague v. CIO*, as well as his friendships with Franklin D. Roosevelt, Brandeis, Broun, and Leffingwell, and his involvement in the Trujillo matter, which had "dismayed" many of his liberal friends.[61] Other newspapers hailed Ernst as the "country's greatest guardian of civil liberties," the "dean of the liberal American bar," and one of America's "best

FIGURE 10. Morris Ernst, sporting his signature bow tie, undated photo probably early 1960s. Courtesy of Harry Ransom Center, University of Texas at Austin.

known lawyers." Summarized the *Los Angeles Times*, "he believed in what he argued, he argued for what he believed, and he served the cause of individual freedom well."[62]

Ernst had no funeral. At the end of the summer, dozens of friends and colleagues gathered for a touching tribute to his quirks and successes, and the tenacity which may have been his most remarkable gift. Morris Ernst, quipped one commentator, was "probably fighting to get *Ulysses* into heaven."[63]

ACKNOWLEDGMENTS

I'm grateful to the archivists, librarians, and scholars who assisted me with this project. Sincere thanks to Paul Mastrangelo of New York Law School, Sylvia Kennick Brown in the Williams College library, Amelia Holmes of the Nantucket Historical Society, Eleanor Drake of the Perry County Historical and Preservation Society in Marion, Alabama, and Rick Watson and Elizabeth Garver at the Harry Ransom Center at the University of Texas in Austin. Many thanks to the entire staff of the Ransom Center for accommodating my frequent visits and requests for material. Sam Walker, Rebecca Erbelding, and Leigh Ann Wheeler provided useful insights into aspects of Ernst's career, and Mary Batten, Jessica Davis, and Stephanie Begen shared their memories of Ernst. I appreciate the attention that Prof. J. H. Schlegel of the University at Buffalo Law School devoted to a draft of the manuscript. The American Philosophical Society, the University at Buffalo Law School, and the Baldy Center for Law and Social Policy contributed much-appreciated research support.

NOTES

INTRODUCTION

1 Quote derived from British case R v. Hicklin L.R. (1868) 3 Q.B. 360 . See "Obscenity Prior to the 1950s: The Restrictive Hicklin Test," in *The Encyclopedia of the Supreme Court*, ed. David Schultz (New York: Facts on File, 2005), 351.
2 Robert Aitken, "United States of America, Libellant, against One Book Entitled *Ulysses* by James Joyce," *ABA Journal* 25 (1998): 53.
3 Alden Whitman, "Morris Ernst, 'Ulysses' Case Lawyer Dies," *New York Times*, May 23, 1976, 40.
4 See Brett Gary, "'Guessing Oneself Into Jail': Morris Ernst and the Assault on American Obscenity Law in the 1930s," in *Obscenity and the Limits of Liberalism*, ed. Loren Daniel Glass and Charles Francis Williams (Columbus: Ohio State University Press, 2011), 50–70.
5 Harry Kalven Jr., *A Worthy Tradition: Freedom of Speech in America* (New York: Harper & Row, 1988), 167.
6 "Says Big Bill," *NYC East Underwriter*, February 28, 1936.
7 Marquis James, "Morris L. Ernst," *Scribner's Magazine*, July 1938, 8.
8 Harrison Salisbury, "The Strange Correspondence of Morris Ernst and John Edgar Hoover, 1939–1964," *Nation*, December 1, 1984, 580.
9 See, e.g., "Ernst Reportedly Aided FBI in Surveillance of ACLU," *Baltimore Sun*, August 6, 1977.
10 Morris L. Ernst (MLE) interview with Mary Batten, September 1, 1973, in Morris Leopold Ernst Papers, MS-1331, Harry Ransom Center, University of Texas, Austin (collection hereafter cited as Ernst Papers).
11 "Harriet Pilpel: Superlawyer," *Boston Globe*, April 10, 1983, 124.

CHAPTER ONE

1 Morris Ernst, *A Love Affair with the Law: A Legal Sampler* (New York: Macmillan, 1968), 128.
2 Leonard Dinnerstein and Mary Dale Palsson, eds., *Jews in the South* (Baton Rouge: Louisiana State University Press, 1973), 3–4.
3 Thomas D. Clark, "The Post-Civil War Economy in the South," in Dinnerstein and Palsson, *Jews in the South*, 166; Anton Hieke, *Jewish Identity in the Reconstruction*

South: Ambivalence and Adaptation (Berlin: De Gruyter, 2013), 108; Dinnerstein and Palsson, *Jews in the South*, 16.

4 Allan Nevins, *Herbert H. Lehman and His Era* (New York: Charles Scribner, 1963), 4, 23.

5 National Register of Historical Places, Uniontown, Perry County, Alabama.

6 History of Ernst family by Magdalen Ernst, 11, box 550, Ernst Papers.

7 Hasia R. Diner, *A Time for Gathering: The Second Migration, 1820–80* (Baltimore: Johns Hopkins University Press, 1992), 66.

8 History of Ernst family by Magdalen Ernst, 11; Stuart Rockoff, "Arthur Mayer and Demopolis, Alabama," *Southern and Jewish*, May 22, 2013.

9 Fred Rodell, "Morris Ernst: New York's Unlawyerlike Liberal Lawyer Is the Censor's Enemy, the President's Friend," *Life*, February 21, 1944, 100.

10 History of Ernst family by Magdalen Ernst, 11.

11 Batten interview.

12 Normal College of the City of New York, *Fifteenth Annual Commencement, Thursday, June 26th, 1884* (New York: J. S. Babcock, 1884), https://library.hunter.cuny.edu/old/sites/default/files/15th_commencement_06261884.pdf.

13 Samuel White Patterson and George N. Shuster, *Hunter College: Eighty-Five Years of Service* (New York: Lantern Press, 1955).

14 History of Ernst family by Magdalen Ernst, 11.

15 *Canebrake Herald*, August 31, 1888, 3.

16 History of Ernst family by Magdalen Ernst, 14.

17 Batten interview; Ernst interview with Harlan Phillips, June 1961, 4, boxes 550.7–551.2, Ernst Papers.

18 On Jews in Harlem at the turn of the twentieth century, see Jeffrey S. Gurock, *The Jews of Harlem: The Rise, Decline, and Revival of a Jewish Community* (New York: New York University Press, 2016), 33–38.

19 Ernst interview with Harlan Phillips, 22.

20 History of Ernst family by Magdalen Ernst, 19–20.

21 Ernst, *Love Affair with the Law*, 124.

22 Stephen Birmingham, *Our Crowd: The Great Jewish Families of New York* (New York: Harper & Row, 1967); see also Barry E. Supple, *A Business Elite: German-Jewish Financiers in Nineteenth-Century New York* (Boston: Business History Review, 1957).

23 Leonard Dinnerstein, *Antisemitism in America* (New York: Oxford University Press, 1994), 39–41; S. Birmingham, *Our Crowd*, 147.

24 Batten interview.

25 Batten interview.

26 See Jeffrey S. Gurock, *When Harlem Was Jewish, 1870–1930* (New York: Columbia University Press, 1979), 19–20; Gurock, *Jews of Harlem*, 38–39.

27 Edward Samuel Greenbaum, *A Lawyer's Job: In Court, in the Army, in the Office* (New York: Harcourt, Brace & World, 1967), 9.

28 Ernst interview with Harlan Phillips, 8.

29 Batten interview.

30 Ernst interview with Harlan Phillips, 8.

31 Batten interview.

32 See drafts, "Love Affair with the Law," box 471, Ernst Papers.

33 Batten interview.

34 Ernst, *Love Affair with the Law*, 7–8.
35 MLE recollections of mother, n.d., box 550.5, Ernst Papers.
36 MLE recollections of mother, n.d.
37 "Mrs. Carl Ernst Dead," *New York Times*, February 15, 1908, 14.
38 MLE recollections of mother, n.d.
39 Leo Mayer, "The Pilgrimage of an Orthopedic Surgeon," 1971, box 539.9, Ernst Papers.
40 On Arthur Mayer, see E. J. Kahn, "Boffos and Bustos," *New Yorker*, December 9, 1974, 46.
41 Rachel Mayer to MLE, August 28, 1939, Ernst Papers.
42 Arthur Mayer to MLE, n.d., Ernst Papers.
43 Sarah Ernst to MLE, n.d., Ernst Papers.
44 MLE recollections of mother, n.d.
45 Hanford Hendersen to Sarah Ernst, September 7, 1904.
46 Ernst interview with Harlan Phillips, 79.
47 Scrapbook, n.d., Ernst Papers; Ernst interview with Harlan Phillips, 83.
48 Williams grade report, scrapbook, n.d.
49 Ernst interview with Harlan Phillips, 23.
50 Ernst interview with Harlan Phillips, 82; Morris L. Ernst, *Untitled: The Diary of My 72nd Year* (New York: R. B. Luce, 1962), 206.
51 On Horace Mann School, see R. A. McCardell, *The Country Day School: History, Curriculum, Philosophy of Horace Mann School* (Dobbs Ferry, NY: Oceana Publications, 1962).
52 Maryellen V. Keefe, *Casual Affairs: The Life and Fiction of Sally Benson* (Albany: State University of New York Press, 2014), 18.
53 Susan E. Tifft and Alex S. Jones, *The Trust: The Private and Powerful Family Behind the New York Times* (Boston: Little, Brown, 2000), 110.
54 William Carlos Williams, *The Autobiography of William Carlos Williams* (New York: New Directions Books, 1980), 44.
55 Richard O'Connor, *Heywood Broun: A Biography* (New York: Putnam, 1975), 23.
56 Dean of Harvard to MLE, July 13, 1904, Ernst Papers.
57 Batten interview.
58 Greenbaum, *Lawyer's Job*, 13.
59 Ernst interview with Harlan Phillips, 83.
60 Ernst interview with Harlan Phillips, 98.

CHAPTER TWO

1 Ernst interview with Harlan Phillips, 114.
2 Frank S. Coan, ed., "College Customs and Freshman Rules," in *Handbook of Williams College for 1910–1911*, Ernst Papers.
3 Ernst interview with Harlan Phillips, 178.
4 Benjamin Aldes Wurgaft, *Jews at Williams: Inclusion, Exclusion, and Class at a New England Liberal Arts College* (Lebanon, NH: University Press of New England, 2013), 113–14.
5 Benjamin Aldes Wurgaft, "Gentleman Jews: A Look at the Forces that Shaped Early Jewish Life at Williams," *Williams Magazine*, Summer 2014.

6 Wurgaft, *Jews at Williams*, 113–14.
7 Ernst interview with Harlan Phillips, 39.
8 Ernst interview with Harlan Phillips, 105.
9 *Williamstown, Mass.: Historical Sketch and Views* (Boston: Ellis, 1904), 27.
10 William Raimond Baird, *Baird's Manual of American College Fraternities* (New York: College Fraternity Pub., 1915), 685; "Installation of Iota Chapter at Williams Very Auspicious," *Phi Gamma Delta* 36 (April 1913): 637.
11 Ernst interview with Harlan Phillips, 102.
12 Ernst interview with Harlan Phillips, 26.
13 Morris Ernst, Banned Books memo, n.d., box 564, Ernst Papers.
14 Morris Ernst, *The Best Is Yet* (New York: Harper and Brothers, 1945), 215.
15 *Greek Letter Fraternities at Williams, with the Story of the Commons Club* (Williamstown, MA: Williams College, 1933), 58.
16 Ernst interview with Harlan Phillips, 102.
17 Ernst interview with Harlan Phillips, 104.
18 Ernst interview with Harlan Phillips, 117.
19 MLE to F. M. Myers, January 17, 1940, Ernst Papers.
20 Ernst, *Best Is Yet*, 263.
21 Leverett Wilson Spring, *A History of Williams College* (Boston: Houghton Mifflin, 1917), 247.
22 Ernst, *Best Is Yet*, 264.
23 Williams grade report, n.d.
24 Ernst interview with Harlan Phillips, 86.
25 Ernst interview with Harlan Phillips, 121.
26 Greenbaum, *Lawyer's Job*, 14; Ernst interview with Harlan Phillips, 122.
27 Ernst interview with Harlan Phillips, 88; Morris L. Ernst, foreword to *The Teacher*, ed. Morris L. Ernst (New York: Prentice Hall, 1967), 11.
28 "Clever College Men on Diamond," *Pittsburgh Press*, August 5, 1911, 16.
29 Mark Sullivan, "Never on Sunday," *University of New Hampshire Magazine*, Spring 2012.
30 Morris Ernst, draft outline of article "People Important To Me," n.d., box 515, Ernst Papers.
31 Michael McGerr, *A Fierce Discontent: The Rise and Fall of the Progressive Movement in America, 1870–1920* (New York: Oxford University Press, 2005), xv. See also Daniel T. Rodgers, "In Search of Progressivism," *Reviews in American History* 10 (December 1982): 113–32.
32 Maureen Flanagan, *America Reformed: Progressives and Progressivisms, 1890s-1920s* (New York: Oxford University Press, 2007), 71.
33 Ernst, "People Important To Me."
34 Ernst, *Teacher*, 11.
35 Ernst, "People Important To Me."
36 "Freshman Oratorial Preliminaries," *Williams Record*, May 3, 1906, 5.
37 *Williams College Class Book*, 1909, in Ernst Papers.
38 "Success Awaits Republican Club," *Williams Record*, October 1, 1908, 1.
39 Ernst interview with Harlan Phillips, 159.
40 Ernst interview with Harlan Phillips, 171.
41 Ernst, *Best Is Yet*, 204.
42 Ernst interview with Harlan Phillips, 172.

43 Ernst, *Best Is Yet*, 2.
44 "Mrs. Carl Ernst Dead."
45 MLE recollections of mother, n.d.
46 *Williams College Class Book*, 1909.
47 Coan, "College Customs and Freshman Rules."
48 Ernst interview with Harlan Phillips, 186.
49 *AZA Society of Williams College*, pamphlet, n.d., Ernst Papers.
50 *Williams College Class Book*, 1909.

CHAPTER THREE

1 "Shirt Notes," *Men's Wear*, November 11, 1908, 81.
2 Ernst interview with Harlan Phillips, 194.
3 New York State Department of Labor, "Register of Factories," in *Industrial Directory* (Albany: New York State Department of Labor, 1912), 143.
4 Ernst interview with Harlan Phillips, 196.
5 Ernst interview with Harlan Phillips, 194–95.
6 "Williams Commencement II," *New York Observer and Chronicle*, July 7, 1910, 5.
7 "The 1912 Mortarboard Acknowledgements," in *The Mortarboard* (New York: Columbia University, 1911), 205.
8 "Society," *New York Times*, January 19, 1909, X2.
9 "March of Trade to the West Side of Town," *New York Journal*, November 21, 1897, 37.
10 Advertisement, *New York Times*, October 30, 1909, 10.
11 Ernst interview with Harlan Phillips, 213; Ernst, *Best Is Yet*, 3.
12 Ernst interview with Harlan Phillips, 214; Ernst, *Best Is Yet*, 4.
13 Proposal for Ernst biography by Mary Batten, box 544, Ernst Papers.
14 Ernst, *Love Affair With the Law*, 2.
15 Ernst, *Best Is Yet*, 3.
16 Ernst, *Love Affair With the Law*, 2.
17 George Chase, "Correspondence: Instructions at The New York Law School," *Central Law Journal* (1892): 12.
18 James A. Wooten, "Law School Rights: The Establishment of New York Law School, 1891–1897," *New York Law School Law Review* 36 (1991): 337.
19 "Two Year Course Best in Law," *New York Times*, September 26, 1909, 15.
20 New York Law School Catalog, courtesy of Paul J. Mastrangelo, acting archivist, New York Law School.
21 Robert Stevens, *Law School: Legal Education in America from the 1850s to the 1980s* (Chapel Hill: University of North Carolina Press, 2016), 74.
22 Harry Sanger Richards, *Progress in Legal Education: Address of the President* (Chicago: Association of American Law Schools, 1915), 63.
23 Jerold S. Auerbach, *Unequal Justice: Lawyers and Social Change in Modern America* (London: Oxford University Press, 1977), 125.
24 Auerbach, *Unequal Justice*, 98.
25 See I. Maurice Wormser, "The Problem of Evening Law Schools," *American Law School Review* 4 (1920): 547.
26 Ernst interview with Harlan Phillips, 207.

27 Ernst interview with Harlan Phillips, 210.

28 "Miss Leerburger Weds," *New York Times*, September 10, 1912.

29 MLE to Margaret Samuels, n.d., Ernst Papers.

30 Susan Leerburger Ernst obituary, *New York Times*, August 25, 1920, 8.

31 Ernst interview with Harlan Phillips, 202.

32 Most Jews employed in law firms worked for firms that were predominantly Jewish. Jerold S. Auerbach, "From Rags to Robes: The Legal Profession, Social Mobility and the American Jewish Experience," *American Jewish Historical Quarterly* 66, no. 2 (1976): 266–68; Melvin M. Fagen, "The Status of Jewish Lawyers in New York City: A Preliminary Report on a Study Made by the Conference on Jewish Relations," *Jewish Social Studies* 1 (1939): 43.

33 Ernst, *Love Affair With the Law*, 11.

34 Arthur S. Link and Richard L. McCormick, *Progressivism* (Wheeling, IL: Harlan Davidson, 1983), 2.

35 Mike Wallace, *Greater Gotham: A History of New York City from 1898 to 1919* (New York: Oxford University Press, 2018), 508.

36 "The City Club," *New York Times*, November 23, 1913, C6; City Club of New York, *Annual Report of the City Club of New York* (New York: City Club, 1911).

37 See David Israel Aronson, "The City Club of New York: 1892–1912" (Ph.D. diss., New York University, 1975).

38 Ernst, *Best Is Yet*, 44.

39 Wallace, *Greater Gotham*, 745.

40 Ernst interview with Harlan Phillips, 221.

41 See, e.g., W. M. Leiserson, "The Problem of Unemployment Today," *Political Science Quarterly* 31 (March 1916): 1–24; Theda Skocpol, *Protecting Soldiers and Mothers* (Cambridge: Harvard University Press, 1992), 304–6.

42 See William M. Leiserson, "The Movement for Public Labor Exchanges," *Journal of Political Economy* 23 (July 1915): 707–16.

43 "Unemployed Invade the Labor Temple," *New York Times*, March 1, 1914, 1.

44 "Bringing Them Together," *New Outlook* 106 (1914): 113.

45 "Unemployed Invade the Labor Temple."

46 John Andrews, "A National System of Labor Exchanges," *New Republic*, December 26, 1914, 1.

47 Wallace, *Greater Gotham*, 746.

48 "Unemployed Invade the Labor Temple."

49 Andrews, "National System of Labor Exchanges."

50 Ernst interview with Harlan Phillips, 220.

51 MLE to James Rosenberg, September 29, 1921, Ernst Papers.

52 "Biography: Morris L. Ernst," transcript of Ernst interview by Malcolm A. Hoffmann, October 26, 1977, Indiana University Center for Documentary Research and Practice, Indiana University–Bloomington.

53 "The Use and Abuse of the Dictograph," *Kane Republican* (Kane, PA), July 13, 1914, 4.

54 Ernst, *Best Is Yet*, 3.

55 Ernst interview with Harlan Phillips, 199.

CHAPTER FOUR

1 Ernst interview with Harlan Phillips, 211.
2 "Justice Greenbaum Dead in 77th Year," *New York Times*, August 27, 1930, 21.
3 *The Reminiscences of Edward S. Greenbaum* (New York: Columbia University Oral History Collection, 1965), 4.
4 Ernst, *Love Affair with the Law*, 13.
5 History of Greenbaum, Wolff, and Ernst, n.d., 36, Ernst Papers.
6 Greenbaum, *Lawyer's Job*, 23. I found no documentation to show whether the team did not know that Eddie also was Jewish or, more likely, the team did know but had made an exception for him because his father was a judge and Columbia was getting a significant amount of money through the tuition of the two Greenbaum sons attending.
7 History of Greenbaum, Wolff, and Ernst, 43.
8 "Versatile Lawyer: Edward Samuel Greenbaum," *New York Times*, April 22, 1967, 10.
9 Walter H. Waggoner, "Herbert A. Wolff, 90; Lawyer who Headed Ethical Culture Society," *New York Times*, February 27, 1980, B5.
10 History of Greenbaum, Wolff, and Ernst, 9.
11 History of Greenbaum, Wolff, and Ernst, 40; Ernst, *Love Affair with the Law*, 13.
12 History of Greenbaum, Wolff, and Ernst, 10; Greenbaum, *Lawyer's Job*, 36.
13 Greenbaum, *Lawyer's Job*, 32–33.
14 MLE to Ted Lewis, April 20, 1915, Ernst Papers.
15 David M. Margolick, "Law Firm That Won Battle to Publish 'Ulysses' Is Closing Its Doors," *New York Times*, March 19, 1982, B4.
16 "Somewhat Personal," *Furniture Manufacturer and Artisan*, April 1915, 205.
17 History of Greenbaum, Wolff, and Ernst, 9.
18 Ernst interview with Harlan Phillips, 199.
19 James, "Morris L. Ernst," 57.
20 Ernst interview with Harlan Phillips, 212.
21 Ernst, *Best Is Yet*, 1.
22 "New Counsel Chosen," *Jewelers' Circular Weekly*, February 13, 1918, 51.
23 History of Greenbaum, Wolff, and Ernst, 10.
24 History of Greenbaum, Wolff, and Ernst, 13.
25 James, "Morris L. Ernst," 57.
26 "Twenty First Annual Banquet of the Jewelers 24 Karat Club," *Jewelers' Circular*, January 24, 1923, 91.
27 MLE to National Manufacturers Association, May 13, 1922, Ernst Papers.
28 Newman Levy, *My Double Life: Adventures in Law and Letters* (Garden City, NY: Doubleday, 1958), 168.
29 "Ten Commandments for Lawyers," n.d., Ernst Papers.
30 History of Greenbaum, Wolff, and Ernst.
31 "Hirshfield Ejects Market Lawyer Again," *New York Herald*, December 8, 1922, 18.
32 Draft Card of Morris L. Ernst, United States World War I Draft Registration Cards, 1917–1918, New York, New York City, NARA microfilm publication M1509 (Washington, D.C.: National Archives and Records Administration).
33 See "General Discussion," *American Labor Legislation Review* 8 (March 1918): 60;

"Enemy Aliens Must Have Jobs or Be Supported," *American Monthly*, December 5, 1917, 318.

34 "The Clearing House for Public Employment Offices," *Report of the Committee on Industry and Employment*, December 21, 1917, 16; "Reorganization of the State Employment Bureau," *Annual Report of the Industrial Commission*, June 30, 1919, 217.

35 *Revenue Bill: Hearings Before the Committee on Ways and Means, House of Representatives with Reference to the New Revenue Bill*, 65th Cong., 2d Sess. 513 (1918).

36 Gloria Garrett Samson, *The American Fund for Public Service: Charles Garland and Radical Philanthropy, 1922–1941* (Westport, CT: Greenwood Press, 1996), 8; David M. Kennedy, *Over Here: The First World War and American Society* (Oxford: Oxford University Press, 1982), 34.

37 W. A. Swanberg, *Norman Thomas: The Last Idealist* (New York: Charles Scribner's Sons, 1983), 46.

38 William A. Donohue, *The Politics of the American Civil Liberties Union* (New Brunswick, NJ: Transaction Books, 1985), 29.

39 Donald Johnson, *The Challenge to American Freedoms* (Lexington: University of Kentucky Press, 1963), 5.

40 Donohue, *Politics of the American Civil Liberties Union*, 29.

41 Peggy Lamson, *Roger Baldwin: Founder of the American Civil Liberties Union* (Boston: Houghton Mifflin, 1976), 72; Robert C. Cottrell, *Roger Nash Baldwin and the American Civil Liberties Union* (New York: Columbia University Press, 2000), 61.

42 National Civil Liberties Bureau, "A Statement to the Members of the American Union Against Militarism from the National Civil Liberties Bureau (Until Recently a Bureau of the Union)," ACLU Papers, Seeley G. Mudd Manuscript Library, Princeton University (collection hereafter cited as ACLU Papers).

43 American Union Against Militarism pamphlet *Constitutional Rights in War-Time*, May 1917, ACLU Papers.

44 D. Johnson, *Challenge to American Freedoms*, 194.

45 Sedition Act of 1918, Pub L. No. 65-150, 40 Stat. 563 (1918).

46 Paul L. Murphy, *The Meaning of Freedom of Speech: First Amendment Freedoms from Wilson to FDR* (Westport, CT: Greenwood, 1972), 22.

47 Murphy, *Meaning of Freedom of Speech*, 27–28; Leon Whipple, *The Story of Civil Liberty in the United States* (Westport, CT: Vanguard Press, 1970), 265.

48 Samuel Walker, *In Defense of American Liberties: A History of the ACLU* (New York: Oxford University Press, 1990), 29.

49 D. Johnson, *Challenge to American Freedoms*, 194.

50 Walker, *In Defense of American Liberties*, 21.

51 Melvyn Dubofsky and Foster Rhea Dulles, *Labor in America: A History* (Wheeling, IL: Harlan Davidson, 2004), 215–24.

52 McGerr, *A Fierce Discontent*, 306.

53 D. Johnson, *Challenge to American Freedoms*, 120.

54 D. Johnson, *Challenge to American Freedoms*, 145.

55 "The Position of the ACLU on the Issues in the United States Today," Addendum to the Letter to the Members of the National Committee, February 6, 1920, ACLU Papers.

56 "Position of the ACLU."

57 Murphy, *Meaning of Freedom of Speech*, 117.
58 Murphy, *Meaning of Freedom of Speech*, 131.
59 Donohue, *Politics of the American Civil Liberties Union*, 31–32; Lucille Bernheimer Milner, *Education of an American Liberal* (New York: Horizon Press, 1954), 123.
60 Milner, *Education of an American Liberal*, 123.
61 Lamson, *Roger Baldwin*, 126.
62 Milner, *Education of an American Liberal*, 122.
63 Murphy, *Meaning of Freedom of Speech*, 131.
64 American Civil Liberties Union, "Statement of Principles," 8, ACLU Papers.
65 Murphy, *Meaning of Freedom of Speech*, 131.
66 Corliss Lamont, *Freedom Is as Freedom Does* (New York: Continuum, 1990), 184; Oliver Jensen and Sam Norkin, "The Persuasive Roger Baldwin," *Harper's*, September 1, 1951, 48; "Arrest Speakers at Street Rally," *New York Times*, October 13, 1920, 17.
67 For many years, online sources such as Wikipedia incorrectly listed Ernst as a founder of the ACLU.

CHAPTER FIVE

1 Susan Leerburger Ernst obituary.
2 "From the Williams 1909 Reunion Report," n.d., Ernst Papers.
3 Arthur S. Link, "What Happened to the Progressive Movement in the 1920s?" *American Historical Review* 64, no. 4 (July 1959): 833–51.
4 Samson, *American Fund for Public Service*, xiii.
5 William Floyd, *Social Progress: A Handbook of the Liberal Movement* (New York: Arbitrator, 1925), 241.
6 "A Good Beginning," *Outlook*, March 1920, 362.
7 Cottrell, *Roger Nash Baldwin*, 1.
8 Murphy, *Meaning of Freedom of Speech*, 117.
9 "Roger Baldwin, 97, Is Dead; Crusader for Civil Rights Founded the ACLU," *New York Times*, August 27, 1981, D18.
10 Samson, *American Fund for Public Service*, 7; D. Johnson, *Challenge to American Freedoms*, 8–13.
11 "Roger Baldwin, 97, Is Dead."
12 On Baldwin's work ethic, see Joseph Freeman, *An American Testament: A Narrative of Rebels and Romantics* (New York: Farrar and Rinehart, 1936), 327. On his energy level, see Travis Hoke, "Red Rainbow," *North American Review* 234 (November 1932): 438.
13 Freeman, *American Testament*, 327.
14 Dwight MacDonald, "The Defense of Everybody-II," *New Yorker*, July 18, 1953, 29.
15 Walker, *In Defense of American Liberties*, 66.
16 Dwight MacDonald, "The Defense of Everybody-I," *New Yorker*, July 11, 1953, 31–32.
17 Cottrell, *Roger Nash Baldwin*, 127.
18 American Civil Liberties Union (ACLU), *Annual Report* (New York: ACLU, 1921), 4.

19 David J. Goldberg, *Discontented America: The United States in the 1920s* (Baltimore: Johns Hopkins University Press, 1999), 42.

20 See Norman Hapgood, ed., *Professional Patriots: An Exposure of the Personalities, Methods and Objectives Involved in the Organized Effort to Exploit Patriotic Impulses in These United States during and after the Late War* (New York: Albert and Charles Boni, 1927).

21 Lynn Dumenil, *The Modern Temper: American Culture and Society in the 1920s* (New York: Hill and Wang, 1995), 226.

22 *A Year's Fight for Free Speech, The Work of the American Civil Liberties Union from Sept. 1921. to Jan. 1923* (New York: American Civil Liberties Union, 1923); MacDonald, "Defense of Everybody–I," 38.

23 "So This Is Liberty" (New York: American Civil Liberties Union, 1924); "The Michigan Communist Trials" (New York: American Civil Liberties Union, 1923).

24 MacDonald, "Defense of Everybody–I," 35.

25 MacDonald, "Defense of Everybody–I," 49.

26 Murphy, *Meaning of Freedom of Speech*, 118, 120.

27 Douglas Colin Post, "Partisanship within the American Civil Liberties Union: The Board of Directors, the Struggle with Anti-Communism, and Elizabeth Gurley Flynn, 1938–1940" (PhD diss., University of Richmond, 1996), 21.

28 Arthur Garfield Hays, *Let Freedom Ring*, quoted in Murphy, *Meaning of Freedom of Speech*, 133.

29 American Civil Liberties Union (ACLU), *Free Speech and the Workers' Party* (New York: ACLU, 1925).

30 Walker, *In Defense of American Liberties*, 63; Cottrell, *Roger Nash Baldwin*, 145–46.

31 Lucille Milner to MLE, April 5, 1921, Ernst Papers.

32 Samson, *American Fund for Public Service*, 1–2; Cottrell, *Roger Nash Baldwin*, 130.

33 *The Reminiscences of Roger Nash Baldwin* (New York: Columbia University Oral History Collection, 1975), 325.

34 D. Johnson, *Challenge to American Freedoms*, 386.

35 John A. Saltmarsh, *Scott Nearing: An Intellectual Biography* (Philadelphia: Temple University Press, 1991), 187–88.

36 *Reminiscences of Baldwin*, 326.

37 Merle Curti, "Subsidizing Radicalism: The American Fund for Public Service, 1921–1941," *Social Science Review* 33 (September 1959): 276.

38 American Fund for Public Service pamphlet, Ernst Papers.

39 Minutes of AFPS Board, August 10, 1925, in American Fund for Public Service Records, 1922–1941, MssCol 74, Manuscript and Archives Division, New York Public Library (hereafter cited as AFPS Records).

40 Roger Baldwin (RB) to MLE, February 8, 1923, Ernst Papers.

41 Samson, *American Fund for Public Service*, 143.

42 Saltmarsh, *Scott Nearing*, 188.

43 History of the Fund, n.d., Ernst Papers.

44 Curti, "Subsidizing Radicalism," 279–80; see also Roger N. Baldwin and Stuart Chase, *Survey of Enterprises in the Liberal, Labor and Radical Movements in the United States, Prepared for the American Fund for Public Service, Inc.* (New York: American Fund for Public Service, 1924).

45 See AFPS press release, 1926, AFPS Records: "It is in this field that the Fund has invested the largest amount, believing it to be of substantial and enduring value."
46 Curti, "Subsidizing Radicalism," 287.
47 "Churchmen Backed by Reds, Claim," *Detroit Free Press*, May 6, 1929.
48 Samson, *American Fund for Public Service*, 61.
49 Lamson, *Roger Baldwin*, 149.
50 Freeman, *American Testament*, 332.
51 Freeman, *American Testament*, 332.
52 RB to MLE, December 20, 1926, Ernst Papers.
53 Ernst interview with Harlan Phillips, 477.
54 Ernst, *Best Is Yet*, 245. See also Cottrell, *Roger Nash Baldwin*, 131.
55 Samson, *American Fund for Public Service*, 220–21.
56 "The Midas Curse," *Pittsburgh Post-Gazette*, October 8, 1925.
57 "Radicals Expend Unearned Money to Fight Capital," *Salt Lake Telegram*, September 25, 1925.
58 History of Greenbaum, Wolff, and Ernst.
59 Levy, *My Double Life*, 167.
60 History of Greenbaum, Wolff, and Ernst, 4.
61 Ernst interview with Harlan Phillips.
62 See Marion Dutton Savage, *Industrial Unionism in America* (New York: Arno and New York Times, 1971), 218; Edwin E. Witte, *Historical Survey of Labor Arbitration* (Philadelphia: University of Pennsylvania Press, 1952), 23, 36–37; James H. Tufts, "Judicial Law-Making Exemplified in Industrial Arbitration," *Columbia Law Review* 21 (May 1921): 405–15; J. H. Wigmore, "A New Field for Systematic Justice," *Illinois Law Review* 10 (1915): 592–95.
63 See E. L. Oliver, "The Arbitration of Labor Disputes," *University of Pennsylvania Law Review* 83 (December 1934): 213. The first voluntarily arbitrations were entered into in 1905. Morton Gitelman, "The Evolution of Labor Arbitration," *DePaul Law Review* 9 (1960): 181–95.
64 Morris Ernst, "The Development of Industrial Jurisprudence," *Columbia Law Review* 21, no. 2 (January 1921): 155–61.
65 Drafts, untitled book manuscript, circa 1921, box 242, Ernst Papers.
66 MLE to Margaret Samuels, n.d. (ca. 1922), Ernst Papers.
67 Ernst interview with Harlan Phillips, 221; Ernst, *Best Is Yet*, 45.
68 Ernst interview with Harlan Phillips, 109.
69 Morris Ernst, *Touch Wood: A Year's Diary* (New York: Atheneum, 1960), 342.
70 See Richard J. Altenbaugh, *Education for Struggle: The American Labor Colleges of the 1920s and 1930s* (Philadelphia: Temple University Press, 1990).
71 Alden Whitman, "Norman Thomas, Socialist, Dies," *New York Times*, December 20, 1968, 1.
72 "Making the Surplus Vote Count by Proportional Representation," *New York Times*, January 7, 1923, X9; "Hylan Foes Adopt 5-Cent Park Fare Plank," *New York Times*, June 10, 1921, 1.
73 John Adam Moreau, "The Often Enraged Heywood Broun: His Career and Thought Revisited," *Journalism Quarterly* 44 (Autumn 1967): 497–507.
74 Geoffrey T. Hellman, "Heywood Broun," *Life*, March 6, 1939.
75 Ernst's behavior as described in a series of undated letters he wrote to Margaret Samuels, Ernst Papers.

76 "Mrs. Morris L. Ernst, Taught History of Words," newspaper clipping, box 561, Ernst Papers.
77 Margaret Samuels to MLE, n.d., Ernst Papers.
78 MLE to Margaret Samuels, n.d., Ernst Papers.
79 MLE to Margaret Samuels, n.d., Ernst Papers.
80 MLE to Margaret Samuels, August 1922, Ernst Papers.
81 MLE to Margaret Samuels, n.d., Ernst Papers.
82 MLE to Margaret Samuels, December 1922, Ernst Papers.
83 MLE to Margaret Samuels, n.d., Ernst Papers.
84 "Miss Samuels to Wed," *New York Times*, February 7, 1923, 15; "Miss Samuels a Bride," *New York Times*, March 2, 1923, 15.
85 Ernst, *Best Is Yet*, 220.
86 MLE interview with Mary Batten.

CHAPTER SIX

1 Rodell, "Morris Ernst," 97.
2 MLE memorial transcript, September 1976, box 548, Ernst Papers.
3 "Biography: Morris L. Ernst."
4 Cottrell, *Roger Nash Baldwin*, 166.
5 Levy, *My Double Life*, 176.
6 Rodell, "Morris Ernst," 107.
7 Levy, *My Double Life*, 168.
8 MLE to Margaret Samuels, August 11, 1922, Ernst Papers.
9 Levy, *My Double Life*, 168.
10 American Civil Liberties Union (ACLU), *Free Speech 1925–1926: The Work of the American Civil Liberties Union* (New York: ACLU, 1926), 4–5.
11 "Shaking the Statue of Liberty," *Christian Work*, April 1925.
12 Charles A. Beard, "Count Karolyi and America," *Nation* 120 (April 1925): 347.
13 "Karolyi Gag Laid to Hughes on Plea of Political Foes," *New York Tribune*, February 17, 1925.
14 MLE to William Castle, February 26, 1925, Ernst Papers.
15 "Karolyi Gag Laid to Hughes."
16 "Fail to Tell Why Karolyi is Silenced," *New York Times*, February 19, 1925, 5.
17 "Says Hughes Aims to Gag Karolyi," *Boston Herald*, February 28, 1925.
18 Beard, "Count Karolyi and America," 347–48. See Michael Karolyi, *Memoirs of Michael Karolyi: Faith Without Illusion* (New York: E. P. Dutton, 1957), 209–11.
19 On the ACLU resolution protesting the gag, see Milner, *Education of an American Liberal*, 159–60. On the approach to Kellogg, see "Asks Kellogg Lift Count Karolyi Gag," *Milwaukee Sentinel*, March 10, 1925; "Lifting Karolyi's Gag Up to Kellogg," *World* (New York), March 19, 1925. See also American Civil Liberties Union (ACLU), "The Tresca and Karolyi Cases," *Foreign Dictators of American Rights* (New York: ACLU, 1925), 3–8.
20 ACLU, *Free Speech 1925–1926*, 3.
21 ACLU, *Free Speech 1925–1926*, 3.
22 Milner, *Education of an American Liberal*, 156.
23 Walker, *In Defense of American Liberties*, 73–75.

24 Walker, *In Defense of American Liberties*, 77–78.
25 Erik Barnouw, *A History of Broadcasting in the United States*, vol. 1 (New York: Oxford, 1966), 197.
26 Whitney v. California, 274 U.S. 357 (1927) at 371.
27 Abrams v. United States, 250 U.S. 616 (1919) at 631.
28 *Whitney v. California*, 274 U.S. at 375.
29 Barton Bean, "Pressure for Freedom: The American Civil Liberties Union" (PhD diss., Cornell University, 1955), 108.
30 RB to MLE, March 13, 1926, Ernst Papers.
31 Ernst, *Best Is Yet*, 52.
32 ACLU, *Free Speech 1925–1926*, 4.
33 Murphy, *Meaning of Freedom of Speech*, 208; ACLU, *Free Speech 1925–1926*.
34 RB to MLE, April 1, 1926; February 16, 1926; June 3, 1926, Ernst Papers.
35 D. Johnson, *Challenge to American Freedoms*, 386.
36 Hays, *Let Freedom Ring*, quoted in Murphy, *Meaning of Freedom of Speech*, 151–52.
37 Relator's Brief, *People of the State of New York v. George Ryan*, May 17, 1926; Walker, *In Defense of American Liberties*, 59; "Liberties Union Fight on School Ban Today," *New York Times*, November 4, 1926, 45.
38 "From Dayton to New York," *Nation*, June 2, 1926, 595.
39 "Free Speech Ban by Schools Upheld," *Brooklyn Daily Times*, December 7, 1926, 19; "Liberties Union Fight on School Ban Today."
40 "Lame Ducks Win Out," *Lincoln (NE) Herald*, March 23, 1928, 2.
41 Milner, *Education of an American Liberal*, 172.
42 Robert J. Goldstein, *Political Repression in Modern American History: From 1870 to the Present* (New York: Schenkman, 1978), 181.
43 Douglas B. Craig, *Fireside Politics: Radio and Political Culture in the United States, 1920–1940* (Baltimore, MD: Johns Hopkins University Press, 2006), 9.
44 D. Craig, *Fireside Politics*, 12.
45 Ithiel de Sola Pool, *Technologies of Freedom* (Cambridge, MA: Harvard University Press, 2009), 113, 124.
46 Donald G. Godfrey, "Senator Dill and the 1927 Radio Act," *Journal of Broadcasting* 23 (Fall 1979): 477–89.
47 Morris Ernst, "Who Shall Control the Air?" *Nation* 122 (April 1926): 443.
48 "Radio Menace to Free Speech, Says Lecturer," *Hartford Courant*, March 30, 1927, 2; "Morris Ernst Warns against Radio Gag," *Leader*, April 9, 1927; both in Ernst Papers.
49 Ernst, "Who Shall Control the Air?"
50 Morris L. Ernst, "Radio Censorship and the 'Listening Millions,'" *Nation* 122 (April 1926): 473.
51 Ernst, "Radio Censorship and the 'Listening Millions,'" 475.
52 Ernst, "Radio Censorship and the 'Listening Millions'"; "House Passes White Bill to Control Radio," *St. Louis Post-Dispatch*, March 15, 1926, 1; "Says Dill Bill Means Radio Censorship," *New York Times*, February 27, 1926, 3.
53 Erik Barnouw, *A Tower in Babel: A History of Broadcasting in the United States to 1933* (New York: Oxford University Press, 1966), 197.
54 See Woody Klein, *Liberties Lost: The Endangered Legacy of the ACLU* (Westport, CT: Praeger, 2006), 189.
55 Ernst, "Radio Censorship and the 'Listening Millions,'" 473.

56 "Radio Menace to Free Speech Says Lecturer."
57 "Right to Be Different Discussed By 'Radicals,'" *Hampshire Gazette*, newspaper clipping, n.d., Ernst Papers.
58 Arthur Sears Henning, *Government by Propaganda* (Chicago: Chicago Tribune, Public Service Office, 1927), 39; "On the Trail of the Serpent," *National Republic*, May 1, 1929, 31.
59 Certificate of Incorporation, Sons and Daughters of the Blacklist, Ernst Papers; "To Incorporate Members of the Blacklist," *Daily Republican*, May 26, 1928, 4.
60 Murphy, *Meaning of Freedom of Speech*, 202.
61 MLE to New York *World*, April 6, 1928, Ernst Papers.
62 MLE to Crane Gartz, December 27, 1949, Ernst Papers.
63 Greenbaum, Wolff, and Ernst (GWE) to *Chicago Tribune*, June 16, 1926, Ernst Papers.
64 James, "Morris L. Ernst," 8.
65 Murphy, *Meaning of Freedom of Speech*, 165–66; O'Connor, *Heywood Broun*, 138.
66 "Edna Ferber, Novelist, 82, Dies," *New York Times*, April 17, 1968, 1.
67 J. E. Smyth, *Edna Ferber's Hollywood: American Fictions of Gender, Race, and History* (Austin, TX: University of Texas Press, 2011), 85.
68 Edna Ferber, *A Peculiar Treasure* (Garden City, NJ: Doubleday, 1960), 307.
69 Julie Goldsmith Gilbert, *Ferber: Edna Ferber and Her Circle, a Biography* (New York: Applause, 1999), 376.
70 "His Name Used in Showboat, He Sues Author," *New York Daily News*, October 26, 1928, 150.
71 Levy, *Double Life*, 232; Damron v. Doubleday, Doran Co., Inc., 133 Misc. 302 (N.Y. Misc. 1928).
72 Ernst, *Best Is Yet*, 181.
73 Ferber, *Peculiar Treasure*, 308.
74 Ernst, *Untitled*, 9.
75 "Lawyer at a Lathe," n.d., Ernst Papers.
76 Kenneth Roman, "Free Speech and Bike Paths: Nantucket's Morris Ernst," *Historic Nantucket* 62, no. 2 (Spring 2012): 18.
77 Roman, "Free Speech and Bike Paths," 18.
78 C. A. Lovelace, *A Nantucket Enclave: Monomoy Heights, 1852–2005; From Sheep Commons to Cottage Colony to Gold Coast* (Nantucket, MA: Mill Hill Press, 2005), 57.
79 MLE to Louis Notkin, November 1, 1938, Ernst Papers.
80 MLE interview with Mary Batten.
81 "Lawyer at a Lathe."
82 MLE to Louise Byber, October 13, 1934, Ernst Papers.
83 MLE to Origen Seymour, July 20, 1932, Ernst Papers.
84 Roman, "Free Speech and Bike Paths," 18.
85 Roman, "Free Speech and Bike Paths," 19.
86 Robert F. Mooney, *The Nantucket Way: Untold Legends and Lore of America's Most Intriguing Island* (Garden City, NY: Doubleday, 1980), 134.
87 Roman, "Free Speech and Bike Paths," 18.
88 Morris L. Ernst, *So Far So Good* (New York: Harper and Brothers, 1948), 4.

CHAPTER SEVEN

1 Frederick Lewis Allen, *Only Yesterday: An Informal History of the 1920s* (New York: Blue Robin Books, 1931), 88.

2 For accounts of literary censorship in the 1920s, see Paul S. Boyer, *Purity in Print: Book Censorship in America from the Gilded Age to the Computer Age* (Madison: University of Wisconsin Press, 2002); Felice Flanery Lewis, *Literature, Obscenity, and Law* (Carbondale: Southern Illinois University Press, 1978).

3 Cottrell, *Roger Nash Baldwin*, 166.

4 Boyer, *Purity in Print*, 2; Heywood Broun and Margaret Leech, *Anthony Comstock: Roundsman of the Lord* (New York: Albert and Charles Boni, 1927).

5 Boyer, *Purity in Print*, 2–9.

6 Flanery Lewis, *Literature, Obscenity, and Law*, 63.

7 John E. Semonche, *Censoring Sex: A Historical Journey Through American Media* (New York: Rowman and Littlefield, 2007), 23.

8 Jay A. Gertzman, *Bookleggers and Smuthounds: The Trade in Erotica, 1920–1940* (Philadelphia: University of Pennsylvania Press, 2002); "An Interview," *New Yorker*, October 17, 1925, 7; Henry F. Pringle, "Comstock the Less," *American Mercury* 10 (January 1927): 56–63; Alva Johnston, "'I'm No Reformer,' Says Sumner," *New York Times*, August 20, 1922, 43.

9 George MacAdam, "Sumner Finds World Growing Better," *New York Times*, July 25, 1926, SM10.

10 Edward De Grazia, *Girls Lean Back Everywhere: The Law of Obscenity and the Assault on Genius* (New York: Vintage, 1992), 7.

11 John S. Sumner, "The Truth About Literary Lynching," *Dial* 71 (July 1921): 65; John S. Sumner, "Criticizing the Critic," *Bookman* 53 (July 1921): 285–88.

12 "The Weather Vane," *Buffalo Evening News*, August 19, 1922, 8.

13 "The Sewing Circle," *Dispatch* (Moline, IL), July 29, 1922, 9.

14 Quote derived from British case R v. Hicklin, L.R. (1868) 3 Q.B. 360. For the American case, see United States v. Bennett, 24 Fed. Cas. 1093 (S.D.N.Y. 1879).

15 Frederic Svoboda, review of *What Happens* by John Herrmann, *Middle West Review* 4 (Fall 2017): 147–50.

16 "Literati in Obscene Book Writer's Trial," *World* (New York), October 4, 1927.

17 Sara Kosiba, introduction to *What Happens*, by John Herrmann (Hastings, NE: Hastings College Press, 2015), xi.

18 Forrest Bailey to Edward S. Greenbaum, July 12, 1926, Ernst Papers.

19 Memorandum on Behalf of John Herrmann in opposition to Seizure and Confiscation of 300 Copies of Novel What Happens, box 233, Ernst Papers.

20 L. C. Andrews, assistant secretary to John J. Wildberg, November 1, 1926, Ernst Papers; Kosiba, introduction to *What Happens*, xii.

21 John J. Wildberg to John Herrmann, March 11, 1927, Ernst Papers.

22 MLE to Arthur Garfield Hays, October 4, 1927, Ernst Papers.

23 "Literati in Obscene Book Writer's Trial."

24 Levy, *My Double Life*, 174.

25 "Literary Experts Evidence Refused," *Gazette* (Montreal), October 4, 1927, 18.

26 "Novelist Faces Libel Charges," *Ogden Standard-Examiner* (Ogden, UT), October 4, 1927, 3.

27 "Knox Rules Out Literary Experts," *World* (New York), October 4, 1927.

28 "Book Declared Obscene," *South Bend Tribune* (South Bend, IN), October 5, 1927, 2.

29 "Condemn Books; Expose Immoral," *Journal and Courier* (Lafayette, IN), October 5, 1927, 12.

30 Ernst, *Love Affair with the Law*, 56; MLE to Hays, October 4, 1927.

31 "William Seagle, NLRB Lawyer, Was Author of Books on the Law," *New York Times*, January 2, 1978, 24.

32 MLE to William Seagle, June 9, 1928, Ernst Papers.

33 Morris L. Ernst and William Seagle, *To the Pure: A Study of Obscenity and the Censor* (New York: Viking Press, 1928), vii.

34 Ernst and Seagle, *To the Pure*, 66.

35 Ernst and Seagle, *To the Pure*, 121.

36 Ernst and Seagle, *To the Pure*, 156.

37 Ernst and Seagle, *To the Pure*, 9.

38 Ernst and Seagle, *To the Pure*, viii.

39 Ernst and Seagle, *To the Pure*, 283.

40 Ernst and Seagle, *To the Pure*, 282.

41 Ferris Greenlet, "Are All Things Pure," *Saturday Review of Literature*, November 10, 1928.

42 "Notes on New Books," *Bookman*, March 1929, xxv.

43 Herschel Brickell, "The Literary Landscape," *North American Review* 225 (December 1928).

44 See "Honor Roll for 1928," *St. Louis Post-Dispatch*, January 3, 1929, 16.

45 Levy, *My Double Life*, 174.

46 See Michael Baker, *Our Three Selves: A Life of Radclyffe Hall* (New York: Quill, 1985); Diana Souhami, *The Trials of Radclyffe Hall* (London: Weidenfeld and Nicolson, 1998); Laura L. Doan and Jay Prosser, *Palatable Poison: Critical Perspectives on the Well of Loneliness* (New York: Columbia University Press, 2001); Kathy March, "Radclyffe Hall (12 August 1880–7 October 1943)," in *Dictionary of Literary Biography: British Novelists Between the Wars*, ed. George M. Johnson (Detroit: Gale, 1998), 147–54.

47 Flanery Lewis, *Literature, Obscenity, and Law*, 109; Souhami, *The Trials of Radclyffe Hall*, 258.

48 On Friede's efforts to get *The Well of Loneliness*, see Donald Friede, *The Mechanical Angel: His Adventures and Enterprises in the Glittering 1920s* (New York: Knopf, 1948), 90.

49 Leslie Taylor, "'I Made up My Mind to Get It': The American Trial of the *Well of Loneliness*, New York City, 1928–1929," *Journal of the History of Sexuality* 10 (2001): 260.

50 Friede, *Mechanical Angel*, 93.

51 "Sumner Waiting with Club to Swat 'Well of Loneliness'," *Brooklyn Daily Eagle*, December 15, 1928, 3.

52 Friede, *Mechanical Angel*, 94.

53 "Sumner Seizes 'Loneliness' in Sex Book Raid," *Daily News* (New York), January 12, 1929, 65.

54 "Hyman Bushel Dies, Ex-Magistrate, 77," *New York Times*, March 10, 1969, 45.

55 "Novel 'Loneliness' Is Ruled Obscene: Magistrate Holds Publishers of Radclyffe Hall Book for Trial on Charge," *New York Times*, January 23, 1929, 11.

56 Quoted in Souhami, *Trials of Radclyffe Hall.*
57 "Novel 'Loneliness' Ruled Obscene," 11.
58 DeGrazia, *Girls Lean Back Everywhere*, 200.
59 "Novel 'Loneliness' Ruled Obscene," 11.
60 "Well of Loneliness Cleared in Court Here," *New York Times*, April 20, 1929, 25.
61 "Book Acquitted," *Honolulu Advertiser*, May 11, 1929, 14.
62 Boyer, *Purity in Print*, 134.

CHAPTER EIGHT

1 Mary Ware Dennett (MWD) to MLE, August 27, 1928, in Mary Ware Dennett papers, Schlesinger Library, Radcliffe Institute for Advanced Study, Harvard University, Cambridge, MA (hereafter cited as Dennett papers). Microfilm version viewed at Library of Congress.
2 Ernst, *Best Is Yet*, 144.
3 Constance M. Chen, *"The Sex Side of Life": Mary Ware Dennett's Pioneering Battle for Birth Control and Sex Education* (New York: New Press, 1996); John Craig, "'The Sex Side of Life'": The Obscenity Case of Mary Ware Dennett," *Frontiers: A Journal of Women Studies* 15 (1995): 145–66.
4 Valerie J. Huber and Michael W. Firmin, "A History of Sex Education in the United States Since 1900," *International Journal of Educational Reform* 23 (2014): 25–51.
5 *The Sex Side of Life*, reprinted in Mary Ware Dennett, *Who's Obscene* (New York: Vanguard Press, 1930), 106.
6 "Sex Education or Obscenity? The Mary Ware Dennett Case," Dennett papers; Dennett, *Who's Obscene.*
7 Dennett, *Who's Obscene*, 8.
8 Arthur Garfield Hays to MWD, May 25, 1926, Dennett papers.
9 MLE to MWD, August 30, 1926, Dennett papers.
10 MLE to MWD, October 2, 1926, Dennett papers.
11 MWD to MLE, October 20, 1926; MWD to MLE, November 8, 1926, Dennett papers.
12 *Washington Times*, May 2, 1929, clipping, Ernst Papers.
13 "Sex Education or Obscenity?"
14 Dennett, *Who's Obscene*, 53.
15 Memorandum in support of motion to quash indictment, box 358, Ernst Papers.
16 Chen, *"Sex Side of Life,"* 271.
17 "Clergy to Help Court in 'Obscene' Book Case," *New York Times*, January 22, 1929, 20.
18 "Sex and Our Children," *Nation*, February 6, 1929, 154–55.
19 "Sex and Our Children," 154–55.
20 Chen, *"Sex Side of Life,"* 289.
21 Chen, *"Sex Side of Life,"* 276.
22 "Sex and Our Children," 155.
23 Wilkinson's argument, in Dennett papers.
24 MLE to MWD, February 18, 1929, Dennett papers.
25 "Moscowitz Probe Delays Sex Trial," *Brooklyn Daily Eagle*, March 6, 1929.

26 "Rules Mrs. Dennett Must Go to Trial," *New York Times*, April 6, 1929, 12.
27 Dennett, *Who's Obscene*, 131–32.
28 "Mrs. Dennett Guilty in Sex Booklet Case," *New York Times*, April 24, 1929, 31.
29 Chen, *"The Sex Side of Life,"* 285.
30 Chen, *"The Sex Side of Life,"* 285.
31 MWD to unknown, n.d., Dennett papers.
32 Dudley Nichols, "Sex and the Law," *Nation*, May 8, 1929, 552–54.
33 "Woman Author of Sex Book YMCA Used, Convicted," *St. Louis Post-Dispatch*, April 24, 1929, 25.
34 "Court Sustains Jury's Conviction of Mrs. Dennett," *World* (New York), April 26, 1929.
35 "Sex Writer to Face Sentence Monday," *New York Evening Journal*, April 25, 1929.
36 "Picking On a Woman," *Indianapolis Times*, April 30, 1929.
37 "This Should Be Fought Out," *Elizabeth Times*, April 30, 1929, newspaper clipping, Ernst Papers.
38 "Mrs. Dennett's Appeal Charges 48 Errors," *World* (New York), October 10, 1929; "Mrs. Dennett Claims 48 Errors in Her Trial," *New York Daily News*, October 20, 1929, 34.
39 Brief for Appellant, United States v. Dennett, 39 F.2d 564 (2d Cir. 1930); "Appeal Is Argued for Mrs. Dennett," *New York Times*, January 16, 1930, 25; "Idealism of Dennett Sex Primer Cited in Appeal from Conviction," *World* (New York), June 16, 1930.
40 *Dennett*, 39 F.2d at 569.
41 "Plan New Appeal in Dennett Case," *World* (New York), March 5, 1930.
42 "Government Accepts Mrs. Dennett Decision," *New York Times*, June 6, 1930, 3.
43 Alexander Lindey (AL) to MWD, June 9, 1930, Dennett papers.
44 Linda Gordon, *The Moral Property of Women: A History of Birth Control Politics in America* (Urbana: University of Illinois Press, 2002), 143.
45 Milner, *Education of an American Liberal*, 158.
46 People v. Sanger, 118 N. E. 637 (NY 1918); James Reed, *From Private Vice to Public Virtue: The Birth Control Movement and American Society Since 1830* (Princeton, NJ: Princeton University Press, 1984), 106–8.
47 Gordon, *Moral Property of Women*, 171.
48 Affidavit of Anna McNamara, box 326, Ernst Papers.
49 Affidavit of Anna McNamara.
50 Margaret Sanger, *The Autobiography of Margaret Sanger* (Mineola, NY: Dover Publications, 2004), 403.
51 "Cops Didn't Even Know How to Pull a Good Raid," *Missoula Northwest*, April 23, 1929.
52 Sanger, *Autobiography*, 402.
53 Lawrence Lader, *The Margaret Sanger Story and the Fight for Birth Control* (Westport, CT: Greenwood Press, 1955), 255; Margaret Sanger, "The Birth Control Raid," *New Republic*, May 1, 1929, 305–6.
54 Sanger, *Autobiography*, 403.
55 Sanger, *Autobiography*, 404–6.
56 "Policewomen Raid Birth Control Clinic," *Brooklyn Times Union*, April 16, 1929, 7. See also "Troublemakers!" Margaret Sanger Papers Project Research Annex,

November 28, 2012, https://sangerpapers.wordpress.com/2012/11/28/trouble makers/.

57 Lader, *Margaret Sanger Story*, 258.

58 "Doctors Decry Birth Control Record Seizure," *New York Medical Week* 8 (March 1929): 5–6.

59 Lader, *Margaret Sanger Story*, 258.

60 "Head Women's Bureau Removed from Office," *Sioux City Journal*, May 12, 1929, 2.

61 "Birth Control Raid Stirs Up Support for Mrs. Sanger," *World* (New York), April 19, 1929; "Birth Control Trial Proves Fun for 400," *Brooklyn Citizen*, April 25, 1929, 2.

62 "40 Physicians Volunteer to Aid Birth Control Clinic," *New York Herald Tribune*, April 18, 1929, 10.

63 "500 in Court to Aid 5 Seized at Clinic," *New York Times*, April 29, 1929, 13.

64 Lader, *Margaret Sanger Story*, 259.

65 *People of the State of New York v. Marcella Sideri, Sigrid Brestwell, Antoinette Field, Elizabeth Pissort, and Hannah M. Stone*, Magistrate's Court, Second District–Borough of Manhattan, City of New York, People's Memorandum of Facts and Law, box 326.5, Ernst Papers.

66 "Court Is Jammed as Birth Control Hearing Starts," *Evening World*, April 19, 1929.

67 "500 in Court to Aid 5 Seized at Clinic."

68 "Birth Control Raid Stirs Up Support"; "Court Is Jammed."

69 Sanger, *Autobiography*, 406.

70 Defendant's memorandum, *People v. Sideri*, box 326.5, Ernst Papers.

71 "Woman Sleuth Blushes at Ruse to Snare Clinic," *Daily News* (New York), April 20, 1929.

72 Brief of defendants, *People v. Sideri*, box 326.5, Ernst Papers.

73 Morris L. Ernst and Alexander Lindey, *The Censor Marches On: Recent Milestones in the Administration of the Obscenity Law in the United States* (New York: Da Capo Press, 1971), 156.

74 Ishbel Ross, "Birth Control Hearing Ends After Turmoil," *New York Herald Tribune*, April 25, 1929.

75 Ross, "Birth Control Hearing Ends."

76 "Women in Birth Clinic Raid Freed," *New York Telegram*, May 14, 1929.

77 Morris Ernst, "Birth Control in the Courts," 1942, box 194, Ernst Papers.

78 "Sanger Clinic Continues Fight," *New York Telegram*, May 15, 1929.

79 Lader, *Margaret Sanger Story*, 261–62.

CHAPTER NINE

1 Morris Ernst, address, "The Law Catches Up with Science," speech to the Society of Medical Jurisprudence, October 14, 1937, typescript, box 528, Ernst Papers.

2 "Summer Again Hits Book on Casanova," *Brooklyn Times Union*, August 9, 1930, 14.

3 James, "Morris L. Ernst," 10.

4 In the Matter of John S. Sumner against Simon and Schuster, Inc., September 25, 1930, box 226, Ernst Papers.

5 Decision of the court, in the Matter of John S. Sumner against Simon and Schuster, Inc., September 25, 1930, box 226, Ernst Papers; "Finds No Obscenity in Schnitzler Book: Magistrate Gottlieb Dismisses Sumner's Action Against 'Casanova's Homecoming,'" *New York Times*, September 26, 1930, 6.

6 James, "Morris L. Ernst," 10.

7 "Sumner as Censor Attacked by Ernst," *New York Times*, December 15, 1929, N2.

8 "Says Vice Society Fears Publishers," *New York Times*, February 12, 1930, 2.

9 "Says Vice Society Fears Publishers."

10 "Morgan Library Silent on Erotica," *New York Times*, February 13, 1930, 10.

11 "Censorship Debaters Want Hays Ousted," *New York Times*, March 1, 1930, 11.

12 "Censorship Loses 3-to-1 in Forum of Publicists," *Pittsburgh Press*, May 21, 1930, 46.

13 Samantha Barbas, "How the Movies Became Speech," *Rutgers Law Review* 64, no. 3 (Spring 2012): 665–745.

14 James, "Morris L. Ernst," 10; "Censorship of the Movies," *New York Times*, March 9, 1930, 72.

15 Boyer, *Purity in Print*, 210.

16 Rodney Dutcher, "Censorship of Books Expected to Be Killed," *Daily Tribune* (Wisconsin Rapids, WI), June 21, 1929, 4.

17 MLE to Bronson Cutting, October 18, 1929; November 14, 1929; November 11, 1929. RB to MLE, February 4, 1930; February 7, 1930; all in Ernst Papers.

18 Boyer, *Purity in Print*, 123.

19 Forrest Bailey to MWD, November 5, 1930, Dennett papers.

20 File memorandum, January 22, 1930, Ernst Papers.

21 Marie Stopes to MLE, January 9, 1930, Ernst Papers.

22 MLE to Marie Stopes, January 31, 1930, Ernst Papers.

23 MLE to Marie Stopes, March 4, 1930, Ernst Papers.

24 Actually, 3 percent on the first 25,000 copies, 2 percent on the next 25,000, and 1 percent on all copies beyond 50,000. AL to MLE, July 19, 1930, Ernst Papers.

25 Ernst interview with Harlan Phillips, n.p.; "Lawyer's 10 Pound Book," *Minneapolis Tribune*, January 11, 1938.

26 MLE to AL, August 29, 1930, Ernst Papers.

27 MLE to Collector of Customs, September 3, 1930, Ernst Papers.

28 AL to Earl Balch, September 26, 1930, Ernst Papers.

29 "Volume Immune from Seizure," *Ogden (UT) Standard-Examiner*, April 6, 1931.

30 United States v. One Obscene Book Entitled *Married Love*, 48 F.2d. 821 (S.D.N.Y. 1931) at 824.

31 *One Obscene Book*, 48 F.2d. at 824.

32 United States v. One Book Entitled *Contraception*, 51 F.2d 525 (1931) at 528.

33 See Walker, *In Defense of American Liberties*, 85.

34 *Announcing the National Council on Freedom from Censorship*, pamphlet, n.d., Ernst Papers.

35 MLE to AL, July 21, 1931, Ernst Papers.

36 Morris Ernst, "Sex Wins in America," *Nation*, August 10, 1932, 124.

37 Ernst, "Sex Wins in America," 122–24.

CHAPTER TEN

1 Eric Foner, *Give Me Liberty! An American History*, vol. 2 (New York: W.W. Norton, 2017), 812.

2 William E. Leuchtenburg, *Franklin D. Roosevelt and the New Deal, 1932–1940* (New York: Harper and Row, 1963), 1–2.

3 Murphy, *Meaning of Freedom of Speech*, 230.

4 Cottrell, *Roger Nash Baldwin*, 206.

5 American Civil Liberties Union (ACLU), *The Fight for Civil Liberty 1930–1931* (New York: ACLU, 1931), 3, 9.

6 ACLU, *Fight for Civil Liberty 1930–1931*, 3, 9.

7 Jerold S. Auerbach, "The Depression Decade," in *The Pulse of Freedom: American Liberties*, ed. Alan Reitman (New York: W. W. Norton, 1975), 67.

8 Milner, *Education of an American Liberal*, 184.

9 Walker, *In Defense of American Liberties*, 86–87.

10 American Civil Liberties Union (ACLU), *Blue Coats and Reds* (New York: ACLU, 1929).

11 Murphy, *Meaning of Freedom of Speech*, 234.

12 American Civil Liberties Union (ACLU), *Police and Official Lawlessness against Communists in New York* (New York: ACLU, 1929).

13 ACLU, *Fight for Civil Liberty 1930–1931*, 17; Harry Ward, Art Hays, Morris Ernst, and others to Mayor Walker, March 11, 1930, Ernst Papers; "500 City Leaders Plan Whalen Fete," *New York Times*, April 9, 1930, 24.

14 Milner, *Education of an American Liberal*, 181; "Mayor's Quiet Gibes Answer Red Tirade of Unemployment," *New York Times*, March 15, 1930, 1; "Whalen Is Assailed for Drive on Reds," *New York Times*, March 12, 1930, 3.

15 Memo, June 14, 1930, Ernst Papers.

16 "Favor Bill to Bar Labor Injunction," *New York Times*, January 21, 1928, 28.

17 Elizabeth Israels Perry, "Rhetoric, Strategy, and Politics in the New York Campaign for Women's Jury Service, 1917–1975," *New York History* 82, no. 1 (2001): 60.

18 MLE to Mrs. Jane Cramer, March 24, 1936, Ernst Papers.

19 Morris L. Ernst, "Divorce-and After: I. Children and Property," *Nation* 130, no. 3371 (February 20, 1930): 172.

20 "Assembly Gets 3-Yr. Divorce Bill," *Daily News* (New York), March 29, 1934.

21 Ernst interview with Harlan Phillips, 375.

22 August Meier and Elliott Rudwick, "Attorneys Black and White: A Case Study of Race Relations within the NAACP," *Journal of American History* 62, no. 4 (March 1976): 937.

23 Ernst, *Best Is Yet*, 50.

24 Unsigned opinion piece in *Nation*, June 8, 1929, clipping in Ernst Papers.

25 For example, *Pittsburgh Courier*, November 27, 1926, and January 22, 1927, clippings in Ernst Papers.

26 See MLE to Ashley Totten, February 15, 1941; Ernst, *Love Affair with the Law*, 128.

27 Samson, *American Fund for Public Service*, 197.

28 Auerbach, *Unequal Justice*, 213.

29 Memo, October 18, 1929, AFPS Records.

30 Memo, October 18, 1929.

31 Memo, October 18, 1929.
32 Richard Kluger, *Simple Justice: The History of Brown v. Board of Education and Black America's Struggle for Equality* (New York: Random House, 2004), 133.
33 Kluger, *Simple Justice*, 133.
34 Kluger, *Simple Justice*, 134.
35 Kluger, *Simple Justice*, 136.
36 A Citizen, letter to the editor, *Palladium Item* (Richmond, IN), February 20, 1931.
37 Walker, *In Defense of American Liberties*, 63.
38 Donohue, *Politics of the American Civil Liberties Union*, 137.
39 MLE to Arthur H. Sulzberger, December 4, 1931, Ernst Papers.
40 Murphy, *Meaning of Freedom of Speech*, 166.
41 Judy Kutulas, *The American Civil Liberties Union and the Making of Modern Liberalism 1930–1960* (Chapel Hill: University of North Carolina Press, 2006), 21.
42 ACLU, *The Fight for Civil Liberty 1930–1931*; Murphy, *Meaning of Freedom of Speech*, 230; Kutulas, *American Civil Liberties Union and Liberalism*, 32.
43 Murphy, *Meaning of Freedom of Speech*, 230.
44 Milner, *Education of an American Liberal*, 183–34.
45 Murphy, *Meaning of Freedom of Speech*, 230.
46 Stromberg v. California, 283 U.S. 359 (1931) at 369. See also Near v. Minnesota, 283 U.S. 697 (1931).
47 See generally Arthur Garfield Hays, *City Lawyer: The Autobiography of a Law Practice* (New York: Simon and Schuster, 1942).
48 Walker, *In Defense of American Liberties*, 53.
49 See Lamson, *Roger Baldwin*, 134.
50 *Reminiscences of Baldwin.*
51 Cottrell, *Roger Nash Baldwin*, 124.
52 Ernst, *Best Is Yet*, 191.
53 Ernst, *Best Is Yet*, 192.
54 S. J. Taylor, *Stalin's Apologist: Walter Duranty; The New York Times Man in Moscow* (New York: Oxford University Press, 1990), 156–57.
55 William Leuchtenburg, *Franklin D. Roosevelt and the New Deal*, 22.
56 Julia Mickenberg, "The New Generation and the New Russia: Modern Childhood as Collective Fantasy," *American Quarterly* 62, no. 1 (March 2010): 103.
57 MLE to Hiram Motherwell, November 20, 1931, Ernst Papers.
58 Morris L. Ernst, *America's Primer* (New York: G. P. Putnam's Sons, 1931), 158.
59 "Chaos a Major Crop," *Journal and Courier* (Lafayette, IN), August 24, 1931, 5.
60 Adelin Hohfeld, "About Books," *Wisconsin State Journal* (Madison), June 28, 1931, 3.
61 "Compact Disgust," review of *America's Primer*, by Morris Ernst, *Time*, September 7, 1931.
62 MLE to Elizabeth Sloane, September 18, 1931, Ernst Papers.
63 MLE to Katherine M. Halle, January 31, 1934, Ernst Papers.
64 Morris Ernst, "If I Were A (Constitutional) Dictator," *Nation*, January 13, 1932, 36–39.
65 "Roosevelt Names New Banking Board," *New York Times*, April 24, 1932, 1.
66 Leonard Lyons, "Lyons Den," *St. Louis Globe-Democrat*, September 21, 1937, 27.
67 Ernst, *Best Is Yet*, 240–41.

68 "Says Big Bill."
69 MLE to John Clark Knox, March 23, 1933, Ernst Papers.
70 MLE to Charles Barnes, February 27, 1932, Ernst Papers.
71 Morris L. Ernst, "The Most Unforgettable Character I've Met," *Reader's Digest*, March 1958.
72 "Supreme Court Honors Brandeis," *New York Times*, October 7, 1941.
73 Greenbaum, *Lawyer's Job*, 78.
74 George Van Schaick to MLE, May 8, 1935, Ernst Papers.
75 Ernst, *Best Is Yet*, 12.
76 Ernst, "Most Unforgettable Character."

CHAPTER ELEVEN

1 Leuchtenburg, *Franklin D. Roosevelt and the New Deal*, 61.
2 Though he would become famous for his affiliation with Roosevelt and the New Deal, as a young man Ernst was a political independent, aligned with progressive, labor-oriented third parties. In 1928, with several noted liberals including Oswald Garrison Villard, W. E. B. DuBois, and John Dewey, Ernst organized the League for Independent Political Action. The league, devoted to the creation of a progressive third party, promoted such reforms as social insurance, progressive taxation, and a cooperatively managed "planned economy" marked by full employment and equitable distribution of wealth. Ultimately, the league never resulted in a political party and was rendered obsolete by the New Deal. See Karel Dennis Bicha, "Liberalism Frustrated: The League for Independent Political Action, 1928–1933," *Mid-America* 48, no. 1 (1936).
3 Samuel Walker, *Hate Speech: The History of an American Controversy* (Lincoln: University of Nebraska Press, 1994), 38. See also Travis Hoke, *Shirts! A Survey of the New "Shirt" Organizations in the United States Seeking a Fascist Dictatorship* (New York: American Civil Liberties Union, 1934).
4 Walker, *Hate Speech*, 41, 43.
5 Walker, *Hate Speech*, 42–45.
6 The phrase was first used by Oliver Wendell Holmes in his dissenting opinion in United States v. Schwimmer, 279 U.S. 644 (1929) at 655.
7 Steven Alan Carr, *Hollywood and Anti-Semitism: A Cultural History up to World War II* (New York: Cambridge University Press, 2001), 115.
8 Carr, *Hollywood and Anti-Semitism*, 116.
9 "WNJ Appeals Denial of License," *New York Times*, January 24, 1933, 15.
10 "Shuler Gets Help in Fight for Radio: Civil Liberties Union to Aid Militant Dry in Battle for His Station License," *New York Times*, January 24, 1933, 21.
11 "Radicals Rally to Support of Shuler," *Modesto News-Herald*, February 4, 1933.
12 "Shuler Renews His Radio Fight," *Los Angeles Times*, February 11, 1933.
13 Brief in Support of Petition for Rehearing, *Trinity Methodist Church v. Federal Radio Commission*, February 10, 1933, Ernst Papers. For the original decision, see Trinity Methodist Church v. Federal Radio Commission, 62 F.2d 850 (1932).
14 Quoted in MLE to *Brooklyn Jewish Examiner*, February 17, 1933, Ernst Papers.
15 J. George Fredman to MLE, February 7, 1933, Ernst Papers.
16 MLE to J. George Fredman, February 10, 1933, Ernst Papers.

17 Bradley W. Hart, *Hitler's American Friends: The Third Reich's Supporters in the United States* (New York: Thomas Dunne Books, 2018).
18 "O'Brien Prohibits Celebration Here of German Society," *New York Times*, October 22, 1933, 1.
19 See Robert G. Waite, "'Hitlerism Invades America': Supporters of Hitler in New York City and the Nazi Threat in America, 1930–1934," *New York History Review* (2016).
20 "Ban on Nazi Rally Upheld by O'Brien," *New York Times*, October 26, 1933, 1.
21 "Ban on Nazi Rally Upheld."
22 "Ban on Nazi Rally Upheld."
23 William Robinson to MLE, October 23, 1933, Ernst Papers.
24 Herman Axelrod to MLE, October 24, 1933, Ernst Papers.
25 MLE to Herman Axelrod, October 25, 1933, Ernst Papers.
26 American Civil Liberties Union (ACLU), *Shall We Protect Free Speech for Nazis in America?* (New York: ACLU, 1934), 2.
27 Drew Pearson to MLE, December 13, 1934, Ernst Papers; William Manchester, *American Caesar: Douglas MacArthur 1880–1964* (New York: Little, Brown, 1978).
28 MLE to Douglas MacArthur, December 6, 1934, Ernst Papers.
29 Drew Pearson to MLE, December 12, 1934, Ernst Papers.
30 MLE to Ike Lowenburg, April 13, 1935, Ernst Papers.
31 Margaret A. Blanchard, *Revolutionary Sparks: Freedom of Expression in Modern America* (New York: Oxford University Press, 1992), 144.
32 Morris Ernst and Roger Baldwin, radio debate, January 27, 1934, NBC Blue Network, transcript, Ernst Papers.
33 Morris Ernst, *The First Freedom* (New York: Macmillan, 1946), 23.
34 Ernst and Baldwin, radio debate.
35 Ernst, *Best Is Yet*, 78.
36 "Conversation with Morris M. Schnitzer," *Rutgers Law Review* 47 (Summer 1995): 1420.
37 Daniel J. Leab, *A Union of Individuals: The Formation of the American Newspaper Guild* (New York: Columbia University Press, 1970), 33–34.
38 Leab, *Union of Individuals*, 35.
39 Dale Benjamin Scott, "Labor's New Deal for Journalism: The Newspaper Guild in the 1930s" (PhD diss., University of Illinois at Urbana-Champaign, 2009), 124.
40 Heywood Broun, "A Union of Reporters," *World-Telegram* (New York), August 7, 1933.
41 Ernst, "People Important To Me."
42 Leab, *Union of Individuals*, 58–59. See also "ABA Rival," *Time*, January 18, 1937, magazine clipping in Ernst Papers; O'Connor, *Heywood Broun*, 183; Ernst, *Best Is Yet*, 82.
43 Ernst, *Love Affair with the Law*, 148.
44 Scott, "Labor's New Deal for Journalism," 126.
45 "News Writers Form Guild under NRA," *New York Times*, September 18, 1933, 4.
46 O'Connor, *Heywood Broun*, 184; Isabelle Keating Savell, "Reporters Become of Age," *Harpers'*, April 1935; Ernst, *Best Is Yet*, 85.
47 Ernst, *Touch Wood*, 106.
48 "Old Nevius Farm in East Millstone Sold to N.Y. Man," *Central New Jersey Home News*, January 7, 1934, 11.

49 MLE interview with Mary Batten interview.
50 Maxine Emelia Hirsch, "Caroline Pratt and the City and Country School: 1914–1945" (EdD diss., Rutgers University, 1978).
51 "Mrs. Morris Ernst, Author and Teacher," *New York Times*, December 4, 1964, 39.
52 Ernst, *Best Is Yet*, 109–10.
53 MLE to Harriet Montague, The Volta Bureau, October 19, 1938, Ernst Papers.
54 MLE interview with Mary Batten interview.

CHAPTER TWELVE

1 MLE to Ben Huebsch, October 21, 1931, Ernst Papers.
2 Michael Moscato and Leslie LeBlanc, *The United States of America v. One Book Entitled Ulysses by James Joyce: Documents and Commentary; A 50-Year Retrospective* (Frederick, MD: University Publications of America, 1984), xvii.
3 Stephen Gillers, "A Tendency to Deprave and Corrupt: The Transformation of American Obscenity Law from Hicklin to Ulysses II," *Washington University Law Quarterly* 85, no. 2 (2007): 253. See also Margaret C. Anderson, *My Thirty Years' War: An Autobiography* (Westport, CT: Greenwood Press, 1971).
4 Richard Ellmann, *James Joyce* (Oxford: Oxford University Press, 2006), 524.
5 Moscato and LeBlanc, *United States of America v. One Book*, xix.
6 Harry Hansen, "The First Reader," *World-Telegram* (New York), December 7, 1933.
7 See Robert E. Spoo, *Without Copyrights: Piracy, Publishing, and the Public Domain* (New York: Oxford University Press, 2016).
8 Moscato and LeBlanc, *United States of America v. One Book*, xix.
9 A. Heymoolen v. United States, August 1, 1928, Customs Court, 1928, cited in Moscato and LeBlanc, *United States of America v. One Book*, 144. The court said that *Ulysses* was "filled with obscenity of the rottenest and vilest character."
10 Kevin Birmingham, *The Most Dangerous Book: The Battle for James Joyce's "Ulysses"* (New York: Penguin Books, 2015), 300.
11 Moscato and LeBlanc, *United States of America v. One Book*, xx.
12 Morris L. Ernst, "Reflections on the *Ulysses* Trial and Censorship," *James Joyce Quarterly* 3, no. 1 (1965): 6.
13 K. Birmingham, *Most Dangerous Book*, 300.
14 AL to MLE, August 6, 1931, Ernst Papers.
15 MLE handwritten comment on letter AL to MLE, August 6, 1931.
16 MLE to Huebsch, October 21, 1931. State-level criminal prosecutions would be forestalled by including, as a foreword to the American edition of the book, the favorable opinion of the federal court. This would "cause censorship societies to hesitate before commencing proceedings," Ernst explained.
17 MLE to Huebsch, October 21, 1931.
18 K. Birmingham, *Most Dangerous Book*, 300.
19 Gillers, "Tendency to Deprave," 276.
20 Gillers, "Tendency to Deprave," 275.
21 Bennett Cerf, *At Random: The Reminiscences of Bennett Cerf* (New York: Random House Trade Paperbacks, 2002), 90.
22 Bennett Cerf (BC) to MLE, March 23, 1932, Ernst Papers.

23 BC to Robert Kastor, March 22, 1932, Ernst Papers.
24 BC to MLE, March 23, 1932.
25 BC to Paul Leon, April 19, 1932, Ernst Papers.
26 MLE to AL, April 20, 1932, Ernst Papers.
27 Proposed Letter to Authors, Critics, Clergymen, n.d., box 364, Ernst Papers.
28 AL to BC, March 29, 1932, Ernst Papers.
29 AL to BC, May 9, 1932, Ernst Papers.
30 Moscato and LeBlanc, *United States of America v. One Book*, xx.
31 Paul Leon to BC, April 27, 1932, Ernst Papers.
32 AL to Collector of Customs, May 2, 1932, Ernst Papers.
33 Ernst, "Reflections on the *Ulysses* Trial," 6.
34 K. Birmingham, *Most Dangerous Book*, 306.
35 AL to H. C. Stewart, Assistant Collector of Customs, May 17, 1932, Ernst Papers.
36 H. C. Stewart to GWE, May 24, 1932, Ernst Papers.
37 AL to MLE, June 14, 1932, Ernst Papers.
38 AL to MLE, July 30, 1932, Ernst Papers.
39 AL to MLE, July 30, 1932.
40 MLE to AL, September 27, 1932, Ernst Papers.
41 AL to MLE, August 12, 1932, Ernst Papers.
42 MLE to AL, September 27, 1932.
43 MLE to BC, November 11, 1932, Ernst Papers.
44 MLE to BC, November 11, 1932.
45 MLE to AL, November 17, 1932; December 21, 1932; January 4, 1933; all in Ernst Papers.
46 AL to MLE, June 6, 1933, Ernst Papers.
47 AL to H. C. Stewart, May 5, 1933, Ernst Papers.
48 H. C. Stewart to AL, May 10, 1933, Ernst Papers.
49 AL to H. C. Stewart, June 1, 1933, Ernst Papers.
50 Petition for Release and Admission of the Book into the United States on the Ground That It Is a Classic, June 2, 1933, box 365, Ernst Papers.
51 "Ban Upon *Ulysses* to be Fought Again," *New York Times*, June 24, 1933, 14. See also MLE to AL, June 30, 1933, Ernst Papers.
52 MLE to AL, June 30, 1933.
53 MLE to Jonas Shapiro, August 25, 1933, Ernst Papers.
54 MLE to AL, August 30, 1933, Ernst Papers.
55 "To Pass on 'Ulysses,'" *New York Times*, August 30, 1933, 16.
56 "The Press: A Welcome to 'Ulysses,'" *Time*, December 18, 1933, 42.
57 S. J. Woolf, "A Judge Who Scans the Drama of Life," *New York Times*, March 11, 1934, SM7.
58 Woolf, "Judge Who Scans the Drama."
59 "Judge Woolsey, Who Searched Ulysses," *World-Telegram* (New York), December 13, 1933.
60 "*Ulysses* Case Reaches Court after Ten Years," *New York Herald Tribune*, November 26, 1933, 17.
61 AL to MLE, September 6, 1933, Ernst Papers.
62 AL to BC, September 14, 1933, Ernst Papers.
63 AL to John Woolsey, October 1, 1933, Ernst Papers. See also AL to MLE, September 5, 1933, Ernst Papers.

64 Claimant's Memorandum in Support of Motion to Dismiss Libel, October 14, 1933, box 365, Ernst Papers.

65 Claimant's Memorandum in Support of Motion to Dismiss Libel.

66 Claimant's Memorandum in Support of Motion to Dismiss Libel.

67 Claimant's Memorandum in Support of Motion to Dismiss Libel.

68 Paula Gross to MLE, October 6, 1933, Ernst Papers.

69 "*Ulysses* Case Reaches Court after Ten Years."

70 "*Ulysses* Case Reaches Court after Ten Years."

71 Irving Younger, *The Irving Younger Collection: Wit and Wisdom from the Master of Trial Advocacy* (Chicago: American Bar Association, 2011), 501.

72 Ernst, *Best Is Yet*, 116.

73 "*Ulysses* Case Reaches Court after Ten Years."

74 "*Ulysses* Case Reaches Court after Ten Years."

75 "*Ulysses* Case Reaches Court after Ten Years."

76 Exchange between Ernst and Woolsey reported in "Court Undecided on Ulysses Ban," *New York Times*, November 26, 1933.

77 Ernst, "Reflections on the *Ulysses* Trial," 6.

78 "Judge Understood 'Ulysses,'" *World-Telegram* (New York), November 25, 1933.

79 Aitken, "United States of America, Libellant"; Ernst, "Reflections on the *Ulysses* Trial," 7; Ernst, *Best Is Yet*, 116.

80 Aitken, "United States of America, Libellant."

81 "*Ulysses* Case Reaches Court after Ten Years."

82 Ernst, "Reflections on the *Ulysses* Trial," 7–8.

83 "Recent Cases: Constitutional Law—Tariff Act—Ban Against Importation of Obscene Books—Standard for Test of Obscenity," *George Washington Law Review* 2, no. 4 (1933): 517.

84 "Recent Cases: Standard for Test of Obscenity."

85 United States v. One Book Called "Ulysses," 5 F. Supp. 182 (S.D.N.Y. 1933) at 184.

86 BC to AL, December 15, 1933, Ernst Papers.

87 *One Book Called "Ulysses,"* 5 F. Supp. 182 at 184–85.

88 *One Book Called "Ulysses,"* 5 F. Supp. 182 at 184–85.

89 Gerald Gunther, *Learned Hand: The Man and the Judge* (New York: Knopf, 1994), 186.

90 Lewis Gannett, "Books and Things," *New York Herald Tribune*, December 9, 1933.

91 AL to John Woolsey, December 16, 1933, Ernst Papers.

92 AL to MLE, December 7, 1933, Ernst Papers.

93 "Statement of Morris L. Ernst Upon the Handing Down of Judge Woolsey's Opinion in Ulysses Case," December 1933, typewritten transcript, Ernst Papers.

94 AL to MLE, December 7, 1933.

95 According to his *New York Times* obituary, Ernst received several hundred thousand dollars from the publication of *Ulysses*. Whitman, "Morris Ernst, 'Ulysses' Case Lawyer Dies," 40.

96 Coleman quoted in "Court Lifts Ban on *Ulysses* Here," *New York Times*, December 7, 1933, 21.

97 "*Ulysses* Ban is Removed by Federal Court," *New York Herald Tribune*, December 7, 1933, 23.

98 "U.S. Will Carry Ulysses Ruling to High Court," *New York Herald Tribune*, March 13, 1934.

99 "Conboy Opens U.S. Appeal to Bar *Ulysses*," *New York Herald Tribune*, May 17, 1934.

100 "*Ulysses*, 'Unchaste and Lustful,' No Lunchtime Story for 3 Judges," *World-Telegram* (New York), May 16, 1934.

101 "Is Conboy's Face Red as He Reads 'Ulysses' in Court," *Daily News* (New York), May 17, 1934.

102 "Conboy Opens U.S. Appeal to Bar *Ulysses*."

103 "*Ulysses*, 'Unchaste and Lustful.'"

104 Paul Vanderham, *James Joyce and Censorship: The Trials of Ulysses* (New York: New York University Press, 1998), 140.

105 "Conboy Recites from 'Ulysses' and Girl Flees," *Daily News* (New York), May 18, 1934.

106 "Ulysses Fate Up to Court as Arguments End," *New York Herald Tribune*, May 18, 1934, 19.

107 United States v. One Book Entitled *Ulysses*, 72 F.2d. 705 (2d Cir. 1934) at 709–11.

108 Gunther, *Learned Hand*, 289.

109 *One Book Entitled "Ulysses,"* 72 F.2d. at 707–9.

110 See Marc Randazza, "Ulysses: A Mighty Hero in the Fight for Freedom of Expression," *University of Massachusetts Law Review* 11, no. 2 (2016): 268.

111 Leo M. Alpert, "Judicial Censorship of Obscene Literature," *Harvard Law Review* 52, no. 1 (1938): 40–76.

112 Conboy to Homer Cummings, August 31, 1934, quoted in Gillers, "Tendency to Deprave."

113 Vanderham, *James Joyce and Censorship*, 148.

114 AL to BC, November 2, 1934, Ernst Papers.

115 BC to Dr. Hellmut Lehmann-Haupt, May 21, 1935, Ernst Papers.

116 *Bevue* means "careless error." James Joyce to MLE, October 1937, Ernst Papers.

CHAPTER THIRTEEN

1 "Books to Be Read or Read About," *Evening Sun* (Baltimore), January 30, 1937.

2 Philip Wylie and Bernard Bergman, *The Smiling Corpse* (New York: Farrar and Rinehart, 1935), 151.

3 Peggy Bacon, *Off With Their Heads!* (New York: R.M. McBride), 1934.

4 Rodell, "Morris Ernst," 107.

5 William Bohn, "Morris Ernst, A Man Misplaced," *New Leader*, December 19, 1960, 5.

6 Description of Ernst's calendar and office from Rodell, "Morris Ernst."

7 Ernest Cuneo, "Heaven on Earth," n.d., clipping, Ernst Papers.

8 "Biography: Morris L. Ernst."

9 DeWitt Stetten, *How My Light Is Spent: The Memoirs of DeWitt Stetten, Jr.* (self-pub., 1983), X2.

10 Peter H. Irons, *The New Deal Lawyers* (Princeton, NJ: Princeton University Press, 1982), 300.

11 In Robert M. Mennel and Christine L. Compston, eds., *Holmes and Frankfurter: Their Correspondence* (Hanover, NH: University Press of New England, 1996), xiv.

12 MLE to Felix Frankfurter (FF), March 5, 1934, Ernst Papers.

13 MLE to FF, March 5, 1934.
14 Ernst, *Best Is Yet*, 224.
15 MLE to FF, March 30, 1934, Ernst Papers.
16 Gardner Jackson to Alexander Sachs, July 24, 1933, Sachs Papers, Franklin D. Roosevelt Presidential Library and Museum, Hyde Park, New York (hereafter cited as FDR Library).
17 MLE to Langdon Post, June 16, 1934, Ernst Papers.
18 MLE to Drew Pearson, September 26, 1933, Ernst Papers.
19 Unknown author to Ernst, October 1933, Ernst Papers. (Isadore Hirschmann, Ernst's friend and a publicist for Lord and Taylor, seems to have been behind this endeavor.)
20 "Roosevelt Ready to Let Conboy Quit," *Daily News* (New York), March 14, 1935.
21 Memorandum, February 4, 1935, Ernst FBI file, as provided in digital form by the FBI in response to author's Freedom of Information Act request.
22 "Call Democrats to a Fusion Fight," *New York Times*, October 20, 1935, 3.
23 Ernst, *Love Affair with the Law*, 158.
24 Ernst, *Love Affair with the Law*, 157.
25 Graham Russell Gao Hodges, *Taxi! A Social History of the New York City Cabdriver* (Baltimore: Johns Hopkins University Press, 2007), 52–55.
26 Ernst, *Best Is Yet*, 178.
27 "Taxi Strike Nears End," *New York Herald Tribune*, February 5, 1934.
28 MLE to Charles Barnes, February 9, 1934, Ernst Papers.
29 Hodges, *Taxi!* 56.
30 See August Hecksher, *When LaGuardia Was Mayor: New York's Legendary Years* (New York: W. W. Norton, 1978), 94.
31 Mark Naison, *Communists in Harlem during the Depression* (Urbana: University of Illinois Press, 1983),140–41.
32 "Housing in Harlem Sharply Debated," *New York Times*, May 23, 1935, 27.
33 Naison, *Communists in Harlem*, 145; "Crowd Turbulent at Harlem Inquiry," *New York Times*, April 7, 1935, 6.
34 Ernst, *Best Is Yet*, 49.
35 MLE to Dorothy Nathan, April 29, 1935, Ernst Papers.
36 Report of Housing Committee, April 1, 1935, box 316, Ernst Papers.
37 See Robert M. Fogelson and Richard E. Rubenstein, eds., *The Complete Report of Mayor LaGuardia's Commission on the Harlem Riot* (repr., New York: Arno Press, 1969).
38 MLE to Langdon Post, March 27, 1935, Ernst Papers.
39 MLE to Herbert Lehman, April 9, 1935, Ernst Papers.
40 Ernst, *Best Is Yet*, 49–50.
41 Harold Lord Varney, "The Civil Liberties Union: Liberalism à La Moscow," *American Mercury*, December 1936, 385.
42 Ellen Schrecker, *Many Are the Crimes: McCarthyism in America* (New York: Little, Brown, 1998), 64.
43 American Civil Liberties Union (ACLU), *Who's Un-American? An Answer to the Patriots* (New York: ACLU, 1935).
44 Milner, *Education of an American Liberal*, 229.
45 Elizabeth Dilling, *The Red Network: A "Who's Who" and Handbook of Radicalism for Patriots* (Chicago: Kenilworth, 1934), 111; ACLU, *Who's Un-American?*

46 Dilling, *Red Network*, 278.
47 MLE to RB, February 3, 1936, Ernst Papers; "Libel Suit Started by Liberties Union," *New York Times*, March 16, 1937.
48 Gunter Lewy, *The Cause That Failed: Communism in American Political Life* (New York: Oxford University Press, 1990), 25–26; Schrecker, *Many Are the Crimes*, 13.
49 Lewy, *Cause That Failed*, 25.
50 Walker, *In Defense of American Liberties*, 119.
51 Kutulas, *American Civil Liberties Union and Liberalism*, 33.
52 American Civil Liberties Union (ACLU), *Report on Interference with Madison Square Garden Meeting Against Austrian Fascism* (New York: ACLU, 1934).
53 Kutulas, *American Civil Liberties Union and Liberalism*, 34.
54 Scottsboro Case Correspondence, September–November 1935, database of NAACP archives, accessed through New York Public Library.
55 Ernst, *Best Is Yet*, 58; see also "Scottsboro Cases," Memorandum, October 14, 1935, database of NAACP archives, accessed through New York Public Library.
56 Percival Roberts Bailey, "Progressive Lawyers: A History of the National Lawyers Guild, 1936–1958" (PhD diss., Rutgers University, 1979), 217.
57 On liberal anticommunism in the 1930s, see Lewy, *Cause that Failed*, 48–49; Judy Kutulas, *The Long War: The Intellectual People's Front and Anti-Stalinism, 1930–1940* (Durham, NC: Duke University Press, 1995).
58 Schrecker, *Many Are the Crimes*, 82.

CHAPTER FOURTEEN

1 MLE to Kenneth McKellar, April 16, 1940, Ernst Papers.
2 Leuchtenburg, *Franklin D. Roosevelt and the New Deal*, 143.
3 William E. Leuchtenburg, "When Franklin Roosevelt Clashed with the Supreme Court—and Lost," *Smithsonian Magazine*, May 2005, https://www.smithsonianmag.com/history/when-franklin-roosevelt-clashed-with-the-supreme-court-and-lost-78497994/.
4 Leuchtenburg, *Franklin D. Roosevelt and the New Deal*, 143.
5 Barry Friedman, "The History of the Countermajoritarian Difficulty: Law's Politics," *University of Pennsylvania Law Review* 148, no. 4 (April 2000): 995.
6 Radio address, Station WOR, April 1935, untitled transcript, Ernst Papers.
7 MLE to FF, September 26, 1935, Ernst Papers.
8 "Heywood Broun," *Courier-Post* (Camden, NJ), May 24, 1935, 5.
9 MLE to Franklin D. Roosevelt (FDR), September 3, 1935, Ernst Papers.
10 FDR to MLE, September 9, 1935, Ernst Papers.
11 MLE to FF, June 8, 1936, Ernst Papers.
12 Leab, *Union of Individuals*, 132–33.
13 Scott, "Labor's New Deal for Journalism," 151.
14 Richard Gid Powers, *Not without Honor: The History of American Anticommunism* (New Haven, CT: Yale University Press, 1995), 121.
15 Robert H. Zieger, *The CIO, 1935–1955* (Chapel Hill: University of North Carolina Press, 1995), 395.
16 Scott, "Labor's New Deal for Journalism," 153.

17 Scott, "Labor's New Deal for Journalism," 159.
18 Irons, *New Deal Lawyers*, 265.
19 Jeff Shesol, *Supreme Power: Franklin Roosevelt v. The Supreme Court* (New York: W. W. Norton, 2010), 423; Irons, *New Deal Lawyers*, 254.
20 Scott, "Labor's New Deal for Journalism," 160.
21 Scott, "Labor's New Deal for Journalism," 161.
22 Scott, "Labor's New Deal for Journalism," 162.
23 Memorandum, April 2, 1936, Ernst Papers.
24 MLE to Bob Buck, October 8, 1935, Ernst Papers.
25 Irons, *New Deal Lawyers*, 265.
26 Richard Cortner, *The Wagner Act Cases* (Knoxville: University of Tennessee Press, 1964), 128.
27 William Henry Harbaugh, *Lawyer's Lawyer: The Life of John W. Davis* (New York: Oxford University Press: 1973), 374.
28 Scott, "Labor's New Deal for Journalism," 166.
29 Cortner, *Wagner Act Cases*, 129.
30 Cortner, *Wagner Act Cases*, 129.
31 Scott, "Labor's New Deal for Journalism," 169.
32 Cortner, *Wagner Act Cases*, 130.
33 Scott, "Labor's New Deal for Journalism," 173.
34 Cortner, *Wagner Act Cases*, 131; Scott, "Labor's New Deal," 179.
35 "AP v. Guild," *Time*, June 29, 1936, 34.
36 Brief for Petitioner, *Associated Press v. National Labor Relations Board*, 99. For the main text of the decision, see Associated Press v. National Labor Relations Board, 301 U.S. 103 (1937).
37 Heywood Broun, "Mr. Davis Comes in Second," *Nation*, February 27, 1937, 241. The dig at Hitler was apparently a reference to the führer's unsuccessful early career as a house painter before turning to politics.
38 Brief on behalf of American Newspaper Guild as Amicus Curiae, *Associated Press v. National Labor Relations Board*, 4–5.
39 Newspaper Guild amicus curiae brief, 26–27.
40 Newspaper Guild amicus curiae brief, 25.
41 MLE to FF, February 3, 1937, Ernst Papers. Ernst is referring to Muller v. Oregon, 208 U.S. 412 (1908).
42 MLE to George Bye, August 28, 1936, Ernst Papers.
43 Schrecker, *Many Are the Crimes*, 35; Sheila Irene Stein, "The American Labor Party: 1936–1944" (PhD diss., University of Chicago, 1964).
44 MLE to John Brachett, October 9, 1937, Ernst Papers.
45 MLE to FF, January 7, 1937, Ernst Papers.
46 Morris Leopold Ernst, *The Ultimate Power* (Garden City, NY: Doubleday, 1937), 262.
47 Ernst, *Ultimate Power*, 326.
48 "Book Notes," review of *The Ultimate Power*, by Morris Ernst, *University of Chicago Law Review*, April 1937, 523.
49 Review of *The Ultimate Power*, by Morris Ernst, *Harvard Law Review*, April 1937, 998.
50 John Chamberlain, "Socrates, Morris Ernst, and the Supreme Court," review of *The Ultimate Power*, by Morris Ernst, *Scribner's Magazine*, February 1937, 78.

51 John Corbin, "The Supreme Court and Popular Will," review of *The Ultimate Power*, by Morris Ernst, *New York Times*, January 24, 1937, 92.
52 "Mr. Ernst's Ultimate Power," *New York Times*, January 27, 1937, 20.
53 MLE to *New York Times*, January 23, 1937, Ernst Papers.
54 Art Sulzberger to MLE, January 25, 1937, Ernst Papers.
55 "Ernst Not Counsel in Wagner Act Case: Misstatement in Review of His Book Described Him as an Administrative Advocate," *New York Times*, January 25, 1937, 57.
56 MLE to Doubleday, January 26, 1937, Ernst Papers.
57 MLE to G. Ernst, December 1, 1936, Ernst Papers.
58 MLE to FDR, January 12, 1937, Ernst Papers.
59 Leuchtenburg, "When Roosevelt Clashed with Supreme Court."
60 Joseph Alsop and Turner Catledge, *The 168 Days* (Garden City: Doubleday Doran, 1938), 73.
61 "Hoover Scores Plan to Alter Supreme Court," *Tampa Bay Times*, February 6, 1937.
62 Alsop and Catledge, *168 Days*, 73.
63 "Forum Speaker Is for Court Change," n.d., clipping, Ernst Papers.
64 "Court Plan Booed by Audience Here," *New York Times*, March 12, 1937, 9.
65 The other cases involved the Fruehauf Trailer Company of Detroit (for discharge of employees for belonging to the American Federation of Labor); the Friedman-Harry Marks Clothing Company in Richmond (for discharge of employees for attending an organizational meeting of the Amalgamated Clothing Workers); the Washington, Virginia, and Maryland Coach Company (for discharge of employees who had requested union recognition), and the Jones and Laughlin Steel Company (discharge of workers belonging to the Steel Workers Organizing Committee).
66 Irons, *New Deal Lawyers*, 283.
67 "Labor Act Scored Before High Court," *New York Times*, February 10, 1937, 1.
68 James McMullin, "New York," *News-Press* (Fort Myers, FL), February 19, 1937.
69 *Associated Press v. NLRB*, 301 U.S. at 132–33.
70 Leuchtenburg, "When Roosevelt Clashed with Supreme Court"; Barry Friedman, *The Will of the People: How Public Opinion Has Influenced the Supreme Court and Shaped the Meaning of the Constitution* (New York: Farrar, Straus, and Giroux, 2009), 232.
71 Ernst, *Love Affair with the Law*, 149.
72 On Communists in the Newspaper Guild, see Leab, *Union of Individuals*, 267. By 1937, Communists had made their way into the hierarchy of the guild on both the national and local levels.
73 Ernst, *Best Is Yet*, 86.
74 Auerbach, "Depression Decade," 77.
75 Jerold S. Auerbach, *Labor and Liberty: The La Follette Committee and the New Deal* (Indianapolis, IN: Bobbs-Merrill, 1966), 28.
76 Kutulas, *American Civil Liberties Union and Liberalism*, 26.
77 Cottrell, *Roger Nash Baldwin*, 229; Cletus E. Daniel, *The ACLU and the Wagner Act: An Inquiry into the Depression-Era Crisis of American Liberalism* (Ithaca, NY: ILR Press, 1981).
78 *Reminiscences of Baldwin*, 176.

79 Walker, *In Defense of American Liberties*, 96. In its first annual report under the New Deal, the ACLU had noted that "alarms are widely expressed over alleged dictatorship by the President." Murphy, *Meaning of Freedom of Speech*, 274.
80 *Reminiscences of Baldwin*, 182.
81 Milner, *Education of an American Liberal*, 242.
82 American Civil Liberties Union (ACLU), *How Goes the Bill of Rights?* (New York: ACLU, 1936).
83 *Reminiscences of Baldwin*, 201.
84 Palko v. Connecticut, 302 U.S. 319 (1937) at 325.
85 Walker, *In Defense of American Liberties*, 134.
86 Murphy, *Meaning of Freedom of Speech*, 276.
87 Milner, *Education of an American Liberal*, 243.
88 Judy Kutulas, "Pretty Darn Chic: The American Civil Liberties Union in the 1930s," *Mid-America* 83, no. 3 (September 2001): 195.

CHAPTER FIFTEEN

1 MLE to [unknown], 1942, Ernst Papers.
2 Morris Ernst, "How We Nullify," *Nation*, January 27, 1932, 113–14.
3 Morris Ernst memorial tribute, 1976, box 548, Ernst Papers.
4 Youngs Rubber Corporation v. C. I. Lee, Inc., 45 F.2d 103 (2d Cir. 1930).
5 Sakae Koyama to Margaret Sanger (MS), October 17, 1931, and March 26, 1932; MS to Sakae Koyama, February 20, 1932, Papers of Morris Leopold Ernst, 1933–1937, MC208, Schlesinger Library, Radcliffe Institute for Advanced Study, Harvard University, Cambridge, MA.
6 H. C. Stewart to MS, June 14, 1932; AL to H. C. Stewart, July 8, 1932; H. C. Stewart to Hannah Stone, January 9, 1933; Papers of Morris Leopold Ernst, Schlesinger Library.
7 AL to Florence Rose, January 25, 1933, Ernst Papers.
8 Florence Rose to AL, January 31, 1933; Florence Rose to MLE, February 8, 1933; MS to MLE, February 16, 1934; AL to Florence Rose, February 10, 1933; all in Ernst Papers.
9 Collector of Customs to GWE, February 8, 1933, Ernst Papers.
10 Trial Memorandum for Claimant, *One Package*. For the text of the district court case, see United States v. One Package, 86 F.2d 737 (1936).
11 Transcript of Record, *One Package*, 86 F.2d .
12 Florence Rose to MS, December 10, 1935, Papers of Morris Leopold Ernst, Schlesinger Library.
13 Transcript of Record, *One Package*, 86 F.2d.
14 United States v. One Package, 23 F. Supp. 334 (E.D.N.Y. 1936) at 336.
15 "'New York Closeup' Featured Morris L. Ernst," *Nantucket Inquirer and Mirror*, December 30, 1950.
16 *One Package*, 86 F.2d at 739; "Physician Upheld on Birth Control," *New York Times*, December 8, 1936, 9.
17 Morris Ernst and Harriet Pilpel, "A Medical Bill of Rights," *Journal of Contraception*, February 1937, 35–37.
18 Ernst and Lindey, *Censor Marches On*, 165.

19 James Boyle, Office of the Commissioner, Bureau of Customs, Circular Letter, February 10, 1937, Ernst Papers.

20 Charles Scribner and Morris Ernst, "Interpretation of the Federal Statutes Relating to Contraceptives," memo, April 30, 1937, Ernst Papers.

21 David J. Garrow, *Liberty and Sexuality: The Right to Privacy and the Making of "Roe v. Wade"* (New York: Macmillan, 1994), 42.

22 MS to MLE, January 9, 1937, Ernst Papers.

23 Margaret Sanger, editorial *National Birth Control News*, February 1937, 3–4.

24 Ernst and Lindey, *Censor Marches On*, viii, ix.

25 "Boys in Court Hear 'Bad Book' Debate," *New York Times*, April 27, 1935; Nicholas J. Karolides, Margaret Bald, and Dawn B. Sova, *One Hundred Banned Books: Censorship Histories of World Literature* (New York: Checkmark Books, 1999), 175.

26 Ernst assisted in appealing the case of Maurice Parmelee, author of *Nudism in Modern Life*, to the U.S. Court of Appeals for the District of Columbia. The court agreed with Ernst's argument that nudism was a valid social movement and that nudist treatises were scientific and "so little erotic in [their] result" that they could not be condemned as obscene. The justices used community standards, rather than the *Hicklin* test, to resolve the case. Brian Hoffman, *Naked: A Cultural History of American Nudism* (New York: New York University Press, 2015), 95.

27 See materials on Dobbins Bill, box 148, Ernst Papers.

28 "Wide Ban on 'Life' for Birth Pictures," *New York Times*, April 9, 1938, 15.

29 Morris Ernst, drafts of *Best Is Yet*, n.d., box 415, Ernst Papers.

30 Ernst, *Best Is Yet*, 139.

31 "Larsen Wins Point in Indecency Trial," *New York Times*, April 20, 1938, 46.

32 "Earle Stands Firm in Ban on Life Magazine," *Shamokin (PA) News-Dispatch*, April 11, 1938.

33 People v. Larsen, 5 N.Y. Supp. 2d 55 (Ct. Spec. Sess., 1938) at 56–57.

34 "Court Clears Life on Baby Pictures," *New York Times*, April 27, 1938.

35 "Doubleday v. Macy," *Time*, November 18, 1935, 62.

36 Brief for Doubleday Doran & Co., Inc. v. R.H. Macy & Co., 269 N.Y. 272 (1936).

37 *Doubleday Doran v. Macy* 269 N.Y. at 282.

38 "Book Men Warned on Fair Trade Acts," *New York Times*, May 17, 1938, 40.

39 Ernst, *Best Is Yet*, 124.

40 MLE to FDR, October 14, 1938, Ernst Papers.

41 "Hails Book Postage Cut," *New York Times*, November 2, 1938, 41.

42 Marvin McIntyre to MLE, October 28, 1939, Ernst Papers.

43 Ernst, *So Far So Good*, 239.

44 MLE to FDR, March 11, 1939, Ernst Papers.

45 "Postal Rates Extended," *Publishers Weekly*, July 8, 1939.

46 An Act to Provide for a Permanent Postage Rate of 3 Cents per Pound on Books, June 30, 1942, Pub. L. No. 636, 56 Stat. 462 (1942).

CHAPTER SIXTEEN

1 "Ten Commandments for Lawyers."

2 Radio address, April 1935.

3 “The Law Lags Behind,” n.d., Ernst Papers.
4 Auerbach, *Unequal Justice*, 199.
5 Drew Pearson and Robert Allen, “Washington Merry Go Round,” *San Bernardino (CA) County Sun*, July 19, 1936.
6 National Lawyers Guild, *A History of the National Lawyers Guild, 1937–1987* (New York: National Lawyers Guild Foundation, 1987), 8, https://www.nlg.org/a-history-of-the-nlg-1937-1987/; Bailey, “Progressive Lawyers,” 1; Christopher Johnson, *Maurice Sugar, Law, Labor and the Left in Detroit, 1912–1950* (Detroit: Wayne State University Press, 1988).
7 Bailey, “Progressive Lawyers,” 20–21.
8 MLE to Jerome Court, October 6, 1931, Ernst Papers.
9 Bailey, “Progressive Lawyers,” 21.
10 Morris Ernst, “A Call to American Lawyers,” n.d., Ernst Papers.
11 Bailey, “Progressive Lawyers,” 22; “History of National Lawyers Guild, 1937–1987.”
12 “Liberal Lawyers Form a New Guild,” *New York Times*, December 16, 1936, 29.
13 “The Bar Association Held Reactionary,” *New York Times*, December 23, 1936, 13.
14 Bailey, “Progressive Lawyers,” 26.
15 MLE to FDR, January 18, 1937, Ernst Papers.
16 MLE to Herbert Ehrman, February 2, 1937, Ernst Papers.
17 Stephen Early to MLE, February 17, 1937, Ernst Papers.
18 “ABA Rival.”
19 “Bar Association Held Reactionary.”
20 Jordan Schwarz, *Liberal: Adolf A. Berle and the Vision of American Era* (New York: Free Press, 1987), 159; Auerbach, *Unequal Justice*, 200.
21 “Uproar at Session of New Law Guild,” *New York Times*, January 8, 1937, 3.
22 Bailey, “Progressive Lawyers,” 106–9.
23 Auerbach, *Unequal Justice*, 201.
24 MLE to Mortimer Riemer, December 3, 1937, Ernst Papers.
25 Schrecker, *Many Are the Crimes*, 83; Bailey, “Progressive Lawyers,” 212.
26 MLE to Mortimer Riemer, December 3, 1937, Ernst Papers.
27 MLE to Thurman Arnold, February 17, 1938, Ernst Papers.
28 Ann Fagan Ginger, *Carol Weiss King: Human Rights Lawyer, 1895–1952* (Niwot: University Press of Colorado, 1993), 220.
29 Ernst, *Best Is Yet*, 51.
30 Walker, *In Defense of American Liberties*, 101; Bean, “Pressure for Freedom,” 278.
31 Post, “Partisanship within the American Civil Liberties Union,” 51.
32 Post, “Partisanship within the American Civil Liberties Union,” 51–52.
33 “Would Defend Employers,” *New York Times*, June 5, 1938, 14.
34 ACLU Board Minutes, March 2, 1938, Ernst Papers.
35 MLE to RB, February 3, June 22, 1938, Ernst Papers.
36 *Reminiscences of Baldwin*, 250.
37 Hays, *City Lawyer*, 230.
38 John Haynes Holmes to Harry Ward, February 8, 1938, Ernst Papers.
39 Jerold Lee Simmons, “The American Civil Liberties Union and the Dies Committee, 1938–1940,” *Harvard Civil Rights-Liberties Law Review* 17 (Spring 1982): 194.
40 MLE to Walter Fisher, October 7, 1938, Ernst Papers.
41 Walker, *In Defense of American Liberties*, 128.

42 Richard Polenberg, "Franklin Roosevelt and Civil Liberties: The Case of the Dies Committee," *Historian* 30, no. 2 (1968): 167.
43 Simmons, "American Civil Liberties Union and the Dies Committee," 184.
44 Leuchtenburg, *Franklin D. Roosevelt and the New Deal*, 278.
45 Simmons, "American Civil Liberties Union and the Dies Committee," 184–85.
46 Post, "Partisanship within the American Civil Liberties Union," 31.
47 Simmons, "American Civil Liberties Union and the Dies Committee," 185.
48 Post, "Partisanship within the American Civil Liberties Union," 31.
49 Cottrell, *Roger Nash Baldwin*, 258–59.
50 Simmons, "American Civil Liberties Union and the Dies Committee," 189.
51 ACLU press release, December 12, 1938, Ernst Papers.
52 Jerold Lee Simmons, "Operation Abolition: The Campaign to Abolish the House Un-American Activities Committee, 1938–1964" (PhD diss., University of Minnesota, 1971), 9–10.
53 "Red Link is Denied by Liberties Union," *New York Times*, January 5, 1939, 9.
54 Post, "Partisanship within the American Civil Liberties Union," 38.
55 "Liberties Union Retorts: Demands Dies Retract Charge Linking It to Communists," *New York Times*, August 22, 1939, 5.
56 ACLU press release, December 12, 1938.
57 "Is America Menaced by Foreign Propaganda?" *Town Meeting of the Air* 20–21 (January 1939).
58 Post, "Partisanship within the American Civil Liberties Union," 39.
59 See Ron Chernow, *The House of Morgan: An American Banking Dynasty and the Rise of Modern Finance* (New York: Grove Press, 1990). Biographical sketches of Leffingwell appear in the *New York Times*, July 8, 1923, and October 3, 1960 (obituary).
60 Ernst, *Best Is Yet*, 238.
61 MLE to Lucy Pulling, December 7, 1960, Ernst Papers.
62 Ernst, *Love Affair with the Law*, 147.
63 MLE to FDR, March 31, 1939, Ernst Papers.
64 MLE to FDR, April 7, 1939, Ernst Papers.
65 FDR to MLE, April 10, 1939, Ernst Papers.
66 MLE memorial transcript.
67 "Washington Merry-Go-Round," *Reading (PA) Times*, December 27, 1937.

CHAPTER SEVENTEEN

1 MLE memorial transcript.
2 James, "Morris L. Ernst," 7–11, 57–58.
3 "Walter Winchell on Broadway," *Tampa Bay (FL) Times*, June 23, 1938.
4 "Washington Merry-Go-Round," *El Paso (TX) Times*, June 25, 1938.
5 John J. Gibbons, "Hague v. CIO: A Retrospective," *New York University Law Review* 52, no. 4 (October 1977): 732.
6 J. Christopher Schnell, "Hague, Frank," in *Encyclopedia of the Great Depression*, vol. 1, ed. Robert S. McElvaine (New York: Macmillan Reference USA, 2004), 419–20; Jack Alexander, "King Hanky-Panky of Jersey," *Saturday Evening Post*, October 26, 1940, 9–11, 122–24.

7 Abraham Isserman, "CIO v. Hague: The Battle of Jersey City," *Guild Practitioner* 36, no. 2 (Spring 1979): 14.
8 Gibbons, "Hague v. CIO," 732.
9 Gibbons, "Hague v. CIO," 733.
10 Gibbons, "Hague v. CIO," 733.
11 Benjamin Kaplan, "The Great Civil Rights Case of Hague v. CIO: Notes of a Survivor," *Suffolk University Law Review* 26 (Winter 1991): 918.
12 Gibbons, "Hague v. CIO," 733.
13 Transcript of Record, *Hague v. CIO*, 1227.
14 Alexander, "King Hanky-Panky," 9; Russell B. Porter, "Portrait of a Dictator, Jersey City Style," *New York Times*, February 13, 1938.
15 "Hague Allied with Brandle When Latter Bossed Labor," *Morning Post* (Camden, NJ), February 7, 1938.
16 Gibbons, "Hague v. CIO," 735.
17 Gibbons, "Hague v. CIO," 735; Russell B. Porter, "Hague at Hearing on His C. I. O. Ban," *New York Times*, June 2, 1938, 1; McAlister Coleman, "New Jersey, the Tory Test-Tube," *New Republic*, February 9, 1938.
18 MLE to John L. Lewis, December 9, 1937, Ernst Papers.
19 Gilbert J. Gall, *Pursuing Justice: Lee Pressman, the New Deal, and the CIO* (Albany: State University of New York Press, 1999), 114–15.
20 Powers, *Not without Honor*, 122; Zieger, *CIO, 1935–1955*, 243.
21 Schrecker, *Many Are the Crimes*, 27–28.
22 "C. I. O. Maps Battle on Jersey City Ban," *New York Times*, December 3, 1937, 5; "Hague Inquiry Weighed," *New York Times*, December 5, 1937, 58; "La Follette Gets Data on Hague Ban," *New York Times*, December 7, 1937, 22.
23 "Tells of Police Terrorism," *Baltimore Sun*, December 10, 1937.
24 "Congressmen and C.I.O in Hague Fight," *New York Times*, December 10, 1937, 1.
25 MLE to Charles Owen Rice, December 15, 1937, Ernst Papers.
26 MLE to Gardner Jackson, December 8, 1937, Ernst Papers.
27 MLE to Hugh Johnson, January 3, 1938, Ernst Papers.
28 "Hague Is Defied by Meeting Call," *New York Times*, December 20, 1937, 8.
29 "Civil Liberties Group to Challenge Hague," *Philadelphia Inquirer*, December 20, 1937.
30 "Mayor Hague Cries Communists in New Attack on CIO Chiefs," *St. Louis Star*, December 13, 1937.
31 "CIO Will Test for Free Press," *American Guardian* (Oklahoma City), December 24, 1937.
32 "Major C.I.O Aim is to 'Lick' Hague, Ernst Tells Law Guild Conference," *New York Times*, December 18, 1937, 5.
33 "Who's News Today," *Dayton (OH) Daily News*, December 31, 1937.
34 Kaplan, "Great Civil Rights Case of Hague v. CIO," 918–19.
35 Text of Hague speech, n.d., typescript, Ernst Papers.
36 Heywood Broun, "Shoot the Works," *New Republic*, February 15, 1939, 44.
37 "Reply to Mayor Hague," Station WOR, January 6, 1938, transcript, Ernst Papers.
38 Neil Brant to MLE, January 7, 1938.
39 Lee Pressman to MLE, December 28, 1937; MLE to Walter Fisher, October 7, 1938; both in Ernst Papers.
40 Lee Pressman to MLE, April 15, 1939, Ernst Papers.

41 MLE to editor of New York *Herald Tribune*, July 13, 1943, Ernst Papers.
42 "C. I. O. Starts Suit to Test Hague Ban," *New York Times*, January 8, 1938, 1.
43 Russell B. Porter, "Hague Issue Slated for the Supreme Court," *New York Times*, July 1, 1938, 1.
44 Kaplan, "Great Civil Rights Case of Hague v. CIO," 915.
45 Kaplan, "Great Civil Rights Case of Hague v. CIO," 924.
46 Gibbons, "Hague v. CIO," 737.
47 "Hague Subpoenas All C.I.O. Records," *New York Times*, June 10, 1938, 2; "C. I. O. Fights Move by Hague to Get All Its Records," *New York Times*, June 12, 1938, 1; "Congressmen Defy Hague's Subpoenas for C.I.O. Inquiry," *New York Times*, June 14, 1938, 1; Kaplan, "Great Civil Rights Case of Hague v. CIO," 916.
48 Kaplan, "Great Civil Rights Case of Hague v. CIO," 918.
49 "Hague Subpoenas All C.I.O. Records."
50 "Excerpts from Cross-Examination of Hague in Injunction Hearing," *New York Times*, June 18, 1938.
51 Russell B. Porter, "Hague Urges Exile of 'Reds' to Alaska to Bar Revolution," *New York Times*, June 15, 1938.
52 "Highlights of Hague's Testimony," *New York Times*, June 17, 1938, 12.
53 "Hague Repudiates Red Aid in Party, Jousts With Ernst," *New York Times*, June 16, 1938, 1.
54 "Hague Accused of Contempt of U.S. Court," *Baltimore Sun*, June 17, 1938.
55 Transcript of Record, *Hague v. CIO*, 1334.
56 Transcript of Record, *Hague v. CIO*, 1051.
57 Transcript of Record, *Hague v. CIO*, 1262–63.
58 "The Nation: Hague Philosophy Defense or Offense?" *New York Times*, June 19, 1938, 2.
59 "A Loyal Patriotic American" to MLE, June 21, 1938, Ernst Papers.
60 "Loyal Patriotic American" to MLE.
61 "Anti-Semitism Is Here," *Nation*, August 20, 1938, 167.
62 Maurice Tishman to MLE, June 23, 1938, Ernst Papers.
63 MLE to Louis Brandeis, June 22, 1938, Ernst Papers.
64 Ernst, *Love Affair with the Law*, 41.
65 Hague v. Committee for Industrial Organization, 25 F. Supp. 127 (D.N.J. 1938).
66 Hague v. Committee for Industrial Organization, 101 F.2d 774 (3d Cir. 1939).
67 "Hague Ban on C.I.O. Barred on Appeal; Court Split, 2 to 1," *New York Times*, January 27, 1939, 1; MLE to John L. Lewis, January 20, 1939, Ernst Papers.
68 Kaplan, "Great Civil Rights Case of Hague v. CIO," 923; MLE to William Clark, December 3, 1940, Ernst Papers.
69 Hague v. Committee for Industrial Organization, 307 U.S. 496 (1939) at 515–16.
70 "Rally Planned in Jersey City," *Asbury Park (NJ) Press*, June 6, 1939.
71 Norman Thomas to MLE, June 16, 1939, Ernst Papers.
72 "Washington Merry Go Round," *Tampa (FL) Tribune*, February 15, 1940.
73 "Walter Winchell on Broadway," *South Bend (IN) Tribune*, April 20, 1940.
74 MLE to Walter Winchell, April 16, 1940, Ernst Papers.
75 MLE to FDR, May 3, 1940, Ernst Papers.
76 FDR to MLE, May 7, 1940, Ernst Papers.

CHAPTER EIGHTEEN

1 Ernst, untitled document (apparently an article draft), April 16, 1940, Ernst Papers.
2 Schrecker, *Many Are the Crimes*, 82.
3 MLE to John Gutknecht, February 25, 1939, Ernst Papers.
4 Ann Fagan Ginger and Eugene M. Tobin, *The National Lawyers Guild: From Roosevelt through Reagan* (Philadelphia: Temple University Press: 1988), 31–32.
5 Schrecker, *Many Are the Crimes*, 83.
6 Joseph Alsop and Robert Kintner, "Lawyers Guild Faces an Argument," *Boston Globe*, February 25, 1939.
7 Bailey, "Progressive Lawyers," 221.
8 Auerbach, *Unequal Justice*, 201.
9 Ginger and Tobin, *National Lawyers Guild*, 32.
10 Bailey, "Progressive Lawyers," 226.
11 Ginger, *Carol Weiss King*, 248.
12 Ginger and Tobin, *National Lawyers Guild*, 32.
13 Ginger and Tobin, *National Lawyers Guild*, 33.
14 MLE to Gutknecht, February 25, 1939.
15 Schwarz, *Liberal: Adolf A. Berle*, 160; MLE to Henry Wallace, October 22, 1943, Ernst Papers.
16 Bailey, "Progressive Lawyers," 253.
17 "Ernst Approval Held Up: Senate Committee Sifts Record of Banking Board Appointee," *New York Times*, March 2, 1939, 2.
18 "Senators Confirm Ernst after Tiff: McNaboe for Reconsideration on Banking Board Choice, but Fails," *New York Times*, March 22, 1939, 14; "Ernst Makes the Grade," *New York Times*, March 27, 1939.
19 "The Boomerang from Red-Baiting," *Daily Worker*, March 3, 1939.
20 "Communist Charge Silly, Ernst Replies to Senator McNaboe," *New York American Banker*, March 3, 1939.
21 "Senators Confirm Ernst after Tiff," 14.
22 "Is America Menaced by Foreign Propaganda?" *America's Town Meeting of the Air*, January 1939, transcript, Ernst Papers.
23 MLE to Jerry Voorhis, August 1, 1939, Ernst Papers.
24 "Social Exchange Commission," proposal, [January 1939], typescript, Ernst Papers.
25 Sidney Hook to MLE, October 21, 1939, Ernst Papers. On the CCF, see Lewy, *Cause That Failed*, 50.
26 Jerold Lee Simmons, "Morris Ernst and Disclosure: One Liberal's Quest for a Solution to the Problem of Domestic Communism, 1939–1949," *Mid-America* 71, no. 1 (January 1989): 21.
27 "Possible Methods of Defeating Legislation in Derogation of the Bill of Rights," position paper, [October 1939], Ernst Papers.
28 Quoted in Simmons, "Morris Ernst and Disclosure," 22.
29 Walker, *In Defense of American Liberties*, 104; Kutulas, *American Civil Liberties Union*, 82.
30 Kutulas, *American Civil Liberties Union*, 39.
31 Post, "Partisanship within the American Civil Liberties Union," 56.

32 Corliss Lamont, *The Trial of Elizabeth Gurley Flynn by the American Civil Liberties Union* (New York: Horizon Press, 1968), 169.
33 Simmons, "American Civil Liberties Union and the Dies Committee," 195.
34 "Peace League Head Says Reds Back It," *New York Times*, October 24, 1939, 13; Donohue, *Politics of the American Civil Liberties Union*, 141. There was apparently no such report. See Lamont, *Freedom Is as Freedom Does*, 286.
35 Simmons, "American Civil Liberties Union and the Dies Committee," 196–97; Michael J. Ybarra, *Washington Gone Crazy: Senator Pat McCarran and the Great American Communist Hunt* (Hanover, NH: Steerforth Press, 2004), 242.
36 Martin Dies, "More Snakes Than I Can Kill," *Liberty*, January 27, 1940.
37 "Alliance Between Dies and Jittery Liberals Grows at Cocktail Party," *Daily Worker*, November 24, 1939.
38 Auerbach, "Depression Decade," 89.
39 Roger Baldwin to Gardner Jackson, December 16, 1939; Roger Baldwin to Alfred Baker Lewis, April 11, 1940; both in ACLU Papers.
40 MLE to Gardner Jackson, November 21, 1939, Ernst Papers.
41 MLE to RB, March 1, 1940, Ernst Papers.
42 Kutulas, *American Civil Liberties Union and Liberalism*, 70; Walker, *In Defense of American Liberties*, 129; Simmons, "American Civil Liberties Union and the Dies Committee," 197. Kutulas writes that "the timing of events . . . lends credence to the notion of some sort of intervention." Walker sees it as consistent with Ernst's style but not Hays's. Simmons believed that there was not an explicit deal but an informal agreement that the anticommunists on the ACLU Board would work to limit communist influence.
43 MLE to Jacob Wilk, December 28, 1939, Ernst Papers.
44 MLE to Jacob Wilk, October 30, 1939, Ernst Papers.
45 MLE to Martin Dies, October 30, 1939, Ernst Papers.
46 Simmons, "American Civil Liberties Union and the Dies Committee," 198.
47 Kutulas, *American Civil Liberties Union and Liberalism*, 71; Simmons, "American Civil Liberties Union and the Dies Committee," 198.
48 Simmons, "American Civil Liberties Union and the Dies Committee," 198.
49 "Report on the Dies Committee," November 14, 1939, Ernst Papers.
50 "Report on the Dies Committee."
51 Simmons, "American Civil Liberties Union and the Dies Committee," 200–201.
52 Lamson, *Roger Baldwin*, 228.
53 Cottrell, *Roger Nash Baldwin*, 266; Burt Neuborne, "Of Pragmatism and Principle: A Second Look at the Expulsion of Elizabeth Gurley Flynn from the ACLU's Board of Directors," *Tulsa Law Review* 41, no. 4 (2013): 806.
54 American Civil Liberties Union, *Crisis in the Civil Liberties Union: A Statement Including the Basic Documents Concerned, Giving the Minority Position in the Current Controversy in the ACLU* (New York: American Civil Liberties Union, 1940), 32.
55 Kutulas, *American Civil Liberties Union and Liberalism*, 72–73; Post, "Partisanship within the American Civil Liberties Union," 80–82.
56 American Civil Liberties Union, *Crisis in the Civil Liberties Union*, 7.
57 MLE to Eleanor Roosevelt, January 31, 1940, Ernst Papers.
58 February 5, 1940, Resolution, quoted in Lewy, *Cause That Failed*, 149.
59 American Civil Liberties Union, *Crisis in the Civil Liberties Union*, 20.

60 Lamont, *Freedom Is as Freedom Does*, 275; Corliss Lamont to Margaret DeSilver, May 16, 1940, Ernst Papers.
61 "Dr. H. F. Ward Quits Liberties Union," *New York Times*, March 4, 1940, 20.
62 Milner, *Education of an American Liberal*, 268.
63 Milner, *Education of an American Liberal*, 272.
64 "Liberties Union Asks Red to Resign," *New York Times*, March 5, 1940, 20.
65 American Civil Liberties Union, "To the Members of the National Committee," June 22, 1940, Ernst Papers.
66 John Haynes Holmes to MLE, March 15, 1940, Ernst Papers.
67 MLE to John Haynes Holmes, March 16, 1940, Ernst Papers.
68 Milner, *Education of an American Liberal*, 273–74.
69 Walker, *In Defense of American Liberties*, 133.
70 Neuborne, "Of Pragmatism and Principle," 810.
71 See the account in Lamont, *Trial of Elizabeth Gurley Flynn*. In 1968, the ACLU Board of Directors finally repealed the resolution and voted to restore Flynn to ACLU Board membership posthumously.
72 Geoffrey Perrett, *Days of Sadness, Years of Triumph: The American People, 1939–1945* (Madison: University of Wisconsin, 1973), 93–94.
73 Schrecker, *Many Are the Crimes*, 84.
74 MLE to J. Edgar Hoover (JEH), July 26, 1938, Ernst Papers.
75 MLE to JEH, March 30, 1939, Ernst Papers.
76 Based on Salisbury, "Strange Correspondence," 576, and other sources.
77 Prohibiting Use of Communication Facilities for Criminal Purposes, S. 3756, 75th Cong. (1938).
78 MLE to JEH, July 26, 1938.
79 Walker, *In Defense of American Liberties*, 126.
80 JEH to Attorney General Frank Murphy, March 29, 1939, Ernst Papers.
81 Ernst, *Best Is Yet*, 233–34.
82 MLE to John Finerty, March 27, 1940, Ernst Papers.

CHAPTER NINETEEN

1 Ernst, *Best Is Yet*, 78–99.
2 O'Connor, *Heywood Broun*, 222.
3 O'Connor, *Heywood Broun*, 221.
4 MLE to John L. Lewis, November 30, 1939, Ernst Papers.
5 FDR to MLE, February 10, 1940, Ernst Papers.
6 MLE to FDR, May 15, 1940, Ernst Papers.
7 Ernst, *So Far So Good*, 145.
8 Rodell, "Morris Ernst," 98.
9 "Group of Writers Backs Roosevelt," *New York Times*, September 14, 1940, 19.
10 Harold L. Ickes, *Secret Diary of Harold L. Ickes* (New York: Simon and Schuster, 1954), 401.
11 MLE to Edwin Watson, December 17, 1941; Edwin Watson to MLE, December 26, 1941; both in Ernst Papers.
12 Ernst, *So Far So Good*, 5.
13 West Virginia Board of Education v. Barnette, 319 U.S. 624 (1943).

14 Walker, *In Defense of American Liberties*, 134.
15 *Publishers Weekly*, January 24, 1942, clipping, Ernst Papers.
16 MLE to Thurman Arnold, September 25, 1942, Ernst Papers; Kutulas, *American Civil Liberties Union and Liberalism*, 89.
17 Ernst's suggestion led to the creation of a "Special Committee to Reconsider and Redefine the Union's Functions Outside Legal Defense" in October 1941, but his proposal was rejected. In later years the ACLU indeed moved in that direction. See Joel Lovell, "Can The A.C.L.U. Become the N.R.A. for the Left?" *New York Times Magazine*, July 2, 2018.
18 "The Forums Hit NY Fifth Columnists," *PM*, February 3, 1941.
19 MLE to Hon. Brown Harris, July 10, 1941, Ernst Papers.
20 "Biddle for Adding Executive Power," *New York Times*, June 25, 1940, 13.
21 Richard W. Steele, "Franklin D. Roosevelt and His Foreign Policy Critics," *Political Science Quarterly* 94, no. 1 (Spring 1979): 23–24; MLE to Missy LeHand, February 7, 1941, Ernst Papers; MLE to Francis Biddle, October 31, 1941, Ernst Papers.
22 Henry Morgenthau to FDR, January 21, 1941, Ernst Papers.
23 MLE to Francis Biddle, January 9, 1942, and April 2, 1942, Ernst Papers; Ernst, *So Far So Good*, 144; Marvin McIntyre to FDR, March 18, 1942, Ernst Papers.
24 MLE to Marvin McIntyre, March 23, 1942, Ernst Papers.
25 MLE to Oscar Cox, April 8, 1942, Ernst Papers.
26 MLE to FDR, May 1, 1942, Ernst Papers.
27 MLE to JEH, March 20, 1942, Ernst Papers.
28 JEH to MLE, March 22, 1942, Ernst Papers.
29 Steele, "Roosevelt and His Foreign Policy Critics," 24.
30 "Civil Liberties Champions Clash," *Editor and Publisher*, December 9, 1944, 7.
31 Morris Ernst, "Freedom to Read, See, and Hear," *Harper's Magazine*, July 1945, 51–53.
32 Michael Stamm, *Sound Business: Newspapers, Radio, and the Politics of New Media* (Philadelphia: University of Pennsylvania Press, 2011), 110.
33 Stamm, *Sound Business*, 104–5.
34 Stamm, *Sound Business*, 122.
35 "Ernst Asks for Ban on Press-Radio Link," *New York Times*, October 3, 1941, 19; Stamm, *Sound Business*, 124.
36 MLE to Hazel Rice, March 19, 1941; MLE to RB, October 3, 1941; both in Ernst Papers.
37 Minutes, ACLU Board Meeting, October 1, 1941, ACLU Papers.
38 Memorandum by Morris Ernst Prepared at the Request of the Board of Directors, October 9, 1941, Ernst Papers.
39 Arthur Garfield Hays, "Comment on Mr. Ernst's Memorandum," November 27, 1941, Ernst Papers.
40 Arthur Garfield Hays to RB, June 29, 1945.
41 MLE to RB, September 1, 1942, October 19, 1942; Memorandum on the Associated Press Case, September 23, 1942; all in Ernst Papers.
42 MLE to RB, November 6, 1942, Ernst Papers.
43 United States v. Associated Press, 52 F. Supp. 362, 372 (1943). The Supreme Court upheld the decision in 1945.
44 MLE to William Draper Lewis, February 4, 1943, Ernst Papers.

45 MLE to John Haynes Holmes, October 7, 1943, Ernst Papers.
46 Hays, "Comment on Mr. Ernst's Memorandum."
47 Ernst, *Best Is Yet*, 12.
48 MLE to Robert Lamont, January 26, 1939, Ernst Papers.
49 MLE to FF, February 3, 1939, Ernst Papers.
50 Robert Lamont to MLE, January 25, 1939, Ernst Papers.
51 MLE to Louis Brandeis, February 9, 1939; February 17, 1939; both in Ernst Papers.
52 MLE to Robert Lamont, February 21,1939, Ernst Papers.
53 Louis Brandeis to MLE, March 3, 1940, Ernst Papers.
54 MLE to Robert Lamont, December 7, 1939, Ernst Papers.
55 MLE to Robert Lamont, December 20, 1939, Ernst Papers.
56 MLE to Robert Lamont, February 8, 1940, Ernst Papers.
57 Louis Brandeis to MLE, May 27, 1940, Ernst Papers.
58 Morris Ernst, *Too Big* (Boston: Little, Brown, 1940).
59 Office of the Marshal of the Supreme Court to MLE, November 6, 1942; December 23, 1942; December 30, 1942; January 9, 1943 (with handwritten note by FF); MLE to Elizabeth Brandeis, January 9, 1943; all in Ernst Papers.
60 Ernst, *Best Is Yet*, 13.
61 Dwight MacDonald, "The Defense of Everybody," *New Yorker*, July 3, 1953, 47.
62 Kutulas, *American Civil Liberties Union and Liberalism*, 93; Walker, *In Defense of American Liberties*, 156.
63 Fred Rodell, "The Best Is Yet," *Harvard Law Review*, September 1945, 1105; Walker, *In Defense of American Liberties*, 157.
64 Peter Irons, *Justice at War* (Berkeley: University of California Press, 1993), 133.
65 MLE to RB, March 19, 1942, Ernst Papers; Walker, *In Defense of American Liberties*, 139.
66 Irons, *Justice at War*, 109; MLE to RB, March 19, 1942. Following a conversation with Justice Harlan Stone, Ernst wrote privately to Roosevelt, counseling him that the Supreme Court would likely strike down his order as unconstitutional. "Dear Governor, I am thoroughly persuaded that the Supreme Court will strike down the concentration of Japanese citizens. Wouldn't it be well to have your Japanese rehabilitation boys prepared with a program to be announced on the day when the Supreme Court declares unconstitutional, as it will and should, our treatment of Japanese citizens." He offered to help Roosevelt develop such a program. MLE to FDR, April 15, 1943, Ernst Papers; Greg Robinson, *A Tragedy of Democracy: Japanese Confinement in North America* (New York: Columbia University Press, 2010), 222.
67 MLE to John Haynes Holmes, March 31, 1943, Ernst Papers.
68 MLE to John Haynes Holmes April 14, 1942, Ernst Papers.
69 MLE to John Haynes Holmes, October 6, 1942, Ernst Papers.
70 Kenneth O'Reilly, *Hoover and the Un-Americans* (Philadelphia: Temple University Press, 1983), 32; Schrecker, *Many Are the Crimes*, 219; Matthew Cecil, *Branding Hoover's FBI: How the Boss's PR Men Sold the Bureau to America* (Lawrence: University of Kansas Press, 2016).
71 MLE to Joseph Patterson, January 2, 1942, Ernst Papers.
72 MLE to Joseph Patterson, March 27, 1940, Ernst Papers.
73 MLE to JEH, December 29, 1941, Ernst Papers.

74 MLE to JEH, October 14, 1941, Ernst Papers.
75 Cecil, *Branding Hoover's FBI*, 144.
76 "Washington Gestapo," *Nation*, July 17, 1943, 64–66.
77 JEH to MLE, August 3, 1943, Ernst Papers.
78 MLE to Freda Kirchwey, August 26, 1943, Ernst Papers.
79 Morris Ernst, "Another Witness," *Nation*, September 25, 1943; I. F. Stone, "XXX and the FBI," *Nation*, September 25, 1943, 342.
80 JEH to MLE, October 22, 1939, Ernst Papers.
81 Baldwin was also to blame; after meeting with Hoover in 1942, Baldwin refused to believe complaints about FBI abuses. Walker, *In Defense of American Liberties*, 191.
82 MLE to FDR, February 19, 1942, Ernst Papers.
83 MLE to FDR, April 24, 1942, Ernst Papers.
84 FDR to Director of the Budget, April 27, 1942, FDR Library.
85 Richard W. Steele, "The Pulse of the People: Franklin D. Roosevelt and the Gauging of American Public Opinion," *Journal of Contemporary History* 9, no. 4 (October 1974): 201.
86 MLE to FDR, September 25, 1942; March 26, 1944, Ernst Papers.
87 MLE to John Hildring, March 26, 1944, Ernst Papers.
88 MLE to Randolph Paul, October 6, 1942, Ernst Papers.
89 MLE to Ed Stettinus, October 10, 1942; December 11, 1942; January 6, 1943; all in Ernst Papers.
90 "British Producer Begins Hollywood Film Invasion," *Spokesman Review* (Spokane, WA), September 22, 1946.
91 MLE to John Pehle, February 11, 1944, Ernst Papers; Memorandum, Pehle, February 19, 1944, Ernst Papers.
92 MLE to John Pehle, February 16, 1944; MLE to FDR, February 26, 1944; both in Ernst Papers. See also letter from Ernst's law partner Harold Stern to J. P. Morgan, March 8, 1944, Ernst Papers.
93 MLE to John Pehle, March 6, 1944; John Pehle to MLE, March 8, 1944; both in Ernst Papers.
94 Rebecca Erbelding, *Rescue Board: The Untold Story of America's Efforts to Save the Jews of Europe* (New York: Doubleday, 2018), 77.
95 MLE to Pehle, March 6, 1944.
96 Harold Stern to John Pehle, May 31, 1944, Ernst Papers; Erbelding, *Rescue Board*, 146.
97 MLE, note, March 14, 1963 ("helped get newsprint to the underground of France"); Henri Bonnet, Ambassador of France, to MLE, November 26, 1951; Legion of Honor certificate, June 1951; all in Ernst Papers.
98 Sweeney v. Schenectady Union Pub. Co., 316 U.S. 42 (1942).
99 Norman Rosenberg, "Taking A Look at 'The Distorted Shape of an Ugly Tree': Efforts at Policy-Surgery on the Law of Libel During the Decade of the 1940s," *Northern Kentucky Law Review* 15, no. 1 (1988): 11–56.
100 Alice Fleetwood Bartee, *Privacy Rights: Cases Lost and Causes Won before the Supreme Court* (New York, Rowman and Littlefield, 2006), 7; Ernst and Lindey, *Censor Marches On*, 175; Leigh Ann Wheeler, *How Sex Became a Civil Liberty* (New York: Oxford University Press, 2013), 57–58.
101 Abraham Stone, "The Social and Legal Status of Contraception," *University*

of North Carolina Law Review 22, no. 3 (April 1944): 212; Commonwealth v. Gardner, 300 Mass. 372 (1940).

102 The book case was abandoned. See Garrow, *Liberty and Sexuality*, 59–60.

103 Bartee, *Privacy Rights*, 8; Garrow, *Liberty and Sexuality*, 84; Harry Kalven Jr., "A Special Corner of Civil Liberties: A Legal View," *New York University Law Review* 1223, no. 31 (1956): 1223–37.

104 Bartee, *Privacy Rights*, 3–10.

105 Bartee, *Privacy Rights*, 12–17.

106 "Birth Control Ban Fought in High Court," *Berkshire Eagle* (Pittsfield, MA), January 14, 1943.

107 Ernst, *Best Is Yet*, 254–45.

108 Garrow, *Liberty and Sexuality*, 104–5.

CHAPTER TWENTY

1 Fred Rodell to MLE, February 24, 1944, Ernst Papers.

2 Fred Rodell to MLE, January 26, 1944, Ernst Papers.

3 MLE to Fred Rodell, January 28, 1944, Ernst Papers.

4 Rodell, "Morris Ernst," 97–98, 100–107.

5 MLE to Eleanor Roosevelt, February 26, 1944, Ernst Papers.

6 MLE to Connie Ernst, March 10, 1944, Ernst Papers.

7 MLE to Roy Larsen, February 18, 1944, Ernst Papers.

8 Edna Ferber to MLE, March 6, 1944, Ernst Papers.

9 MLE to Hector Holmes, November 9, 1948, Ernst Papers.

10 Russell Leffingwell to MLE, February 25, 1944, Ernst Papers.

11 MLE to Russell Leffingwell, February 28, 1944, Ernst Papers.

12 Fred Rodell, "Ernst at His Worst," *Progressive*, May 21, 1945.

13 MLE to Edna Ferber, August 31, 1944, Ernst Papers.

14 MLE to Eleanor Roosevelt, August 29, 1944, Ernst Papers.

15 Ernst, *Best Is Yet*, 235.

16 Helen Hirsch, review of *The Best Is Yet*, by Morris Ernst, *Jewish Forum*, n.d., clipping, Ernst Papers.

17 Bruce Bliven, "Ernst Himself," *New Republic*, May 29, 1945, 717.

18 MLE to Joseph Ball, November 29, 1944, Ernst Papers.

19 MLE to Sir David J. M. D. Scott, July 10, 1945, Ernst Papers.

20 Victor Pickard, *America's Search for Media Democracy* (New York: Cambridge University Press, 2014), 124. The Hutchins Commission on Freedom of the Press, a commission of eminent academics and journalists funded by Time-Life publisher Henry Luce, had been recently formed to explore the function of the media in modern democracy. Ernst's book preceded by a year the Hutchins Commission's report, issued in book form as *A Free and Responsible Press*. The commission recognized that the concentration of control over the media industries was problematic but did not treat that factor as the main evil of the press, instead targeting the main difficulties as excessive sensationalism, publishers' conservative bias, and their priority of profit over the public good. See Sam Lebovic, "When the Mainstream Media Was Conservative: Media Criticism in the Age of Reform," in *Media Nation: The Political History of News in Modern America*, ed. Bruce J.

Schulman and Julian E. Zelizer (Philadelphia: University of Pennsylvania Press, 2017).

21 Ernst, *First Freedom*, xiv.

22 Arthur J. Goldberg, "The First Freedom," *University of Chicago Law Review* 13, no. 4 (June 1946): 536.

23 MLE to Joseph Ball, November 29, 1944, Ernst Papers.

24 MLE to Elinor Timberg, November 12, 1945, Ernst Papers.

25 "To Safeguard Speech," *Hartford (CT) Courant*, March 26, 1946.

26 Sterling North, "Freedom of Press in Peril Under Monopolies, Is View," *Cincinnati Enquirer*, March 16, 1946.

27 MLE to Joseph Ball, September 26, 1946, Ernst Papers.

28 Ben H. Bagdikian, "Conglomeration, Concentration, and the Flow of Information," in *Proceedings of the Symposium on Media Concentration* (Washington: Bureau of Competition, Federal Trade Commission, 1978), 7.

29 John O'Donnell, "Capitol Stuff," *Daily News* (New York), April 16, 1945.

30 MLE to Eleanor Roosevelt, May 1, 1945, Ernst Papers.

31 Wheeler, *How Sex Became a Civil Liberty*, 105.

32 Morris Ernst, "The Kinsey Report and the Law," *Scientific Monthly* 70, no. 5 (May 1, 1950): 280–81.

33 Ernst, *Love Affair with the Law*, 114.

34 Morris Ernst and David Loth, *The People Know Best: The Ballots vs. the Polls* (Washington, DC: Public Affairs Press, 1949), 11.

35 Drew Pearson, "Washington Merry Go Round," *Freeport (IL) Journal Standard*, February 17, 1949.

36 Leslie Midgley, *How Many Words Do You Want? An Insider's Story of Print and Television Journalism* (Secaucus, NJ: Carol Publishing Group, 1989), 86; MLE to George Sokolsky, October 11, 1955, Ernst Papers.

37 Sidis v. F. R. Publishing, 113 F.2d 806 (1940); Koussevitsky v. Allen, Towne, and Heath, 188 Misc. 479 (1947).

38 MLE to Clifford Forster, June 15, 1948, Ernst Papers.

39 Hannegan v. *Esquire*, 327 U.S. 146 (1946); Winters v. New York, 333 U.S. 507 (1948).

40 "Ernst Calls on Pic Industry to Fight Pre-Censorship," *Variety*, February 13, 1946, 3.

41 MLE to Howard Dietz, November 27, 1941, Ernst Papers.

42 MLE to JEH, November 29, 1948, Ernst Papers.

43 Curt Gentry, *J. Edgar Hoover: The Man and the Secrets* (New York: Norton, 1991), 235.

44 Cecil, *Branding Hoover's FBI*, 140.

45 MLE to JEH, June 13, 1947, Ernst Papers.

46 Salisbury, "Strange Correspondence," 578.

47 See, e.g., James Lawrence Fly, "The Wire-Tapping Outrage," *New Republic*, February 6, 1950; Jan Hasbrouck, "J. Edgar Hoover's Gossip Mill," *New Republic*, December 15, 1947; Harold Ickes, "A Dirtier 'Dirty Business,'" *New Republic*, January 9, 1950.

48 JEH to MLE, October 17, 1946, Ernst Papers.

49 JEH to MLE, October 17, 1946.

50 Morris Ernst, letter to the editor, *Time*, November 11, 1946.

51 MLE to JEH, February 10, 1947, Ernst Papers.
52 MLE to JEH, February 13, 1948, Ernst Papers.
53 MLE to JEH, February 10, 1947.
54 MLE to Clyde Tolson, September 29, 1948, Ernst Papers.
55 Morris Ernst, "Miasma of Suspicion," *Saturday Review*, May 5, 1949, 19.
56 MLE to JEH, April 28, 1947, Ernst Papers.
57 Salisbury, "Strange Correspondence," 582.
58 Schrecker, *Many Are the Crimes*, 237.
59 Mickie Edwardson, "James Lawrence Fly, The FBI, and Wiretapping," *Historian* 61, no. 2 (Winter 1999): 361–81; Walker, *In Defense of American Liberties*, 192.
60 Quoted in Kenneth O'Reilly, "The Bureau and the Committee: A Study of J. Edgar Hoover's FBI, The House Committee on Un-American Activities, and the Communist Issue" (PhD diss, Marquette University, 1981), 235.
61 MLE to James Fly, February 7, 1950; Walker, *In Defense of American Liberties*, 192.
62 James Fly to MLE, November 10, 1949, Ernst Papers.
63 JEH to MLE, December 1, 1949, Ernst Papers; Salisbury, "Strange Correspondence," 579; O'Reilly, *Hoover and the Un-Americans*, 142.
64 MLE to JEH, November 25, 1949, Ernst Papers.
65 Edward Tamm to JEH, November 10, 1947, Ernst FBI file.
66 John D. Morris, "Truman Creates Civil Rights Board," *New York Times*, December 6, 1946, 26.
67 William E. Juhnke, "President Truman's Committee on Civil Rights: The Interaction of Politics, Protest, and a Presidential Advisory Commission," *Presidential Studies Quarterly* 19, no. 3 (Summer 1989): 593–610.
68 William E. Juhnke, "Creating a New Charter of Freedom: The Organization and Operation of the President's Committee on Civil Rights, 1946–48" (PhD diss., University of Kansas, 1974), 75.
69 Juhnke, "Truman's Committee on Civil Rights," 596.
70 Simmons, "Morris Ernst and Disclosure," 26.
71 MLE to Robert K. Carr, April 29, 1947, Ernst Papers; Juhnke, "Creating a New Charter of Freedom," 102.
72 "Historical Document Calls for US Action," *Pittsburgh Courier*, November 8, 1947.
73 Juhnke, "Truman's Committee on Civil Rights," 603; Edith S. Riehm, "Forging the Civil Rights Front: How Truman's Committee Set the Liberal Agenda for Reform, 1947–1965" (PhD diss., Georgia State University, 2012), 235.
74 Juhnke, "Creating a New Charter of Freedom," 141.
75 JEH to Charlie Wilson, September 9, 1947, Ernst Papers.
76 Juhnke, "Truman's Committee on Civil Rights," 606.
77 MLE to JEH, November 19, 1947, Ernst Papers; Tamm to Hoover, November 10, 1947.
78 *To Secure These Rights: The Report of the President's Committee on Civil Rights* (Washington, DC: U.S. Government Printing Office, 1947), 53.
79 "Ernst Asks Forcing of Groups Into Open," *New York Times*, December 9, 1947, 23.
80 Robert Bendiner, "Civil Liberties and the Communists," *Commentary* 6 (January 1, 1948): 423–31.
81 "Reds Oppose Plan for Identifying Secret Agents," *Dayton (OH) Daily News*, December 12, 1947.
82 "Ernst's 'Registration' Trap," *Daily Worker*, December 10, 1947.

83 "Issues on Rights Sharply Debated," *New York Times*, March 20, 1949, 61; Simmons, "Morris Ernst and Disclosure," 29.
84 Dorothy Thompson, "Knowledge a Public Right," *Fort Worth (TX) Star-Telegram*, December 15, 1947.
85 Arthur Garfield Hays, "Full Disclosure, Dangerous Precedent," *Nation*, January 29, 1949, 121–23.
86 Draft of memorandum "Approach to Loyalty Program," October 20, 1947, Ernst Papers.
87 MLE to Ben Kaplan, October 18, 1947, Ernst Papers.
88 Victor S. Navasky, *Naming Names* (New York: Viking Press, 1980); Mary Sperling McAuliffe, *Crisis on the Left: Cold War Politics and American Liberals, 1947–1954* (Amherst: University of Massachusetts Press, 1978), 90; American Civil Liberties Union (ACLU), *It's Not Only Communists' Rights* (New York: ACLU, 1948).
89 Corliss Lamont, *Yes to Life: Memoirs of Corliss Lamont* (New York: Horizon Press, 1981), 136.
90 "Rules Proposed by Morris Ernst to House Un-American Activities Committee," February 18, 1948, Ernst Papers.
91 MLE to Richard Nixon, September 30, 1948, Ernst Papers.
92 MLE to Charles Wyzanski, February 16, 1948, Ernst Papers.
93 Zechariah Chafee Jr., foreword to *A Letter to the House Un-American Activities Committee on the Mundt-Nixon Bill* (New York: American Civil Liberties Union, 1950).
94 MLE to Clifford Forster, January 8, 1948, Ernst Papers.
95 MLE to Richard Nixon, January 26, 1948, Ernst Papers.
96 *Hearings of the Subcommittee on Legislation of the Committee on Un-American Activities, House of Representatives*, 80th Cong., 1st Sess. (1948), 283.
97 MLE to Richard Nixon, May 11, 1948, Ernst Papers.
98 Simmons, "Morris Ernst and Disclosure," 29.
99 Morris Ernst, "Liberals and the Communist Trial," *New Republic*, January 31, 1949, 7; MLE to JEH, October 31, 1948, Ernst Papers.
100 "Memorandum of Morris L. Ernst on the Clear and Present Danger Rule," October 21, 1948, Ernst Papers.
101 "Additional Memorandum in view of Dr. Holmes letter," January 24, 1949, Ernst Papers.
102 Morris Ernst, "Supreme Court Expands Clear and Present Danger," *Saturday Review*, [ca. 1948], clipping, box 142, Ernst Papers.
103 MLE to Harold Medina, September 12, 1949, Ernst Papers.
104 Roger Baldwin, "Liberals and the Communist Trial," *New Republic*, January 31, 1949, 8.
105 MLE to Medina, September 12, 1949.
106 Simmons, "Morris Ernst and Disclosure," 29.

CHAPTER TWENTY-ONE

1 See, e.g., Bridges v. California, 312 U.S. 252 (1941); Thomas v. Collins, 323 U.S. 516 (1945).
2 Quoted in Jensen and Norkin, "Persuasive Roger Baldwin," 55.

3 See Donohue, *Politics of the American Civil Liberties Union*, 242–43.
4 Wheeler, *How Sex Became a Civil Liberty*, 93–105.
5 Walker, *In Defense of American Liberties*, 168.
6 Baldwin, Hays, and Forster quoted in MacDonald, "Defense of Everybody—II," 52.
7 Arthur Garfield Hays to MLE, December 27, 1951, Ernst Papers.
8 MLE to Ernest Angell, January 4, 1954, Ernst Papers.
9 See Walker, *Hate Speech*, 83–86.
10 Ernst, *Best Is Yet*, 65.
11 MLE to Lionel Bernstein, November 15, 1948, Ernst Papers.
12 Irving Spiegel, "Ernst Warns Jews of 'Making' Ghetto," *New York Times*, April 23, 1950, 43.
13 "Should Minority Groups Exercise Censorship over Books and Films?" *Town Meeting of the Air*, May 10, 1949, transcript, Ernst Papers.
14 MLE to Henry Spitz, State Commission Against Discrimination, March 16, 1951, Ernst Papers.
15 MLE to Russell Leffingwell, January 11, 1951, Ernst Papers.
16 MLE to Mrs. Edward Burke, February 15, 1951, Ernst Papers.
17 MLE to Leffingwell, January 11, 1951.
18 MLE to Russell Leffingwell, December 13, 1950; MLE to Henry Spitz, March 16, 1951; both in Ernst Papers.
19 *Person to Person*, television program episode broadcast January 6, 1956, video recording provided to author by private source.
20 Walker, *In Defense of American Liberties*, 209–11; McAuliffe, *Crisis on the Left*, 98.
21 MLE to Ernest (Angell), February 4, 1960, Ernst Papers.
22 "Comic Book Bill Assailed," *New York Times*, March 11, 1949, 23.
23 Brief of the National Council on Freedom from Censorship as Amicus Curiae, Superior Films, Inc. v. Department of Ed. of Ohio, 346 U.S. 587 (1954).
24 Wheeler, *How Sex Became a Civil Liberty*, 70.
25 Roth v. United States, 237 F. 2d 796 (1956) at 827.
26 Harriet Pilpel to Florence Frank, March 22, 1957, Ernst Papers.
27 Brief of Morris L. Ernst as Amicus Curiae, Roth v. United States, 354 U.S. 476 (1957).
28 *Roth v. United States*, 354 U.S. 476 at 489.
29 Garrow, *Liberty and Sexuality*, 157–58.
30 In the 1960s, Ernst also campaigned for the legalization of abortion. Ernst envisioned a "liberalization of abortion law by judicial opinions," and he wrote and lectured on the topic. He believed that the initiative to reform abortion law must come from doctors rather than lawyers. He urged physicians to act, telling them that "the health of our nation in this area of abortion awaits no more than some simple dignified and thoughtful leadership. Only men in the health discipline are fit to so lead our people." See Morris Ernst, "There is a Desperate Need of Medical Wisdom to Deal with the Problem of Abortion," *New Medica Materia*, January 1962, 21.
31 Cecil, *Branding Hoover's FBI*, 170.
32 Athan Theoharis and John Stuart Cox, *The Boss: J. Edgar Hoover and the Great American Inquisition* (Philadelphia: Temple University Press, 1988), 206–7.
33 Clyde Tolson to Louis B. Nichols, March 8, 1951, Ernst FBI file; Ralph Engelman, *Friendlyvision: Fred Friendly and the Rise and Fall of Television Journalism* (New

York: Columbia University Press, 2009), 111; A. M. Sperber, *Murrow: His Life and Times* (New York: Fordham University Press, 1999), 371.

34 JEH to MLE, February 29, 1952, Ernst Papers.

35 Introduction to Morris Ernst, "Why I No Longer Fear the FBI," *Reader's Digest*, December 1950, 135.

36 Athan Theoharis, *J. Edgar Hoover, Sex, and Crime: An Historical Antidote* (Chicago: Ivan R. Dee, 1995), 263.

37 JEH to MLE, September 6, 1950, Ernst Papers; Gentry, *J. Edgar Hoover*, 386.

38 MLE to Louis B. Nichols, September 22, 1950, Ernst Papers.

39 Morris Ernst, "Why I No Longer Fear the FBI," *Reader's Digest*, December 1950, 135–39.

40 William Sullivan, *The Bureau: My Thirty Years in Hoover's FBI* (New York: Norton, 1979), 94.

41 JEH to MLE, November 20, 1950, Ernst Papers.

42 MLE to Groucho Marx, October 7, 1952, Ernst Papers.

43 MLE to Louis B. Nichols, June 12, 1952, Ernst Papers; William Sullivan to A. H. Belmont, January 19, 1959, Ernst FBI file; O'Reilly, *Hoover and the Un-Americans*, 187.

44 Morris L. Ernst and David Loth, *Report on the American Communist* (New York: Holt, 1952).

45 MLE to Clayton Fritchey, June 26, 1952; MLE to Charles Murphy, November 28, 1950; both in Ernst Papers.

46 Ernst and Loth, *Report on the American Communist*, 223, 226.

47 "Walter Winchell of New York," *El Paso (TX) Times*, January 21, 1953.

48 "Winchell in New York," *Jackson (TN) Sun*, February 8, 1953.

49 "Walter Winchell," *Argus-Leader* (Sioux Falls, SD), January 19, 1953.

50 On the ACLU position, see McAuliffe, *Crisis on the Left*, 103.

51 MLE to Ethel Goldberg, January 23, 1953, Ernst Papers; Salisbury, "Strange Correspondence," 584.

52 Joyce Milton and Ronald Radosh, *The Rosenberg File: A Search for the Truth* (New York: Holt, Rinehart, and Winston, 1983), 357–58; Louis B. Nichols to Clyde Tolson, December 20, 1952, Ernst FBI file.

53 MLE to Eleanor Roosevelt, December 29, 1952, Ernst Papers.

54 MLE to Eleanor Roosevelt, January 23, 1953, Ernst Papers.

55 Milton and Radosh, *Rosenberg File*, 379.

56 MLE to E. Roosevelt, January 23, 1953.

57 Milton and Radosh, *Rosenberg File*, 358.

58 Milton and Radosh, *Rosenberg File*, 358.

59 Richard Harris, "Worse than Murder: The Lawyers and the Rosenbergs," *Grand Street* 3, no. 2 (Winter 1984): 169.

60 Alan M. Dershowitz, "Spies and Scapegoats," *New York Times*, August 14, 1983, BR1.

61 Morris L. Ernst and Malcolm A. Hoffmann, *Back and Forth: An Occasional, Casual Communication* (Mount Vernon, NY: Peter Pauper Press, 1969), preface.

62 MLE interview with Mary Batten.

63 Ernst, *Touch Wood*, 7.

64 See Joel Silverman, "Pursuing Celebrity, Ensuing Masculinity: Morris Ernst, Obscenity, and the Search for Recognition" (PhD diss., University of Texas at Austin, 2006), 242–43.

65 MLE to Marie Jahoda, August 20, 1958, Ernst Papers.
66 Review of *Utopia 1976*, by Morris Ernst, *Austin (TX) American Statesman*, November 5, 1955.
67 MLE to Betty Glass, October 15, 1956, Ernst Papers.
68 *Person to Person*, January 6, 1956.
69 "Story of a Dark International Conspiracy," *Life*, February 23, 1957, 24.
70 MLE to George Cornish, May 12, 1959, Ernst Papers.
71 See MLE to Franklin D. Roosevelt Jr., January 7, 1957; Franklin D. Roosevelt Jr. to MLE, December 26, 1956; MLE to Biagio DiVenuti, January 31, 1957; all in Ernst Papers.
72 MLE to Ambassador Temistocles Messina, January 11, 1957, Ernst Papers.
73 Wayne Phillips, "Ernst to Conduct Galindez Inquiry," *New York Times*, July 21, 1957, 1.
74 RB to Edward S. Greenbaum, August 22, 1957, Ernst Papers.
75 Salisbury, "Strange Correspondence," 586.
76 Salisbury, "Strange Correspondence," 586.
77 Morris Ernst, *Report and Opinion in the Matter of Galindez* (New York: Sidney Baron, 1958).
78 Stuart A. McKeever, *The Galindez Case* (Bloomington, IN: AuthorHouse, 2013), 227.
79 MLE to Allen Lane, September 11, 1957, Ernst Papers.
80 A. H. Belmont to S. B. Donahoe, June 19, 1959, Ernst FBI file.
81 McKeever, *Galindez Case*, 265.
82 McKeever, *Galindez Case*, 236.
83 Belmont to Donahoe.
84 Salisbury, "Strange Correspondence," 587.
85 Salisbury, "Strange Correspondence," 587; Alan U. Schwartz, "Ernst and the Galindez Case," letter to the editor, *New York Times*, June 1, 1976, 34.
86 Morris Ernst and Alan Schwartz, "The Galindez Mystery," memo, September 5, 1961, Ernst Papers.
87 Ernst, *Report and Opinion in the Matter of Galindez*; Peter Kihss, "Ernst Report on Galindez Clears Dominican Dictator," *New York Times*, June 2, 1958, 1.
88 Cecil, *Branding Hoover's FBI*, 169; "Whitewash for Trujillo," *Time*, June 9, 1958.
89 Salisbury, "Strange Correspondence," 588; Ernst and Schwartz, "Galindez Mystery."
90 "Costly Whitewash of Black Charges," *Life*, June 9, 1958, 105.
91 Alan Reitman to Mrs. H. L. Romanick, April 3, 1959, ACLU Papers.
92 Charles O. Porter, "Ernst and Galindez," *New Leader*, July 10, 1958, 8.
93 "Anguish in the Ranks," *Newsweek*, July 7, 1958.
94 "An Old Friend" to MLE, July 2, 1958, Ernst Papers.
95 Fred Rodell to MLE, June 25, 1958, Ernst Papers.
96 MLE to Marie Jahoda, July 1, 1958, Ernst Papers.
97 MLE to Jahoda, August 20, 1958.
98 MLE to Bernard Knollenberg, August 27, 1958.
99 MLE to Abraham Muller, July 2, 1958; MLE to Ben Kaplan, July 10, 1958; both in Ernst Papers.
100 "Ernst Urges Inquiry on Galindez by U.S.," *New York Times*, July 3, 1958, 1.

101 McKeever, *Galindez Case*, 266.
102 Salisbury, "Strange Correspondence," 588.
103 L. V. Boardman to A. H. Belmont, April 21, 1954, Ernst FBI file; Gentry, *J. Edgar Hoover*, 235.
104 Toledano, reporting through Nichols: Louis B. Nichols to Clyde Tolson, April 14, 1954, Ernst FBI file.
105 MLE to JEH, December 22, 1955, Ernst Papers; Gentry, *J. Edgar Hoover*, 438.
106 Salisbury, "Strange Correspondence," 585.
107 JEH to Louis B. Nichols, July 11, 1957, Ernst FBI file.
108 MLE to Louis B. Nichols, August 7, 1957, Ernst FBI file.
109 Salisbury, "Strange Correspondence," 585.
110 Helen Gandy to MLE, April 14, 1959, Ernst Papers.
111 MLE to JEH, February 6, 1958, Ernst Papers.
112 MLE to Louis B. Nichols, May 20, 1959, Ernst Papers.
113 MLE to JEH, February 15, 1960, Ernst Papers.
114 JEH to C. D. DeLoach, March 10, 1961, Ernst FBI file.
115 Anthony Marro, "F.B.I. Files Disclose '50s Tie to ACLU," *New York Times*, August 4, 1977, 1.
116 "Surprising ACLU Link to the FBI," *San Francisco Examiner*, August 5, 1977, reprinting the story from *Chicago Daily News*.
117 Gentry, *J. Edgar Hoover*, 440.
118 Aryeh Neier, *Taking Liberties: Four Decades in the Struggle for Rights* (New York: Public Affairs, 2003), 140.
119 Walker, *In Defense of American Liberties*, 333–34.
120 Gentry, *J. Edgar Hoover*, 236.
121 "Rosenberg Case: Ernst Did Not Act for ACLU," *New York Times*, October 7, 1983, A30.
122 Salisbury, "Strange Correspondence," 575.
123 Advertisement, *Nation*, December 1984.

CHAPTER TWENTY-TWO

1 MLE to Mae Goodman, October 30, 1958, Ernst Papers.
2 MLE to Horace Lyon, October 11, 1962, Ernst Papers.
3 "Morris Ernst Sees Moral Breakdown," n.d., Ernst Papers.
4 "Ernst Calls News Media Evil Influence in Society," *Editor and Publisher*, January 27, 1968.
5 "A Limit to Obscenity," *Akron Beacon Journal*, January 8, 1970.
6 "One Year in the Life of Morris Ernst," *San Francisco Examiner*, October 23, 1960, 20.
7 Ernst, *Untitled*, 2.
8 Ernst, *Untitled*, 217.
9 Ernst, *Untitled*, 239–40.
10 Ernst, *Untitled*, 171.
11 *Untitled*, 171. On April 3, 1968, his friends gave him a party, gloating because he was proven in error.
12 MLE to Roger Ernst, February 21, 1962, Ernst Papers.

13 MLE to Roger Ernst, November 22, 1963, Ernst Papers.
14 "ML Ernst's Publishings," *Variety*, December 4, 1963.
15 "Words for Mrs. Morris L. Ernst," *Villager*, December 10, 1964, 9.
16 Paula Gross to Edna Ferber, December 10, 1964, Ernst Papers.
17 Diary, n.d., Ernst Papers.
18 Diary, September 2, 1967, Ernst Papers.
19 Diary, September 9, 1967, Ernst Papers.
20 MLE to Edna Ferber, September 5, 1967, Ernst Papers.
21 MLE to Roger Ernst, May 27, 1966, Ernst Papers.
22 MLE to Marie Jahoda, November 16, 1972, Ernst Papers.
23 MLE to Jean [last name unknown], September 17, 1975, Ernst Papers.
24 Diary, 1967, Ernst Papers.
25 "Busy Lawyer Sums Up Case against Boredom," New York *World-Telegram*, n.d., clipping, Ernst Papers.
26 Diary, 1967, Ernst Papers.
27 MLE to Roger Ernst, April 18, 1969, Ernst Papers.
28 [Morris Ernst], *Pandect of C. L. D.* (Mount Vernon, NY: Peter Pauper Press, 1965), 8.
29 MLE to Arnold Gingrich, March 9, 1964, Ernst Papers. "Two of my most valued book editor friends did not catch on that I was trying to pull a J.M. Barrie kind of hoax."
30 MLE to Ambassador Hannes Kjertansson, June 16, 1966, Ernst Papers.
31 Edna Ferber to MLE, July 1966, Ernst Papers.
32 Leonard Lyons, "Lyons Den," *New York Post*, April 14, 1969.
33 "Village Vagrants Routed by Police," *New York Times*, August 10, 1968, 15.
34 Jane Allison, "Hoosier in Manhattan," *Indianapolis News*, October 21, 1971, 35.
35 Ernst, "Reflections on the *Ulysses* Trial," 3. Ernst never believed it was an important case; as he wrote to Bennett Cerf, "the literati and you have made it important." MLE to BC, June 4, 1969, Ernst Papers.
36 Ernst, "Reflections on the *Ulysses* Trial," 11.
37 MLE to Monroe Freedman, April 8, 1967, Ernst Papers.
38 MLE to Thomas Smith, March 21, 1966, Ernst Papers.
39 Morris Ernst, "We're Getting Murdered by TV," *Variety*, June 12, 1968.
40 "News Media Called an Evil Influence," *Publishers' Auxiliary*, May 1968.
41 Morris Ernst, *Utopia 1976* (New York: Rinehart, 1955), 11.
42 MLE to Governor Paul Johnson, February 16, 1965, Ernst Papers.
43 MLE to Benno Schmidt, March 23, 1973, Ernst Papers; Morris Ernst, "Malice: Try to Prove It," *Variety*, January 3, 1968.
44 MLE to Alexander Bickel, December 7, 1972, Ernst Papers.
45 MLE to Whitney North Seymour, June 23, 1972, Ernst Papers.
46 "Veteran Foe of Censorship Sees Need for Limit with in a Free Culture," *Variety*, January 7, 1970.
47 MLE to Leonard Granato, November 11, 1971, Ernst Papers.
48 MLE to William Brennan, April 20, 1966, Ernst Papers.
49 Irving Spiegel, "Censors' Foe Sees Need for Limits to Freedom," *New York Times*, January 5, 1970, 46; see also Walter Berns, "Pornography vs. Democracy: The Case for Censorship," *Public Interest* 22 (Winter 1971): 3–24.
50 "Highest Freedom," *Christian Science Monitor*, February 4, 1970, B16.

51 Raymond Haberski, *Freedom to Offend: How New York Remade Movie Culture* (Lexington: University Press of Kentucky, 2007), 218.

52 Rosalind Massow, "Life Begins at 80," *New York Daily News*, August 12, 1973.

53 "Morris Ernst, at 82, Enters Party Politics," *New York Daily News*, May 19, 1970. The newspaper got his age wrong; he was eighty-one at the time, having not yet reached his eighty-second birthday in August.

54 Untitled press release, May 22, 1973, Ernst Papers. It is unclear whether any newspaper published it.

55 Elin Odzemir to John Sawyer, January 26, 1973, Ernst Papers, referring to Morris Ernst and David Loth, *The Taming of Technology* (New York: Simon and Schuster, 1972).

56 MLE to Schmidt.

57 Descriptions of Ernst's activities based on readings of his personal diary, Ernst Papers, and other sources.

58 Morris Ernst memorial tribute.

59 Morris Ernst memorial tribute.

60 Herb Wolff, "Memorial for Morris L. Ernst," n.d., Ernst Papers.

61 Whitman, "Morris Ernst, 'Ulysses' Case Lawyer Dies," 40.

62 "Morris Ernst—On Behalf of Freedom," *Los Angeles Times*, May 26, 1976, 50.

63 Jack O'Brian, "Broadway," *Asbury Park (NJ) Press*, January 13, 1977.

INDEX

Page numbers in italics refer to figures.

abortion, 405n30

Abrams v. United States, 72

Academy of Medicine, 112

Agricultural Adjustment Act, 191

Alabama, 7–9, 342

Algonquin Round Table, 63

Alice in Wonderland (Dodgson), 346

Allen, Frederick Lewis, 84

Allen, Robert, 145–46, 232, 249

Alpha Zeta Alpha (fraternity), 19–20, *25*

Amalgamated Textile Workers of America, 59

American Association of Labor Legislation, 35–36

American Association of Obstetricians, Gynecologists, and Abdominal Surgeons, 214

American Bar Association, 29–30, 130, 219–22

American Birth Control League, 3, 108–15, 208–18, 288–89

American Civil Liberties Union (ACLU): anti-Communism and, 309–11; Baldwin's leadership and, 51–53; changing public opinion and, 49; Clear and Present Danger Committee, 311–13; Communism and, 4, 71–72, 79, 186–89, 226–29, 242, 250, 256–60, 319; Ernst's "spying" and, 285, 322, 337–40; expulsion of Flynn and, 264–66; Ford controversy and, 225–27; founding of, 5, 47–48; free speech and, 1–2, 48; Great Depression and, 127–28, 133; *Hague v. Committee for Industrial Organization* and, 232–49; Japanese American internment and, 282; Karolyi affair and, 68–70; literary censorship and, 85; as a mainstream institution and, 315–16; media monopolies and, 277–78; National Committee on Labor Injunctions and, 129; National Council on Freedom from Censorship and, 104, 124, 213; New York City Board of Education and, 73–74; pornography and, 124–25; positions on free speech and, 315; positions on obscenity and, 320; promotion of Ernst to general counsel, 72–73; radio, regulation of, 74–77; resolution on civil liberties abroad and, 261–64; Roosevelt's reelection and, 206–7; sex education and, 104; sexual matters and, 301; silk workers strike and, 70–71; support for controversial groups and, 54–55, 132–33, 142, 144–45, 187–89; Wagner Act and, 206; wiretapping and, 268, 285, 305; Wise report and, 260–61; World War II and, 281–83

American Communist Party, 47. *See also* Communism

American Fund for Public Service. *See* Garland Fund

American Labor Party (ALP), 199–200, 271, 299

American League for Peace and Democracy, 257

American Newspaper Guild, 3, 150, 193–96, 205–6, 250

American Newspaper Publishers Association (ANPA), 148, 195

American Protective League, 45–47

American Sexual Behavior and the Kinsey Report (Ernst and Loth), 300

American Tragedy, An (Dreiser), 95–96

American Union Against Militarism (AUAM), 44–45

America's Primer (Ernst), 135

Andrews, John B., 35

anti-injunction laws, 128–29

antilynching laws, 130

anti-Semitism, 10, 14, 19, 129–30, 317–18

Associated Press, 194–99, 204–5, 278–79

Atlantic Monthly, 178

Atlantic Monthly Press, 279

Atlas, Nicholas, 159

Axelrod, Herman, 145

Bacon, Peggy, 176

Baker, Helen Bartlett, 16

Balch, Earl, 122

Baldwin, Roger: AUAM and, 44–45; Communism and, 227; conservatism and, 281; creation of the ACLU and, 47–49, 51–53; "disclosure" and, 256; on Ernst, 150; Ernst's promotion to general counsel and, 72–73; expansion of ACLU activities and, 128; expulsion of Flynn

Baldwin, Roger (*continued*)
from the ACLU and, 266; the FBI and, 284; Ford controversy and, 226; free speech and, 314; Galindez affair and, 331; the Garland Fund and, 55–57; HUAC and, 258; Ku Klux Klan and, 54; National Civil Liberties Bureau, 45–47; obscenity law and, 85; resignation from the ACLU and, 316; rivalry with Ernst and, 61; silk workers strike and, 70–71; split with Ernst and, 328; viewpoint-neutral position on free speech and, 142; Wagner Act and, 206
Bancroft, Frederic Wolcott, 210
Barnes, Charles, 60–61
Baron, Sidney, 331
Baumann, Charlie, 27
Baumann's (furniture store), 27–28, 31–32, 40
Beach, Sylvia, 153–55
Bentley, Elizabeth, 304
Berle, Adolf, 206
Bernheim, Eli, 26
Bernheim, Henry, 9
Bessie, Simon Michael, 302
Best Is Yet, The (Ernst), 295–97
Bible-reading laws, 73
Biddle, Francis, 274
birth control, 3, 108–15, 208–18, 288–89, 314, 321. See also *Contraception* (Stopes); Sanger, Margaret
Birth Control Clinical Research Bureau. *See* Sanger, Margaret
Birth of a Baby, The (film), 214–15
Bliven, Bruce, 296
Bloch, Manny, 326–27
Bondy, William, 196
Bonus March, 141
Brandeis, Louis, 71–72, 139–40, 143, 215–16, 231, 245, 279–81
Brant, Neil, 239
Brennan, William, 349
Brestwell, Sigrid, 111
Bromley, Dorothy Dunbar, 265
Brooklyn Jewish Examiner, 143
Brotherhood of Sleeping Car Porters, 130
Broun, Heywood: American Newspaper Guild and, 3; *Casanova's Homecoming* case and, 117–18; Daughters of the American Revolution and, 78; death of, 270–71; *Hague v. Committee for Industrial Organization* and, 238; Horace Mann School and, 16; relationship with Ernst and, 63, 147–48; Sacco and Vanzetti columns, 79–80; Supreme Court and, 191–92; unionizing journalists and, 148–50; Wagner Act and, 196, 198
Browder, Earl, 55
Brownell, Herbert, 332
burlesque, 214
Burrows, Warren, 105–6
Bushel, Hyman, 97
cabbies, 182–83
Campbell, Marcus, 104–5
capitalism: Garland Fund and, 56; Great Depression and, 127, 135
Cardozo, Benjamin N., 207
Carlebach, Herbert, 28–29
Carr, Robert K., 306
Casanova's Homecoming (Schnitzler), 116–17
case method of study, 29
Casey, Daniel, 237, 242
Censored: The Private Life of the Movies (Ernst and Lorentz), 119
Censor Marches On, The (Lindey and Ernst), 213
censorship. *See* film censorship; freedom of the press; free speech; literature; radio, regulation of
Central Intelligence Agency, 333–35
Cerf, Bennett, 155–56, 162, 175
Chafee, Zechariah, 71, 241
Chicago Daily News, 338
Chicago Tribune, 79
Child Labor Amendment, 223
City Club, 33–35
civil liberties: censorship of the arts and, 124; Communism and, 250, 255–57, 262–64; the Constitution and, 200; evolution of, 2; the FBI and, 4, 301–5; freedom of sexual education and, 104; the Great Depression and, 127–28, 141; Greenbaum, Wolff, and Ernst and, 79; National Civil Liberties Bureau and, 45; New Deal and, 181, 207; organized labor and, 226–27; police and, 128; President's Commission on Civil Rights and, 305–9; race and, 131; radicals and, 71; Rosenberg trial and, 326; the Wagner Act and, 206; wiretapping and, 266–69, 285, 301–6. *See also* American Civil Liberties Union (ACLU); freedom of the press; free speech; *Hague v. Committee for Industrial Organization*; New Deal; organized labor
Civil Rights Act of 1871, 241
Clark, Charles, 196
Clark, Tom, 309
Clark, William, 242, 245–46
Clean Books Bill, 118
Coleman, Frank J., 159
Coleman, McAlister, 62
Coleman, Samuel, 158–60, 172
Columbia Law Review, 212
Committee for Cultural Freedom, 255
Committee for Industrial Organization, 193–94. See also *Hague v. Committee for Industrial Organization*
Committee on Civil Liberties in Jersey City. See *Hague v. Committee for Industrial Organization*
Commonwealth v. Nelson, 289
Communications Act of 1964, 267
Communism, 47; ACLU and, 54–55, 132–33, 226–

27, 242, 250, 256–60, 263–66, 319; American Labor Party and, 200; American Newspaper Guild and, 205–6, 250; "clear and present danger" rule and, 311–13; "disclosure" and, 253–55, 258, 273–75, 301, 306–13; formation of the American Communist Party and, 47; front organizations and, 187–89, 227–29, 251; Garland Fund and, 57; Great Depression and, 127, 135–36; HUAC and, 227–29, 309–11; National Lawyers Guild and, 224–25, 250–53; organized labor and, 187–88, 235, 240; President's Commission on Civil Rights and, 306; *Report on the American Communist* and, 324–25; Supreme Court and, 207; US federal employees and, 304. See also *Hague v. Committee for Industrial Organization*
Communist Party of America, 51, 183. *See also* Communism
Comstock, Anthony, 85–86
Comstock laws: birth control and, 208–13, 289, 321; demise of, 118–19; judicial liberalization and, 94; obscene material and, 84–85; *People v. Sanger* and, 108–15; sex education material and, 99–108; Tariff Act and, 88; *Ulysses* and, 1. *See also* New York Society for the Suppression of Vice (NYSSV)
Conboy, Martin, 172–73, 175, 181–82
Connecticut, 289–91, 314, 321
Contact Editions of Paris, 89
contraception. *See* birth control
Contraception (Stopes), 124–25
Cookman, Joseph, 134–35
Cooper, Isabel Rosario, 146
Cooper, Kent, 194, 197
Coplon, Judith, 304
Corbin, John, 201–2
Costello, Frank, 300–301
Covici, Pascal, 95–98
Covici-Friede publishing company, 95–98
Croly, Herbert, 36
Cummings, Homer, 181, 191, 268
Cuneo, Ernest, 177, 252
curse of bigness, 139–40, 297–99
Cutting, Bronson, 120

Daily Worker, 57, 189, 225, 253, 308
Damron, Wayne, 80–81
Darrow, Clarence, 70, 78
Daughters of the American Revolution, 78. *See also* professional patriots
Davis, John W., 195–98, 205
Deep Throat, 350
DeJonge v. Oregon, 207
DeLoach, C. D., 337
Denis, Holly Beach, 154
Dennett, Mary Ware, 99–108
Dershowitz, Alan, 328
DeSilver, Albert, 48, 51, 55, 73
DeSilver, Margaret, 142
De Toledano, Ralph, 336
Devaney, John, 223
Dewey, John, 255
Dewey, Thomas, 315
Dickinson, Robert, 111
Dies, Martin, 227–29, 250, 257–60
Dill, Clarence, 75–76
Dilling, Elizabeth, 186–87
"disclosure," 253–55, 258, 273–75, 301, 306–13
"Dissenting Opinions," 134–35
divorce laws, 129
Dodgson, Charles, 346
Doty, Madeleine Zabriskie, 47
Doubleday, Doran (publisher), 215–16
Doubleday, Nelson, 216
Dwight, Theodore, 29

Eastman, Crystal, 44
Eisenhower, Dwight, 146
Emerson, Thomas, 223
Ernst, Carl (father), 8–12, 24
Ernst, Constance (daughter), 31, 60, 63, 151, 267, 302, 318, 329
Ernst, George Goodman (brother), 9, 203
Ernst, Joan (daughter), 66, 151, 318
Ernst, Magdalen (sister), 9, *17*
Ernst, Margaret (second wife), 60, 63–66, 150, 229, 330, *339*, 343, *353*
Ernst, M.L. (uncle), 8
Ernst, Morris, *354*; abortion and, 405n30; ACLU involvement and, 1–2, 5, 49, 55, 72–73, 273, 282, 315–16, 319; American Labor Party and, 199–200; anti-Communism and, 189, 250–69; appointment to the NY State Banking Board and, 138–39, 253; approach to law of, 42–43; autobiographies and diaries of, 295–97, 299, 342–43; bar exam and, 31–32; Baumann's and, 27–28, 30–31, 40; birth control movement and, 108–15, 208–18; book industry matters and, 215–18; Brandeis's lamps and, 281; carpentry and, *312*; causes and, 2–3, 6, 37, 128–29; *Censored: The Private Life of the Movies* and, 119; City Club and, 33–35; coauthorship of books with Loth, 299–300; as cocounsel with Hays, 133–34; college years, 16–25, *25*; Communism and, 4, 132–33, 240, 243–44, 324–25; conservatism and, 302, 341; criticism of the legal profession and, 219–20; curse of bigness and, 139–40, 279–81, 297–99; death of, 4, 352–55; debate team and, 23–24; *Dennett* case and, 99–108; descriptions of, 2–3, 5, 14–15, 36, 67, 177, 293–94; "disclosure" and, 253–55, 258, 273–75, 301, 306–13; "diversity" and, 275–76; divorce laws and, 129; early life of, 7, 9–11, 14–18, *17*; evolution of First Amendment law and, 314–15; exhibitionism and, 23, 40; fading influence of, 316–17; failing health and, 343–44, 351–52; FBI falling out and, 336–37; FBI support and, 4, 283–86, 321 28; female

Ernst, Morris (*continued*)
law associates and, 211; film censorship and, 119, 214–15; finances of, 1–2, 81, 172; *The First Freedom* and, 297–99; Ford controversy and, 225–27; free speech and, 1–2; the French Resistance and, 287–88; Galindez affair and, 330–36; Gargoyle and, 24–25; Garland Fund and, 56–58; glandular optimism and, 6, 14, 342; grandchildren and, 329; Greenbaum, Wolff, and Ernst and, 3, 38–43, 300–301, 316; Greenwich Village and, 318–19, 346–47; *Hague v. Committee for Industrial Organization* and, 232–49, *248*; Harlem Riots and, 184–87; Harvard and, 16; heroes of, 15, 20; on his own biography, 5; image and, 3–4, 69; Joan's hearing and, 151; James Joyce and, 175; Karolyi affair and, 68–70; "law in the vernacular" book series and, 345; law school and, 28–31; League for Independent Political Action and, 379n2; libel threats and, 78, 136–37; as a liberal pundit, 134–35; *Life* article, 292–95; lifestyle of, 3, 23–24, 61–63, 81–83, 150, 176–78, 229–32, 342; literary censorship and, 116–26, 213–14, *217*; *Married Love* and, 120–23; media monopolies and, 277–78; membership in organizations and, 36, 51; M&M Books and, 343; mother's death and, 24; mother's influence on, 11–13; Nantucket Island and, 82–83, *290*, *339*, 344, *353*; National Lawyers Guild and, 221–25; Nazis and, 142, 144; New Deal and, 141, 178–80, 190–207; "new morality" and, 349–50; obscenity law and, 88–92; President's Commission on Civil Rights and, 306; profanity and, 67, 69; professional patriots and, 77–78; public positions and, 180–81; racial equality and, 317–18; radio censorship and, 74–77, 142–43; relationship with Brandeis and, 279–81; relationship with Broun, 63, 270–71; relationship with father and, 11; relationship with FDR and, 192–93, 271–72, 286–88; relationship with Hoover and, 266–69, 286–88, 302–5, 321, 336; relationship with Jahoda, 329; relationship with La Guardia and, 182–86; relationship with Margaret Ernst and, 60, 63–66, 343–44; relationship with Susan Ernst and, 27, 31; religion and, 11; rivalry with Roger Baldwin and, 61; Rosenberg case and, 326–28; sailing, 83, *339*; sexual ideas and, 124–26; "spying" on the ACLU and, 285, 322, 337–40; as a student, 15, 20; suicide and, 345; Susan Ernst's passing and, 50, 60; Truman and, 299; *Utopia 1976*, 329–30; views on government and, 21; Wagner Act and, 193–205; women's issues and, 129; work for the press and, 145–47; World War I and, 43–46
Ernst, Roger (son), 66, 151, 318, 329, 346
Ernst, Sarah (mother), 9–15, 24
Ernst, Susan (wife), 27, 31, 50, 60
evolution, teaching of, 73
fascism, 142, 255
Federal Bureau of Investigation (FBI): Ernst's falling out with, 336–37; Ernst's support of, 4, 283–86, 321–28, 337–40; Galindez affair and, 332–33; President's Commission on Civil Rights and, 307; wiretapping and, 266–69, 285, 305–6
Federal Bureau of Investigation, The (Lowenthal), 323
Federal Communications Commission, 76, 276
Federal Radio Commission, 76, 142–43
Feld-Crawford Fair Trade Act, 215–16
feminism, 84, 109. *See also* Sanger, Margaret
Ferber, Edna, 80–81, 83, 295, 346
Ferman, Irving, 338
Field, Antoinette, 111
film censorship, 119, 214, 301, 319–20
First Amendment. *See* "disclosure"; freedom of the press; free speech; *Hicklin* test; libel; literature; radio, regulation of; Supreme Court
First Freedom, The (Ernst), 297–99
First National Congress on Unemployment, 35
flag salute regulations, 73
Flaubert, Gustave, 213
Fleischmann, Raoul, 19
Fly, James Lawrence, 276–77, 304–5, 319, 322
Flynn, Elizabeth Gurley, 264–66
For Better or for Worse (Ernst and Loth), 300
Ford, Henry, 225–27
Ford Motor Company, 225–27
Forever Amber (Winsor), 301
Forster, Clifford, 316
Forsyte, Malachi, 135. *See also* Ernst, Morris
Foster, William Z., 54, 141
Fourteenth Amendment, 46, 71, 133, 241, 245–46, 290, 321
Foxworth, Percy, 284
Fraenkel, Osmond, 16, 261, 273, 282
Frank, Jerome, 179, 286, 320, 328
Frankfurter, Felix, 128–29, 131, 178–80, 206, 281
fraternities, 19–20, *25*
Frazer, E. Franklin, 184–86
Frazer, Spaulding, 235, 240, 242–43
freedom of assembly, 232–49
freedom of the press, 45, 145–47, 197, 276–79, 301. *See also* Associated Press; libel
free speech: ACLU's impact on, 314; censorship and, 2; "clear and present danger" rule and, 311–13; "diversity" in media ownership and, 275–76; in education, 73–74; Ernst and, 1–2; *Hague v. Committee for Industrial Organization* and, 233; Karolyi and, 68–70; libel and, 146–47; police and, 128; radio and, 74–77; Scopes "monkey trial" and, 70; silk workers strike and, 70–71; *United States v. Associated Press* and, 279; World War I and, 45–46; World War II and, 272–73. *See also* freedom of the press; literature
Freudianism, 84

Frey, Alexander, 252
Friede, Donald, 95–98
Friends of New Germany, 144
Fusion Party, 180

Galindez, Jesus de, 330–36
Gannett, Lewis, 130
Garland, Charles. *See* Garland Fund
Garland Fund, 55–58, 62, 78–79, 130–32, 238, 244
Garrett, Eileen, 346
Genius, The (Dreiser), 87
George, David Lloyd, 22
Gitlow v. New York, 71
Glass-Steagall Act, 138–39
Glynn, Martin, 35
Goldman, Emma, 52
Gottesman, Callman, 197
Gottlieb, Maurice, 117
Great Depression, 127–28, 133, 135, 142, 182–83, 220–21. *See also* New Deal; Roosevelt, Franklin Delano
Greenbaum, Eddie, 24, 38–40, 363n6
Greenbaum, Laurie, 39, 328
Greenbaum, Samuel, 11, 38
Greenbaum, Wolff, and Ernst (law firm): Frank Costello and, 300–301; creation of, 38–43; female associates and, 211; Galindez affair and, 331; growth of, 58–60; literary law and, 79–81, 213; media and publishing lawsuits, 301; the mortgage crisis and, 140; pro bono work and, 3; support for progressive causes and, 79; *What Happens* case and, 88–91. *See also* Ernst, Morris
Gregg, Abel, 105–6
Griswold v. Connecticut, 321
Gutknecht, John, 252

Hague, Frank, 232–49
Hague v. Committee for Industrial Organization, 232–49
Hall, Radclyffe, 95
Hand, Augustus, 107–8, 172–74, 211–12
Hand, Learned, 172–74, 211–12, 279
Hannegan v. Esquire, 301
Hansen, Harry, 153
Harlem Riots, 184–87
Harper and Brothers, 296
Harris, Lewis, 114
Harris, Maurice, 11
Harris, Richard, 327–28
Harvard Law Review, 175, 201
Hays, Arthur Garfield: cocounsel partnership with Ernst and, 133–34; Daughters of the American Revolution and, 78; Dennett case and, 101; "disclosure" and, 308–9; expulsion of Flynn from the ACLU and, 266; Ford controversy and, 225–27; *Hague v. Committee for Industrial Organization* and, 233, 241; Harlem riots and, 184–86; HUAC and, 229, 258–60; legal work for the ACLU and, 273, 316; media monopolies and, 277–78; Nazis and, 142; resignation from the ACLU and, 316; Scopes "monkey trial" and, 70; Wagner Act and, 206; working with Communists and, 54–55; World War II and, 282
Hearst, William Randolph, 186
Henderson, Leon, 231
Herndon v. Lowry, 207
Herrick, Elinor, 195
Herrmann, John, 89–91
Hicklin test, 88, 105, 108, 116, 152–53, 162, 170, 173, 175, 321
Hiss, Alger, 336
Hitler, Adolf, 142, 187
Hoffmann, Malcolm, 67, 328–29, 352
Hold Your Tongue! Adventures in Libel and Slander (Ernst and Lindey), 146
Holmes, John Haynes, 46, 49, 188, 260, 264–65, 282
Holmes, Oliver Wendell, Jr., 71
homosexuality, 125
Hook, Sidney, 255
Hoover, J. Edgar: "disclosure" and, 275; Ernst's autobiography and, 296; Galindez affair and, 333; investigation of Ernst's Communist ties and, 181; relationship with Ernst and, 266–67, 283–86, 302–5, 321, 336–40; wiretapping and, 267–69
Horace Mann School, 15–16, 38
Horthy, Miklos, 68
House Un-American Activities Committee (HUAC), 227–29, 253, 257–61, 308–11
Howard, Roy, 271
HUAC. *See* House Un-American Activities Committee (HUAC)
Huebsch, Ben, 52, 154–55
Hughes, Charles Evans, 69, 133, 204
Hunt, Henry, 223
Hutchins Commission, 401n20

Ickes, Harold, 206, 236, 272, 276
Ilin, M., 135–36
In A Word (Ernst), 150
Industrial Workers of the World (IWW), 45, 264
injunctions, 128–29
Internal Revenue Service, 274
In the Court of Public Opinion (Hiss), 336

Jackson, Gardner, 228
Jackson, Robert, 223, 272
Jahoda, Marie, 329
James, Marquis, 232
Japanese American internment, 282, 399n66
Jersey City, NJ. See *Hague v. Committee for Industrial Organization*
jewelry industry, 41–42
Jews: anti-Semitism and, 10, 14, 19, 243–45, 306, 318–19; bar admissions and, 30; fraternitics

Jews (*continued*)
and, 19; Nazis and, 144; radicalism and, 245; in the South, 7–8; Williams College and, 18–19
Johnson, Donald, 46
Johnson, James Weldon, 130
Josephson, Matthew, 178
Journal of Contraception, 212
Joyce, James. See *Ulysses* (Joyce)
Jungle, The (Sinclair), 22

Kalven, Harry, Jr., 2
Karolyi, Michael, 68–70
Kastor, Robert, 155
Katz, Joel, 328
Kelley, Edmond, 33
Kellogg, Herbert, 108
Kennedy, Foster, 113, 209
Kennerley, Mitchell, 86
Kenyon, Dorothy, 16
Kern, Paul J., 223
Kinsey Report, 300
Kirkpatrick, William, 122
Kluger, Richard, 132
Knopf, Alfred, 86–87, 95
Knox, John, 90
Koussevitsky v. Allen, Towne, and Heath, 301
Koyama, Sakae, 209
Koyama Suction Pessary, 209
Ku Klux Klan, 54
Kun, Bela, 68

labor colleges, 62
Lader, Lawrence, 112
La Guardia, Fiorello, 182–86, 200
Lamont, Corliss, 257, 264
Lamont, Robert, 280
La Ronde, 320
Larsen, Roy, 214, 292, 294–95
Lawyers' Security League, 220–21
League of Women Voters, 51
Leerburger, Susan. *See* Ernst, Susan (wife)
Leffingwell, Russell, 229–31, 295
legal realism, 42, 179, 219
Legion of Honor, 287–88
Lehman, Herbert, 18–19, 138, 140
Lehman, Mayer, 7
Leibowitz, Samuel, 189
Leon, Paul, 156–57
lesbianism, 95–97
Levy, Newman, 42, 67, 69, 80, 90, 117
Levy, Salvyn, 27
Lewis, Edward "Ted" Morgan, 20–23, 33
Lewis, John L., 193, 230–31, 235
libel, 78, 136–37, 145–47, 187, 303, 348–49
Liberty, 258
Life, 214, 292–95, 330–31, 334
Liggett's Drug Store, 137
Lindey, Alexander, 108, 122, 154, 158, 162, 175, 209, 213
Lippman, Walter, 36
literature: censorship and, 1–2, 84–85, 116–26, 213–15, 314–15, 319; "community mores" test and, 175; New York Society for the Suppression of Vice (NYSSV) and, 86–87; postage rate for books and, 216–19; "work as a whole" standard, 175. See also *Ulysses* (Joyce)
Little Review, 87, 152
Lorentz, Pare, 119
Loth, David, 299–300, 324, 345
Lowenthal, Max, 323
Luce, Henry, 231
Ludwig, Edward, 81
Lusk Committee, 53–54
lynching, 130

MacArthur, Douglas, 146
Macmillan, 345
Macy's, 215–16
mandamus actions, 131–32
Manton, Martin, 172–74
Margold, Nathan, 131–32
Married Love (Stopes), 120–25
Marro, Anthony, 337–38
Marx, Groucho, 78
Massachusetts, 289–91, 301, 314, 321
Mastick-Goodrich bill, 129
Matthews, John A., 242–43
Mayer, Art, 13–14, 16, 23–24
Mayer, Leo, 13–14, 16, 27
Mayer, Rachel (aunt), 13
Mayer, Simon, 8–9, 13
McAlmon, Robert, 89
McCarran Internal Security Act of 1950, 311
McCarthy, Joseph, 319
McCormick, Robert, 276
McNaboe, John T., 253
McNamara, Anna, 110, 113
McReynolds, James, 246
Mead, James, 218
Medalie, George Z., 158–59
media monopolies, 277–78, 297–99, 341–42, 347–48, 401n20
Medical Review of Reviews, 100, 102
Mencken, H. L., 89
Metro-Goldwyn-Mayer, 301
Miller, Herman, 213
Milner, Lucille, 48, 70, 128, 133, 207
Milton, Joyce, 327–28
M&M Books, 343
Mooney, Tom, 138
Morgan, J. P., 118
Morgenthau, Henry, 62, 274–75
"Morris Ernst: New York's Unlawyerlike Liberal Lawyer is the Censor's Enemy, the President's Friend," 292–95
mortgage crisis, 139–40
Moscowitz, David, 196
Moscowitz, Grover, 102–3, 105, 209–10

Moses, Robert, 62
Mundt-Nixon Bill of 1948, 310–11
Munson, William, 331–32
Murphy, Frank, 272
Murphy, Gerald, 330–36
Murrow, Ed, 322, 330
Muste, A. J., 59, 61

NAACP, 3, 129–32
Nardone v. United States, 268
Nantucket Island, 82–83, *290*, 296, *339*, 344, *353*
Nation, 80, 94, 103–4, 130, 134, 284–85, 338–39
National Civil Liberties Bureau (NCLB), 45
National Committee on Federal Legislation for Birth Control, 208
National Committee to Abolish Postal Discrimination Against Books, 218
National Industrial Recovery Act (NIRA), 148, 190–91
National Jewelers' Board of Trade, 41
National Labor Relations Act. *See* Wagner Act
National Labor Relations Board (NLRB), 193–97, 225–28
National Lawyers Guild, 3–4, 221–25, 235, 250–53, 276
National Organization for Decent Literature, 319
National Recovery Administration (NRA), 148–49
National War Labor Board, 47
Nazis, 2, 142, 144–45, 250, 255, 262, 271
Nazi-Soviet Pact, 250, 255, 262, 271
Nearing, Scott, 56–58
Near v. Minnesota, 133
Nelles, Walter, 55
New Deal: American Liberty League and, 195; conservative lawyers and, 219–20; Ernst's support for, 178–80, 190–207; Roosevelt and, 141; *Schechter Poultry Corp. v. United States* and, 190–91; Supreme Court and, 190; *United States v. Butler* and, 191; Wagner Act and, 193–99, 204–5
New Leader, 325, 334
New Masses, 57
New Republic, 36, 51, 178, 284
New Russia's Primer (Ilin), 135–36
Newsweek, 334
New York City: Board of Education, 73–74; burlesque houses and, 214; Progressive movement and, 33; unemployment and, 35
New York County Medical Society, 112
New Yorker: on Baldwin, 53; financial backing for, 19
New York Evening Journal, 106
New York Evening Post, 134–35
New York Journal American, 135
New York Law School, 29–31
New York Market Growers Association, 43
New York Post, 31
New York Society for the Suppression of Vice (NYSSV), 86, 116–19, 152, 172, 213, 314. *See also* Comstock laws; obscenity
New York Star, 303
New York State Banking Board, 138–39
New York Times, 11, 43, 86–87, 98, 119, 161, 201–2, 338
New York Times v. Sullivan, 288, 348–49
New York World, 78–80
New York World-Telegram, 149
Nichols, Louis B., 283, 302, 321–23, 337
Nixon, Richard, 310
Norris, George, 128–29
Norris-La Guardia Act, 129
November (Flaubert), 213, *217*

O'Brien, John, 144–45
Obscene Publications Act, 95
obscenity: Comstock laws and, 85–88; Customs cases and, 119–20; *Hicklin* test and, 88; literature and, 85; New York Society for the Suppression of Vice (NYSSV) and, 86; *The Sex Side of Life* and, 99–108; *To the Pure* and, 91–95; *The Well of Loneliness* and, 95–98. *See also* sex
O'Connell, Jerry, 241
O'Donnell, John, 299
Off With Their Heads (Bacon), 176
Oliver Twist, 317–18
One Package case, 211–12, 289
organized labor: America, 193; auto workers and, 225–27; Communism and, 187–88, 235, 240; *Hague v. Committee for Industrial Organization* and, 232–49; injunctions and, 128–29; journalists and, 148–50, 193–99, 204–5; labor unions, 3, 47–48, 53; Wagner Act and, 193–99. *See also* American Newspaper Guild
Outlook, 51

Palko v. Connecticut, 207
Pandect of C.L.D. (Ernst), 346
Panic of 1907, 24
Patterson, Joseph, 284
Pearson, Drew, 145–46, 180, 229, 232, 249, 288
Pecora, Ferdinand, 251–52
Pehle, John, 287
People Know Best, The (Ernst and Loth), 300
People v. Sanger, 108–15
Perrett, Geoffrey, 266
Perry, Lewis, 20
Pilpel, Harriet, 211–12, 216, 315, 321
Pioneer Press, 121
Pissort, Elizabeth, 111
planned economies, 135–36, 138
Planned Parenthood. *See* American Birth Control League
Poe v. Ullman, 321
police, 128
pornography. *See* obscenity; sex
Porter, Charles, 334

Postal Rate Proclamation, 216–18
President's Commission on Civil Rights, 305–9
Pressman, Lee, 235
professional patriots, 45–46, 53, 77–78
Progressivism (progressive movement): in the 1920s, 50–54; Brandeis and, 139; Great Depression and, 127; Greenbaum, Wolff, and Ernst and, 79; National Lawyers Guild and, 221–22; New York City and, 32–37; private power and, 22; as a response to social problems, 21; World War I and, 44–46
propaganda, 124, 227, 254, 261, 274
Proskauer, Joseph, 32
public forums. See *Hague v. Committee for Industrial Organization*
Pulitzer, Ralph, 80
Putnam, G. P., 121–22

Quinn, John, 152

race, 129–32, 184–87, 305–9, 317–18
radio, regulation of, 74–77, 142–43, 276–77
Radosh, Ronald, 327–28
Randolph, A. Philip, 130, 184–86
Random House, 155, 157, 174. See also *Ulysses* (Joyce)
Rank, J. Arthur, 287
rantumscooting, 83
Readers' Digest, 322–24
red flag laws, 47. *See also* Communism
Red Network, The: A "Who's Who" and Handbook of Radicalism for Patriots (Dilling), 186–87
Reed, Stanley, 204
Regina v. Hicklin, 88
Reiss, Sigmund, 27
Remington, William, 304
Report on the American Communist (Ernst and Loth), 324–26
reproductive rights. *See* Sanger, Margaret
Retail Jewelers' Association of Greater New York, 41
Riemer, Mortimer, 221–22, 224
Rodell, Fred, 292–95, 335
Roosevelt, Eleanor, 263, 326
Roosevelt, Franklin Delano: banking reform and, 138; "disclosure" and, 274–75; Ernst's autobiography and, 296; Ernst's work for, 286–88; Hague and, 233; National Lawyers Guild and, 221–22; New Deal and, 141, 148, 178–79, 190–202; Postal Rate Proclamation and, 216–18; press support for, 276–77; relationship with Ernst and, 138, 271–72; Spanish Civil War and, 223–24; Supreme Court expansion and, 203–4; wiretapping and, 268
Roosevelt, Teddy, 15, 32
Rose, Florence, 209–10
Rosenberg case, 326–28
Rosenbluth, Abraham, 111–12, 114
Roth, Samuel, 153, 320
Roth v. United States, 320–21

Sacco and Vanzetti, 79–80, 178
Salisbury, Harrison, 4
Samuels, Margaret. *See* Ernst, Margaret (second wife)
Sanger, Margaret, 3, 108–15, 208–18
Saturday Review of Literature, 94
Schackno Act, 140
Schaick, George Van, 140
Schechter Poultry Corp. v. United States, 190–91
Schwartz, Alan, 328, 332
Scopes "monkey trial," 70
Scottsboro Boys, 189
Seagle, William, 91–95
Second Circuit Court of Appeals, 107, 122, 152, 172, 175, 197, 208–11, 279, 320
segregation. *See* race
Selective Service Act, 47
Seligman, Joseph, 7–8
sex: ACLU and, 301; homosexuality and, 92, 95, 125, 300; "new morality" and, 349–50; pornography and, 85, 93–94, 124–25, 153, 314; sex education and, 12, 93, 99–109, 294; sexual freedoms and, 84, 349. *See also* obscenity
Sex Side of Life, The, 99–108
Shall We Defend Free Speech for Nazis in America? (ACLU position statement), 145
Shapiro, Jonas, 161
Sherman Antitrust Act, 278
Shipstead bill, 128–29
Show Boat (Ferber), 80–81
Shuler, Robert, 142–43
Sideri, Marcella, 111
Sidis v. F.R. Publishing, 301
silk workers strike of 1926, 70–71
Simon and Schuster, 116, 199
Smiling Corpse, The (Bergman and Wylie), 175
Smith, T. C., 20
Smith Act, 311
Smoot Amendment, 120
So Big (Ferber), 80
social hygiene, 100
socialism, 45, 51, 57, 71, 78, 109, 127, 187–88, 262
Socialist Party, 51, 127
Social Register, 18
So Far So Good (Ernst and Loth), 299
Soviet Union, 135–36, 187, 189, 250, 255, 262, 271
Spanish Civil War, 223–24
Spanknoebel, Heinz, 144
stare decisis, 42
Steele, Walter, 228
Stone, Hannah, 110–11, 209
Stone, Harlan Fiske, 39, 268
Stopes, Marie, 120–25
Stratton, Lloyd, 196–97

Stripling, Robert, 228
Stromberg v. California, 133
Strong, Charles H., 34
Subversive Activities Control Act, 310–11
Sugar, Maurice, 220
Sullivan, Mary, 111
Sullivan, William, 324
Sulzberger, Arthur, 11, 43, 202
Sulzberger, Cyrus, 11
Sumner, John, 86–87, 96–98, 103, 116–19, 213. *See also* Comstock laws; New York Society for the Suppression of Vice (NYSSV); obscenity
Superior Films v. Ohio, 320
superpatriots. *See* professional patriots
Supreme Court: *Abrams v. United States*, 72; "clear and present danger" rule and, 311–14; Communism and, 207; *DeJonge v. Oregon*, 207; expansion of, 203–4; film censorship and, 301, 320; First Amendment and, 46; freedom of expression and, 207; free speech tests and, 71–72, 88, 108, 116, 152–53, 162, 173, 175, 311–14, 321; *Gitlow v. New York*, 71; *Hague v. Committee for Industrial Organization* and, 2, 246; *Herndon v. Lowry* and, 207; *Hicklin* test and, 88, 108, 116, 152–53, 162, 173, 175, 321; Hughes court and, 133; "immoral" magazines and, 301; New Deal and, 190–92, 197–202, 204–5; *New York Times v. Sullivan*, 288, 348–49; *Palko v. Connecticut*, 207; *Roth v. United States*, 320–21; *Tileston v. Ullman*, 289–91; *Whitney v. California*, 72; wiretapping and, 268
Swan, Thomas, 211–12

"Take Your Choice," 135
Tariff Act, 88, 120, 122, 158–60, 208–10
taxi industry, 182–83
Temple Israel, 11
Third Circuit Court of Appeals, 246
Thomas, Norman, 49, 58, 62, 188, 233, 241, 247, 262, 319
Thompson, Dorothy, 145
Thurber, James, 150, 176
Tileston, Wilder, 289–91
Tileston v. Ullman, 289–91
Time, 303
Tishman, Maurice, 245
Tolson, Clyde, 303, 336
Too Big (Ernst), 279–81
To Secure These Rights. *See* President's Commission on Civil Rights
totalitarianism, 255
To the Pure: A Study of Obscenity and the Censor (Ernst and Seagle), 91–95, 320
Touch Wood (Ernst), 342
Trujillo, Rafael, 330–36
Truman, Harry S., 299–300, 304–9, 314–15, 351
Two Worlds Monthly, 153

Ullman, Abraham, 290
Ultimate Power, The (Ernst), 193, 199–202
Ulysses (Joyce): 25th anniversary of the decision and, 347; appeal to the Second Circuit and, 172–75; critical acclaim and, 153; decision to prosecute and, 158–59; hearing and, 164–68; history of suppression in the US, 152–53; Joyce's search for a publisher and, 153; Judge Woolsey and, 161–63; legalization of, 1; publication of, 171–72; search for a US publisher and, 154–55; securing a favorable hearing and, 159–61; setting the case in motion, 156–58; Sumner and, 87; Woolsey's opinion, 168–71
unemployment, 34–35
"Union of Reporters, A," 149
Union Theological Seminary, 101
United Auto Workers of America, 225–27
United German Societies, 144
United Shoe Workers of America, 234. See also *Hague v. Committee for Industrial Organization*
United States, 399n66; capitalism and, 135–36, 138; culture wars and, 84–99; Department of Justice, 47, 204, 257, 272, 274–75, 278, 328, 332; Department of Labor, 214–15; Espionage Act of 1917, 45, 47; federal customs censorship and, 119–26; interstate commerce and, 190–91, 194–201, 205; Japanese American internment and, 282, 399n66; loyalty of federal employees and, 304, 309–11; Post Office Department and, 85, 88, 99–102, 119, 152, 212, 214, 216–19, 256, 301; Progressivism and, 21–22; Sedition Act of 1918, 45; Tariff Act, 88; Treasury Department, 275; World War I, 43–46. *See also* New Deal
United States Shipping Board, 44
United States v. Associated Press, 279
United States v. Bennett, 88
United States v. One Book Entitled Contraception. *See* Stopes, Marie
United States v. Three Packages of Bound, Obscene Books, 88–91
Untitled: The Diary of My 72nd Year (Ernst), 342–43
US Customs Department, 88–91, 119–26, 153–54
Usona ("United States of North America" shirt company), 26–27
Utopia 1976 (Ernst), 329–30

Vanderbilt, Arthur, 241
Varney, Harold Lord, 186
Viking Press, 91, 94, 154–55
Villard, Oswald Garrison, 184–86
Voorhis, Jerry, 258

Wagner Act, 193–95, 197–99, 204–6
Wald, Lillian, 44–45
Wallace, Mike, 33
Walsh, Frank P., 221–22
Ward, Harry F., 48, 188, 226, 257, 259–60, 264

War Refugee Board, 287
Watson, Edwin, 272
Watson, Morris, 194–96. *See also* American Newspaper Guild
Well of Loneliness, The (Hall), 95–98
West Coast Hotel Company v. Parrish, 204
West Virginia Board of Education v. Barnette, 272–73
Whalen, Grover, 112, 128
What Do You Mean—Free Speech? (ACLU pamphlet), 74
"What Every Girl Should Know," 109
What Happens (Herrmann), 89–91
White, Wallace, 75–76
Whitney, Charlotte Anita, 71
Whitney v. California, 72, 143
Wildberg, John, 89
Wilkinson, James A., 102, 104–5
Williams College, 16–25, 351–52
William Sloane Associates, 323
Willkie, Wendell, 231, 271
Wilson, Charlie, 306
Wilson administration, 45–47
Winchell, Walter, 249
Winters v. New York, 301
Wolff, Herb, 38–40
Woman Rebel, 109. *See also* Sanger, Margaret
Woolsey, John, 1, 122–24, 159–61, 208
Works Progress Administration, 220
World War I, 43–46
World War II, 272–73, 281–88

Young Men's Christian Association (YMCA), 100, 105
Youngs Rubber Corporation v. C. I. Lee, Inc., 208–9, 211

Zionism, 317